BASIC READINGS IN THEOLOGY

BASIC READINGS IN THEOLOGY

EDITED BY

A. D. GALLOWAY

LONDON

GEORGE ALLEN & UNWIN LTD

RUSKIN HOUSE MUSEUM STREET

FIRST PUBLISHED IN 1964

PRINTED IN GREAT BRITAIN
in 11 point Bembo type
BY UNWIN BROTHERS LIMITED
WOKING AND LONDON

CONTENTS

THE PERIOD OF EXPERIMENTAL THEOLOGY

NEW BEGINNINGS

INTRODUCTION

I hope that this book will be useful to at least two classes of people—to students reading the history of theology who would profit from direct acquaintance, however brief, with some of the major theologians whom they have not as yet had the opportunity to read at greater length—and to the general reader who wishes to taste where he cannot drink deeply. I hope that the effect of this book will be to stimulate a desire for fuller acquaintance with at least some of the authors represented.

A surprising number of alleged theological novelties of contemporary literature have in fact been investigated and put in their proper perspective a very long time ago. In this respect the major 'classics' of theology retain perpetual relevance.

Some of the material will make fairly heavy reading for the beginner. But take courage! Facility comes as one acquires familiarity with the concepts involved. I know of no quicker way of acquiring this than through direct encounter with the great seminal thinkers of the church.

The field from which these readings have been selected is mainly restricted to that of doctrinal theology. Philosophy of religion is a separate subject already served by its own anthologies. But there have been periods in the history of the church when theology and philosophy became so closely intertwined that it has not been possible to apply this principle rigorously. However, even a generous interpretation of this principle has meant that in some cases, particularly in the eighteenth century, essentially philosophical works which were of fateful moment for theology have had to be excluded.

Within the still vast field of theology several principles of selection commended themselves. Firstly, the readings should as far as possible reflect the movement and changing ethos of theology through the centuries. Secondly, they should represent the typical teachings of the authors selected. Thirdly, they should give fair coverage to the major doctrinal themes. Fourthly, the issues represented should be those which remain live, or impinge upon the live theological problems of our contemporary situation. These principles are often in tension with one another. For instance, one might have wished to represent St Augustine by his characteristic teaching on Grace, but it was found necessary to use his treatment of the doctrine of the Trinity to balance the less mature treatment of it in earlier writers.

The readings have tended to form a loose unity round a Christological and soteriological centre of interest. This has not come about by premeditated design, but has emerged as a reflection of an over-all pattern in the historical development of theology.

The arrangement of the material is historical and falls into five main periods: (1) The Early Formative Period, running up to the declining years of Hellenistic and Roman civilization, in which the fundamental concepts of Christian theology were forged and the basic problems formulated. (2) The Period of Catholic Consolidation, running from Augustine to Aquinas, in which the work of the early period was tested and refined into a massive, stable structure which, in the main, continues to serve the Roman Catholic Church to this day. These two periods are exceedingly rich and it is in them that the necessary omissions have been most reluctantly made. (3) The Reformation Period: To a far greater extent than is generally realized, this period is theologically continuous with the preceding ages and is simply a continuation and exacerbation of Mediaeval debates. But, quite apart from its fateful ecclesiastical consequences, there are certain crucial respects in which the theology of the Reformers constitutes a quite new departure. It is as though the basic concepts of the theological tradition had been put back into the fire in which they were first forged. The old debates take on a new, yet at the same time more primitive and original significance. In this section, I have placed Richard Hooker in rather closer association with Luther and Calvin than is usual. I have done so because he represents the more moderate, conservative type of reform. (4) The Period of Experimental Theology: This covers most of the eighteenth and nineteenth centuries and contains a wide variety of theological types. In suggesting that their common feature is the experimental character of their theology, I use the word in two senses. Firstly, it is experimental in the common sense that all manner of novel interpretations and approaches are being tried out. The continuity of Reformed theology with the Mediaeval and primitive debates has been largely lost. But secondly, it is experimental in an older sense of the word in that the theological interpretation of man's religious *experience* tends to be the centre of interest. (5) New Beginnings: No attempt has been made to represent the prodigious theological developments that are taking place in our own century. But in this brief final section, perhaps a little invidiously, I have set apart three theologians who, along with others, seem to me to have set the stage and provided the jumping-off point for some of the developments that are taking place in our own times—Kierkegaard, for the inspiration he provided for existentialist and confessional theology; Maurice, for the influence he has had upon our renewed Christological understanding of man's corporate existence in the church and in society; Newman, not only for his association with the Oxford Movement, but also for the fillip which he gave to a new kind of Catholic apologetic, especially among English-speaking peoples.

I am conscious of the fact that, apart from Newman, no Roman Catholic theologian has been included after Aquinas. I do not wish to suggest that Catholic theologians were idle during this long period. But, mainly for historical reasons which are obvious enough, there was little strikingly creative or novel Catholic theology during these centuries. I hasten to add, however, that if we were to attempt to include the twentieth century within our purview, this situation would be found to have altered dramatically.

The brief statements with which each writer is introduced have been kept to a minimum. The whole point of a volume such as this is that the authors should be left to speak for themselves. Similarly, I have resisted the temptation to attempt to justify the actual selections. They must justify themselves.

I should like to express my grateful indebtedness to Professor H. D. Lewis, from whose original suggestion this project arose.

I am grateful to those publishers who have given permission to use the following translations still in copyright: *Origen on First Principles*, tr. G. W. Butterworth, S.P.C.K., 1936; St Athanasius, *The Incarnation of the Word of God*, tr. by a Religious of C.S.M.V.S.Th., Geoffrey Bles, 1944; *Augustine: Later Works*, tr. John Burnaby, *The Library of Christian Classics*, S.C.M. Press, 1955; St Thomas Aquinas, *Summa Theologica*, literally translated by Fathers of the English Dominican Province, Thomas Baker, 1915; *Martin Luther on the Bondage of the Will*, tr. J. I. Packer and O. R. Johnston, James Clarke & Co., 1957; G. W. F. Hegel, *The Phenomenology of Mind*, tr. J. B. Baillie, Allen & Unwin, 1910 and 1931; Friedrich Schleiermacher, *The Christian Faith*, tr. and ed. H. R. Mackintosh and J. S. Stewart, T. and T. Clark, 1928; Albrecht Ritschl, *The Christian Doctrine of Justification and Reconciliation*, tr. and ed. H. R. Mackintosh and A. B. Macauley, T. and T. Clark, 1902; S. Kierkegaard, *Philosophical Fragments*, tr. David F. Swenson, Princeton University Press, 1936.

Where no source is acknowledged the translation is my own.

THE EARLY FORMATIVE PERIOD

I

IRENAEUS

St Irenaeus of Lyons came originally from Asia Minor. But his life-work was performed in the Latin west. He thus combined in himself something of both the eastern and the western traditions. He became bishop of the important see of Lyons in 177. It is reported by Gregory of Tours that he died a martyr about 202; but this is uncertain.

Irenaeus' literary activity was chiefly directed against the Gnostic and Montanist heresies of his day. To some extent this determines the emphasis of his teaching. Against all heretics he emphasizes the authority of those writings which the whole church recognized as apostolic. (The canon of Scripture had not yet been formally defined.) Equally he emphasizes the authority of the apostolic tradition, under the guarantee of apostolic succession in the episcopate.

He strongly upholds the biblical tradition of the significance of the material creation against the Greek tendency to regard matter as essentially evil. As a correlate of this, he defends the reality of the inacrnation of the Christ in truly human flesh, the reality of the sacraments, the resurrection of the body and the restoration of the physical conditions of paradise in the final consummation of the work of Christ.

He gave form and precision to the concept of catholicity and in this respect can be regarded as, in a sense, the father of Catholic dogmatics.

Apart from fragments, only two major works survive.

(1) *Presentation of the Apostolic Preaching* (English translation, J. P. Smith, Ancient Christian Writers, 1946 ff., Westminster).

(2) *Five books against Heresies* (English translation, M. Hitchcock, S.P.C.K., 2 vols., 1916).

See also selections in *Alexandrian Christianity* (J. E. L. Oulton and H. Chadwick, Library of Christian Classics, S.C.M., 1954).

THE TRADITION OF THE CHRISTIAN FAITH

Book 3, Chapter 1

We have come to know the pattern of our salvation through none other than those through whom the Gospel reached us. They at one time proclaimed the Gospel. Then, by the will of God, they passed it on to us in the Writings. These Writings were to become the foundation and pillar of our faith. Some people, who have the effrontery to boast that they can improve upon the Apostles, assert that they preached before they had complete knowledge. This is quite wrong. For after our Lord rose from the dead and they were invested with the power of the Holy Spirit, coming from on high, they were brought to fulfilment in all respects and had complete knowledge. They went to the ends of the earth proclaiming those good things which are from God and for us. They declared peace in heaven towards men. Each singly and all together they were in possession of the Gospel of God.

So Matthew, among the Hebrews, published a written version of the Gospel in their own language. In the meantime Peter and Paul were preaching the Gospel in Rome and founding the church. After they had departed this world, Mark, who was a disciple of Peter's and his interpreter, himself handed on to us in writing those things which Peter had proclaimed. And Luke, too, the follower of Paul, set down in a book the Gospel which had been preached by him. Afterwards John, the disciple of our Lord, the very one who lay upon his breast, published a Gospel while he was living at Ephesus in Asia.

All of these handed on to us the tradition of one God, maker of heaven and earth, declared by the law and the prophets, and of one Christ, the Son of God. Anyone who does not assent to these things shows disrespect for those who shared our Lord's life and disrespect to the Lord Christ himself. Such a one is self-condemned. He resists and repudiates his own salvation. That is what all heretics do. . . .

So the tradition of the Apostles is openly available throughout the world. It is present throughout the whole church to be seen plainly by all who care to look upon the truth. We can actually recount those whom the Apostles made bishops and their successors right up to our own times. . . . But it would be a very lengthy business, in such a volume as this, to list all those in the chain of succession in every church.

Therefore we point to the tradition of the greatest and oldest of the churches, the church of Rome. It was founded and established by the two most glorious Apostles, Peter and Paul. It received its tradition from the Apostles and has declared the faith to men through a succession of bishops right up to the present time. Thus we confound all those who, in whatever manner, either wickedly to suit themselves or from empty pride or from blindness and perversity of mind, form unsanctioned associations. For every church, that is to say, the faithful everywhere, inasmuch as the apostolic tradition is preserved by them (and there are people everywhere by whom the apostolic tradition is preserved) is inevitably in agreement with this church because of its stronger fundamental grounding (*propter potentiorem principilitatem*).[1] . . .

[There follows an account of the successive bishops of Rome from the Apostles up to Irenaeus' own day.]

Book 3, Chapter 4

So, since so many demonstrations are available, we ought not to look among others for the truth, when we can so easily obtain it from the church. The Apostles, in the fullest manner, bestowed the whole truth upon the church, as a rich man does in a treasure house. So whoever wishes may freely partake of the water of life[2] therefrom. For the church is the entrance to life. All the others are thieves and robbers.[3] For this reason we should certainly avoid them. We should, on the other hand, firmly favour whatever belongs to the church and lay hold upon the tradition of the truth. Even if there were disagreement over some proper question, surely we ought to turn to the oldest churches, with which the Apostles were associated, and to learn from them the sure and clear answer to the question at issue.

Suppose the Apostles had not left us any written documents. Would we not then be obliged to follow the rule of the tradition which they handed on to those to whom they entrusted the care of the churches? Many nations of those uncivilized people who believe in Christ accept this rule without paper or ink, having salvation written in their hearts by the Spirit. They have carefully preserved the ancient tradition, believing in one God, maker of heaven and earth and all that is therein, by Jesus Christ, Son of God. He, on account of his exceeding love for what he had made, took upon himself all that was involved in being born of the Virgin, in his own person uniting man to God. He suffered under Pontius Pilate. He rose again and was received in splendour. He will come in glory as the saviour of those who are saved and the judge of those who are judged. He will send into eternal fire those who distort the truth, and those who disparage his Father and his own coming.

In respect of our language, those people who have believed this faith in the absence of written documents are uncivilized; but in respect of belief, usage and morals, because of faith, they are extremely wise and pleasing to God, being just and chaste and wise in their dealings. If anyone were to preach the inventions of heretics to these people, speaking in their own language, they would immediately close their ears and flee as far as possible rather than subject themselves to hearing blasphemous talk.

[1] It is impossible to reproduce the tantalizing ambiguity of this phrase in English.

[2] cf. *John* 22. 17. [3] cf. *John* 10. 8.

Thus by means of the ancient apostolic tradition they do not even admit the pretentious talk of these men to their minds. For among these men there was neither church founded nor doctrine established.

THE FOUR GOSPELS

Book 3, Chapter 2

These, then, are the fundamentals of the Gospel: the declaration that there is one God, who is maker of this universe, who was proclaimed by the prophets and who established the dispensation of the law through Moses and who is the Father of our Lord Jesus Christ. There is no knowledge in the Gospels of any other God or any other Father. The Gospels have such solid ground about them that even the heretics themselves bear witness in their favour. Everyone of them makes the Gospel his starting point in attempting to establish his doctrine. The Ebionites,[1] who entertain false preconceptions about the Lord and use only the Gospel according to Matthew, are refuted out of that very same Gospel. Marcion[2] cuts out passages from the Gospel according to Luke, yet by those very portions which he retains he is shown to be a blasphemer against the only existent God. Those who separate Jesus from the Christ, and assert that the Christ remained incapable of suffering while Jesus really suffered, give pride of place to the Gospel according to Mark. They could be corrected if they read it with love of truth. The Valentinians[3] make the fullest use of the Gospel according to John in order to prove their 'conjunctions'. They will be exposed by that very same Gospel as saying nothing right, as I have shown in Book 1. And so, since the opposition lends us support in using these Gospels, our case is true and well founded.

The Gospels can neither be more nor less in number than they are. There are four regions of the world in which we live and four winds which blow throughout the whole world. The church is spread over all the world and the pillar and mainstay of the church is the Gospel and the spirit of life. It therefore follows reasonably that the church should have four pillars from which blow the winds of immortality giving life to men. So plainly, he who is the maker of all things, the Word, he who

[1] An unorthodox group with strong Jewish associations. According to Irenaeus, they held that Jesus was an ordinary man on whom the heavenly 'Christ' descended at his baptism.

[2] Leader of a strongly anti-Jewish movement. He denied that the God of the Old Testament was the God and Father of Jesus Christ.

[3] Valentinus was the leader of a school of thought which attempted to combine Christianity with oriental and Greek religious thought. There were many such movements in the second and third centuries. They are collectively known as the Gnostics. The Valentinians believed in a vast hierarchy of spiritual beings, arranged in pairs. Each pair was produced by the union or *conjunction* of the pair above them in the hierarchy.

sits above the cherubim and holds all things together in his power, being disclosed to men, has given us a fourfold gospel bound together in a single spirit. So David, praying insistently for his advent says, 'Thou that sittest upon the cherubim, shine forth'.[1] The cherubim had four faces. Their faces are images of the ordered work of the Son of God. 'For the first beast', it says, 'was like a lion.'[2] This signifies his efficacious, commanding, royal character. 'The second is like a calf', signifying his sacrificial, priestly office. 'And the third beast had a face as a man.' This plainly describes his advent as a man. 'And the fourth was like a flying eagle', showing the gift of the Spirit flying towards the church.

Now the Gospels are in harmony with those creatures among whom the Christ is seated. For the Gospel according to John describes the sovereign, efficacious and glorious generation, saying thus, 'In the beginning was the Word and the Word was with God, and the Word was God'[3] and 'All things were made by him and without him was not anything made that was made.'[4] For this reason that Gospel is full of complete confidence, for such is his person. The Gospel according to Luke, being of a sacerdotal character, began with Zacharias, the priest, offering a sacrifice to God. For already the fatted calf was being prepared, the one to be sacrificed for the finding of the younger son. Matthew tells of the human aspect of his birth, saying 'The book of the generation of Jesus Christ, the son of David, the son of Abraham'[5] and again 'Now the birth of the Christ was on this wise:'[6] So this is the Gospel of his human aspect and on this account throughout the whole Gospel a meek, humble-minded man is kept in mind. Mark began with the prophetic spirit coming to men from on high. He says 'The beginning of the gospel of Jesus Christ as it is written in the Prophet Esaias'[7] indicating the winged image of Gospel. So his proclamation is abbreviated and fast-moving, for this is the prophetic style.

The Word of God himself held conversation with the Patriarchs before Moses in his divine and glorious aspect. For those under the law he singled out his priestly, ministerial office. After that he became man and sent the gift of the Holy Spirit into all the world, sheltering us with his own wings.

Such, then, is the ordered work of the Son of God and such are the forms of the beasts, and the character of the Gospels corresponds to the forms of the beasts. The beasts are fourfold, the Gospel is fourfold, and the ordered work of the Lord is fourfold. For this reason four catholic covenants were given to mankind. The first, that of the flood of Noah, on the occasion of the rainbow; the second, that of Abraham, under the

[1] *Psalm* 80. 1. [2] *Revelation* 4. 7. [3] *John* 1. 1. [4] Ibid. 3.
[5] *Matthew* 1. 1. [6] cf. *Matthew* 1. 18. [7] cf. *Mark* 1. 1–2.

sign of circumcision; the third, that of the giving of the law under Moses; and the fourth, that of the Gospel, established by our Lord, Jesus Christ.

These things being so, all who disregard the form of the Gospel, those who amend the aspects of the Gospel, making them more or less than they are said to be, are vain, ignorant and presumptuous. The former attempt to appear to have discovered more than the truth. The latter attempt to set aside the divine plan. . . .

RESURRECTION AND RESTORATION

Book 4, Chapter 36

In these last days, when the fullness of the time of liberty came, the Word himself, through himself, 'washed away the filth of the daughters of Zion',[1] and with his own hands washed the feet of his disciples. This is the completion of man's inheritance of God. As in the beginning we were all brought into slavery through the debt of death by the first men, so in the last times and in the last man, all who from the beginning had been disciples, being cleansed and washed of the concomitants of death, entered into the life of God. For he who washed the feet of the disciples made the whole body holy and brought it into a state of purity. For this reason, too, he administered food to the disciples when they were in a recumbent posture, symbolizing those who are lying in the ground. It was to them that he came to impart life. As Jeremiah says: 'The holy Lord has remembered his dead in Israel, who have been asleep in the land of the grave, and he came down to them to declare his salvation to them so that they might be saved.'[2]

It was for this reason also that the eyes of the disciples were weighed down when the Christ was coming to his passion. When he found them sleeping, he let it pass the first time, thus signifying the patience of God with slumbering humanity. But when he came the second time, he awakened them and got them to their feet, signifying that his passion is the awakening of those of his disciples who are asleep. On their account 'he also descended into the lower parts of the earth'[3] to see with his own eyes the passivity of those laid to rest.[4] Concerning them, he said to his disciples, 'Many prophets and righteous men have desired to see and hear what ye do see and hear'.[5]

[1] *Isaiah* 4. 4.

[2] This alleged quotation appears elsewhere in the *Five Books Against Heresies*. It is there attributed not to Jeremiah but to Isaiah. The curious thing is that in no extant manuscript of either prophet can any trace of this saying be found.

[3] *Ephesians* 4. 9.

[4] Something like this appears to be the sense of a phrase which defies translation.

[5] *Matthew* 13. 17.

For the Christ came not only for the sake of those who believed in him in the time of Tiberius Caesar and the Father did not make provision only for those men who are alive now. He made provision for the whole number of all men who, from the beginning, according to their virtue in their own generation feared and loved God and were just and pious in their dealings with their neighbours and desired to see the Christ and to hear his voice. So in his second coming he will arouse all such men from their sleep. He will raise them up. Equally he will raise up the remainder, who will be judged, and he will establish his kingdom.

Since there is one God who guided the patriarchs into his ways, it is he who 'has justified the circumcision by faith and the uncircumcision through faith.'[1] For as we are prefigured in the former, so they in turn are represented in us—that is, in the church—and they receive the reward of their accomplishment. . . .

Book 5, Chapter 2

Those who deny that the flesh can be saved and are scornful about its regeneration, alleging that it is not capable of becoming incorruptible, are utterly mistaken. They treat the whole providence of God as though it were of no account. If the flesh is not saved then, obviously, neither did the Lord redeem us with his blood, nor is the cup of the Eucharist the communion of his blood, nor the bread which we break the communion of his body. Blood does not exist except in veins and flesh and everything else that goes to make a man. Being made just such flesh as this, the Word of God redeemed us by his blood. Thus his Apostle says: 'In whom we have redemption through his blood, even the remission of our sins.'[2]

We are his members and we draw our nourishment from the created order. He himself bestows the creation upon us. He causes his sun to rise and the rain to fall according to his will. He affirmed that that cup, which is part of the created order, is his blood which was shed. With it he infuses our blood. He has assured us that that bread, which is part of the created order, is his body. With it he builds up our bodies.

So, when the cup which is mixed and the bread which is made receive the Word of God, and the Eucharist becomes the body of Christ, and the substance of our flesh is sustained and increased by them, how can they say that the flesh is not capable of receiving the gift of God, which is eternal life?—Why, when the flesh is nourished by the body and blood of Christ and is a member of him? As the blessed Apostle Paul also says in his letter to the Ephesians, 'For we are members of his body, of his flesh, and of his bones.'[3] He does not say this with reference to some kind

[1] *Romans* 3. 30. [2] *Colossians* 1. 14. [3] *Ephesians* 5. 30.

of spiritual, invisible man, for a spirit has neither bones nor flesh. He is referring to the constitution of an actual man, made up of flesh and nerves and bones. It is this flesh which is nourished by the cup which is his blood and receives growth from the bread which is his body. . . .

Book 5, Chapter 36

Since men really exist, their renewal must be something that really exists—not a departure into nothingness, but an actual advance in the real world. It is not the substance or essence of creation that is brought to an end. (For he who established it is true and constant.) But 'the fashion of this world passeth away'[1]—that is to say, those aspects in which transgression has been committed, for in them man grows old. For this reason the present fashion of the world has been made temporary, since God has foreknowledge of everything. (I showed this in the previous book and, so far as possible, disclosed the reason for the creation of the temporal world.)

But when this present fashion passes away and man is renewed and flourishes to the point of incorruptibility so that he can no longer grow old, there shall be the new heaven and the new earth. In this new heaven and earth, the new humanity will remain perpetually in communion with God. As this will continue without end, Isaiah says: 'For as the new heaven and the new earth, which I make, remain before me, saith the Lord, so shall your seed and your name remain.'[2] As the Presbyters say: Then those who are judged worthy of a life in heaven shall go there, others shall enjoy the delights of paradise, others shall have the splendour of the city. For the Saviour shall be seen everywhere according as those who see him shall be worthy. . . .

[1] *I Corinthians* 7. 31. [2] *Isaiah* 66. 22.

II

TERTULLIAN

Quintus Septimius Florens Tertullianus was born in Carthage of pagan parents about AD 160. He received a very thorough education and went to practise law in Rome, where he became a Christian. About 195 he returned to Carthage. It is unlikely that he was ever a priest, but after his return to Carthage he devoted his whole time to the service of the church.

He was of a severe, uncompromising turn of mind. This made him critical of what appeared to him as the laxity of the Catholic church. He became a member of the Montanist sect. The Montanists attached crucial importance to the ecstatic possession of its leaders by the Holy Spirit. They also entertained a severely puritanical interpretation of Christian ethics. In spite of the official condemnation of Montanism as a heresy, Tertullian continued to be their most distinguished champion.

In spite of his heretical, sectarian connexions in the later part of his life, Tertullian made important contributions to orthodox theology. He was, above all, a master of language. The terse brilliance of his language is largely lost in translation, however. He argues his case with the suave brilliance of a distinguished barrister. Much of the technical terminology, in terms of which the theology of the West was worked out, was coined by him.

The treatise *Against Praxeas*—the opening section of which is reproduced below—was written after Tertullian became a Montanist. Praxeas was largely responsible for the exclusion of Montanus and his followers from the communion of Rome. But it is not on this score that Tertullian attacks him so much as his doctrine that God the Father and God the Son may be identified. This heresy is sometimes known as Patripassianism.

Tertullian comes far short of settling any of the fundamental problems of trinitarian doctrine; but with the precision of his legal mind he disclosed the issues in terms of which the West was to discuss this problem in the centuries to come.

He was very prolific and his extant writings are too numerous to list here.

English translations of the treatise *Against Praxeas: Tertullian's Treatise*

Against Praxeas, the text edited with introduction, translation and commentary by Ernest Evans, London, S.P.C.K., 1948.

See also *The Writings of Tertullian*, 2 vols., Ante-Nicene Christian Library, Edinburgh, T. and T. Clark, 1849, and selections from the writings of Tertullian in *Early Latin Theology*, editor S. L. Greenslade, Library of Christian Classics, London, S.C.M.

AGAINST PRAXEAS

(1) The devil has vied with the truth in various ways. At times he has tried to shake it by defending it. He is the advocate of one Lord, the almighty Creator of the world, only in order to make a heresy out of the unity. He alleges that the Father himself came down into the Virgin; that the Father himself was born of her; that the Father himself suffered. In short, he alleges that the Father himself *is* Jesus Christ.

But the serpent has forgotten himself, for when he tackled Jesus Christ after the baptism of John, it was as the Son that he tempted him. He knew that God had a Son. He knew it on the basis of those very Scriptures out of which he framed the temptation. 'If thou art the Son of God, command these stones to be made bread.[1] And again, 'If thou art the Son of God, cast thyself down from hence, for it is written that he (the Father of course) hath given his angels charge concerning thee, that in their hands they should bear thee up lest in any place thou dash thy foot against a stone'.[2] Or does he accuse the Gospels of lying? Does he say, 'Let Matthew and Luke answer for that. The fact is that I made my approach to God himself. It was the Almighty himself that I tempted—face to face. This was the intention of the approach. This was the intention of the temptation. Indeed, had it been the Son of God, I might never have demeaned myself'?

But the truth is rather that he himself has been a liar from the very first. So is any man who has been suborned to support his case, such as Praxeas.

Praxeas was the first to introduce this kind of perversion from Asia into Rome. He has always been an unstable character. He is puffed up, too, with the grand boast that he is a martyr, all because of the mere tedium of a short period of ordinary imprisonment. Even if this man had given his body to be burned, it would have profited him nothing, for he has nothing of the love of God in him. He has altogether obliterated God's gracious gifts of the spirit. For at that time, the Bishop of Rome was on the very point of recognizing the prophecies of Montanus, Prisca and

[1] *Matthew* 4. 3. [2] Ibid. 4. 6; cf. *Psalm* 91. 11–12.

Maximilla.[1] On the basis of this recognition he was offering peace to the churches of Asia and Phrygia. But this man, by telling lies about the prophets themselves and their churches, and by upholding the pronouncements of the bishop's predecessors, forced him to revoke the letters of peace already sent upon their way, and to abandon the proposal to recognize the spiritual gifts.

So Praxeas successfully negotiated two items of the devil's business in Rome. He expelled prophecy and introduced heresy. He put the Holy Spirit to flight and crucified the Father.

The field was oversown with Praxean tares. They flourished here also, while most people slumbered in the simplicity of true doctrine. The presence of these tares was disclosed by those whom God had appointed to do so. They even seemed to have been weeded out. Indeed the teacher gave assurance that he would mend his ways by returning to his former opinions. His written statement is still lodged with those natural men[2] among whom the transaction took place. After that, not another word is heard of him.

It was after this that we dissociated ourselves from the natural men over the issue of our acknowledgment and defence of the Holy Spirit. In the meantime those tares had scattered their seed everywhere. For a time it lay concealed, its vitality deceptively disguised. Now it has burst forth afresh. But, if God be willing, it will be weeded out again in the time at my disposal. If not, then in his own time, every rank growth will be gathered in and, along with everything else that is offensive, it will be burned in inextinguishable fire.

(2) So, in spite of the lapse of time, we still have a Father who was born, a Father who suffered—the Lord God Almighty himself, declared to be Jesus Christ. Now we have always believed that God is one. We are all the more sure of it now that we are better informed through the agency of the Holy Spirit, who leads us into all truth. But we conceive this unity in terms of an 'inner nature' (*dispensatio*)—which is our expression for οἰκονομία. The one only true God has a Son, who proceeded from himself, 'by whom all things were made and without whom was not anything made that was made'.[3] He was sent by the Father into the Virgin, Son of man and Son of God. He was called Jesus Christ. He suffered, died and was buried, according to the Scriptures. He was raised up by the Father and taken back into Heaven. He sits at the right hand

[1] Tertullian's point here is that had it not been for Praxeas' interference, the Montanist sect to which he belonged might have been in full communion with the Roman church.

[2] This is the name by which the Montanist sect referred to the non-Montanists, who did not recognize the charismatic gifts of the spirit in the same sense as they did.

[3] *John* I. 3.

of the Father and will come again to judge the living and the dead. Thereafter, according to his promise, he sent the Holy Spirit from the Father—the Holy Spirit, who is the Paraclete, the sanctifier of the faith of those who believe in the Father and in the Son and in the Holy Ghost.

This rule of faith has come down to us from the beginning of the Gospel. It antedates even the early heretics, to say nothing of Praxeas, who is but a man of yesterday. This is demonstrable from the lateness of all heresies, as well as from the sheer novelty of Praxeas' recent contribution. So I submit that we should oppose all heresies with this maxim: Whatever is original is genuine; whatever is secondary is counterfeit.

But apart from this maxim, it is always proper to make room for a critical review of heresies, if only to brief and arm people against them. Besides, it might otherwise seem that each particular perversion of the truth had been condemned without examination, the issue being merely prejudged. This is especially so in the case of this heresy, which imagines itself to be in possession of the pure truth in the belief that the oneness of God can be affirmed only by saying that the Father, the Son, and the Holy Spirit are one and the same person.

They appear not to realize that since all proceed out of one, they are one in respect of substance; yet at the same time the mystery of the *οἰκονομία* (inner nature), which distinguishes the unity into a trinity, is preserved. The doctrine of the 'inner nature' sets out three, however, not in status, but in order, not in substance but in aspect, not in power but in manifestation. But they are one in substance, one in status and one in power, for there is one God from whom these orders, these aspects, these manifestations are reckoned out in the name of the Father and of the Son and of the Holy Ghost.

How they admit of plurality without division, the argument will show as it proceeds.

(3) Simple people (not to say the foolish and ignorant)—for the majority of the faithful have always been such—fail to understand that along with the unity of God, one should believe also in his 'inner nature'. Since the rule of faith converts them from the many gods of the world to the one true God, they are frightened off by the idea of an inner nature in God. They claim that the plurality and structure of the trinity divides the unity. But a trinity which derives from unity itself does not destroy unity but arranges it.

So they allege that we preach two or even three gods while they claim that they worship one—as though unity irrationally conceived did not make a heresy and trinity rationally worked out did not constitute the truth. 'We hold', they say, 'to the principle of undivided rule (*monarchia*).' Even the Latins pronounce this [Greek] word '*monarchia*' with such deliberation and expertise that you would think they understood it as well as they pronounce it. But while the Latins at least try to pronounce '*monarchia*', the Greeks themselves won't even try to understand οἰκονομία (inner nature).

In so far as I have gathered any small knowledge of both languages I know that '*monarchia*' signifies neither more nor less than a single, unitary rule. Yet the fact that undivided rule pertains to one man does not necessarily mean that he to whom it pertains may not have a son or must have made himself his own son or may not administer his monarchy by the agency of whomever he chooses. I submit that in such a sense, no dominion so belongs to a single person as his own, with such singularity of title, or in such a sense of monarchy, that it is not administered by other persons intimately associated with it, whom it has provided as its own agents. If, moreoever, he to whom the monarchy belongs has a son, it is not thereby divided, nor does it cease to be a monarchy if the son is appointed a partner in the rule. It remains ultimately in the hands of him who bestows it on his son. So long as it is his, it still remains a monarchy, though held by two who are thus united.

The undivided rule of God is administered by so many legions and hosts of angels (as it is written, 'ten thousand times ten thousand stood before him and a thousand thousands ministered unto him')[1]; this does not mean that it ceased to be the rule of one. A monarchy does not cease to be a monarchy because it is administered by so many officials. If this is so, why should it be thought that God suffers division and dispersion in the Son and in the Holy Spirit, who have the second and third places assigned to them, and who even share the substance of the Father.

Do you seriously suggest that the members of the body politic, the family relationships, the institutions, the power itself, the whole establishment of monarchy is in fact its overthrow. Surely not! I should much prefer it if you would exercise your wit upon the significance of the facts rather than the sound of the word. You must understand the overthrow of a monarchy to occur only when another power which has a different basis and acts on its own authority, and which features thus as a rival, is superimposed. This happens, for instance, when another god is introduced to oppose the Creator, as by Marcion—or when many gods are introduced, as by people like Valentinus and Prodicus. When the destruction of the Creator is involved, then you have the overthrow of the undivided rule.

[1] *Daniel* 7. 10.

(4) But I derive the Son from no other source than the substance of the Father. He does nothing apart from the Father's will. His whole authority derives from the Father. How, then, in the matter of the faith, can I be destroying that undivided rule which was committed by the Father to the Son and which, I insist, remains a unity in the Son. I would maintain the same principle with regard to the third order, for I believe that the Spirit proceeds from no other source than the Father through the Son.

Have a care, then, lest it is you who are destroying the undivided rule which has been constituted in its own order and arrangement under just as many names as God pleased. So firmly does the unity maintain its place, that even though it admits the introduction of trinity, yet the kingdom must be restored to the Father by the Son. So the apostle writes with reference to the last things, 'When he shall have delivered up the kingdom to God the Father; for he shall reign until God put all his enemies under his feet'.[1] It is clearly stated in the Psalm, 'Sit thou at my right hand until I make thine enemies the footstool of thy feet'.[2] 'But when all things have been made subject to him (except him who put all things under him), then shall the Son himself be subject to him who put all things under him, that God may be all in all.'[3]

We see, then, that the Son does not prejudice the principle of undivided rule, although, for the time being, it is vested in the Son. Its condition remains unaltered in the Son, and in that same condition it will be restored to the Father by the Son. Thus no one is destroying it just because they admit that there is a Son, since plainly it is committed to him by the Father and restored to the Father by him.

From this one passage of the apostolic Epistle we have been able to show that the Father and the Son are two in number. Furthermore, we have been able to show that, since one is called Father and the other is called Son, since there is one who bestows the kingdom and one upon whom it is bestowed, since, also, there is one who subjects it and one to whom it is subject, they must of necessity be two in number.

(5) But since people will have it that the two are but one, so that the Father and the Son are deemed to be one and the same, the whole question of the Son needs investigation. We must ask whether there really is such a being, who he is and how he exists. In this way the actual facts of the case will themselves justify the formula of their description. This will be done from the Scriptures and from a correct interpretation of them.

There are even some who say that the Book of Genesis begins, in the Hebrew, 'In the beginning God made himself a Son'. However, since there are no adequate grounds for this reading, it is by other arguments that I am influenced. These arguments are based on God's own inner

[1] *I Corinthians* 15, 24f. [2] *Psalm* 110. 1. [3] *I Corinthians* 15. 27–8.

nature, which existed before the foundation of the world, until the Son was begotten.[1] For before everything, God was alone, being in himself, for himself, his own world, his own place and all things. But he was alone only in the sense that there was nothing extrinsic to him. And yet he was not alone. He had with him the reason which he possessed in himself. For God is rational. Reason was first in him. It is because this is so that all things come from him. This reason is his consciousness. The Greeks call it *Logos*. We translate this term as 'Word'.[2] So now, as a result of the *naïveté* of the translation, it is usual for our people to say that the Word was in the beginning with God. But it would be more appropriate to think of reason as prior; for God was not so much articulate as rational before the beginning. Besides, the Word itself is grounded in reason. This shows that reason is prior as being the substance of the Word.

But ultimately this makes no difference. For although God had not yet uttered his Word, he nonetheless had it with him in his reason and within his very self. He was silently thinking and ordering within himself those things which he would soon declare through the Word. When he was thinking out and ordering those things with his reason, his private discourse was, in effect, the employment of his Word.

To understand this more easily, consider what takes place within yourself. You are made in the image and likeness of God, and so have reason within yourself. You are a rational animal, not merely as having been made by a rational creator, but actually being made a living soul out of his substance. Note how, when you reason with yourself, the same process takes place within you. In every movement of thought you find discourse. It is involved in every act of consciousness. Your every thought involves a word. Every act of consciousness involves reason. You have to speak it in your mind, and while you speak it you have to recognize the discourse as your interlocutor. This discourse contains within itself the same reason by which you think. You think in company with it and you think by means of it. So there is, in a sense, a second person within you, through whom you speak when thinking and through whom you think when speaking. The discourse itself is something other than yourself.

How much more completely does this take place in God, whose image you are reckoned to be? He has reason within himself even when he is silent; and in reason is his Word. So I am not being at all rash when I conclude that even before the foundation of the world, God was not

[1] It is clear from what follows that Tertullian did not intend to deny the eternal generation of the Son. Here, as throughout the whole treatise, we see how the theologians of the church were still only feeling their way into the delicate problem of the precise definition of trinitarian doctrine.

[2] *Sermo*, i.e. 'word' in the sense of connected discourse.

alone. Within himself he always had reason. Within reason was the Word. In the employment of that Word he distinguished it as something beside himself.

(6) In the Scriptures this power and structure of the divine consciousness is also designated by the name 'Wisdom'. For what is wiser than the reason or Word of God? Listen, then, to Wisdom herself, established as a second person. 'The Lord created me as the beginning of his ways for his works' sake, before he made the earth, before the mountains were set in their places; yea, before all the hills he begat me'[1]—that is, creating and begetting in his own consciousness. Now note that she stands beside him as a separate being. 'When he was preparing the heavens', she says, 'I was present with him; and when he made his strong places upon the winds, which are the clouds above; and when he secured the fountains which are beneath the sky, I was with him arranging all things with him. I was she in whose presence he delighted. Daily did I delight in his person.'[2] When God first willed to produce those things which, by Wisdom and Reason and Word, he had ordained within himself, giving to each its own substance and form, he first of all sent forth the Word who had within him his inseparable wisdom and reason. He did this so that the universe should come into existence by the agency of the very one who had thought it out and ordained it. Indeed the universe was already made in the sense that it was already in the consciousness of God. All that was wanting was for each thing to be manifest, recognized and apprehended, each in its own form and substance.

This, then, is where the Word takes on his own form and outward vesture. He became sound and voice when God said, 'Let there be light'. This is the perfect birth of the Word when he proceeds from God. He was first established by God under the name of Wisdom. 'The Lord established me as the beginning of his ways.'[3] Then he was begotten as effective agent, 'When he prepared the Heavens I was present with him'.[4] Thus he makes God his Father by proceeding from him. He was made the Son, the first begotten, begotten before all things. He is the only-begotten; for he alone is begotten in the true sense out of the womb of God's heart. The Father himself testifies to this, saying, 'My heart has brought forth a most excellent word'.[5] Thereafter the Father delights in him and rejoices in his person. 'Thou art my beloved Son, this day have I begotten thee'[6] and 'Before the daystar I begat thee'.[7] The Son likewise acknowledges the Father, speaking in his own person under the name of Wisdom. 'The Lord formed me as the beginning of his ways for his own works' sake; before all the hills did he beget me.'[8] It is Wisdom

[1] *Proverbs* 8. 22–5. [2] Ibid. 8. 27–30. [3] Ibid. 8. 22. [4] Ibid. 8. 27.
[5] *Psalm* 45. 1. [6] *Psalm* 2. 7. [7] *Psalm* 110. 3. [8] *Proverbs* 8. 22, 25.

who seems here to say that she was established by the Lord for the sake of his works and ways. But elsewhere it is made clear that all things were created by the Word and without him was not anything made.[1] And also in another place, 'By his word were the heavens established and all the powers thereof by his spirit'.[2] That means the Spirit which is within the Word. It is therefore clear that it is one and the same power which is sometimes referred to as Wisdom, sometimes as Word. He received the beginning of the ways of God's works. It is he who established the heavens. It is he by whom all things were made and without whom was not anything made that was made.

There is no need to dwell on this point any longer. For it is quite clear that under the name of Wisdom and of Reason and of the whole divine mind or spirit, we are to understand the Word. He becomes the Son of God when, by proceeding from him, he was begotten.

'So', you say, 'you make the Word some kind of substance made up of spirit, wisdom and reason.' Certainly I do! But you will not admit that he is substantial, having a being of his own. In this way he could be regarded as a real being, a person. Thus he could be another beside God, so making two—Father and Son, God and the Word. You will say, 'What is a word but a voice, the sound emitted by a mouth? It is, as the grammarians say, air that has been struck and is intelligible to the ear. Apart from that it is an empty I-know-not-what, a void, an incorporeal thing.'

But I maintain that nothing void or empty can come forth from God. He from whom it has been brought forth is not empty or void. Whatever has proceeded from so great a substance cannot lack substance. That which is the maker of such great substances cannot lack substance—for he himself is the maker of the things that were made through him. How can he himself amount to nothing when no single thing was made without him? Could a void create solid objects? Could an empty thing create things that are full? Could an incorporeal thing create corporeal things? Admittedly there are instances in which a thing can produce its opposite, but a mere void can produce nothing at all. Is the Word of God, who is called the Son, who is even called God, a mere nothing? 'And the Word was with God and the Word was God.'[3] It is written 'Thou shalt not take the name of God as an empty thing (*in vanum*)'.[4]

Surely we are here concerned with the one who, 'being in the form of God, thought it not robbery to be equal with God'. In what sense was he in the form of God? He must certainly have been God in some form, not in no form at all; for who will deny that God is a body although

[1] *John* 1, 3. [2] *Psalm* 33. 6. [3] *John* 1. 1. [4] *Exodus* 20. 7.

he is spirit?[1] Spirit has corporeal existence of its own kind and in its own form. If, then, even invisible entities have body and shape so that they are visible to God alone, surely what has been put forth from God's own substance will not lack substance. Whatever the substance of the Word was, I call him Person and I claim for him the name of Son. And so long as I call him Son, I claim that he is distinguishable as another beside the Father.

[1] The view that although God was a spiritual, immaterial substance, he was nonetheless corporeal was common in antiquity prior to the time of St Augustine. It arises from the fact that the church was dependent on the terminology of popular Stoic philosophy as a medium of expression.

III

ALEXANDRIAN THEOLOGY

The catechetical school of Alexandria was the oldest and most famous of the ancient theological schools. We first hear of it under the leadership of Pantaenus about AD 180. The city of Alexandria had, since its foundation by Alexander the Great, been a centre of intellectual activity where all cultures met. The Christian school of Alexandria was always led by men of broad culture who made full—sometimes daring—use of all the resources of Greek philosophy. The Alexandrian scholars were much given to allegorical interpretations of scripture. This tradition had already been established in Alexandria by such Jewish scholars as the great Philo. It was typical of the Alexandrians that they made full and ingenious use of the freedom in interpreting the Bible which this method allowed.

The scholars of Alexandria were also prepared to find Christian doctrine in Greek philosophy. Much of their ingenuity was devoted to an attempted reconciliation of the essentially Hebraic ethos of the biblical writings with Greek modes of thought.

Clement and Origen were by far the most outstanding scholars of this school. It reached its zenith in the work of Origen. After his departure it fell progressively into decay.

CLEMENT

Clement of Alexandria (Titus Flavius Clemens) was born in Athens of pagan parents about the middle of the second century. He travelled widely and eventually settled in Alexandria, first as a pupil of Pantaenus and finally as his successor as head of the school. During the persecutions under the Emperor Septimus Severus, he left Alexandria about 202 and settled in Asia Minor where he died about ten years later.

Clement has been called the first Christian scholar. He not only had a scholarly knowledge of the Scriptures and the writings of Hellenistic Judaism, but also was thoroughly acquainted with the whole body of Greek philosophy and literature. In arguing his case for Christianity, he uses this pagan source almost as readily as the Bible. He saw all true knowledge and wisdom, whatever its source, as a preparation for Christianity, and the Christian faith as the fulfilment of all learning.

His work lacks the systematic completeness of his successor, Origen; but it was he who established the theological method and created the distinctive character of the Alexandrian school. In spite of attitudes and presuppositions which seem strange to us today, his work retains a fine spiritual quality, especially in the way he combines a severely puritanical ethic with a sensitive appreciation of the gentleness and love of God.

Works

Apart from fragments, only three major works survive.

(1) *Exhortation to the Gentiles*—An appeal to the Greeks to recognize the fulfilment of the best insights of their culture in Christianity.

(2) *The Pedagogue*—Christ as the teacher of humanity.

(3) *The Miscellanies*—A loosely connected treatment of various topics in eight books.

It is from this work that I have strung together a few passages on the theme of philosophy and faith—a topic which once more in our own day has become crucial.

English Translations

W. Wilson, *Clement of Alexandria*, 2 vols., Ante-Nicene Christian Library, T. and T. Clark, Edinburgh, 1869.

L. Oulton and H. Chadwick, *Alexandrian Christianity*, Library of Christian Classics, S.C.M. Press, 1954—selected passages.

PHILOSOPHY AND FAITH

(Passages from the *Miscellanies*)

From Book 1, Chapter 5

Before the advent of the Lord, philosophy was necessary to the Greeks as a means to righteousness. Now it serves as a means to piety. It is a kind of preparatory training for those who wish to attain to faith through demonstration. 'For thy foot shall not stumble',[1] it is said, if you refer all that is good, whether it pertains to the Greeks or to us, to Providence. God is the cause of everything that is good. Of some things he is the immediate cause, as in the case of the Old and New Testaments. Of other things he is the indirect cause, as in the case of philosophy. Perhaps he even gave philosophy directly to the Greeks, before the Lord had extended his call to them. For philosophy informed the Hellenistic mind, just as the law did for the Hebrews, to lead them to the Christ. Philosophy is a preparatory discipline, opening the way for him whom the Christ will bring to perfection.

[1] *Proverbs* 3. 23.

Solomon says, 'Defend wisdom and she will exalt thee; she will arm thee with a crown of delight'.[1] Indeed, when you have fortified her round about with the coping stone of philosophy, then, given honest, unstinted effort, you will be able to keep her impregnable to the Sophists. The way of truth is one, but it is like an ever-flowing river into which there flow streams from all sides. So, in inspired words, it is said: 'Hear, my son, and receive my words, so that you may have many ways into life. I teach you the ways of wisdom so that the fountains may not dry up on you.'[2] These are fountains which flow from the earth itself. It was not for one righteous man that he says there are many ways of salvation; but for many righteous men there are many ways of salvation. Thus we should understand 'The ways of the righteous shine like a light'.[3] So this preparatory training as well as the law is to be regarded as a way and a point of departure into life.

'Jerusalem, Jerusalem, how often would I have gathered thy children, as a hen her chickens!'[4] Now the name 'Jerusalem' means 'vision of peace'. So, in the language of inspiration, he shows that those who enjoy the vision of peace are trained for their calling in many different ways. It is said that he would but could not. How often and where?—Twice!—in the coming of the prophets and in his own coming. So the expression 'how often' shows that wisdom is manifold. In all ways, however numerous and however excellent, it certainly saves some, both in time and in eternity. . . .

Just as education in the liberal arts is a means of approach to philosophy, their mistress; so philosophy is a means of approach to wisdom. Philosophy is the study of wisdom, and wisdom is the knowledge of things divine and human and their causes. Wisdom is therefore mistress of the preparatory culture. . . .

All I am really saying here is that philosophy is dedicated to the pursuit of truth and reality. This is the truth to which the Lord himself referred when he said, 'I am the truth'. The preparatory training for the life in Christ rouses the intellect, and induces an inquiring sagacity by means of true philosophy, which the initiated possess, having found it, or rather received it, from the truth himself. . . .

From Book 1, Chapter 8

But the art of sophistry, which the Greeks cultivate, is a specious power which makes false opinions like true by means of words. It produces rhetoric as a means of persuasion and argument for the sake of disputation. Now if these arts are practised without philosophy, they will be injurious to everyone. Plato roundly denounces sophistry as a fraudulent art.

[1] cf. *Proverbs* 4. 8–9. [2] cf. *Proverbs* 4. 10–11. [3] *Proverbs* 4. 18. [4] *Matthew* 23. 37.

Aristotle follows him in exposing it as a thieves' device, for it speciously usurps the whole function of wisdom and professes a wisdom which it has not studied. In short, rhetoric begins from the specious; its business is argumentation; its aim is persuasion. Similarly, the art of argument begins from matters of opinion; its business is disputation; its aim is victory. So sophistry always begins from the mere appearance of things and operates by a twofold method. One part is rhetoric—that is, continuous discourse. The other part is dialectic—using the method of question and answer. The purpose of the whole process is to win admiration.

As for the famous dialectic of the schools, it does no more than exercise philosophers in matters of opinion for the sake of disputation.

The truth is not in any of these. So the Apostle is quite right in deprecating this useless game of words, saying, 'If any man do not give heed to wholesome words, and is puffed up by some kind of teaching, knowing nothing, but doting about questions and strifes of words, whereof cometh contention, envy, railings, evil surmisings, perverse disputings of men of corrupt minds, destitute of truth'.[1]

You see how he is moved against them. Their method of reasoning—in which all the sophists, whether Greeks or Barbarians, who love this wordy and fraudulent art, take such pride—he treats as diseased. The tragic poet Euripides puts it well in the *Phoenissae*, 'Unrighteous speech is a disease, standing in need of the remedies of wisdom'. Indeed, the saving Word is called 'wholesome', because it is the truth itself, and whatever is wholesome does not die. But whatever declines from health and from the divine is sheer impiety and mortal sickness. . . .

From Book 1, Chapter 9

On the other hand there are some people who think themselves so well endowed that they can choose to dispense with philosophy and reason and even to ignore natural science. They demand bare faith alone. It is as if they wished to harvest the grapes immediately without having cultivated the vine. By 'the vine' I mean, allegorically speaking, the Lord. His fruits can be harvested only by painstaking and skilful culture involving the employment of reason.

We must cut, cultivate and train and perform all the other operations. We must use the pruning hook and the hoe and all the other implements of cultivation in order to care for this vine, if we expect it to yield us good fruit. In agriculture and in medicine, unless we have undergone the training which enables us to cultivate and to cure, we are quite incompetent. So, in the matter with which we are here concerned, I call a

[1] I *Timothy* 6. 3–5.

man competent if he relates all his activities to the truth; so that he takes from geometry, from music, from grammar, from philosophy, whatever is useful, and at the same time guards his faith against every attack.

We look askance at the athlete who arrives at the contest untrained. We respect the experienced navigator who has seen the 'cities of many men', and we respect the doctor who has treated many cases. Some call this the 'empiric'.[1] The man who brings all experience to bear on the good life, drawing his examples from the Greeks as well as other sources, is an experienced seeker after truth. He is a man of discrimination. He is like the touch-stone—that Lydian stone which is believed to have the power of distinguishing between spurious and genuine gold. Our well-informed man of learning, our gnostic, can thus distinguish sophistry from philosophy, just as he can distinguish beauty-treatment from gymnastics and cookery from medicine, rhetoric from reasoned argument, and, among other things, he can distinguish heresy from truth within that philosophy which does not derive from the Greeks [i.e. the Christian faith]. So it is surely essential for the man who wishes to discover the power of God that he should know his way about intellectually and that he should achieve this by philosophical study. Surely he needs to be able to distinguish between the same word used in two different senses in the Testaments. On the occasion of his temptation, it was by distinguishing the two senses of an expression that the Lord rebutted the Devil. (In this connexion, I fail to see how the inventor of philosophy and rational enquiry, as some believe the Devil to be, could be deceived by an ambiguity.)

Admittedly the prophets and apostles were unfamiliar with the techniques of philosophical enquiry. But the thought of the prophetic and teaching Spirit is expressed in difficult language. Therefore, since all people do not have the same powers of understanding, a clear technique of exposition is called for. The prophets and disciples of the Spirit understood with perfect comprehension. For the Spirit communicated with them in faith rather than through facility of comprehension. But those who are not thus directly instructed cannot receive the faith in the same way. 'Write my commandments doubly,' it is said, 'in counsel and knowledge, that you may be able to answer the questions that are put to you with a true saying.'[2] What is this answering knowledge? Is it not also questioning knowledge? Surely it is dialectic.

Speech itself is a deliberate act, and all deliberate action proceeds from the inner word of reason. If we do not act on the basis of the word of reason, we act irrationally. To act rationally is to act in accord with God.

[1] The reference is to a school of medicine which laid great stress on clinical experience.

[2] cf. *Proverbs* 22. 20, 21. This reading represents neither the Septuagint nor the Hebrew.

'Nothing', it is said, 'was made without him'—i.e. the reasonable Word of God. Did the Lord not make all things through his own Word of reason? By contrast, the irrational animals act only under the compulsion of fear. Similarly, those persons who merely enjoy a reputation for holding the correct opinions have been induced to do the right thing, but they lack the faintest notion of what they are doing. . . .

From Book 2, Chapter 4

But, on the other hand, we, who know from the Scriptures that men have received the faculty of autonomous choice or refusal from the Lord, base our position upon the infallible criterion of faith. We show a willing spirit in that we have chosen life and have believed God simply because it is *he* who has spoken. Whoever believes the Word knows that it is genuine, for the Word is Truth. But he who disbelieves when God speaks has disbelieved God.

The Apostle says: 'By faith we understand that the world was created by the Word of God, so that what is seen was made out of things which do not appear. By faith Abel offered to God a more acceptable sacrifice than Cain, through which he received approval as righteous, God bearing witness by accepting his gifts; he died, but through his faith he is still speaking', and so on down to '. . . than to enjoy the fleeting pleasures of sin.'[1] So faith has justified even those who lived before the giving of the law made them heirs of God's promise. What need is there, then, to bring forward further examples of faith from the history available to us and to cite them as examples? 'For time would fail me to tell of Gideon, Barak, Samson, Jephthah, of David and Samuel and the prophets . . .' and the rest of the passage.[2]

There are four things in which the truth resides—sense experience, the intellect, knowledge and opinion. Among these, intellect has a natural primacy. But in our case and in our circumstances, sense experience comes first. Knowledge is brought into being out of both sensation and intellect. Taken together, their common product is evidence. But sensation merely opens the way to knowledge. Faith, on the other hand, after it has traversed the path provided by sense experience, leaves mere opinion behind, pressing on towards what is no mere appearance. It comes to rest in those things which are true.

If anyone should maintain that knowledge rests entirely upon demonstration by pure reason, he must be told that first principles are incapable of demonstration. They are known neither by skill nor by reflection. Reflection is concerned with mutable things. Skill is purely practical,

[1] *Hebrews* 11. 3–25. [2] Ibid. 11. 32.

not theoretical. So faith alone can attain to the ultimate principle on which everything rests.

All knowledge can be taught; and whatever can be taught is founded upon prior knowledge. Now the fundamental principle of the Universe was not known to the Greeks, neither to Thales who thought that water was the first cause, nor to the other natural philosophers who came after him. Even Anaxagoras, who was the first to give mind primacy over matter, was not referring strictly to the creative cause. He speaks of non-intelligent vortices acting in consort with inert, non-intelligent mind. That is why the Word says, 'Do not call yourselves masters upon the earth'.[1]

Knowledge is a state of mind resulting from demonstration, but faith is a grace which begins with what is undemonstrable and rises to what is both universal and simple—to something which is not matter, is not with matter and is not under matter. But the unbelieving, as it seems to Plato, 'try to drag everything heavenly and invisible down to earth, grasping clumsily at rocks and trees with their hands. For, clinging to all such things, they hold that only the things which can be touched and handled exist. They think that body and being are co-extensive.

'But their opponents in this matter argue carefully, basing their case upon the invisible realm. They try to establish that true being consists in intelligible, incorporeal forms.'[2] 'Behold I make new things', says the Word, 'which eye hath not seen nor ear heard, nor hath it entered the heart of man.'[3] Whatever is seen or heard or experienced, is received with new eyes and new ears and in a new heart with faith and understanding, and the disciples of the Lord hear and act spiritually. There is genuine coin and counterfeit coin. The counterfeit deceives the inexpert, but not the bankers. They are able to distinguish and separate the counterfeit from the genuine, because they have learned how. So the banker simply tells the inexpert that his money is counterfeit. How this is done, only the man who works under a banker's direction and is trained for the job knows. Aristotle says that such a capacity, resulting from sound knowledge, to judge what is true, is really faith.[4] So faith is more fundamental than knowledge and is the criterion of knowledge.

The mere parroting of opinions is only an imitation of faith. It is a feeble shot in the dark. It counterfeits faith as a flatterer counterfeits a friend, as a wolf counterfeits a dog. We know that it is only by learning his trade that the carpenter becomes a craftsman and the helmsman learns to navigate. It is not enough for them simply to want to do the

[1] cf. *Matthew* 23. 8 (?).
[2] cf. Plato, *Sophist*, 246.
[3] cf. *Isaiah* 43. 19; 64. 4; I *Corinthians* 2. 9.
[4] No such saying can be traced in any extant work of Aristotle.

right thing. They must learn by obedience. Now to be obedient to the reasonable Word, to him whom we have called the Teacher, is to believe in him unreservedly. (How, indeed, can one offer resistance to God?) So, by a divinely ordained reciprocity, knowledge assumes the character of faith, and faith assumes the character of knowledge (Book 2, Chapter 4) . . .

ORIGEN

Origen (*c.* 185–254) was born of Christian parents in Alexandria. His father was martyred in the persecutions of 202. He led a severely ascetic life—an asceticism which he carried to the mistaken extreme of castrating himself on the grounds of a misunderstanding of *Matthew* 19.12. He became the greatest and most learned teacher of the great Alexandrian school. Under the persecution of Caracalla he was forced to migrate for a short time to Caesarea in 215, but returned to Alexandria shortly afterwards. During another visit to Caesarea he was ordained priest in 230, despite his self-mutilation which should have disqualified him. The Alexandrian synod, which did not look so kindly upon him, deposed him from his position in the theological school and excommunicated him for unlawful ordination. He then moved permanently to Caesarea where he established another school. He was eventually imprisoned and tortured there in the Decian persecution and, though he survived this ordeal, he died shortly afterwards.

He is the greatest scholar among the early Fathers, but his teachings have always been highly controversial. Catholic theology owes a great deal to the creative originality of his thought, but this same originality led him into many theological novelties which have never been accepted. He was much given to a free, allegorical interpretation of Scripture and, in common with others of the Alexandrian school, expended a great deal of ingenuity integrating Platonic and Stoic philosophy with the Christian faith. Controversy over his doctrines continued after his death and some of his teachings were finally condemned in the sixth century.

His literary output was enormous (it is said that he kept seven stenographers fully employed) though by no means all of it has survived. His main writings are: (1) The *Hexapla*—a critical edition of the Hebrew and various Greek versions of the Old Testament set out in parallel columns. (2) Commentaries and sermons on every book of the Bible of which only a few survive. (3) *Against Celsus*—a systematic refutation of the powerful attack on Christianity published by the philosopher Celsus. (4) Spiritual works such as *On Prayer* and *Exhortation to Martyrdom*. (5) *De Principiis* (or *On the Fundamentals*).

De Principiis, from which the reading below is taken, is the most systematic statement of his doctrine. Unfortunately, apart from a few fragments which have come to us in Greek, we are mainly dependent for the text on a Latin translation published by Rufinus *c.* AD 400. There can be no doubt that Rufinus considerably modified the original text to bring it into line with orthodox views. This is clearly shown in Paul Koetschau's edition. I have used G. W. Butterworth's translation of this edition though I have simplified or omitted much of the annotation.

Some distinctive aspects of Origen's doctrine are: that creation is an eternal act since God's love must always have had an object; that all souls will eventually be restored to their original perfection; that the gross material nature of the universe is the result of the Fall; that eventually this material world and many worlds beyond it will be restored to the perfect condition in which they were created. He made important contributions to trinitarian doctrine and christology, though his tendency to subordinate the Christ to the Father is suspected of being one of the roots of the Arian heresy.

For further reading see:

G. W. Butterworth, Litt.D., *Origen on First Principles*, S.P.C.K., 1936.

F. Crombie, *The Writings of Origen*, Ante-Nicene Christian Library, T. and T. Clark, Edinburgh, 1869–72.

L. Oulton and H. Chadwick, *Alexandrian Christianity*, Library of Christian Classics, S.C.M. Press, 1954 (where a fuller bibliography is given).

THE CHRIST

First we must know this, that in Christ there is one nature, his deity, because he is the only-begotten Son of the Father, and another human nature, which in very recent times he took upon him to fulfil the divine purpose. Our first task therefore is to see what the only-begotten Son of God is, seeing he is called by many different names according to the circumstances and beliefs of the different writers. He is called Wisdom, as Solomon said, speaking in the person of Wisdom: 'The Lord created me the beginning of his ways for his works. Before he made anything, before the ages he established me. In the beginning before he made the earth, before the springs of waters came forth, before the mountains were settled, before all the hills he begets me.'[1] He is also called Firstborn, as the apostle Paul says: 'who is the firstborn of all creation'.[2] The Firstborn is not, however, by nature a different being from Wisdom, but is one and the same. Finally, the apostle Paul says, 'Christ, the power of God and the wisdom of God'.[3]

[1] *Proverbs* 8. 22–5. [2] *Colossians* 1. 15. [3] I *Corinthians* 1. 24.

Let no one think, however, that when we give him the name 'wisdom of God' we mean anything without hypostatic existence, that is, to take an illustration, that we understand him to be not as it were some wise living being, but a certain thing which makes men wise by revealing and imparting itself to the minds of such as are able to receive its influence and intelligence. If, then, it is once rightly accepted that the only-begotten Son of God is God's wisdom hypostatically existing, I do not think that our mind ought to stray beyond this to the suspicion that this hypostasis or substance could possibly possess bodily characteristics, since everything that is corporeal is distinguished by shape or colour or size. And who in his sober senses ever looked for shape or colour or measurable size in wisdom, considered solely as wisdom? And can anyone who has learned to regard God with feelings of reverence suppose or believe that God the Father ever existed, even for a single moment, without begetting this wisdom? For he would either say that God could not have begotten wisdom before he did beget her, so that he brought wisdom into being when she had not existed before, or else that he could have begotten her and—what it is profanity even to say about God—that he was unwilling to do so; each of which alternatives, as everyone can see, is absurd and impious, that is, either that God should advance from being unable to being able, or that, while being able, he should act as if he were not and should delay to beget wisdom.

Wherefore we recognize that God was always the Father of his only-begotten Son, who was born indeed of him and draws his being from him, but is yet without any beginning, not only of that kind which can be distinguished by periods of time, but even of that other kind which the mind alone is wont to contemplate in itself and to perceive, if I may so say, with the bare intellect and reason. Wisdom, therefore, must be believed to have been begotten beyond the limits of any beginning that we can speak of or understand. And because in this very subsistence of wisdom there was implicit every capacity and form of the creation that was to be, both of those things that exist in a primary sense and of those which happen in consequence of them, the whole being fashioned and arranged beforehand by the power of foreknowledge, wisdom, speaking through Solomon in regard to these very created things that had been as it were outlined and prefigured in herself, says that she was created as a 'beginning of the ways' of God, which means that she contains within herself both the beginnings and causes and species of the whole creation.

Now just as we have learned in what sense wisdom is the 'beginning of the ways' of God and is said to have been created, in the sense, namely, that she fashions beforehand and contains within herself the species and causes of the entire creation, in the same manner also must wisdom be understood to be the Word of God. For wisdom opens to all other beings, that is, to the whole creation, the meaning of the mysteries and secrets which are contained within the wisdom of God, and so she is called the Word, because she is as it were an interpreter of the mind's secrets. Hence I consider that to be a true saying which is written in the Acts of Paul, 'He is the Word, a living being'.[1] John, however, uses yet more exalted and wonderful language in the beginning of his gospel, when by an appropriate declaration he defines the Word to be God: 'And the Word was God, and he was in the beginning with God.'[2] Let him who assigns a beginning to the Word of God or the wisdom of God beware lest he utters impiety against the unbegotten Father himself, in denying that he was always a Father and that he begat the Word and possessed wisdom in all previous times or ages or whatever else they may be called.

This Son, then, is also the truth and the life of all things that exist; and rightly so. For the things that were made, how could they live, except by the gift of life? Or the things that exist, how could they really and truly exist, unless they were derived from the truth? Or how could rational beings exist, unless the Word or reason had existed before them? Or how could they be wise, unless wisdom existed? But since it was to happen that some should fall away from life and bring death upon themselves by the very fact of their falling (for death is nothing else but a departure from life), and yet it would certainly not have been logical that beings once created by God for the enjoyment of life should utterly perish, it was needful that before the existence of death there should exist a power capable of destroying the death that was to come, and that there should exist a resurrection, the figure of which was shown in our Lord and Saviour, which resurrection should have its ground in the very wisdom and word and life of God. Or again, since it was to happen that some of those who were created would prove unable, in consequence of the good being within them as an accident and not by nature, that is not essentially, to remain firm and steadfast and to abide for ever in the just and temperate use of their original blessings, but would turn and change and fall away from their first state, the word and wisdom of God became the way. And it is called the way for this reason, that it leads to the Father those who walk along it.

Whatever then we have said of the wisdom of God will also fitly apply to and be understood of him in his other titles as the Son of God, the life, the word, the truth, the way and the resurrection. For all these

[1] *The Acts of St Paul* is mentioned by Eusebius (*Hist. Eccl.*, III. 3. 25) as a writing used in some parts of the Church but not considered authoritative.

[2] *St John* I. 1–2.

titles are derived from his works and powers, and in none of them is there the least reason to understand anything corporeal, which might seem to denote either size or shape or colour. But whereas the offspring of men or of the other animals whom we see around us correspond to the seed of those by whom they were begotten, or of the mothers in whose womb they are formed and nourished, drawing from these parents whatever it is that they take and bring into the light of day when they are born, it is impious and shocking to regard God the Father in the begetting of his only-begotten Son and in the Son's subsistence as being similar to any human being or other animal in the act of begetting; but there must needs be some exceptional process, worthy of God, to which we can find no comparison whatever, not merely in things, but even in thought and imagination, such that by its aid human thought could apprehend how the unbegotten God becomes Father of the only-begotten Son. This is an eternal and everlasting begetting, as brightness is begotten from light. For he does not become Son in an external way through the adoption of the Spirit, but is Son by nature.

Let us now see how our statements are also supported by the authority of divine Scripture. The apostle Paul says that the only-begotten Son is 'the image of the invisible God', and that he is the 'firstborn of all creation';[1] and when writing to the Hebrews he says of the Son that he is the 'brightness of God's glory and the express image of his substance'.[2] But we also find, in the Book of Wisdom which is said to be Solomon's, a certain description of the wisdom of God in the following terms: 'For she is a breath of the power of God, and a pure effluence (that is, emanation) of the glory of the Almighty.' Therefore 'nothing that is defiled can enter into her. For she is the brightness of the eternal light and an unspotted mirror of the working of God and an image of his goodness.'[3] Now as we said above, the wisdom of God has her substance nowhere else but in him who is the beginning of all things, from whom also she took her birth. And because he himself, who alone is a Son by nature, is this wisdom, he is on this account also called the only-begotten.

Let us now see what we ought to understand by the expression 'image of the invisible God', in order that we may learn therefrom how God can rightly be called the Father of his Son; and let us first of all consider what things are called images in ordinary human speech. Sometimes the term 'image' is applied to an object painted or carved on some material, such as wood or stone. Sometimes a child is said to be the image of its parent, when the likeness of the parent's features is in every respect faithfully reproduced in the child. Now I think that the first of these illustrations may be fitly applied to him who was made 'in the image

[1] *Colossians* 1. 15. [2] *Hebrews* 1. 3. [3] *Wisdom* 7. 25 f.

and likeness of God',[1] that is, man. Of man, however, we shall inquire more carefully, with God's help, when we come to the exposition of this passage in Genesis.[2]

But in regard to the Son of God, of whom we are now speaking, the image may be compared to our second illustration; for this reason, that he is the invisible image of the invisible God, just as according to the scripture narrative we say that the image of Adam was his son Seth. It is written thus: 'And Adam begat Seth after his own image and after his own kind.'[3] This image preserves the unity of nature and substance common to a father and a son. For if 'all things that the Father doeth, these also doeth the Son likewise',[4] then in this very fact that the Son does all things just as the Father does, the Father's image is reproduced in the Son, whose birth from the Father is as it were an act of his will proceeding from the mind. And on this account my own opinion is that an act of the Father's will ought to be sufficient to ensure the existence of what he wills: for in willing he uses no other means than that which is produced by the deliberations of his will. It is in this way, then, that the existence of the Son also is begotten by him.

This point must above all be upheld by those who allow nothing to be unbegotten, that is unborn, except God the Father only. Moreover, we must take care not to fall into the absurd fables of those who imagine for themselves certain emanations, splitting the divine nature into parts and, so far as they can, dividing God the Father. For it is not only the utmost impiety, but also the depth of folly, to entertain the slightest suspicion that such a thing could happen to an incorporeal being; nor is it at all consistent with our intelligence to think that a physical division of an incorporeal being is possible. Rather we must suppose that as an act of will proceeds from the mind without either cutting off any part of the mind or being separated or divided from it, in some similar fashion has the Father begotten the Son, who is indeed his image; so that as the Father is invisible by nature, he has begotten an image that is also invisible.

For the Son is the Word, and therefore we must understand that nothing in him is perceptible to the senses. He is wisdom, and in wisdom we must not suspect the presence of anything corporeal. 'He is the true light, which lighteth every man that cometh into the world',[5] but he has nothing in common with the light of our sun. Our Saviour is therefore the image of the invisible God, the Father, being the truth, when considered in relation to the Father himself, and the image, when con-

[1] *Genesis* 1. 26. [2] *Hom. in Gen.*, I. 13. [3] *Genesis* 5. 3.
[4] *John* 5. 19. [5] Ibid. 1. 9.

sidered in relation to us, to whom he reveals the Father;[1] through which image we know the Father, whom 'no one' else 'knoweth save the Son and he to whom the Son hath willed to reveal him'.[2] And he reveals the Father by being himself understood; for whoever has understood him understands as a consequence the Father also, according to his own saying, 'He that hath seen me, hath seen the Father also'.[3]

But we quoted the saying of Paul in which he speaks of Christ as being the 'brightness of God's glory, and the express image of his substance'; let us see, therefore, what we are to learn from this. 'God is light',[4] according to John. The only-begotten Son, therefore, is the brightness of this light, proceeding from God without separation, as brightness from light, and lightening the whole creation. For by the same method of exposition which we have used above, to show how he is the way and leads to the Father, and how he is the Word who interprets and presents to the rational creation the secrets of wisdom and the mysteries of knowledge, and how he is also the truth and the life and the resurrection, must we arrive at the meaning of his being the brightness; for it is through its brightness that the nature of the light itself is known and experienced. This brightness falls softly and gently on the tender and weak eyes of mortal man and little by little trains and accustoms them, as it were, to bear the light in its clearness; and when it has removed from them all that darkens and obstructs their vision, in accordance with the Lord's saying, 'Cast out the beam out of thine eye',[5] it renders them capable of enduring the glory of the light, becoming in this respect even a kind of mediator between men and the light.

Christ is said, however, by the apostle to be not only 'the brightness of God's glory' but also 'the express image of his substance', or subsistence. I do not think it superfluous, therefore, to turn our attention to this point, namely, how there can be said to exist, besides the actual substance or subsistence of God (whatever that substance or subsistence means), something else which is an image of his substance. See, then, whether the Son of God, who is called God's word and wisdom, and who alone knows the Father and reveals him to whom he will, to those, namely, who become capable of receiving his word and wisdom, may not perhaps be said to express the image of God's substance or subsistence

[1] This passage provides a good example of the tendency of Rufinus (on whose Latin translation we are mainly dependent for our knowledge of this work) to alter the sense of his Greek original whenever it seemed to deviate from orthodoxy. From a quotation made by Jerome in *Ep. ad Avitum* 2, it appears that what Origen may actually have said was: 'The Son, who is the image of the invisible Father, is not the truth when compared with the Father; but in relation to us, who are unable to receive the truth of God almighty, he is a shadow and semblance of the truth.'

[2] *Matthew* 11. 27. [3] *John* 14. 9. [4] 1 *John* 1. 5. [5] *Matthew* 7. 5; *Luke* 6. 42.

for this reason, that he makes God understood and known; that is, when wisdom outlines first in herself the things which she wishes to reveal to others, by means of which they are to know and understand God, then she herself may be called the express image of God's substance.

In order, however, to understand still more completely how the Saviour is 'the image of God's substance' or subsistence, let us use an illustration which, although it does not fully or properly represent the subject under discussion, we may yet be allowed to employ for the sole purpose of showing that when the Son, 'who was in the form of God, emptied himself',[1] his desire was by means of this very emptying to display to us the fullness of the godhead. Let us suppose, for example, that there existed a statue of so great a size as to fill the whole world, but which on account of its immensity was imperceptible to anyone, and that another statue was made similar to it in every detail, in shape of limbs and outline of features, in form and material, but not in its immense size, so that those who were unable to perceive and behold the immense one could yet be confident that they had seen it when they saw the small one, because this preserved every line of limbs and features and the very form and material with an absolutely indistinguishable similarity.

It is by some such likeness as this that the Son, in emptying himself of his equality with the Father, and showing to us a way by which we may know him, becomes an 'express image' of God's substance; so that, through this fact of his becoming to us the brightness, we who were not able to look at the glory of pure light while it remained in the greatness of his godhead, may find a way of beholding the divine light through looking at the brightness. Needless to say, a comparison with statues, taken from the region of material things, is to be allowed for no other purpose but to show that the Son of God, though brought within the very narrow compass of a human body, yet gave indications, in the likeness of his power and works to those of God the Father, of the immense and invisible greatness that was in him; witness the words which he said to his disciples, 'He that hath seen me hath seen the Father also',[2] and, 'I and the Father are one';[3] along with which we must also interpret that similar saying of his, 'the Father in me, and I in the Father'.[4]

Let us now see what is the meaning of that passage which we find written in the Wisdom of Solomon, who speaks of wisdom as follows: 'She is a breath of the power of God and a pure effluence (that is, emanation) of the glory of the Almighty and the brightness of the eternal light and an unspotted mirror of the working or power of God and an image of his goodness.'[5] He gives here five definitions of God and from each

[1] *Philippians* 2. 6–7. [2] *John* 14. 9 [3] Ibid. 10. 30. [4] Ibid. 10. 38. [5] *Wisdom* 7. 25–6.

of them in turn he indicates a certain characteristic belonging to God's wisdom; for he speaks of God's 'power' and 'glory' and 'eternal light' and 'working' and 'goodness'. He says, however, that wisdom is a breath not of the glory of the Almighty, nor of the eternal light, nor of the working of the Father, nor of his goodness, since it was not suitable to apply the term breath to any one of these; but in all appropriateness he says that wisdom is a breath of the 'power' of God. Now the power of God must mean that by which he is strong, that by which he both established and also preserves and controls all things visible and invisible, and that by which he is sufficient for all things which are the objects of his providence and with all of which he is present as if they were joined in one. The breath, then, or if I may so call it, the strength of all this power, so great and so immense, comes to have a subsistence of its own; and although it proceeds from the power itself as will proceeding from mind, yet nevertheless the will of God comes itself to be a power of God. There comes into existence, therefore, another power, subsisting in its own proper nature, a kind of breath, as the passage of Scripture calls it, of the first and unbegotten power of God, drawing from this source whatever existence it has; and there is no time when it did not exist.

For if anyone is inclined to describe it as being non-existent at first but coming into existence afterwards, let him tell us why the Father who caused it to exist did not do so before. And if he lays it down that there was one definite beginning when this 'breath' first proceeded from the power of God, we shall ask again why it did not so proceed before this beginning of which he has spoken. Thus by ever inquiring what happened before and going further back with our questions, we shall reach the conclusion that, since God always had both the power and the will, there was never the slightest reason or possibility that he should not always have had this good thing that he desired. This proves that there always has existed that breath of the power of God, having no beginning but God himself. Nor indeed could it have fitly had any other beginning except him from whom it takes its existence and birth, that is, God. And in regard to the apostle's saying that 'Christ is the power of God',[1] this power must be called not merely a breath of the power of God but a power proceeding from the power.

Let us now look into the saying that wisdom is 'an effluence', that is, an emanation, 'of the clear glory of the Almighty', and if we first consider what 'the glory of the Almighty' is, we shall then understand what its 'effluence' is. Now as one cannot be a father apart from having a son, nor a lord apart from holding a possession or a slave, so we cannot even call God almighty if there are none over whom he can exercise his

[1] I *Corinthians* I. 24.

power. Accordingly, to prove that God is almighty we must assume the existence of the universe. For if anyone would have it that certain ages or periods of time, or whatever he cares to call them, elapsed during which the present creation did not exist, he would undoubtedly prove that in those ages or periods God was not almighty, but that he afterwards became almighty from the time when he began to have creatures over whom he could exercise power. Thus God will apparently have experienced a kind of progress, for there can be no doubt that it is better for him to be almighty than not to be so.

Now how does it seem anything but absurd that God should at first not possess something that is appropriate to him, and afterwards by a kind of progress should come to possess it? But if there was no time when he was not almighty, then of necessity those things must always have existed, in virtue of which he is called almighty; and he must always have had creatures over which he exercised his power and which were controlled by him as king and ruler.

Of these we shall treat more fully in the proper place, when we come to discuss the subject of God's creatures. Yet even now, since we are dealing with the question how wisdom is a pure effluence, or emanation, of the glory of the Almighty, I deem it necessary to give warning, however briefly, to prevent anyone from thinking that the title of the Almighty belonged to God before the birth of wisdom, through which he is called Father; for wisdom, which is the Son of God, is said to be a 'pure effluence of the glory of the Almighty'. Let him who is inclined to believe this hear what the Scriptures plainly proclaim; for it says that 'thou hast made all things in wisdom'[1] and the Gospel teaches that 'all things were made by him and without him was not anything made';[2] and let him understand from this that the title of Almighty cannot be older in God than that of Father, for it is through the Son that the Father is Almighty.

But the passage speaks of a glory belonging to the Almighty, of which glory wisdom is the effluence. From this we learn that wisdom, through which God is called Almighty, has a share even in the glory of omnipotence. For it is through wisdom, which is Christ, that God holds power over all things, not only by his own authority as Master, but also by the voluntary service of his subjects. And to prove to you that the omnipotence of the Father and the Son is one and the same, just as God and the Lord are one and the same as the Father, listen to the manner in which John speaks in the Apocalypse: 'These things saith the Lord God, which is and which was and which is to come, the Almighty.'[3] For he who 'is to come', who else is it but Christ? And just as no one ought to be offended

[1] *Psalm* 104. 24. [2] *John* 1. 3. [3] *Revelation* 1. 8.

because, while the Father is God, the Saviour also is God; so too ought no one to be offended because, while the Father is called Almighty, the Son also is called Almighty.

Moreover we shall in this way see the truth of that saying which Christ utters to the Father: 'All things that are mine are thine, and thine are mine, and I am glorified in them.'[1] Now if all things which are the Father's are Christ's, and among all that the Father is, he is Almighty, then undoubtedly the only-begotten Son must also be Almighty, that the Son may have all that the Father has. 'And I am glorified', he says, 'in them.' For 'in the name of Jesus every knee shall bow, of things in heaven, and things on earth, and things under the earth; and every tongue shall confess that Jesus is Lord in the glory of God the Father'.[2] He is therefore the 'effluence of the glory of God' in this respect, that he is Almighty, God's pure and clear wisdom itself, glorified as being the effluence of omnipotence or glory.

We add the following, however, to make it more clearly understood what the glory of omnipotence is. God the Father is almighty because he holds dominion over all things, that is, over heaven and earth, sun, moon and stars and everything contained in them. This dominion he exercises through his Word, for 'in the name of Jesus every knee bows, of things in heaven, and things on earth, and things under the earth'. Now if every knee bows to Jesus, then undoubtedly it is Jesus to whom all things have been subjected, and it is he who wields dominion over all things, and all things have been subjected to the Father through him; for it is through wisdom, that is by word and reason and not by force and necessity, that they are subject. His glory, therefore, lies in the very fact that he possesses all things; and this is the purest and brightest glory of omnipotence, that the universe is held in subjection by reason and wisdom, and not by force and necessity. It is called the 'purest and brightest' glory of wisdom as the most suitable way of distinguishing it from that glory which is not pure or sincere.

For every nature which is alterable and changeable, even though it may be glorified in works of righteousness or wisdom, cannot be said to possess a glory that is sincere and bright, by reason of the fact that its righteousness and wisdom are accidents, and whatever is accidental may also be separated and lost. But since the wisdom of God, which is his only-begotten Son, is in all respects unalterable and unchangeable, and since every good quality in him is essential and can never be changed or altered, his glory is on that account described as pure and sincere.

In the third place, wisdom is said to be the brightness of the eternal light. The force of this expression we have explained in a previous

[1] *John* 17. 10. [2] *Philippians* 2. 10–11.

passage, where we introduced the illustration of the sun and the brightness of its rays and showed to the best of our ability how the expression should be understood. We will add, however, this one point. The term everlasting or eternal properly denotes that which had no beginning of existence and can never cease to be what it is. This is the idea underlying the passage in John, where he says that 'God is light'. Now God's wisdom is the brightness of that light, not only in so far as it is light, but in so far as it is everlasting light. His wisdom is therefore an everlasting brightness, enduring eternally. If this point is fully understood, it is clear proof that the Son's existence springs from the Father himself, yet not in time, nor from any other beginning except, as we have said, from God himself.

Wisdom is also called an 'unspotted mirror of the *energy* or working of God'. We must first understand, therefore, what the 'working' of God's power is. It is a kind of strength, so to speak, by means of which the Father works, whether in his acts of creation, or of providence, or of judgment, or in the ordering and superintendence of every detail of the universe at his own appointed time. And when wisdom is called the 'unspotted mirror' of the Father's power and working, she would have us understand her nature to be like the image reflected in a mirror, which moves and acts in correspondence with the movements and actions of him who looks into the mirror, not deviating from them in any way whatever. So too the Lord Jesus Christ, who is the wisdom of God, speaks of himself when he says, 'the works which the Father doeth, these also doeth the Son in like manner';[1] and again, 'the Son can do nothing of himself, but what he hath seen the Father doing'.[2]

As regards the power of his works, then, the Son is in no way whatever separate or different from the Father, nor is his work anything other than the Father's work, but there is one and the same movement, so to speak, in all they do; consequently the Father has called him an 'unspotted mirror', in order to make it understood that there is absolutely no dissimilarity between the Son and the Father. Some indeed have said that the Son's acts are to be compared with a pupil's work in likeness to or imitation of his master, or that such things as the Father has first formed in their spiritual essence are made by the Son in bodily material; yet how can these opinions be reconciled with the Gospel, which says, not that the Son does like things, but that he does the same things 'in like manner'?

There remains the inquiry, what is the 'image of his goodness'? Here, I think, we do well to adopt the same line of reasoning which we used above in regard to the image formed in a mirror. The original goodness is undoubtedly the Father; and from this is born the Son, who is in every

[1] *John* 5. 19. [2] Ibid.

respect an image of the Father, and who may also without any doubt be properly called an 'image of his goodness'.[1] For there is no other second goodness existing in the Son, besides that which is in the Father. So the Saviour himself rightly says in the Gospel that 'none is good save one, God the Father',[2] the purpose of this statement being to make it understood that the Son is not of some other 'goodness', but of that alone which is in the Father; whose image he is rightly called, because he neither springs from any other source than from original goodness itself—for if that were so, there would seem to be a different goodness in the Son from that which is in the Father—nor has the goodness that is in him any dissimilarity or divergence from that of the Father. Accordingly we ought not to imagine that there is some kind of blasphemy, as it were, in the saying that 'none is good save one, God the Father', as if these words were to be taken as a denial that either Christ or the Holy Spirit is good; but, as we said before, the original goodness must be believed to reside in God the Father, and from him both the Son and Holy Spirit undoubtedly draw into themselves the nature of that goodness existing in the fount from which the one is born and the other proceeds.

If then there are any other things called good in the Scriptures, such as an angel, or a man, or a slave, or a treasure, or a good heart, or a good tree, all these are so called by an inexact use of the word, since the goodness contained in them is accidental and not essential. And it would be a long business, demanding another time and another work, to collect all the titles of the Son of God, such for example as the true light, or the door, or righteousness, or sanctification, or redemption, and countless others, and to explain for what reasons either in regard to his powers or his moral qualities each of these names is given to him.

[1] Here again we can see how the Latin translation of Rufinus, on which we must depend, is really a paraphrase, and how the more venturesome aspects of Origen's thought have been toned down. A Greek quotation in Justinian (*Ep. ad Mennam*) of this passage translates: 'In the same way, therefore, I consider that in the case of the Saviour it would be right to say that he is an image of God's goodness, but not goodness itself. And perhaps also the Son, while being good, is yet not good purely and simply. And just as he is the image of the invisible God, and in virtue of this is himself God, and yet is not he of whom Christ himself says "that they may know thee, the only true God"; so he is the image of the goodness, and yet not, as the Father is, good without qualification.'

[2] *Mark* 10. 18.

IV

ATHANASIUS

Athanasius 'The Great' (296–373) was born in Alexandria. He received a full education and as a young man was taken into the household of the bishop Alexander. As the bishop's secretary he accompanied him to the great Council of Nicea in 325, when the Nicene Creed was adopted. In 328 he became bishop of Alexandria. In spite of the conclusions of the Council of Nicea, Arianism (which made the divinity of the Christ significantly inferior to that of the Father) was still an active force with official imperial support. In the face of this opposition Athanasius lived a stormy life, being forced from his see into exile no less than five times. Throughout a life of loyal and industrious struggle in support of the Nicene formula that the Christ is 'of one substance' with the Father he contributed decisively to its final triumph over Arianism.

There was still at this time a danger that Christianity might have degenerated into a mere school of philosophy—especially in the Eastern half of the Empire. In spite of his continuous concern with abstract theological metaphysics, Athanasius countered this tendency by placing the personal existence of the Christ, the Incarnate Son, at the very centre of all his theology. This is illustrated in the passages reproduced below from his treatise *On the Incarnation of the Word of God*. These passages also illustrate what is sometimes known as the 'classical' view of the atonement, emphasizing the victory of the Christ over the demonic forces and his capacity to sum up or 'recapitulate' all mankind in himself.

So great did the fame and prestige of St Athanasius become that many writings which were not his came to be ascribed to him. In particular, the so-called Athanasian Creed is not his composition—though it does reflect some of his theological influence.

On the Incarnation of the Word of God is the second half of a two-volume work, the first part being his *Contra Gentes*. These are his earliest works, dating from about 319. His main anti-Arian writings are: *Orationes contra Arianos* (only part of which is likely to be genuine), *Apologia contra Arianos* and *Historia Arianorum*. There is ascribed to him a *Life of St Antony* which in spite of some doubts, may well be genuinely his.

For further reading see:

Select Writings and Letters of Athanasius, tr. J. H. Newman, Nicene and Post-Nicene Fathers (Second Series), Vol. IV, Oxford, 1892.

Christology of the Later Fathers, ed. Edward Rochie Hardy, Library of Christian Classics, Vol. III, S.C.M. Press, 1954.

The Incarnation of the Word of God, translated by a Religious of C.S.M.V. S.Th., with introduction by C. S. Lewis, Geoffrey Bles, 1944 (from which the passages below are reproduced).

THE INCARNATION OF THE WORD OF GOD

In our former book[1] we dealt fully enough with a few of the chief points about the heathen worship of idols, and how those false fears originally arose. We also, by God's grace, briefly indicated that the Word of the Father is himself divine, that all things that are owe their being to his will and power, and that it is through him that the Father gives order to creation, by him that all things are moved and through him that they receive their being. Now, Macarius, true lover of Christ, we must take a step further in the faith of our holy religion, and consider also the Word's becoming Man and his divine Appearing in our midst. That mystery the Jews traduce, the Greeks deride, but we adore; and your own love and devotion to the Word also will be the greater, because in his Manhood he seems so little worth. For it is a fact that the more unbelievers pour scorn on him, so much the more does he make his Godhead evident. The things which they, as men, rule out as impossible, he plainly shows to be possible; that which they deride as unfitting, his goodness makes most fit; and things which these wise-acres laugh at as 'human' he by his inherent might declares divine. Thus by what seems his utter poverty and weakness on the cross he overturns the pomp and parade of idols, and quietly and hiddenly wins over the mockers and unbelievers to recognize him as God.

Now in dealing with these matters it is necessary first to recall what has already been said. You must understand why it is that the Word of the Father, so great and so high, has been made manifest in bodily form. He has not assumed a body as proper to his own nature, far from it, for as the Word he is without body. He has been manifested in a human body for this reason only, out of the love and goodness of His Father, for the salvation of us men. (pp. 25–6) . . .

. . . It is we who were the cause of his taking human form, and for our salvation that in his great love he was both born and manifested in a human body. For God had made man thus (that is, as an embodied

[1] i.e. the *Contra Gentes*.

spirit), and had willed that he should remain in incorruption. But men, having turned from the contemplation of God to evil of their own devising, had come inevitably under the law of death. Instead of remaining in the state in which God had created them, they were in process of becoming corrupted entirely, and death had them completely under its dominion. For the transgression of the commandment was making them turn back again according to their nature; and as they had at the beginning come into being out of non-existence, so were they now on the way to returning, through corruption, to non-existence again. The presence and love of the Word has called them into being; inevitably, therefore, when they lost the knowledge of God, they lost existence with it; for it is God alone who exists, evil is non-being, the negation and antithesis of good. By nature, of course, man is mortal, since he was made from nothing; but he bears also the Likeness of him who is, and if he preserves that Likeness through constant contemplation, then his nature is deprived of its power and he remains incorrupt. So is it affirmed in Wisdom: 'The keeping of his laws is the assurance of incorruption.'[1] And being incorrupt, he would be henceforth as God, as Holy Scripture says, 'I have said, Ye are gods and sons of the Hightest all of you: but ye die as men and fall as one of the princes'.[2] (pp. 29–30) . . .

. . . Man who was created in God's image and in his possession of reason reflected the very Word himself, was disappearing, and the work of God was being undone. The law of death, which followed from the Transgression, prevailed upon us, and from it there was no escape. The thing that was happening was in truth both monstrous and unfitting. It would, of course, have been unthinkable that God should go back upon His word and that man, having transgressed, should not die; but it was equally monstrous that beings which once had shared the nature of the Word should perish and turn back again into non-existence through corruption. It was unworthy of the goodness of God that creatures made by him should be brought to nothing through the deceit wrought upon man by the devil; and it was supremely unfitting that the work of God in mankind should disappear, either through their own negligence or through the deceit of evil spirits. As then, the creatures whom he had created reasonable, like the Word, were in fact perishing, and such noble works were on the road to ruin, what then was God, being Good, to do? Was he to let corruption and death have their way with them? In that case, what was the use of having made them in the beginning? Surely it would have been better never to have been created at all than, having been created, to be neglected and perish; and, besides that, such indifference to the ruin of his own work before his very eyes

[1] *Wisdom* 6. 18. [2] *Psalm* 82. 6 f.

would argue not goodness in God but limitation, and that far more than if he had never created men at all. It was impossible, therefore, that God should leave man to be carried off by corruption, because it would be unfitting and unworthy of himself.

Yet, true though this is, it is not the whole matter. As we have already noted, it was unthinkable that God, the Father of Truth, should go back upon his word regarding death in order to ensure our continued existence. He could not falsify himself; what, then, was God to do? Was he to demand repentance from men for their transgression? You might say that that was worthy of God, and argue further that, as through the Transgression they became subject to corruption, so through repentance they might return to incorruption again. But repentance would not guard the Divine consistency, for, if death did not hold dominion over men, God would still remain untrue. Nor does repentance recall men from what is according to their nature; all that it does is to make them cease from sinning. Had it been a case of a trespass only, and not of a subsequent corruption, repentance would have been well enough; but when once transgression had begun men came under the power of the corruption proper to their nature and were bereft of the grace which belonged to them as creatures in the Image of God. No, repentance could not meet the case. What—or rather *Who* was it that was needed for such grace and such recall as we required? Who, save the Word of God himself, who also in the beginning had made all things out of nothing? His part it was, and his alone, both to bring again the corruptible to incorruption and to maintain for the Father his consistency of character with all. For he alone, being Word of the Father and above all, was in consequence both able to recreate all, and worthy to suffer on behalf of all and to be an ambassador for all with the Father.

For this purpose, then, the incorporeal and incorruptible and immaterial Word of God entered our world. In one sense, indeed, he was not far from it before, for no part of creation had ever been without him who, while ever abiding in union with the Father, yet fills all things that are. But now he entered the world in a new way, stooping to our level in his love and Self-revealing to us. He saw the reasonable race, the race of men that, like himself, expressed the Father's Mind, wasting out of existence, and death reigning over all in corruption. He saw that corruption held us all the closer, because it was the penalty for the Transgression; he saw, too, how unthinkable it would be for the law to be repealed before it was fulfilled. He saw how unseemly it was that the very things of which he himself was the Artificer should be disappearing. He saw how the surpassing wickedness of men was mounting up against them; he saw also their universal liability to death. All this he saw and, pitying our race, moved with compassion for our limitation, unable to endure that death should have the mastery, rather than that his creatures should perish and the work of his Father for us men come to nought, he took to himself a body, a human body even as our own. Nor did he will merely to become embodied or merely to appear; had that been so, he could have revealed his divine majesty in some other and better way. No, he took *our* body, and not only so, but he took it directly from a spotless, stainless virgin, without the agency of human father—a pure body, untainted by intercourse with man. He, the Mighty One, the Artificer of all, himself prepared this body in the virgin as a temple for himself, and took it for his very own, as the instrument through which he was known and in which he dwelt. Thus, taking a body like our own, because all our bodies were liable to the corruption of death, he surrendered his body to death instead of all, and offered it to the Father. This he did out of sheer love for us, so that in his death all might die, and the law of death thereby be abolished because, having fulfilled in his body that for which it was appointed, it was thereafter voided of its power for men. This he did that he might turn again to incorruption men who had turned back to corruption, and make them alive through death by the appropriation of his body and by the grace of his resurrection. Thus he would make death to disappear from them as utterly as straw from fire.

The Word perceived that corruption could not be got rid of otherwise than through death; yet he himself, as the Word, being immortal and the Father's Son, was such as could not die. For this reason, therefore, he assumed a body capable of death, in order that it, through belonging to the Word who is above all, might become in dying a sufficient exchange for all, and itself remaining incorruptible through his indwelling, might thereafter put an end to corruption for all others as well, by the grace of the resurrection. It was by surrendering to death the body which he had taken, as an offering and sacrifice free from every stain, that he forthwith abolished death for his human brethren by the offering of the equivalent. For naturally, since the Word of God was above all, when he offered his own temple and bodily instrument as a substitute for the life of all, he fulfilled in death all that was required. Naturally also, through this union of the immortal Son of God with our human nature, all men were clothed with incorruption in the promise of the resurrection. For the solidarity of mankind is such that, by virtue of the Word's indwelling in a single human body, the corruption which goes with death has lost its power over all. You know how it is when some great king enters a large city and dwells in one of its houses; because of his dwelling in that single house, the whole city is honoured, and enemies and robbers cease to molest it. Even so is it with the King of all; he has come into our country and dwelt in one body amidst the many, and in consequence the designs of the enemy against mankind have been foiled and the corruption of death, which formerly held them in its power, has simply ceased to be. For the human race would have perished utterly had not the Lord and Saviour of all, the Son of God, come among us to put an end to death.

This great work was, indeed, supremely worthy of the goodness of God. A king who has founded a city, so far from neglecting it when through the carelessness of the inhabitants it is attacked by robbers, avenges it and saves it from destruction, having regard rather to his own honour than to the people's neglect. Much more, then, the Word of the All-good Father was not unmindful of the human race that he had called to be; but rather, by the offering of his own body he abolished the death which they had incurred, and corrected their neglect by his own teaching. Thus by his own power he restored the whole nature of man. The Saviour's own inspired disciples assure us of this. We read in one place: 'For the love of Christ constraineth us, because we thus judge that, if One died on behalf of all, then all died, and he died for all that we should no longer live unto ourselves, but unto him who died and rose again from the dead, even our Lord Jesus Christ.'[1] And again another says: 'But we behold him who hath been made a little lower than the angels, even Jesus, because of the suffering of death crowned with glory and honour, that by the grace of God he should taste of death on behalf of every man.' The same writer goes on to point out why it was necessary for God the Word and none other to become Man: 'For it became Him, for Whom are all things and through Whom are all things, in bringing many sons unto glory, to make the Author of their salvation perfect through suffering.'[2] He means that the rescue of mankind from corruption was the proper part only of him who made them in the beginning. He points out also that the Word assumed a human body expressly in order that he might offer it in sacrifice for other like bodies: 'Since then the children are sharers in flesh and blood, he also himself assumed the same, in order that through death he might bring to nought him that hath the power of death, that is to say, the Devil, and might rescue those who all their lives were enslaved by the fear of death.'[3] For by the sacrifice of his own body he did two things: he put an end to the law of death which barred our way; and he made a new beginning of life for us, by giving us the hope of resurrection. By man death has gained its power over men; by the Word made Man death has been destroyed and life raised up anew. That is what Paul says, that true servant of Christ: 'For

[1] II *Corinthians* 5. 14 f. [2] *Hebrews* 2. 9 ff. [3] Ibid. 14 f.

since by man came death, by man came also the resurrection of the dead. Just as in Adam all die, even so in Christ shall all be made alive',[1] and so forth. Now, therefore, when we die we no longer do so as men condemned to death, but as those who are even now in process of rising we await the general resurrection of all, 'which in its own times He shall show',[2] even God who wrought it and bestowed it on us.

This, then, is the first cause of the Saviour's becoming Man. There are, however, other things which show how wholly fitting is his blessed presence in our midst; and these we must now go on to consider.

When God the Almighty was making mankind through his own Word, he perceived that they, owing to the limitation of their nature, could not of themselves have any knowledge of their Artificer, the Incorporeal and Uncreate. He took pity on them, therefore, and did not leave them destitute of the knowledge of himself, lest their very existence should prove purposeless. For of what use is existence to the creature if it cannot know its Maker? How could men be reasonable beings if they had no knowledge of the Word and Reason of the Father, through whom they had received their being? They would be no better then the beasts, had they no knowledge save of earthly things; and why should God have made them at all, if he had not intended them to know him? But, in fact, the good God has given them a share in his own Image, that is, in our Lord Jesus Christ, and has made even themselves after the same Image and Likeness. Why? Simply in order that through this gift of God-likeness in themselves they may be able to perceive the Image Absolute, that is the Word himself, and through him to apprehend the Father; which knowledge of their Maker is for men the only really happy and blessed life.

But, as we have already seen, men, foolish as they are, thought little of the grace they had received, and turned away from God. They defiled their own soul so completely that they not only lost their apprehension of God, but invented for themselves other gods of various kinds. They fashioned idols for themselves in place of the truth and reverenced things that are not, rather than God who is, as St Paul says, 'worshipping the creature rather than the Creator'.[3] Moreover, and much worse, they transferred the honour which is due to God to material objects such as wood and stone, and also to man; and further even than that they went, as we said in our former book. Indeed, so impious were they that they worshipped evil spirits as gods in satisfaction of their lusts. They sacrificed brute beasts and immolated men, as the just due of these deities, thereby bringing themselves more and more under their insane control. Magic arts also were taught among them, oracles in sundry places led men

[1] I *Corinthians* 15, 21 f. [2] I *Timothy* 6. 15. [3] *Romans* 1. 25.

astray, and the cause of everything in human life was traced to the stars, as though nothing existed but that which could be seen. In a word, impiety and lawlessness were everywhere, and neither God nor his Word was known. Yet he had not hidden himself from the sight of men nor given the knowledge of himself in one way only; but rather he had unfolded it in many forms and by many ways.

God knew the limitation of mankind, you see; and though the grace of being made in his Image was sufficient to give them knowledge of the Word and through him of the Father, as a safeguard against their neglect of this grace, he provided the works of creation also as means by which the Maker might be known. Nor was this all. Man's neglect of the indwelling grace tends ever to increase; and against this further frailty also God made provision by giving them a law, and by sending prophets, men whom they knew. Thus, if they were tardy in looking up to heaven, they might still gain knowledge of their Maker from those close at hand; for men can learn directly about higher things from other men. Three ways thus lay open to them, by which they might obtain the knowledge of God. They could look up into the immensity of heaven, and by pondering the harmony of creation come to know its Ruler, the Word of the Father, Whose all-ruling providence makes known the Father to all. Or, if this was beyond them, they could converse with holy men, and through them learn to know God, the Artificer of all things, the Father of Christ, and to recognize the worship of idols as the negation of the truth and full of all impiety. Or else, in the third place, they could cease from lukewarmness and lead a good life merely by knowing the law. For the law was not given only for the Jews, nor was it solely for their sake that God sent the prophets, though it was to the Jews that they were sent and by the Jews that they were persecuted. The law and the prophets were a sacred school of the knowledge of God and the conduct of the spiritual life for the whole world.

So great, indeed, were the goodness and the love of God. Yet men, bowed down by the pleasures of the moment and by the frauds and illusions of the evil spirits, did not lift up their heads towards the truth. So burdened were they with their wickednesses that they seemed rather to be brute beasts than reasonable men, reflecting the very Likeness of the Word.

What was God to do in face of this dehumanising of mankind, this universal hiding of the knowledge of himself by the wiles of evil spirits? Was he to keep silence before so great a wrong and let men go on being thus deceived and kept in ignorance of himself? If so, what was the use of having made them in his own Image originally? It would surely have been better for them always to have been brutes, rather than to revert to that condition when once they had shared the nature of the Word. Again, things being as they were, what was the use of their ever having had the knowledge of God? Surely it would have been better for God never to have bestowed it, than that men should subsequently be found unworthy to receive it. Similarly, what possible profit could it be to God himself, who made men, if when made they did not worship him, but regarded others as their makers? This would be tantamount to his having made them for others and not for himself. Even an earthly king, though he is only a man, does not allow lands that he has colonized to pass into other hands or to desert to other rulers, but sends letters and friends and even visits them himself to recall them to their allegiance, rather than allow his work to be undone. How much more, then, will God be patient and painstaking with his creatures, that they be not led astray from him to the service of those that are not, and that all the more because such error means for them sheer ruin, and because it is not right that those who had once shared his Image should be destroyed.

What, then, was God to do? What else could he possibly do, being God, but renew his Image in mankind, so that through it men might once more come to know him? And how could this be done save by the coming of the very Image himself, our Saviour Jesus Christ? Men could not have done it, for they are only made after the Image; nor could angels have done it, for they are not the images of God. The Word of God came in his own Person, because it was he alone, the Image of the Father, who could recreate man made after the Image.

In order to effect this re-creation, however, he had first to do away with death and corruption. Therefore he assumed a human body, in order that in it death might once for all be destroyed, and that men might be renewed according to the Image. . . . (pp. 31–41) . . . The body of the Word, then, being a real human body, in spite of its having been uniquely formed from a virgin, was of itself mortal and, like other bodies, liable to death. But the indwelling of the Word loosed it from this natural liability, so that corruption could not touch it. Thus it happened that two opposite marvels took place at once: the death of all was consummated in the Lord's body; yet, because the Word was in it, death and corruption were in the same act utterly abolished. Death there had to be, and death for all, so that the due of all might be paid. Wherefore, the Word, as I said, being himself incapable of death, assumed a mortal body, that he might offer it as his own in place of all, and suffering for the sake of all through his union with it, 'might bring to nought him that had the power of death, that is, the devil, and might deliver them who all their lifetime were enslaved by the fear of death'.[1]

[1] *Hebrews* 2. 14 f.

Have no fear, then. Now that the common Saviour of all has died on our behalf, we who believe in Christ no longer die, as men died aforetime, in fulfilment of the threat of the law. That condemnation has come to an end; and now that, by the grace of the resurrection, corruption has been banished and done away, we are loosed from our mortal bodies in God's good time for each, so that we may obtain thereby a better resurrection. Like seeds cast into the earth, we do not perish in our dissolution, but like them shall rise again, death having been brought to nought by the grace of the Saviour. That is why blessed Paul, through whom we all have surety of the resurrection, says: 'This corruptible must put on incorruption and this mortal must put on immortality; but when this corruptible shall have put on incorruption and this mortal shall have put on immortality, then shall be brought to pass the saying that is written, "Death is swallowed up in victory. O Death, where is thy sting? O Grave, where is thy victory?"'[1] (pp. 49–50) . . .

[1] I *Corinthians* 15. 53 ff.

THE PERIOD OF CATHOLIC CONSOLIDATION

V

AUGUSTINE

St Augustine (Aurelius Augustinus) (354–430) was born at Tagaste in North Africa. Whether he was of pure Roman or partly Berber or Punic stock is uncertain. He went to school locally and then to the great school of rhetoric in Carthage. His early life and the manner of it up to a time shortly after his conversion is well known from his *Confessions*. He was an excellent Latin scholar, but acquired only a poor understanding of Greek. The references which he makes in the *Confessions* to the sins of his youth, when closely examined, are evidence of a sensitive conscience rather than of abandoned or dissolute life. The life he lived at Carthage was rather better and certainly no worse than that of other students of his day. At the age of 17 he took a mistress with whom he lived in faithful concubinage until shortly before his conversion some eighteen years later. She bore him one son to whom he was greatly devoted. Though much influenced by his Christian mother, Monica, he was not at this time a Christian. He became professor of Rhetoric first at Carthage, then at Rome and finally at Milan.

For nine years he was a follower, though never a full member, of the Manichaean sect. (A syncretistic religion containing Persian, Greek and Christian elements.) Religious disquiet and philosophical doubts led him to abandon this position. For a time he toyed with the purely sceptical philosophy then fashionable in Rome. When he moved to Milan, he came under the influence of Bishop Ambrose, in whom he encountered a more robust and sophisticated kind of Christianity than he had previously known. At the same time Ambrose allayed some of his difficulties by introducing him to Greek philosophy. His well-known dramatic conversion took place shortly afterwards. He retired from public life, seeking a monastic existence with a few friends. But he was soon pressed into active service as a priest in North Africa and then consecrated Bishop of Hippo. In spite of the heavy ecclesiastical burdens imposed upon him, he studied and wrote prodigiously.

St Augustine completely dominated the thought of Europe for five centuries after his death. He is best known as the doctor of Grace—chiefly because of his distinguished and victorious part in the controversy with Pelagius and his followers over questions of merit and free-will. Because of his position in this struggle he is acclaimed and revered by Protestant as much as by Roman Catholic theologians.

But it is not by his teaching on Grace that I have represented him here. His greatest and most profound work is his fifteen books on *The Trinity*. The passages from this work reproduced below show the degree of maturity which Trinitarian doctrine had attained when compared with the early gropings of Origen and Tertullian. The text here used is *Augustine: Later Works*, ed. John Burnaby, Library of Christian Classics, Vol. VIII, S.C.M. Press, 1945. (See also Vols. VI and VII in the same series: J. H. S. Burleigh (ed.), *Augustine: Early Writings*; Albert Cook Outler (ed.). *Augustine: Confessions and Enchiridion*.) Most of Augustine's major works are available in a variety of English translations.

THE TRINITY

Book 8

The Search for God by the Understanding

We have already observed that the only terms which can strictly be applied to distinguish the several Persons of the Trinity are those which denote their mutual relations: Father, Son and Holy Spirit, Gift of both. The Trinity is neither Father nor Son nor Gift. But the terms applicable to the several Persons, regarded in themselves, denote not three beings in the plural, but one, that is, the Trinity itself: thus the Father is God, the Son God, the Holy Spirit God; the Father is good, the Son good, the Holy Spirit good; the Father almighty, the Son almighty, the Holy Spirit almighty; yet there are not three Gods, or three good, or three almighty; but one God, good, almighty—the Trinity itself; and so for every other term which denotes not a mutual relation, but the several Persons regarded in themselves. We may describe such terms as 'essential'; for the essence or being of God is the same as his being great, good, wise, and anything else which is true either of each several Person or of the Trinity itself. We use the expression three Persons, or three substances, not to suggest any difference in essence, but to furnish ourselves with some one word by which to answer the question: *What* are these 'three'?

In this Trinity there is an absolute equality. In divinity the Father is not greater than the Son; nor are the Father and Son together greater than the Holy Spirit; nor is any single Person of the three anything less than the Trinity itself. All this has been said before, and repetition may familiarize our minds with the idea. But there must be a limit to repetition. Let us now beseech God, with reverent devotion, that he will open our understandings, and remove from us all contentiousness of spirit, so that our mind may contemplate the essence of truth, free from all thought of physical mass or motion. It is now our purpose, so far as the Creator's own wonderful mercy may assist us, to address ourselves to the same theme as before, but by a more inward method of approach: still observing the same rule, that the truth which has not yet become luminous to our understanding be still held fast by faith.

We say that in this Trinity two or three Persons are not any greater thing than one of them. Our material habit of thought fails to grasp this, simply because, while it is aware according to its capacity of those truly existing things which have been created, it cannot perceive the Truth itself which has created them. If it could, the fact of which we have spoken would be as clear as the light of day. Only Truth itself has true being: in its substance there is nothing 'greater' but that which more truly is. But in the realm of the spiritual and the changeless there cannot be degrees of truth; for all is equally changeless and eternal. What is called 'great' is great only because it truly is. If then 'greatness' is truth itself, to have more greatness must mean to have more truth: that which has not more truth cannot have more greatness. Whatever has more truth is the truer, just as whatever has more greatness is the greater. In this realm therefore the truer is the greater. But Father and Son together have no more true being than the Father alone or the Son alone. Both together, then, are no greater a thing than either of them singly. And since the Holy Spirit no less truly is, no more are Father and Son together anything greater than the Spirit, because they are nothing that more truly is. The Father and the Holy Spirit together, since they do not surpass the Son in truth (for they have no more true a being), do not surpass him in greatness. So the Son and the Holy Spirit together are as great a thing as the Father alone, because they no less truly are. And the Trinity itself has the same greatness as any one Person: the Person who is not truer is not greater, where truth itself is greatness. In the essential being of truth, to be true is to be: to be is to be great. To be great, therefore, is to be true. Here, therefore, what is equally true must be equally great.

In the case of material things, one piece of gold may be as true as another, and yet not as great, because here greatness is not the same thing as truth: it is one thing to be gold, another to be great. Similarly with the soul, we do not call a soul true in respect of the same quality which makes us call it great. A true soul belongs no less to him who is not great-souled. For the essence of body and soul is not the essence of truth itself, as the Trinity is God, one, sole, great, truly real, really true, true reality. If we would conceive of him, so far as he allows and vouchsafes, we must conceive of no spatial contact or connection, no conjoined structure like that of the three-bodied Geryon in the legend. Any image of that kind, greater in its three parts than in any one of them, less in one than in two, must be unhesitatingly rejected, even as we reject everything that is material. Even in the world of spirit, nothing that is changeable must be taken for God. When we rise from the deep submergence in which we live, and draw breath towards the heights of heaven, it will be a matter of no small knowledge for us, before we are yet able to know what God is, if we can at least know what he is not. Certainly he is neither earth nor sky, nor of the nature of earth and sky or of anything that we see in the sky or that may perhaps exist there though we see it not. Multiply in your imagination the light of the sun, make it greater and brighter as you will, a thousand times or times out of number: God will not be there. Conceive of the being of pure angelic spirits, animating celestial bodies, changing and turning them at will for the service of God: not if all those thousand thousands were brought together and made one, will God be any such thing—not even if you could conceive those same spirits as bodiless, difficult as that is for our materially determined thinking. Behold, if thou canst, thou soul heavily burdened by the body of corruption, laden with earthly conceits many and diverse, behold if thou canst: God is Truth. It is written, 'For God is light'—not the light seen by these eyes of ours, but that which the heart sees upon hearing of the words 'He is Truth'. Ask not, What is Truth? At once will rise the fogs of material images, the thick clouds of phantasm, and darken that clear empyrean which shone forth for a single instant upon your sight at that word 'Truth'. In that instant, that flash of vision that touches you with the word 'Truth', hold fast—if you can. But you cannot: you fall back into this familiar world of earthly things. And what—I ask you—is the weight that pulls you down again, but the defilements contracted from the mire of passion and the delusions of your wanderings?

Try once again, and consider the matter this way. Nothing draws your love but what is good. Good is earth with its lofty mountains, its gentle hills, its level plains. Good is the beauteous and fertile land, good the well-built house with its symmetry, its spaciousness and light. Good are the bodies of living things, good is the temperate and wholesome air, good is the pleasant and healthful food, good is health itself free from pain and weariness. Good is the human face with its regular features, its cheerful expression, its lively colouring; good is the heart of a friend whose comradeship is sweet and whose love is loyal; good is a righteous man, good is wealth for the things it can enable us to do, good is the sky with its sun, moon, and stars, good are the angels of holy obedience; good is the speech that instructs the hearer winningly and counsels him appropriately, good is the poem of musical rhythm and profound thought. But enough! This is good and that is good: take away 'this' and 'that' and look if you can upon Good itself: then you will see God, good not by the possession of any other good thing, but the goodness of every good. For among all these good things, those I have named and any others you may see or conceive, we could not pronounce with a true judgment any one better than another, were there not imprinted on our mind the idea of Good itself, as the standard by which we should either approve or prefer. So our love must rise to God, not as we love this or that good thing, but as the Good itself. The soul must needs seek that Good over which it will not range superior as judge but to which it will cleave in love. And what is that Good but God?—not the good soul, the good angel, the good heavens, but the good Good!

Perhaps this may make it easier to grasp what I mean. When I hear, for instance, the phrase 'good soul', those two words convey two things to my mind: that there is a soul, and that it is good. It was no act of its own that made it a soul, for it was not there to bring itself into being. But for it to be a good soul, I can see that voluntary action of its own was needed: not that there is no good in its very existence as soul, for then it could not be called and truly called, better than a body. But it is not yet to be called a good soul, because there needs yet the activity of will to give it excellence. If that activity is neglected, it rightly incurs blame and is properly called no good soul. It differs from the soul that is so active, and since the latter deserves praise, clearly the former's failure so to act must deserve censure. But when a soul sets itself to this purpose and is becoming good, it cannot achieve its end unless it be directed towards something which is not itself. Yet to what may the soul turn so as to become good, but to *the* Good, loving, pursuing, attaining it? If it turn away again, and lose its goodness by the very act of turning away from good, there will be nothing to which it may return once more (if it desire to amend), unless that Good from which it is declining abides still in itself.

It follows that there could be no changeable goods, were there not a Good that is changeless. You hear the word 'good' applied to this and that, things which at another time may be called not good. See then if you can pass beyond the things which are good by virtue of their share in goodness, and rise to the vision of that Good whose partial presence makes them good. You must know the meaning of Good itself, when you hear that this or that is good. If then you can set them aside and reach the sight of Good in itself, you will have reached the sight of God; and if you shall cleave to him in love, you will in that moment receive beatitude. Other things are loved only because they are good. It were shame to stay cleaving to them and not to love the Good itself which makes them good. A soul may not yet have the goodness of conversion to the changeless Good; but simply as a soul, we may give it a value (if we rightly apprehend) higher than that of any material luminary. Yet its value for us lies not in itself but in the creative art that made it: it is our seeing that it was worth the making that makes us approve it as made.

This is the Truth, the absolute Good—nothing else but Good itself, and therefore the highest good; for the only good that can be diminished or increased is that whose goodness is derived from another good. The soul's goodness, then, comes from its conversion to that same Source which has made it a soul. The soul's perfecting in goodness comes from the conforming of will to nature, when the will turns in love towards that Good from which is derived the existence that cannot be lost, even if the will turns away from its Source. When it turns away from the highest Good, the soul ceases to be a good soul, but not to be a soul—which is itself a good that is superior to body. The will loses what the will gains; for the soul already existed, with power to will its turning towards its Source, but it was not there to will to be a soul before it existed. The good for us is to see how it was or is right for that thing to be, the rightness of which we can understand; and if there is anything of which we cannot understand the rightness, to see that it could not have been unless it was right for it to be. And this Good is not far from each one of us: for 'in him we live and move and have our being'.

But we have to stand fast by that Good in love, and cleave to it, that we may enjoy the presence of him from whom we have our being, and in whose absence we could not be at all. 'We walk by faith, as yet, and not by sight': not yet do we see God, as the same apostle says, 'face to face'. But unless we already love him, we shall never see him.

Yet how can we love what we do not know? A thing may be known and not loved; but we may question whether that which is not known can be loved: if it cannot, no one can love God before he knows him. To know God means to perceive him with the grasp of the mind: he is not a body to be observed with the eye of flesh. But to see and apprehend God, as he may be seen and apprehended, is given to the pure in heart: they, we read, are 'blessed, for they shall see God'. And before we have gained strength for that seeing, there can be no purifying of the heart to make it fit to see him, unless he be loved by faith. Faith, hope, and charity, those three virtues for whose building up is mounted all the scaffolding of the Bible, are only in the soul that believes what it sees not yet, and hopes and loves what it believes. Therefore there can be love even of him who is not known, if yet he is believed. Doubtless, we must beware lest the soul, believing what it does not see, feign for itself an image of that which is not, and put its hope and love upon a lie. Then there will not be that 'charity from a pure heart and a good conscience and a faith unfeigned, which is the end of the commandment', as Paul says.

When we acquire beliefs from the reading or hearing of material things which we have not seen, the mind cannot but form for itself some image in outline and shape such as may present itself to thought. But it will not be a true image: or if it is, as may very exceptionally happen, there will be no advantage in retaining it for the maintenance of our belief, though it may serve a purpose in suggesting to us something else. Most people who read or hear the writings of Paul or his history will form some picture of his appearance, and of that of all the other persons whose names occur in connection with his. Of all the many people who know his letters, one will picture the forms and features of these persons in one way, one in another: but none can say whose picture is the nearest resemblance. Our belief is not concerned with the outward appearance of the men, but only with the fact that by the grace of God their lives and doings were what the Scripture tells us. That is the belief which is both profitable and attainable, and the belief we should seek for. The bodily appearance of the Lord himself is represented by an innumerable variety of mental images: but whatever it actually was, it was not more than one. In our faith concerning the Lord Jesus Christ, the salutary element is not in the mental image, which may be a long way from the facts, but in the idea of Man: fixed in our knowledge is a definite standard of human nature, by which we immediately recognize, upon seeing that which conforms to it, that this is a man or a human form.

By this knowledge our thought is shaped, when we believe that God was made man for us, to be an example of humility, and to prove God's love towards us. What is good for us to believe and to keep firm and unshaken in our hearts, is that the humility whereby God was born of a woman and brought by mortal men that shameful way to death, is the supreme medicament for the healing of the cancer of our pride, and the profound mystery that can loose the fetters of sin. So also it is because we have the idea of omnipotence that we believe the power of his miracles and of his resurrection to have come from the omnipotent God; and we think of such facts in accordance with our systematic knowledge of general and specific notions, whether innate or acquired by experience, so that our faith be not feigned. We do not know the appearance of the virgin Mary, of whom Christ was marvellously born, so that both in conceiving and in giving birth her virginity was preserved. We do not know the figure of Lazarus; we have not seen Bethany, the grave or the stone which Christ made them take away when he raised him from the dead, nor that new tomb cut in the rock from which he himself rose, nor the mount of Olivet where he ascended into heaven. And if we have not seen them, we are wholly ignorant whether they are as we imagine them: indeed we suppose it the more likely that they are not. For if ever a place or a person or any physical object presents to our eyes the same appearance as it had in our imagination before we saw it, we are struck with astonishment—so rarely does it happen, if ever. Yet we have a most firm belief in the Gospel story, because we conceive it in accordance with our assured knowledge of general and specific notions. We believe that the Lord Jesus Christ was born of a virgin called Mary: but what is a virgin, what is to be born, what is a proper name, we do not believe but simply know. Whether Mary had that form which comes to our mind when we tell or remember the story, we neither know nor believe. And so without damage to faith we may say, 'Perhaps she was like this, perhaps she was not'. But 'Perhaps Christ was born of a virgin' is what no-one can say without damage to his Christian faith.

Now it is our desire to gain such understanding as may be granted us of the Trinity, its eternity, its equality, its unity. But before we can understand, we have to believe, and we must take care that our faith be not feigned; for our happiness rests upon the fruition of the Trinity, and if our belief about it be false, our hope will be vain and our love not pure. How then can we love, through believing, the Trinity which we do not know? The love which we can have for Paul is based upon a knowledge of general and specific ideas. We may be entirely ignorant of his appearance, which may have been quite different from our imagination of it. Yet we know what a man is, for we need go no further than what we are ourselves. Plainly, Paul was a man: his soul was linked to a body and lived a mortal life. We believe of him what we find in ourselves according to the genus or species in which every human nature is equally contained. But knowledge of genus and species can tell us nothing of the transcendent Trinity: there are not a number of such trinities, experience of some of which could enable us to form a generalized notion, and believe that the divine Trinity is similar; and so, by analogy with what we know, love that which not yet knowing we believe. No: we can love our Lord Jesus Christ's resurrection from the dead, although we have never seen anyone so rise again; but we cannot in the same way love, through believing, the Trinity which we do not see and the like of which we have never seen. We know that death and life are, because we are alive and we have seen and experienced the death and the dying of others. To rise again, then, is simply to return to life. But when we say and believe that the Trinity exists, we know indeed what the word 'Trinity' means, since we know the meaning of 'three'; but that is not what we love. We can have 'three' whenever we like, by holding up three fingers. Is that which we love, then, not *any* Trinity but the Trinity which is God? Is it God in the Trinity that we love? but we neither have seen nor know any other God; for there is but one only God whom we have not yet seen, whom through believing we love. The question is, what likeness or comparability in things we know can form the belief by which we may love God, before he is known?

Let us go back, and consider why we love the apostle. Not, surely, because of that form of humanity which is familiar to us and which we believe he shared. If it were so, our love would now have no object, for his soul and body are divided and he exists no longer in human form. That which we love in him, we believe is now living: for we love the righteous soul. But this implies reference to a pattern of genus or species —that we know what a soul is, and what 'righteous' is. Now we may properly say that we know what a soul is, because we ourselves have a soul. We have never seen it with our eyes or formed a generic conception from a number of things seen; we know it because we have it. I know nothing more intimately than that which I am aware of being, that by which I am aware of all things else—the soul itself. The bodily movements by which we are aware of the life of others, we recognize from their likeness to our own: life makes us move our bodies as we observe other bodies moving. When a living body moves, our eyes do not find their way in to a vision of the soul, which eyes cannot see; but we are aware that in that bodily mass there is something of the same kind as we have in ourselves to move our own bodily mass—namely, life and soul. And this is not peculiar to human intelligence and reason: animals are aware of life not only in themselves but in one another and in us. They do not see our souls, but become aware of them from movements of the body with simple and instinctive immediacy. From our own soul then we draw the knowledge of soul in anyone else and the belief of it when we do not know it. We are not only aware of the soul but are able to know what soul is by the consideration of our own; for we *have* a soul.

But how do we know what is 'righteous'? We said that the only reason for our love of the apostle is that he is a 'righteous soul': we must know then what 'righteous' is, as well as what is 'soul'. What 'soul' is, we know from ourselves as we have said; for there is soul in us. But how do we know what is 'righteous', if *we* are not righteous? If none but he who is righteous knows what 'righteous' is, none can love the righteous but the righteous. The mere belief that a man is righteous cannot make you love him, if you do not know what 'righteous' is. As we have already shown, one can only love what one believes without seeing, on the basis of some standard conception of genus or species. If then none can love the righteous but the righteous, how can anyone who is not yet righteous desire to be so? For no one desires to be what he does not love. Yet it is impossible to become righteous without willing it; and to will it one must love the righteous. It follows that a man not yet righteous himself can love the righteous; but this cannot be if he does not know what 'righteous' is. We must allow that a man not yet righteous may know the meaning of the word; and we ask whence such knowledge comes. Clearly not by the visual sense: a body is not righteous, as it is white or black, square or round; and nothing but bodies are seen by the eyes. The righteous element in man is the soul, and a man is called righteous in virtue of his soul and not his body. Righteousness is a beauty of the soul which can exist in men whose bodies are deformed or ugly; and the soul's beauty no more than the soul itself is visible to the outward eye. Whence then can a man not yet righteous learn the meaning of the word, and through loving the righteous become righteous himself? Bodily movements might give indications of righteousness in this or that man; but if one were wholly ignorant of the meaning of 'righteous', one could not recognize that such were signs of a righteous soul. The problem remains. Somehow or other we know what 'righteous' means, before we are righteous ourselves. If that knowledge comes from the external world, it must be derived from some bodily source; but its object does not belong to the bodily realm at all. It must therefore be *in ourselves* that we learn the meaning of the term 'righteous'. When I look for the proper way to describe it, I can find the answer nowhere but in my own mind. If I ask another man, he must look within for his answer; and no one can give a true answer unless he has found it in himself. When I want to describe Carthage, I enquire of myself and I find an image of Carthage in my own mind. But I have got it by way of sense perception, having been in the town in bodily presence, seen it and remembered it, so that the right word will be at my disposal whenever I want to describe it. Its 'word' is the actual image in my memory—not the sound of two syllables when I say 'Carthage', nor the silent passing of the name through the mind: it is the object of my inward vision, when I pronounce, or before I pronounce, the two syllables 'Carthage'. Similarly, if I want to describe Alexandria which I have never seen, an image of it is at my disposal. I have been credibly informed that it is a great city, and have constructed a picture of it as described to me to the best of my ability. And that is the 'word' of it in my mind, when I want to speak of it, before I pronounce the five syllables of the well-known name. But if I could display my mental picture to people who know Alexandria, they would assuredly say 'That is not it!'—or if they said 'It is', I should be greatly surprised, and when I considered the picture in my mind I should still not *know* that it was Alexandria: I should only believe those who had seen it.

But this is not how I enquire the meaning of 'righteous'; it is not how I find it or contemplate it when I describe it, how my description is accepted or how I accept another's description. It is not as though I had seen anything of the kind or perceived it, by any bodily sense, or heard of it from others who had their knowledge in that way. When I say, and say with knowledge, that 'the righteous soul is that which by rational principle in life and conduct assigns to each his own',[1] I am not thinking of an absent object like Carthage, or imagining one like Alexandria correctly or incorrectly. I perceive something *present*, perceive it in myself, though I am not myself what I perceive. Many, on hearing me, may accept my description; but whoever does so knowledgeably will himself be perceiving in himself the same thing, though he be not himself what he perceives. When a righteous man says it, he is perceiving and saying what he himself is; but he too perceives it 'in himself'. That is natural enough: where should he see himself but in himself? The surprising thing is that the mind or soul should see in itself what it has seen nowhere else, that it should see truly, see the truly righteous soul, being itself soul yet not the righteous soul which it sees in itself. We can hardly suppose the presence of *another* righteous soul in the soul which is not yet righteous. But then what *is* present to the soul when it sees and defines the righteous soul, and sees it entirely in itself though itself is not righteous? Our answer is, that what it sees is an *inward truth* present to the soul that has the power to contemplate it. Not all have the power; and those that have are not all themselves what they contemplate—not all themselves righteous souls, though they can see and define the righteous soul. They can only become it themselves, by cleaving to that same form or pattern which they contemplate, being conformed to it and becoming righteous souls: not only perceiving and declaring that the righteous soul is 'that which by rational principle in life and conduct assigns to each his own', but by making righteous life and conduct their own, assigning to each his own, 'owing no man anything but to love one another'. The only way of cleaving to that pattern is by love. If we love another man whom we believe righteous, we cannot but love the pattern itself which shows us what the righteous soul is, in order that we too may become righteous. Indeed, did we not love the pattern, we could have no love for the man; for our love for him is based upon the pattern: it is only that so long as we are not righteous our love of it is insufficient to make us righteous.

Our conclusion is that love for the man who is believed righteous is based upon that pattern and truth which the lover perceives and apprehends in himself. But love for the pattern and the truth itself cannot be based upon anything extraneous. We cannot find anything outside itself, so that our belief in it and our love for it, when it is still unknown, might be based on a previous knowledge of anything of the kind. It is

[1] The definition of *Justitia* given by Cicero in *De Finibus* V.33 and set at the beginning of Justinian's *Institutes* as the basis of Roman law.

itself the thing you behold wherever you behold anything of the kind: indeed there is nothing else 'of the kind', for it alone is what it is. Accordingly our love for men must have their righteousness either as the cause or as the purpose of our love. In the same way a man's own righteousness must be either cause or purpose of his love for himself; only so can he safely love his neighbour as himself. If his self-love has any other ground, it is an unrighteous self-love, for he will be loving himself so as to be unrighteous—and therefore to be evil, so that it will be no real self-love; for 'he who loves iniquity, hateth his own soul'.

It follows that in this enquiry concerning the Trinity and our knowledge of God, the first thing for us to learn is the nature of true love—or rather the nature of love; for only the love which is true deserves the name. All other is covetousness: it is a misuse of language when the covetous are said to love, as it is when those who love are said to covet. The aim of true love is the life of righteousness in cleaving to the truth; and this means that nothing in this world should have any weight for us beside the love of men, which means the will that they may live righteously. That gives all the value to the readiness to die for our brethren, which the Lord Jesus Christ taught us by his example. There are two commandments on which hang all the Law and the Prophets: love of God and love of neighbour; but it is not without reason that the Scripture often puts one of them for both. Sometimes it is the love of God. 'We know that all things work together for good to them that love God.' 'Whosoever loveth God, he is known of God.' 'The love of God is shed abroad in our hearts by the Holy Spirit which is given to us.' In such sayings it is implied that he who loves God must do what God has commanded, that his love depends upon his doing, and so he must love his neighbour also, because this is what God has commanded. Sometimes Scripture mentions only the love of neighbour. 'Bear ye one another's burdens, and so shall ye fulfil the law of Christ.' 'The whole law is fulfilled in one saying, namely, Thou shalt love thy neighbour as thyself.' Or as in the Gospel, 'Whatsoever ye would that men should do unto you, even so do unto them; for this is the Law and the Prophets'. There are many other places in Holy Writ, where it seems that the love of neighbour is alone enjoined for our perfecting, and nothing is said of the love of God; though the Law and the Prophets hang on both commandments. The reason for this is that he who loves his neighbour must necessarily have first the love for love itself. But 'God is love, and he who abideth in love, abideth in God'. It follows that he must have first the love of God.

Those who seek God by way of the spiritual powers set over the world or its parts, drift far away from him—separated not by space but by difference of affection. They strive towards the external, and desert what lies within them, though God is more inward than the innermost. They may have heard or conceived of some holy celestial power; but what draws them is the admiration that human weakness feels for the works of such a power, rather than the model of reverent submission which attains to the rest of God. They choose rather the pride of angelic potency than the devotion of angelic being. No holy person rejoices in his own power, but in the power of him from whom is derived all potency for fitting action. He knows that it is mightier to be united in willing worship to the omnipotent, than to display in his own power and will a potency which is fearful to those who have it not. So when the Lord Jesus Christ himself wrought miracles, he sought to convey to those who marvelled a fuller truth, to turn them from their absorption in temporal portents to things inward and eternal. 'Come unto me, all ye that labour and are heavy laden, and I will refresh you: take my yoke upon you.' He does not say 'Learn of me, for I raise up them that have been dead four days'; but 'Learn of me, for I am meek and lowly of heart'. The firm ground of humility is stronger and safer than any windy elevation. So he goes on, 'And ye shall find rest for your souls'. For 'Love is not puffed up': 'God is love': 'the faithful in love shall rest in him', called back from the noisy outer world to the joyful silences.

'God is love.' Why should we go speeding to the height of heaven and the nethermost parts of the earth, seeking for him who is with us, if we would but be with him? Let none say: 'I do not know what I am to love.' Let him love his brother, and he will love that same love: he knows the love whereby he loves better than the brother whom he loves. God can be more known to him than his brother—really more known, because more present; more known because more inward; more known, because more sure. Embrace the love that is God: through love embrace God. He is the very love that links together in holy bond all good angels and all God's servants, and unites them and us to one another and in obedience to himself. The more we are clean from the cancer of pride, the more are we filled with love; and he who is filled with love is filled with God.

But now you will say: 'Charity indeed I see; I fix my mind's eye upon it as best I may; I believe the word of Scripture, that God is charity, and he that abideth in charity abideth in God. But my vision of charity is not a vision of the Trinity.' Well, let me try to make you see that it is, trusting that Charity itself be present to move us to a good end. The charity that we love is a loving charity, and it is because it loves that we love it. What then is the object of charity's love, which makes charity itself lovable? If it loves nothing, it is not charity. If it loves itself, it cannot love itself *as charity*, unless itself have some object. A transitive word denotes itself as well as connotes its object, but it does not denote itself *as transitive word*, unless it denotes itself as connoting an object; similarly charity may love itself, but only if it love itself as having an object of its love will it be loving itself *as charity*. The object of charity's love must be something which charity makes us love; and that, if we are to start from what is nearest, is our brother. Remember the apostle John's commendation of brotherly love: 'Whosoever loveth his brother, abideth in the light, and there is no cause of stumbling in him.' Evidently he has set the perfection of righteousness in the love of brother: he in whom there is no cause of stumbling is plainly perfect. Yet he seems to have said nothing of the love of God. The only explanation of that is that he means God to be comprehended in brotherly love itself. And a little later in the Epistle he says explicitly: 'Beloved, let us love one another; for love is of God; and everyone that loveth is born of God and knoweth God. He that loveth not, hath not known God; for God is love.' The train of thought makes it clear enough, that this same brotherly love (the love wherewith we love another) is being proclaimed with apostolic authority to be not only 'of God', but 'God'. It is God, then, that causes us to love our brother, when love causes us to do so; and the first object of our love must needs be that very love wherewith we love our brother.

We infer from this that the Two Commandments cannot be separated. 'God is love.' He who loves love, assuredly loves God: he who loves his brother, must necessarily love love. So we read soon after: 'He that loveth not his brother whom he sees, cannot love God whom he seeth not.' The reason of his not seeing God is that he does not love his brother. He who does not love his brother is not in love, and he who is not in love is not in God, for God is love. Again, he who is not in God is not in the light: for 'God is light, and there is no darkness in him'. Naturally, then, he who is not in the light does not see the light, which means that he does not see God; because he is in darkness. He sees his brother with the outward human vision to which God is invisible. But if he loved with spiritual charity the brother whom his outward vision sees, he would see God, who is Charity itself, with the inward vision whereby God can be seen. Thus he who loves not the brother whom he sees cannot love God, whom he does not see just because God is the love which he lacks. We need not be disturbed by the question, How much charity ought we to give to our brother and how much to God? The answer is, To God incomparably more than to ourselves, and to our brother as much as to ourselves; ourselves we love the more, the more we love God. It is, then, out of one and the same charity that we love God and our neighbour: but we love God for God's sake, and for God's sake ourselves and our neighbour.

What is it, I would ask, that kindles the fire in our hearts, when we hear or read such words as these?—'Behold, now is the acceptable time, behold, now is the day of salvation: giving no occasion of stumbling in anything, that our ministration be not blamed, but in everything commending ourselves as God's ministers: in much patience, in afflictions, in necessities, in distress, in stripes, in imprisonments, in tumults, in labours, in watchings, in fastings; in pureness, in knowledge, in long-suffering, in kindness, in the Holy Ghost, in charity unfeigned, in the word of truth, in the power of God; by the armour of righteousness on the right hand and on the left, by glory and dishonour, by evil report and good report; as deceivers and yet true, as unknown and yet well known, as dying, and behold, we live; as chastened, and not killed, as sorrowful, yet always rejoicing, as poor, yet making many rich, as having nothing, and yet possessing all things.'—If the love of Paul the apostle is kindled in us at this reading, surely it is because we believe that his life was like that. But that God's ministers *ought* so to live, is not a thing we believe on hearsay: it is what we see within ourselves, or rather above ourselves, in very truth. The Paul whom we believe so to have lived, we love because of what we *see*. And were it not that above all we loved that pattern which we perceive in everlasting fixity and changelessness, we should not love the apostle because we retain the faith that his life in the flesh was correspondent and accordant to that pattern. Yet we find that we are somehow stirred more largely to love of the pattern itself, through the faith by which we believe that a man has lived in accord with it, and by the hope which forbids us, since there have been men who so lived, to despair of ourselves who are men like them being able to live like them; so that we desire it more ardently and pray for it more confidently. What makes us love their life is the love of that pattern according to which we believe they lived; and their life, when we believe it, stirs in us towards the same pattern a more burning charity. So that the stronger burns our love for God, the more sure and unclouded is our vision of him; because in God we behold the changeless pattern of righteousness, in accord with which we make our judgment that a man should live.

Faith then avails for the knowledge and the love of God, not as though he were wholly unknown or wholly unloved before, but that he may be known more clearly and loved more steadfastly. Now the charity praised and preached with such energy by divine Scripture, what is it but love of the good? Love is the activity of a lover, and it has a certain object. There, then, we have three things: the lover, that which is loved, and love. Love itself is nothing but a kind of life which couples together or seeks to couple some two entities, the lover and the loved. This is so in the carnal loves of the external world; but let us leave the flesh beneath our feet and rise to the soul, where we may drink of a purer and more limpid spring. What does any friend love in his friend but the soul? There too are the three: the lover, the loved, and love. A further ascent still remains for us, a higher realm in which our search is to be pursued, so far as men may. But here we may pause—not supposing we have found what we seek, but having found (as seekers do) the place in which to look. We have found, not the thing itself, but where it is to be sought; and that will suffice to give us a point from which a fresh start may be undertaken.

Book 15, Para. 10

We may recall that it was in the eighth Book that the manifestation of the Trinity to our understanding began. There we essayed to lift up, so far as might be, the effort of our mind to the understanding of that most excellent and changeless being which is other than our mind. In contemplation we were aware of it as not far from us and yet above us—not spatially but by its own most reverend and wonderful excellence, so that we found it present in us in virtue of its own pervading light. But so far we had no glimpse of the Trinity, because we could not in that dazzling brightness direct our mind's eye steadily to look for it. All that we could with some clearness distinguish was that it was no measurable mass in which the quantity of two or three must be believed greater than that of the two. Only when we came to consider charity, which in Holy Scriptures is called God, the light began to break upon a Trinity, consisting in lover, the beloved and love. But from that ineffable light our gaze flinched away: we had to confess that our mind in its weakness was not yet strong enough to be conformed to it. And therefore, in order to recruit our labouring efforts, we paused in the pursuit of our undertaking and turned back to the more familiar consideration of that same mind of ours, in which man has been made in the image of God; and from the ninth to the fourteenth Book we occupied ourselves with our own creaturely nature, in order that we might be able to apprehend and perceive the invisible things of God through the things that are made.

And now the time has come, when after this exercise of our understanding in a lower sphere for so long as need required (and maybe for longer), we would lift ourselves up to perceive the supreme Trinity which is God. Yet our strength fails us. Many trinities we can see most surely. There are those which are produced by the action of bodily objects on the outward senses, and those which occur when the sense perception becomes matter of thought. There are trinities when things arising in the mind apart from the bodily senses are distinguished by clear reasoning and comprehended in knowledge, such as our faith, and those virtues which are ways of living. There are trinities when the mind itself, by which we know all that we truthfully claim to know, is known to itself or thinks of itself, or when it perceives an eternal and unchanging object rather than itself. In all these processes we see trinities with assurance since they occur or exist in us as we remember, regard, and will. But can we perceive therein by an act of understanding a Speaker and his Word, the Father and the Son, and proceeding thence the Charity common to both which is the Holy Spirit? It may be urged that while trinities belonging to the sphere of sense or mind are for us objects of sight rather than belief, the fact that God is Trinity must be believed rather than seen. If that be so, it must follow, either that the invisible things of him are nowhere apprehended and perceived by us through the things that are made; or, that in none of them which we perceive can we perceive the Trinity—that there is something in that sphere which we may perceive, but something also which we are obliged to believe though unperceived. Yet the eighth Book showed that we do perceive a changeless good, other than ourselves; and the same was indicated in the fourteenth Book when we spoke of the wisdom which comes to man from God. Why then can we not recognize there the Trinity? It is impossible to maintain that this wisdom which is called God neither understands nor loves itself; and it is patent that where there is no knowledge there cannot possibly be wisdom. That the wisdom which is God knows or loves other things but neither knows nor loves itself, cannot be asserted or believed without foolishness and impiety; and if so, here surely is Trinity: wisdom, its knowledge of itself and its love of itself. That was how we discovered a trinity in man: the mind, the knowledge whereby it knows itself, and the love whereby it loves itself.

But these three are *in* man, without by themselves constituting man; for if we follow the definition of the ancients, man is a rational and mortal animal. The three things named are then man's highest part, but not by themselves man. Moreover, the one person which is the individual man possesses those three in his mind. Even if we adopt a different definition of man, to the effect that he is a rational substance composed of soul and body, it remains indubitable that man possesses a soul which is not body and a body which is not soul. And then our triad is not equivalent to man but belongs to man or is in man. If we set aside the body and think of the soul alone, we find that the mind is a part of it, as it might be its head or eye or face—though we may not think of the soul's parts as bodies. Thus it is not the soul but the highest thing in it which we call the mind. But we cannot say that the Trinity is in God in this manner —a part of God but not itself God. The individual man, who is called the image of God not in respect of all that belongs to his nature but in respect of his mind alone, is a personal unity, having the image of the Trinity in his mind. But the Trinity of whom he is image is as a whole nothing but God, is as a whole nothing but Trinity. Nothing belongs to God's nature that does not belong to this Trinity. The three Persons are of one essence, not like the individual man one person.

In another respect also there is a wide difference to be noted. In man, whether we speak of mind, its knowledge and its love or of memory, understanding, and will, nothing in the mind is remembered but through memory, or understood but through understanding, or loved but through will. In the divine Trinity, reverence forbids us to say that the Father understands neither himself nor his Son nor the Holy Spirit, save through the Son, nor loves save through the Holy Spirit; or that through himself he does no more than remember either himself or the Son or the Holy Spirit. Or similarly, that the Son remembers himself and the Father only through the Father and loves only through the Holy Spirit; while through himself he can only understand both the Father and himself and the Holy Spirit. Or in the same way that it is through the Father that the Holy Spirit remembers Father, Son, and himself, through the Son that he understands the Father, the Son and himself, while through himself he can only love himself, the Father and the Son. This would amount to saying that the Father is memory of himself, Son and Holy Spirit, the Son is understanding of himself, Father, and Holy Spirit, the Holy Spirit is charity to himself, Father and Son. But to hold or express such opinions concerning the divine Trinity would be extreme presumption. If only the Son understands for himself and the Father and the Holy Spirit, we are back in the irrational notion that the Father is wise not in himself but by the Son: that wisdom has not begotten wisdom, but the Father is called wise in virtue of the wisdom he has begotten. For where understanding is lacking, there can be no wisdom: if the Father understands not for himself but the Son for the Father, clearly the Son makes the Father wise. And if for God to be is to be wise, and his essence is his wisdom, it will not be the Son who has his essence from the Father (as he truly does), but the Father who has his essence from the Son—which is entirely irrational and false. We may be satisfied with our discussion, refutation and rejection of this irrationality in the seventh Book. God the Father is wise by that same wisdom which is his own being; and the Son is the wisdom of the Father, as being derived from the wisdom which is identical with the Father of whom he is begotten. And accordingly the Father is understanding by the same understanding which is his own being; for wisdom implies understanding; and the Son is the understanding of the Father, as begotten of the understanding which is the Father's being. The same may properly be said of memory. He who remembers nothing, or does not remember himself, cannot be wise. Since therefore the Father is wisdom, and the Son is wisdom, the Son will remember himself no less than the Father remembers himself; and just as the Father remembers himself and the Son with a memory that is his own and not the Son's, the Son will remember himself and the Father with a memory that is not the Father's but his own. Finally, we cannot predicate wisdom where there is no love; from which it follows that the Father is his own love, no less than his own understanding and his own memory. We seem forced to the conclusion that our triad of memory, understanding and love or will, in that supreme and changeless essence that is God, are not to be identified with Father, Son and Holy Spirit, but with the Father by himself. And because the Son is wisdom begotten of wisdom, it is equally true that he understands for himself and not the Father or the Holy Spirit for him, and that neither does the Father remember nor the Holy Spirit love for him, but he does both for himself; for he is his own memory, his own understanding, his own love, though that property comes to him from the Father of whom he is begotten. Again, since the Holy Spirit is wisdom proceeding from wisdom, it is not true that the memory which belongs to him is the Father, the understanding the Son, and the love himself; for he would not be wisdom if another remembered for him, and another understood for him, while for himself he did no more than love. All three belong to him, and in such a manner that he *is* all three; but this property comes to him from that Source from which he proceeds.

No man can comprehend the wisdom by which God knows all things, a wisdom wherein that which we call past does not pass, and that which we call future is not awaited as though not yet available, but both past and future are all together present with what is present: a wisdom wherein there is no thinking on particular things severally, or movement of thought from one thing to another, but the whole universe is presented simultaneously in one single view. No man, I say, can comprehend such a wisdom, which is both foresight and knowledge; inasmuch as even our own wisdom passes our comprehension. We can perceive, in various ways, what is present to our senses or our understanding: what is absent but was once present, we know by memory if we have not forgotten it. We conjecture, not the past from the future, but the future from the past, though we cannot have certain knowledge of it. To some of our thoughts we look forward with a degree of clearness and assurance as about to occur in the immediate future; but when we do so with maximum of security, we do it by an act of memory, which is evidently concerned not with what is going to happen but with what is past. This is open to experience in the case of speeches or songs which we render from memory in a certain order: did we not foresee in thought what comes next, we could not speak it. But what enables us to foresee is not pre-vision but memory. Until the whole speech or song is ended, there is nothing in its recitation that was not foreseen and looked forward to. Yet in the process our singing and speaking is not ascribed to pre-vision but to memory; and we remark, in those who display exceptional powers of such extended recitation, a strength not of foresight but of memory. We know, without any doubt, that such processes are carried on in our mind, or by our mind; but the more closely we try to observe the manner of the process, the more surely does description fail us and effort exhaust itself in the attempt to reach lucidity of understanding, if not of language. Can we expect then that our feeble minds will be able to comprehend the identity of God's providence with his memory and understanding—the providence of God who does not regard each thing severally in discursive thought, but embraces all that he knows in one eternal, changeless and ineffable vision? In the strait of such perplexity we may well cry out to the living God: 'From myself thy knowledge has become wonderful: its strength is shown, and I shall not be able to reach it.' For from myself I understand how marvellous and incomprehensible is thy knowledge whereby thou hast made me; and yet in my meditation the fire is kindled, so that I seek thy face evermore.

I know that wisdom is an incorporeal substance, a light in which are seen things not seen by the eye of flesh. And yet a man of such spiritual greatness as Paul says that 'we see now through a mirror, in an enigma; but then face to face'. If we ask of what manner or of what nature is this mirror, we think immediately of the fact that in a mirror what is seen is no more than an image. What we have tried to do is to gain through this image which is ourselves some vision, as through a mirror, of him who made us. We find the same sense in other words of the apostle's: 'We with unveiled face beholding in a mirror the glory of the Lord, are transformed into the same image from glory unto glory, as by the Spirit of the Lord.'

Para. 44 ff.

When the promised vision 'face to face', has come, we shall behold the Trinity—that Trinity which is not only incorporeal but perfectly inseparable and truly changeless—far more clearly and surely than we now behold its image in ourselves. This present vision, through a mirror and in an enigma, as vouchsafed to us in this life, belongs not to any who can perceive in their own mind all that we have here set out by our analysis; but to those who see the mind as an image, and so are able to achieve a certain relating of what they see to him whose image it is; to reach through their actual vision of the image a presumptive vision of the original which cannot yet be seen face to face. The apostle does not say, 'We see now a mirror', but 'We see now through a mirror'. Those who see the mind as it may be seen, and in it that trinity of which I have attempted to give a variety of descriptions, yet without believing or understanding it to be the image of God: they are seeing a mirror, but so far from seeing through the mirror him who is now to be seen only in that way, they are unaware that the mirror seen *is* a mirror—which is to say, an image. If they knew it, they might be conscious of the need to seek and in some measure even now to see, through this mirror, him whose mirror it is: their hearts being purified by faith unfeigned, so that he who is seen now through a mirror may at last be seen face to face. But if they despise the faith that purifies hearts, no understanding of the most subtle analysis of our mind's nature can serve but to condemn them, on the testimony of their own understanding itself. The failure to reach any firm assurance despite all the struggles to understand, can be caused only by envelopment in a darkness which is punishment, and the burden of a corruptible body which presseth down the soul. Such evil can have been incurred only by the guilt of sin; and the gravity of evil should be their warning to follow the Lamb that taketh away the sin of the world. For men in his keeping, whose gifts of intellect are far less than theirs, when released from the body at this life's end are clear of all claim upon them by the powers of malice: those powers which the Lamb whom they slew without debt of sin vanquished by the right of his blood before overthrowing them by the might of his power. Free from the power of the devil, they have welcome from the holy angels, delivered from every evil through the Mediator of God and men, the man Christ Jesus: for the Holy Scriptures old and new are at one, both those that foretell the Christ and those that forth-tell him, in knowing 'no other name under heaven whereby men must be saved'. Thus cleansed from every taint of corruption, the elect are established in peaceful dwelling-places until their bodies be given back to them, bodies corruptible no longer, for beauty not for burdening. For so the perfect goodness and perfect wisdom of the Creator has ordained, that the spirit of man in dutiful subjection to God should possess a body blessedly subject to itself, and that this blessedness should abide for ever.

There without any impediment shall we see the truth and enjoy it in perfect clarity and assurance. The mind will not pursue a knowledge by reasoning, but in contemplation will discern why Holy Spirit is not Son, though he proceed from the Father. In that light all such questioning will cease; though here its difficulty has been proved so great for me, and doubtless for all who read with care and understanding what I have written. In my second Book I promised to discuss the question in another place; but whenever I would have pointed out some likeness to that truth in our creaturely being, I found no form of words adequately corresponding to such understanding as I had reached—though even in that understanding I am aware of more endeavour than success. Again, when I found in the single person of a man an image of the supreme Trinity, I sought to make the likeness more easily apprehended in the sphere of things changing, and to display it (particularly in the ninth Book) as existing in temporal succession. But, as we have shown in this fifteenth Book, our human way of thinking cannot fit the three entities in one person to the three divine Persons. Moreover, in the supreme Trinity that is God there is no temporal successiveness, whereby the question whether first the Son is born of the Father and then the Holy Spirit proceeds from both, could be answered or even asked. Holy Scripture, indeed calls him Spirit of both. It is he of whom the apostle says: 'Because ye are sons, God hath sent the Spirit of his Son into your hearts'; and it is he of whom the Son himself says: 'For it is not ye that speak, but the Spirit of your Father that speaketh in you.' And there are many other texts of Scripture which prove that he who in the Trinity has the special title of Holy Spirit is Spirit both of Father and of Son. The Son again says of him, 'whom I will send to you from the Father'; and elsewhere, 'whom the Father will send in my name'. That he proceeds from both may be learnt, first from the saying of the Son, that he 'proceedeth from the Father', and secondly, in that after his rising from the dead and appearing to his disciples, he breathed on them and said, 'Receive ye the Holy Spirit': so showing that the Spirit proceeds from himself. The Spirit is that same 'virtue', which (as we read in the Gospel) 'went from him and healed them all'.

If one ask why it was that after his resurrection he first gave the Holy Spirit on earth and afterwards sent him from heaven, my answer would be that by this gift is shed abroad in our hearts the charity whereby we love God and our neighbour—according to those two commandments on which hang all the law and the prophets. To signify this, the Lord Jesus gave the Spirit twice: once on earth for the love of neighbour, and again from heaven for the love of God. But if the double gift of the Holy Spirit should be otherwise explained, at least we may not doubt that it was the same Holy Spirit, given in the breathing of Jesus, of whom afterwards he says, 'Go, baptize all nations in the name of the Father and of the Son and of the Holy Spirit'. It is the same Spirit, then, that was also given from heaven on the day of Pentecost, ten days after the Lord's ascension into heaven. He who gives the Holy Spirit must assuredly be God: nay, how great a God must he be who gives God! None of his disciples gave the Holy Spirit: they prayed that the Spirit should come upon those on whom they laid their hand, but they did not themselves give him. And the church keeps now the same rule in her officers. Even Simon Magnus, when he offers money to the apostles, does not say, 'Give me also this power, that I may give the Holy Spirit', but 'that on whomsoever I lay my hands, he may receive the Holy Spirit'. The words of Scripture preceding were not: 'Simon seeing that the apostles gave the Holy Spirit', but: 'Simon seeing that by the laying on of the apostles' hands the Holy Spirit was given.' Accordingly the Lord Jesus himself not only gave as God the Holy Spirit, but also received him as man; and therefore he is said to be 'full of grace', and 'full of the Holy Spirit'. More expressly is it written of him in the Acts of the Apostles: 'for God hath anointed him with the Holy Spirit'—with no visible oil, but with the gift of grace, which is signified by the visible unction wherewith the Church anoints the baptized. Doubtless, Christ's own anointing with the Holy Spirit was not at that time when the Spirit descended upon him as a dove at his baptism. Then, it was his body that he deigned to represent, his church in which particularly at baptism the Holy Spirit is received. The mystical and invisible anointing of him we must recognize at the moment when the Word of God was made flesh: that is, when human nature, with no preceding merits of good works, was so linked with God the Word in the virgin's womb as to become one person with him. Therefore we confess him born of the Holy Spirit and the virgin Mary. It would be incongruous indeed to suppose that he received the Holy Spirit when he was already thirty years old, at which age he was baptized by John: he must have come to baptism, as altogether without sin, so not without the Holy Spirit. If it is written of John his minister and fore-runner that 'he shall be filled with the Holy Spirit from his mother's womb'—since though engendered by the Father he yet received the Holy Spirit when he was formed in the womb—how are we to think or believe concerning the man Christ, the very conception of whose flesh was not fleshly but spiritual? When it is written of him that he received from the Father the promise of the Holy Spirit and poured it forth, both natures are displayed, the human and the divine. He received as man, he poured forth as God. We can receive indeed the gift according to our capacity; but pour it forth upon others we cannot: for that, we must invoke upon them the God by whom it is performed.

We cannot then ask whether the Holy Spirit had already proceeded from the Father when the Son was begotten, or had not yet so proceeded but upon the begetting of the Son proceeded from both. For here nothing takes place in time. When we come to deal with the temporal we can suppose will first to proceed from the human mind, making a search for what may be called an offspring when it is found: with the 'getting' or 'begetting' of this, the act of will is completed, coming to rest in its object, so that the pursuit of the will that sought becomes the love of the will that enjoys; and this love now proceeds from both, from the begetting mind and the begotten idea, as from parent and offspring. But it is impossible to look for parallels to this in a region where there are no temporal beginnings that can reach completion in the process of time. Thus, given the power to understand the timeless generation of the Son from the Father, one must likewise understand the timeless procession of the Holy Spirit from both. Given power to understand, in the saying of the Son, 'as the Father hath life in himself, so hath he given to the Son to have life in himself', that the Father's gift of life is not to a Son previously existing without life, but that by this timeless generation the life given by the Father in his begetting is co-eternal with the life of the Father who gave it: one must likewise understand that as the Holy Spirit's procession from the Father belongs to the Father's own being, so has he given to the Son that the same Holy Spirit should proceed from him—in both cases timelessly. When it is said that the Holy Spirit proceeds from the Father, we understand that his procession from the Son comes likewise to the Son from the Father. If it is from the Father that the Son has all that he has, it must be from the Father that he has the proceeding from him of the Holy Spirit. We must think here of no temporal before or after; for here there are no times at all. It would be wholly irrational to call the Spirit the Son of both; for while the Son receives his being, with no temporal origin and no mutability of nature, by generation from the Father, the Holy Spirit receives his being, with no temporal origin and no mutability of nature, by procession from both. We do not call the Holy Spirit begotten, but neither may we presume to call him unbegotten, lest the words suggest either two Fathers in the divine Trinity, or two Persons underived. The Father alone is underived, and therefore alone called unbegotten—not indeed in Scripture, but in the common usage of theologians, making discourse on such high matters as fitly as they can. The Son is begotten from the Father; and the Holy Spirit proceeds, ultimately from the Father, and by the Father's gift at no temporal interval from both in common. He could be called son of Father and of Son, only if both had begotten him—a notion intolerable to all sound feeling. Thus he is not begotten of both, but proceeds from the one and the other as the Spirit of both.

To distinguish generation from procession in the divine Trinity, co-eternal, co-equal, incorporeal, beyond all expression changeless and inseparable, is indeed most difficult. For readers who find their thought here at the end of its tether, it may suffice for the moment to repeat what we have said in a sermon addressed to our Christian congregation, and afterwards put in writing. I had shown by texts of Holy Scripture that the Holy Spirit proceeds from both. 'If then,' I said, 'the Holy Spirit proceeds both from the Father and from the Son, why has the Son said that he "proceedeth from the Father"? It can only be after his manner of ascribing that which belongs to himself to him from whom he has his own being. For example: "My doctrine is not mine, but his that sent me." Here, the doctrine he says is not his own but the Father's must yet be understood as *his* doctrine. No less must we understand in the text before quoted, where he says that the Spirit "proceedeth from the Father" (not "proceedeth not from me"), that the Spirit proceeds also from himself. The Son is God from God; and he from whom is derived the Godhead of the Son is the same from whom is derived the Holy Spirit's proceeding from the Son. So it is from the Father that the Holy Spirit has his procession from the Son, even as he proceeds from the Father. And this may enable us to understand, so far as understading is possible for men like us, why the Holy Spirit is not called begotten, but is said to proceed. For if he also were called Son, he must be son of both the other Persons—which would be altogether irrational. A son can be son of two only if they be father and mother; and between God the Father and God the Son no relation of the kind is even to be thought of. Indeed no human son proceeds at one and the same time from father and mother; he does not proceed from the mother when he proceeds from the father into the mother, and he does not proceed from the father at the time of his proceeding from the mother into visible existence. Whereas the Holy Spirit does not proceed from the Father into the Son, and then from the Son to sanctify the creature: he proceeds at once from both, although his proceeding from the Son as from the Father is the Father's gift to the Son. We cannot say that while the Father is life and the Son is life, the Holy Spirit is not life. As, then, the Father who has life in himself has given to the Son to have life in himself, so has he given to the Son that life should proceed from him even as it proceeds from himself.' I insert this passage from a sermon into the present Book: it is addressed of course to the faithful and not to unbelievers.

Unbelievers indeed may lack the power to contemplate God's image in them, and to see the reality of the three elements in their own mind, which are three not as three persons but as all pertaining to the one person of a man. Then they had best believe what the holy Books contain concerning the supreme Trinity that is God, instead of demanding for themselves a perfectly clear and rational account such as weak and sluggish human minds cannot take in. By all means, once they have an unshakable belief in the truth of Holy Scripture's witness, let them go on by prayer and enquiry and right living to the pursuit of understanding—which means the seeing with the mind (so far as seeing is possible) of what is firmly held by faith. Who should forbid them? Who indeed would not encourage them to do so? But if they suppose that the reality must be denied because their minds are too blind to perceive it, then the blind from birth may with equal right deny the existence of the sun. The light shineth in darkness: if the darkness comprehend it not, let those who are darkness first become enlightened by the gift of God into believing, and so begin in comparison with the unbelieving world to be light. Upon that foundation they may be built up to see what they believe, and in due course gain the power of sight. There are certain matters of belief, the sight of which is no longer possible. Christ can never again be seen upon the cross. But without belief in that which once happened and was seen, though there can be no expectation of its happening or being seen again, we can never reach that vision of the Christ which shall be without end. As for such discernment as is possible for the understanding of the supreme, ineffable, immaterial and changeless being of God: there is no field wherein the human mind can better train its insight, under the guidance of the rule of faith, than in that possession of human nature which is better than anything in the beasts, and better than any other part of the human soul, namely the mind itself. To it has been granted a certain vision of things invisible; it is the authority, raised upon the seat of honour in its inner chamber, for whose judgment the bodily senses deliver all their messages; above it there is none to whose ruling it is subject, save God.

In all this long discourse, I dare not claim to have said anything worthy of the unspeakable greatness of the supreme Trinity. I confess rather that 'from myself his knowledge has become wonderful: its strength is shown and I cannot attain unto it'. And thou, soul of mine, where in all this dost thou find thyself, where liest thou, where standest thou, waiting for him who has shown mercy upon all thine iniquities to heal all thy sicknesses? Doubtless thou seest thyself in that inn, whither the Samaritan brought him that was found half dead from the many wounds laid on him by the robbers. Yet thou hast seen many truths, not with the eyes that see the hues of bodily things, but with those for which the Psalmist made his prayer: 'Let mine eyes look upon equity.' Thou hast seen many truths indeed, and not confused them with that Light that enabled thee to see them. Lift thine eyes to the Light itself and fix them upon it, if thou canst. Then only shalt thou see the difference of the begetting of God's Word from the procession of God's Gift: wherefore the only-begotten Son has said that the Holy Spirit proceeds from the Father, and is not begotten of him so as to be his brother. Being a certain consubstantial communion between Father and Son, the Spirit is called the Spirit of both, never the son of both. But to perceive this plainly and clearly, thou art not able to keep thine eye fixed firmly: I know thou art not able. I speak truth to myself, I know what exceeds my power. Yet the light itself displays to thee those three elements in thyself, wherein thou mayest recognize the image of the supreme Trinity, whom thou hast not yet the strength to contemplate with unwavering eyes. The light itself shows thee that a true word is in thee, when it is begotten of thy knowledge, that is, when we say what we know; though it be with no people's tongue that we utter or think a sound with meaning, but our thought receives a form from the object of our knowledge. In the view of the thinker arises an image nearly alike to that knowledge which memory contained, while the will or love unites the two to one another as parent and offspring. That will proceeds from knowledge, for no one wills a thing of whose being or nature he is altogether ignorant; yet it is not an image of knowledge. And thus there is a suggestion in this mental reality of the difference between begetting and proceeding, inasmuch as to view in thought is not the same as to pursue or to enjoy with the will. So much is to be perceived and discerned by him who is able. And thou too hast been able to perceive it, although thou couldst not and canst not set forth in adequate expression that truth which through the mists of material similitudes, that never cease to invade men's thinking, thou didst hardly see. Yet the light which is not thyself shows thee also that the immaterial likeness of material things are wholly other than the reality which our understanding contemplates when they are rejected. This and the like certainties are manifested by that light to thine inward eye. Is there any reason why thou canst not behold the light itself with a gaze unwavering, but thine own infirmity? And what has made thee infirm but thine own iniquity? Therefore there is none that can heal all thy sicknesses, but he that has mercy upon all thine iniquities. So were it better to bring this Book at last to an end, not with argument but with prayer.

O Lord our God, we believe in thee, Father, Son, and Holy Spirit. If thou wert not Trinity, the Truth would not have said: 'Go ye, baptize all nations in the name of the Father and of the Son and of the Holy Spirit.' Nor wouldst thou, Lord God, have commanded us to be baptized in the name of one who was not Lord and God. Yet, Trinity as thou art, wert thou not one Lord God, the divine word would not have said: 'Hear, O Israel, the Lord thy God is one God.' Moreover, if thou wert thyself God the Father, and thyself Jesus Christ, the Son, thy Word, and the Holy Spirit, his Gift and thine, we should not read in the book of truth that 'God sent his Son'; nor wouldst thou, the only-begotten one, have said of the Holy Spirit: 'whom the Father shall send in my name', and 'whom I will send to you from the Father'.

Guiding the effort of my mind by this rule of faith, I have sought thee with all my power, with all the power thou hast created in me: I have desired greatly to see with my understanding that which I have believed; I have made much discourse, and much toil therein. O Lord my God, my one hope, hear me, that weariness may not lessen my will to seek thee, that I may seek thy face evermore with eager heart. Do thou give strength to seek thee, as thou hast made me to find thee, and given hope of finding thee ever more and more. My strength and my weakness are in thy hands: preserve the one, and remedy the other. In thy hands are my knowledge and my ignorance: where thou hast opened to me, receive my entering in; where thou hast shut, open to my knocking. Let me remember thee, understand thee, love thee: increase in me all these, until thou restore me to thy perfect pattern.

I know that it is written: 'In much speaking thou shalt not escape sin.' Would that all my speaking were the preaching of thy word and the praise of thee! Then should I not only escape sin, how much soever I spoke, but gain desert of goodness. For it could not have been sin that a man blessed of thee enjoined upon his own son in the faith, to whom he wrote: 'Preach the word, be instant in season, out of season.' In him who neither in season nor out of season kept back thy word, none can say there was not much speaking. And yet it was not much, when so much was needful. Deliver me, O God, from the plague of much speaking within mine own soul, a soul miserable in thy sight and fleeing unto thy mercy. For my thoughts are not always silent, though I keep silence from words. From this much speaking I would not ask for deliverance, if my thought were only such as should please thee. But my thoughts are many, thoughts such as thou knowest, vain as thou knowest the thoughts of men to be. Grant me not to give way to them, but to reject them even when they delight me, and not to dwell upon them like a man falling asleep. Let them not have such power with me that aught of my working proceed from them; but let my mind at least and my conscience be kept safe from them by thy safe-guarding. A wise man, in that book of his we name Ecclesiasticus, spoke thus concerning thee: 'We speak many things, and yet attain not: and the whole consummation of our discourses is himself.' When therefore we shall have attained to thee, all those many things which we speak, and attain not, shall cease: one shalt thou abide, all things in all; one shall we name thee without end, praising thee with one single voice, we ourselves also made one in thee. O Lord, one God, God the Trinity, whatsoever I have said in these Books that comes of thy prompting, may thy people acknowledge it: for what I have said that comes only of myself, I ask of thee and of thy people pardon.

VI

ANSELM

St Anselm of Canterbury (1033–1109) was born in Piedmont. His father intended a career in politics for him, but Anselm chose the monastic life. His natural inclination was to scholarship and devotion. However, the circumstances of his later life forced him to become a politician as well as a scholar. He entered the Benedictine monastery of Bec in 1056. Under his influence it became a great centre of learning. He visited England several times in connection with the administration of properties gifted to the Benedictines by William the Conqueror. On one such visit, William II appointed him Archbishop of Canterbury. Anselm accepted reluctantly and from then on became involved in a long struggle to restore the church lands and revenues usurped by the crown and the nobility, to affirm the rights and independence of the church against the claims of the state, and to reform the church from within. His successful policies not only set the pattern for the relations between church and state in England during the following centuries, but also influenced the outcome of similar controversies throughout Europe.

His scholastic and theological achievements were of even more lasting importance than his political and administrative activities. He provided the first clear statement of the ontological argument for the existence of God. This argument, which purports to deduce the existence of God from our bare intuition of perfection, though it has been rejected as invalid by many eminent philosophers such as St Thomas Aquinas and Immanuel Kant, nonetheless retains a tantalizing fascination for philosophers to this day. The Argument is stated in his *Proslogion* (1078). The *Monologion*, written a year earlier, is an examination of the attributes of God, who is presented as the necessary norm of all value judgments. The *De Veritate* (1080) expounds his theory of knowledge. His *Cur Deus Homo*, of which a small part is reproduced below, is the classic statement of one of the main interprepations of the Atonement. It is from this work that the passages below have been selected in the translation of Edward S. Prout (Christian Classics Series, London Religious Tract Society, n.d.).

For further reading see:

E. Fairweather, ed. *A Scholastic Miscellany, Anselm to Ockham* (1956);

N. S. Dean, *St Anselm* (1935); J. McIntyre, *St Anselm and his Critics a Re-interpretation of Cur Deus Homo* (1954).

WHY DID GOD BECOME MAN?
(CUR DEUS HOMO?)

Chapter XX. *That satisfaction must be according to the measure of sin; and that man cannot make this of himself.*

Anselm. I suppose you will not doubt this, too, that satisfaction must be made according to the measure of sin.

Boso. Otherwise sin would remain to a certain extent not subject to law, which cannot be; for God leaves nothing beyond control in his kingdom. But it has been already settled that the slightest inconsistency in God is impossible.

Anselm. Tell me, then, what will you pay to God for your sin?

Boso. Repentance, a contrite heart, humility, fastings, and many kinds of bodily labours, mercy in giving and forgiving, and obedience.

Anselm. In all these things what do you give to God?

Boso. Do not I honour God when, because of the fear and love of him, in the contrition of my heart I reject the joy of this world; by fastings and labours I trample on the delights and repose of this life; by giving, and forgiving what is due to me, I freely spend my substance; by obedience I subject myself to him?

Anselm. When you render anything which you owe to God, even if you have not sinned, you ought not to reckon this as a debt which you owe on account of sin. But all these things which you mention you do owe to God. For there ought to be in this mortal life such great love as this; and also (for which prayer is appropriate) a longing to attain to the end for which you were created; and a grief that you have not yet reached it; and a fear lest you should not attain to it; so that you ought to feel no real pleasure except in regard to those things which are either a help to you or give you the hope of attaining. For you do not deserve to have what you do not love and long for in proportion to its real worth, and respecting which you do not grieve that you have not yet obtained it, and are still in such uncertainty as to whether you will gain it or not. And for this object it is your place to flee repose and worldly pleasures, which draw off the mind from the true repose and pleasure, except so far as you learn that they serve to promote your purpose of attaining that end. As to what you give, you ought to consider it as part of what you owe, since you know that what you give you obtain not from yourself, but from him whose servants both you and he to whom you give are. Nature itself also teaches you that you should do to your fellow-servant, man to man, as you wish to be done to by him, and that he who is not willing to give what he has, ought not to receive what he has not. As to forgiveness, I speak quite briefly, because vengeance does not at all belong to you, as we said above, since neither art thou thine own, nor is he who did thee the wrong thine own or his own; but you are servants of one Lord, made by him out of nothing. And if you take vengeance on your fellow-servant, you proudly claim over him a power of judgment which belongs to the Lord, the Judge of all. And when you render obedience, what do you give to God that you do not owe to him, to whose command you owe all that you are and have and can become?

Boso. I dare not now say that in all these things I give to God anything I do not owe.

Anselm. What, therefore, will you pay to God for your sin?

Boso. If I owe to him myself and all I can give, even when I do not sin, lest I should sin, I have nothing to render to him in compensation for sin.

Anselm. What, then, will become of you? In what way can you be saved?

Boso. If I think over your reasonings I do not see how. But if I have recourse to my belief in the Christian faith, 'which worketh by love', I hope it is possible for me to be saved, because we read that if the unrighteous man is turned from his unrighteousness and doeth righteousness, all his unrighteousnesses shall be forgotten.

Anselm. This is only said to those who either looked for Christ before he came, or believed in him after he came. But we have been regarding Christ and the Christian faith as though they did not exist. For we have purposed to inquire by reason alone whether his advent was necessary for the salvation of men.

Boso. So we did.

Anselm. Let us proceed, therefore, by pure reason.

Boso. Although you lead me into some difficulties, still I very much wish you to advance as you began.

Chapter XXI. *What a heavy weight sin is.*

Anselm. Let us grant that you do not already owe all those things which you just now declared you are able to pay for your sin; and let us see if they can suffice as satisfactions for a single sin, however small, as, for example, a single look in opposition to the will of God.

Boso. Except that I hear you bring this into question, I should suppose that I blotted out this sin by one single pang of sorrow for it.

Anselm. Have you not yet considered what a heavy weight sin is?

Boso. Pray show it to me now.

Anselm. If you were to see yourself in the presence of God, and someone should say to you, 'Look thither', and God, on the other hand, were to say, 'I wish you on no account to look', ask now in your heart, now what is there in all things that exist for the sake of which you ought to take that look contrary to the will of God?

Boso. I know of no reason why I ought to take that look, unless I were perchance placed under the necessity of committing either this or some greater sin.

Anselm. Put that necessity out of the case, and consider in regard to that sin alone, whether you might do it even for your own redemption.

Boso. I see clearly that I cannot.

Anselm. Not to detain you too long: what if it were necessary either that the whole world, and all that is not God, perish and be reduced to nothing, or that you should do so slight an act against the will of God?

Boso. When I think of the act itself I see that it is a very trifling one. But when I look at what it is in opposition to the will of God, I perceive that it is exceedingly grave, and not to be compared with any loss that might be sustained. But we are wont sometimes to do a thing against the will of someone, yet without blame, that his property may be preserved; and we do against his will what afterwards he is pleased with.

Anselm. This is done for a man who sometimes does not understand what is for his advantage, or who cannot restore what he has lost. But God is in need of no one, and could restore all things, were they to perish, just as He made them.

Boso. I must confess that in order to preserve the whole creation, I ought not to do anything against the will of God.

Anselm. What if there were more worlds full of creatures as this is?

Boso. If they were infinitely multiplied, and were placed before me in like manner, I should give the same answer.

Anselm. You can do nothing better. But suppose it happened that you did take that look against the will of God, what could pay for that sin?

Boso. I have nothing more than I have said above.

Anselm. Thus seriously do we sin whenever we knowingly do anything, however slight, against the will of God. For we are always in his sight, and he is always bidding us not to sin.

Boso. As I understand, we live in an exceedingly dangerous condition.

Anselm. It is clear that God requires satisfaction according to the amount of sin.

Boso. I cannot deny it.

Anselm. You do not, therefore, make satisfaction unless you return something greater than that for the sake of which you were under obligation not to have committed the sin.

Boso. I see that reason requires it, and yet, that it is altogether impossible.

Anselm. Neither can God take to a state of blessedness anyone bound to any extent by the debt of sin, because he ought not.

Boso. This decision is exceedingly serious.

Chapter XXV. *That of necessity man may be saved by Christ.*

Anselm. Is it not clearly enough proved that man can be saved by Christ, since even unbelievers do not deny that man may in some way be made blessed; and yet it has been sufficiently proved, that if we assume that Christ does not exist, no way of salvation for man can be discovered by any means. For man can be saved either by Christ, or in some other way, or in no way at all. Wherefore, if it is false that he cannot be saved at all, or in some other way, it is necessary that he be saved by Christ.

Boso. If anyone, seeing the reason why man cannot be saved in any other way, and yet not understanding how he may be saved by Christ, should assert that he can be saved neither by Christ nor in any way at all, what shall we answer him?

Anselm. What should be our answer to a man who asserts that a thing which is seen to be necessary is impossible, because he does not know how it can be?

Boso. That he is a fool.

Anselm. So that what he says may be set at nought.

Boso. That is true. But we ought to prove to him in what way the thing is true which he thinks impossible.

Anselm. Do you not understand from what we have said above, that it is necessary some men should attain to blessedness? For if it is inconsistent for God to bring man with any stain on him to that state for which he created him without any stain, lest he should seem either to repent of his good undertaking, or not to be able to fulfil his plan; much more impossible is it, on account of the same inconsistency, that no man at all should be promoted to that state for which he was created. Therefore, either some satisfaction for sin must be found, apart from the Christian faith, such as we have shown above ought to be made—a thing which no reasoning can point out—or without hesitation it ought to be believed to exist in the Christian faith. For what we conclude to be undoubtedly true by necessary reasoning, ought not to be brought into any uncertainty, although the reason why it is so is not clearly seen.

Boso. What you say is quite true.

Anselm. What, then, do you ask further?

Boso. I did not come to you that you might remove any hesitation in my own faith, but that you might show me the reason for my certainty. Wherefore, as you have led me by reasoning to this point, that I see man the sinner owes to God, on account of sin, what he cannot repay, and unless he repays it he cannot be saved, so now I wish you to lead me on to the following point, viz., that I may understand, by necessary reasoning, how all those things must be true which the Catholic faith bids us believe respecting Christ, if we wish to be saved; also, the efficacy they have in the salvation of man; and in what way God saves man by his mercy, since he does not remit his sin unless he pays what he owes on account of it. . . .

Book II

Chapter V. . . .

Anselm. . . . Let us, however, say that, on account of God's unchangeableness, it is necessary that his goodness bring to perfection in man what he has begun, although all the good that he does is of grace.

Boso. I grant it.

Chapter VI. *That no one but one who is God-man can make the satisfaction by which man is saved.*

Anselm. But this [good] cannot be accomplished unless there be some one to pay to God in compensation for the sin of man something greater than everything that exists, except God.

Boso. That is certain.

Anselm. It is needful, too, that he who can give to God of his own something of more value than everything which is below God, must himself be greater than all that is not God.

Boso. I cannot deny it.

Anselm. But there is nothing above all that is not God except God himself.

Boso. True.

Anselm. There is no one, therefore, who can make this satisfaction except God himself.

Boso. That follows.

Anselm. But no one *ought* to make it except man; otherwise man does not make satisfaction.

Boso. Nothing seems juster than this.

Anselm. If, therefore, as is certain, it is needful that that heavenly state be perfected from among men, and this cannot be unless the above-mentioned satisfaction be made, which no one *can* make except God, and no one *ought* to make except man, it is necessary that one who is God-man should make it.

Boso. Blessed be God! Already we have discovered one great truth on the subject of our enquiry. Go on, therefore, as you have begun; for I hope that God will help us.

Chapter XIV. *How his death outweighs the number and greatness of all sins.*

Boso. Now, I ask you to teach me how his death outweighs the number and greatness of all sins, since you show that one sin (which we think very trifling) is so infinite, that if an infinite number of worlds were placed before us, as full of creatures as this is, which could not be saved from annihilation unless some one took a single look contrary to the will of God, yet it ought not to be taken.

Anselm. If that Man we are speaking of were before you, and you were told that unless you killed him this whole world and all that is not God would perish, would you do this for the sake of preserving every other creature?

Boso. I would not do it even if an infinite number of worlds were placed before me.

Anselm. What if it were said to thee again, Either kill him or all the sins of the world will come upon thee?

Boso. I would answer that I would prefer to endure all the sins past and future, not only of this world, but also all that, in addition to these, can be conceived, rather than do that single act. And I think I ought to give the same answer not only respecting his death, but in regard to any slight injury that might be done to him.

Anselm. You think rightly. But tell me why your heart judges that it would dread one sin that would injure that Man more than all other sins that can be conceived, since all sins that are committed are against Him.

Boso. Because a sin which is committed against his person surpasses beyond comparison all those which can be conceived of apart from his person.

Anselm. What will you say on this point? That one often willingly suffers some injuries in his own person lest he should suffer more serious injuries in his property?

Boso. That God, to whose power all things are subject, does not need to endure such a loss, as you answered before to one of my questions.

Anselm. You answer well. We see, therefore, that no magnitude or multitude of sins apart from the person of God can be compared to an injury done to the bodily life of this Man.

Boso. That is very clear.

Anselm. How great a good does this life seem to be, since its destruction is so evil!

Boso. If its existence is as great a good as its destruction is an evil, this good is, beyond comparison, far greater than is the evil of those sins, which are yet surpassed beyond estimation [in wickedness] by the destruction of that life.

Anselm. You say the truth. Consider, also, that sins are as hateful as they are evil, and that life is as precious as it is good. Whence it follows that that life is more precious than sins are hateful.

Boso. I cannot fail to see this.

Anselm. Do you think that a good so great, so precious, can suffice to pay what is due for the sins of the whole world?

Boso. Verily it is worth infinitely more.

Anselm. You see, then, how this life may overcome all sins if it is given for them.

Boso. Plainly.

Anselm. If, then, to give life is the same as to accept death, just as the giving of this life outweighs all the sins of men, so too, does the accepting of death.

VII

PETER ABELARD

Peter Abelard [Abailard, Abaelard] (1079–1142) was the son of the Lord of Le Pallet in Brittany. He studied philosophy in Parish and Brittany, but tended always to outshine his masters in brilliance and learning. He taught Logic and Theology at Notre Dame in Paris. It was there that he became involved in his tragic love-affair with his pupil Héloise. His theological work was continuously under suspicion of heresy. He was a purist, a reformer and above all a man of surprising modernity, anticipating many of the insights of later humanism. He was finally forced to submit to the condemnation of his theological doctrines by the council of Sens just before his death.

Abelard's contributions to logic and ethics and to the methodology of dialectic were perhaps more important than his theological achievements. He was one of the founders of the scholastic method of disputation as it broke free of the traditional Augustinianism of previous centuries. There can be no question that his theology—particularly his treatment of the Trinity and his Christology—exhibited tendencies which the Catholic Church rightly regarded with suspicion. Yet he represents a valid and important element within the dialectic of Catholic theological development and did much to prepare the way for the great synthesis which found expression in the work of St Thomas Aquinas.

Among his more important works are *Historia Calamitatum*, edited and translated by J. T. Muckle under the title *The Story of Abelard's Adversities* (Pontifical Institute of Mediaeval Studies, Toronto, 1954); *Scito teipsum*, translated by J. R. McCallum as *Abailard's Ethics* (Blackwell, Oxford, 1935). The best Latin edition of his work is *Petri Abaelardi Opera*, edited by Victor Cousin, 2 vols., Paris 1849–1859. The short passage below is translated from his *Commentary on the Epistle to the Romans* in that edition (Vol. 2, pp. 203–7). This passage is selected because it illustrates briefly his distinctive views on the atonement—views which will be seen to contrast sharply with those of Anselm.

A good general introduction is that of J. G. Sikes, *Peter Abailard* (University Press, Cambridge, 1932).

COMMENTARY ON THE EPISTLE TO THE ROMANS ON ROMANS 3. 21–26

[Here, in the *Authorized King James Version*, is the passage on which Abelard is commenting:

21. But now the righteousness of God without the law is manifested, being witnessed by the law and the prophets; 22. Even the righteousness of God which is by faith of Jesus Christ unto all and upon all them that believe: for there is no difference; 23. For all have sinned, and come short of the glory of God; 24. Being justified freely by his grace through the redemption that is in Christ Jesus: 25. Whom God hath set forth to be a propitiation through faith in his blood, to declare his righteousness for the remission of sins that are past, through the forbearance of God; 26. To declare, I say, at this time his righteousness: that he might be just, and the justifier of him which believeth in Jesus.

Abelard's text is, of course, with some slight deviation, the *Vulgate*.]

3. 21. *But now* . . . I have said that no one is justified before God by the special works of the written law—i.e. by those formal regulations which are unknown in natural law.—*But now*!—that is, in the time of the gift of God's righteousness—righteousness which God has approved and through which we are justified before him—love is shown forth through the teaching of the gospel. Righteousness is manifested *apart from the law* —i.e. apart from its unspiritual, specific legislation. Nonetheless, *the law and the prophets bear witness* to this righteousness and enjoin it. He shows us on what this righteousness depends when he immediately adds: 3. 22 *It is the righteousness of God*. He refers to the faith of Christ which we hold concerning him; either believing him or believing in him. When he adds *those that believe*, he makes no specific reference to any one of them in order that it may apply equally to all.

Love is generated in us by the faith which we hold concerning Christ, because, through this faith—that God in Christ united our nature to himself, and, by suffering in that nature, showed forth the supreme love of which he himself says, *greater love hath no man than this*[1]—we are united with him in the closest possible way by indissoluble bonds of affection. Somewhat further on it is written: *Who, then, shall separate us from the love of God*? *Shall tribulation* . . .?[2] And again, *For I am persuaded that neither death* . . .[3] There is, I say, a righteousness invested upon all the faithful, in the higher part of their being, in the soul, where alone love can exist—not in a show of outward works.

For there is no [*difference*] . . . I was right to speak of all, both Jews and

[1] John 15. 13. [2] *Romans* 8. 35. [3] Ibid. 8. 38.

Gentiles alike, for there is no distinction between them with regard to this righteousness of God through the faith of Christ—though there was once such a distinction with regard to the works of the law. For, since all have sinned, so all alike are justified through this supreme grace which God has shown towards us. This is what is meant by, [3. 23] *All have sinned and are in need of the grace of God.*[1] This means that they have a duty, a kind of obligation, to glorify the Lord.

[3. 24] They are justified without any previous merit of their own. They are justified by his grace, the grace of God who first loved us. He tells us what it really is, this grace which is God's own free spiritual gift, when he goes on to say: *Through our redemption accomplished by Christ,* [3. 25] *whom God the Father put forward as a propitiation for us.* He is the reconciler *in his blood*, that is, by his death. And since this propitiation is put forward and established by God, not on behalf of all, but only for those who believe, he adds, *by faith*, for this reconciliation relates only to those who believed it and hoped for it.

This was to show God's righteousness. That is, his love, which justifies us before him—To show his love to us, or to teach us how much we should love him who *did not spare his own Son*[2] for our sakes.

For the remission . . . That is, that we might obtain remission of sins through this righteousness—through this love. As the Truth himself says, of that blessed woman who was a sinner: *Many sins are forgiven her because she has loved much.*[3] I maintain emphatically that remission is granted even for previous sins *in the forbearance of God*—because of the patience of God, who does not immediately punish the guilty and destroy the sinners, but waits for a long time so that they may return to him again through penitence, leave off sinning, and so obtain forgiveness.

[3. 26] *In order to show* . . . First he said simply that it was in order to show forth his righteousness. Now he adds, *in this time* of grace—meaning the time of love rather than fear. So, when he says, *his righteousness in this present time* of grace, he clearly teaches how he primarily understands this righteousness to be love. It is a love which perfectly befits the condition of the men of our time—the time of grace.

It is possible that when he says, *in the forbearance of God*, this should be taken in conjunction with the following clause, *that he might show his righteousness in this present time*. The point, then, would be that the Lord forbore or delayed in this respect, in order that he might disclose his righteousness—the righteousness of which we have been speaking—the righteousness which is love in this present time—in order to be righteous

[1] The Vulgate here reads 'glory' or 'praise' of God, which is perhaps what Abelard himself intended. It would fit better with the following sentence.

[2] *Romans* 8. 32. [3] *Luke* 7. 47.

himself, in his will, and the cause of righteousness, in his actions; that is to say, in order that he might both will the fulfilment through Christ of that which he had promised in regard to redemption or justification and at the same time implement it in act.

[He justifies] *him who has faith in Jesus Christ.*—i.e. him who believes in him as Jesus (which means salvation) because he is the Christ (which means to be both God and man).

A Question

A question of the utmost importance arises at this point. What is this redemption which we have through the death of Christ? In what way does the Apostle say that we are justified in his blood? We seem rather to be worthy of still greater punishment because, like the wicked servants, we have been the active cause of the death of our innocent Lord.

So we must first ask why it was necessary for God to take human nature upon himself so that he might redeem us by dying in the flesh. From whom did he redeem us? Did this being hold us captive justly or tyrannously? By what manner of justice did he free us from this being who laid down those conditions which he willingly accepted in order to release us.

It is said that he has redeemed us from the dominion of the Devil. The Devil had the right of universal dominion over mankind, through the sin of the first man who thereby willingly placed himself in subjection to him. So the Devil had this right of dominion in perpetuity unless a liberator came. But since he liberated only the elect, when did the Devil ever possess them either in this present age or in the age to come or at any other time? Has the Devil been tormenting that poor man resting in the bosom of Abraham, just as he does the rich man who was damned—through perhaps he has tortured him a bit less? Has he been holding Abraham himself and all the rest of the elect in his power? When did that evil tormentor have power over him of whom it is said that he was borne by angels to Abraham's bosom? Abraham himself gives testimony concerning him, when he says: *But now he is comforted and thou art tormented.*[1]

He says, moreover, that a great chasm is fixed between the elect and the reprobate, so that neither can ever cross over to the other. Still less can the Devil, who is more evil than all, hold dominion in that place where no evil person has either place or access.

What right of possession over man could the Devil possibly have if he had not received him with the Lord's permission, or even from the Lord's own hands, for torment? If a slave wanted to leave his master and

[1] *Luke* 16. 25.

place himself under the power of some other person, would he be allowed to do this in such a way that his master could not justly, if he so wished, send for him and bring him back? Who could doubt, then, that if it were someone else's slave whose persuasions seduced his loyalty and who caused him to depart from obedience to his real master, the seducer will be much more guilty than the seduced in the master's eyes? It would be unjust indeed if he who seduces another should thereby gain some right or power over him. Surely, rather, by the mere act of seduction, he should forfeit any right which he might formerly have had over him. It is written: 'He who abuses his power deserves to lose his privilege.'[1] If one of these slaves is to be set above the other and given power over him, it would be most unfitting that the more wicked, who had no right to it whatsoever, should have the preferment. It makes better sense that he who is seduced should have the right to claim damages against the seducer. Besides, the Devil has been unable to bestow the immortality which he promised to man as the fruit of his transgression. As if this could give him any just rights!

So, on these grounds, it seems to be established, that the Devil, by the mere fact of seduction, acquires no rights over man, whom he seduces; except perhaps, as we have said, in so far as the Lord permits it. He hands man over to him as jailer or tormentor for punishment. Man had sinned against no one but his own Lord, whose obedience he had deserted. So, if the Lord should choose to remit his sin, as in the case of the Virgin Mary, and as he did in many cases before his passion—as, for instance, is reported of Mary Magdalene and in the saying of the Lord to the paralytic: *Take heart, my son, your sins are forgiven.*[2] Now, if our Lord chose thus to ignore the sins of men apart from his passion, and to say to his tormentor, 'Punish him no more!', what right would the tormentor retain to torment him further? As we have shown, he had received no right to inflict torment without express permission from the Lord. So if the Lord withdrew this permission, the tormentor would retain no right whatever. If he were to complain or grumble against the Lord, the Lord could well reply, *Is thine eye evil because I am good*?[3] The Lord did the Devil no injustice when, for the sake of the sinful masses, he took upon himself pure flesh and sinless humanity.

It was not his merit as a man that secured for him a sinless conception and birth and sinlessness throughout his life, but the grace of the Lord sustaining him. Surely, then, if he wished to remit the sins of the rest of humanity by that same grace, it was in his power to free them from punishment. Once the sins for which they were being punished were

[1] The source of this commendable saying is unknown.

[2] *Matthew* 9. 2. [3] Ibid. 20. 15.

remitted, there seems no reason why they should be punished for them any further. He who showed such love towards man that he united him in personal being to himself could surely do him the lesser favour of forgiving his sins.

If, then, by merely showing his divine compassion he was able to release man from the Devil, what necessity, what reason, what need was there for the Son of God to become incarnate, to suffer so many and great privations, insults, scourgings, spittings and finally a harsh and shameful death upon the cross, bearing the cross of punishment with the malefactors, for our redemption? In what way does the Apostle say that we are justified or reconciled to God through the death of his Son? Ought not his wrath rather to have been directed against man in that man sinned far more gravely in crucifying his Son than when he transgressed his original commandment in paradise by tasting a single apple? The more man multiplies transgression, the more justifiable God's wrath would have been. If the sin of Adam was of such magnitude that only the death of Christ could expiate it, what expiation will there be for the murder of the Christ and all the crimes committed against him and his? How could the death of his innocent Son be so pleasing to God that, through it, he is reconciled to us—to us who, in our sin, have committed those very acts on account of which our innocent Lord was put to death?

If this ultimate sin had not been perpetrated, could he not have overlooked the less grievous sin? Could he not have done this good thing for us without the multiplication of evil? In what respect are we made any more righteous than we were before by the death of the Son of God, so that we ought now to be released from punishment? To whom is this blood-price paid for our redemption if not to him in whose power we were? But we have declared that we were in God's power and it was he who had handed us over to his tormentor. Now it is not the tormentors, but the masters of their captives who settle for or receive [a ransom]. How did he release these captives for ransom if he himself fixes or exacts the price of their release? It certainly does seem cruel and wicked that anyone should demand innocent blood as the price of anything, or that the execution of an innocent person should give him any pleasure—the more so that God should consider the death of his own Son so acceptable as to be reconciled to the whole world by it.

These and similar considerations seem to me to present no small problem in relation to our redemption or reconciliation through the death of Christ.

The Solution

It seems to me that we are justified through the blood of Christ and reconciled to God in that, through the disclosure to us of such unique grace—that his Son took our nature upon him, and has persisted in teaching us by word and example even unto death—he has bound us more closely to himself by love. When we are thus enkindled by such a gift of divine grace, there is nothing which true love is afraid to undergo for him. Moreover, we have no doubt that the ancient fathers, who looked forward in faith to this gift, were enkindled with the supreme love of God, just as the men of this time of grace. It is written, *And they that went before and they that followed cried out 'Hosanna to the Son of David'*.[1] And after the passion of Christ, everyone becomes still more righteous—i.e. everyone loves the Lord more completely—than ever before; for a gift actually received moves us to greater love than one merely hoped for. So our redemption is that supreme love inspired in us by the passion of Christ. It not only frees us from slavery to sin, but obtains for us the true freedom of the sons of God. So we are obedient in every respect not from fear, but for love of him, who has shown such love towards us that no greater can be found. As he says himself: *Greater love hath no man than this, that he lay down his life for his friends.*[2] Of this same love, Our Lord says elsewhere: *I came to cast fire upon the earth and how I wish that it were already kindled.*[3] So he testifies that he came to spread the true liberty of love among men. Later on, the Apostle fully acknowledges this, when he says, *for the love of God has been poured into our hearts through the Holy Spirit who has been given to us; for did not Christ . . .*[4] or again: *God shows his love for us in that while yet . . .*[5] We shall expound these verses more fully in their proper place. Meantime, let this statement—compressed though it must be, in view of the brevity of this commentary—suffice as an account of how the manner of our redemption appears to me.

[1] *Mark* 11. 9. [2] *John* 15. 13. [3] *Luke* 12. 49.
[4] *Romans* 5. 5–6. [5] Ibid. 5. 8.

VIII

AQUINAS

St Thomas Aquinas (1225–1274) was born in Italy near Monte Cassino, where he went to school. He was a big, powerfully-built man. He distinguished himself as a young scholar in the University of Naples and entered the Dominican order. The Dominicans sent him to Cologne where he continued his studies under Albertus Magnus. He subsequently taught for many years in the University of Paris and was finally summoned to Rome as a theological adviser to the Pope. He was canonized by Pope John XXII in 1323.

It was not until the sixteenth century that St Thomas began to be the dominant figure which he has since remained in Roman Catholic theology. His teaching has twice received official approval in papal encyclicals in 1879 and 1923. But in his own lifetime and in the immediately succeeding centuries, his doctrines were hotly contested.

Until the twelfth century or thereabout the philosophical background to Christian theology had been mainly Neo-Platonic. The dominant figures were Augustine, Boethius and Pseudo-Dyonisius. Philosophical enquiry was an exercise conducted almost entirely within the context of the Christian faith. But when the philosophy of Aristotle, firstly through Arabic sources and then in direct translation, began to make its impact felt, the possibility of an independent, secular philosophy became a much more serious consideration. St Thomas wedded this new scientific philosophy to traditional doctrine in a synthesis which has stood the tests of time better than any of his early opponents or even his supporters could have anticipated. The structure of the synthesis is reflected in the co-operative relationship which he established between the natural and the super-natural, reason and revelation, nature and grace.

Of his many works, the two most important are *Summa contra Gentiles* —a Christian apologetic addressed to unbelievers—and *Summa Theologica* —a systematic and magnificently ordered presentation of the whole Christian faith. The power of the *Summa Theologica* consists partly in its sheer completeness and thoroughness. It therefore suffers even more than most works from being represented by a necessarily brief selection. The passages below are from the *Summa Theologica*, literally translated by

Fathers of the English Dominican Province, Thomas Baker, London, 1915.

Several selections from the work of St Thomas Aquinas in English translation are available: A. M. Fairweather, tr. and ed., *Nature and Grace* (Library of Christian Classics, S.C.M. 1954); A. C. Pegis, *Basic Writings of St Thomas*, New York, 1954; T. Gilby, St Thomas Aquinas; *Philosophical Texts* (1951), *Theological Texts* (1955).

EXTRACTS FROM THE *SUMMA THEOLOGICA*

Part I, Question 1

The Nature and Extent of Sacred Doctrine

Article 1: Whether, besides Philosophy, any further doctrine is required?

Objection 1. It seems that, besides philosophical science, we have no need of any further knowledge. Man should not seek to know what is above reason: 'Seek not the things that are too high for thee' (*Ecclesiasticus* 3. 22). But whatever is not above reason is fully treated of in philosophical science. Therefore any other knowledge besides philosophical science is superfluous.

Objection 2. Further, knowledge can only be concerned with being, for nothing can be known, save what is true; and all that is, is true. But everything that is, is treated of in philosophical science—even God himself; so that there is a part of philosophy called Theology, or the Divine Science, as Aristotle has proved. Therefore, besides philosophical science, there is no need of any further knowledge.

On the contrary, It is said, 'All Scripture inspired of God is profitable to teach, to reprove, to correct, to instruct in justice' (II *Timothy* 3. 16). Scripture, inspired of God, is no part of philosophical science, which has been built up by human reason. Therefore it is useful that besides philosophical science there should be other knowledge—i.e. inspired of God.

I answer that, It was necessary for man's salvation that there should be a knowledge revealed by God, besides philosophical science built up by human reason. Firstly, indeed, because man is ordained to God, as to an end that surpasses the grasp of his reason; 'The eye hath not seen, besides Thee, O God, what things Thou hast prepared for them that wait for Thee' (*Isaiah* 44. 4). But the end must first be known by men who are to direct their thoughts and actions to the end. Hence it was necessary for the salvation of man that certain truths which exceed human reason should be made known to him by Divine Revelation. Even as regards those truths about God which human reason could have discovered, it was necessary that man should be taught by a Divine Revelation; because the Truth about God such as reason could discover, would only be known by a few, and that after a long time, and with the admixture of many errors. Whereas man's whole salvation, which is in God, depends upon the knowledge of this Truth. Therefore, in order that the salvation of men might be brought about more fitly and more surely, it was necessary that they should be taught Divine Truths by Divine Revelation. It was therefore necessary that, besides philosophical science built up by reason, there should be a sacred science learnt through Revelation.

Reply Objection 1. Although those things which are beyond man's knowledge may not be sought for by man through his reason, nevertheless, once they are revealed by God, they must be accepted by faith. Hence the sacred text continues, 'For many things are shown to thee above the understanding of man' (*Ecclesiasticus* 3. 25). And in this the Sacred Science consists.

Reply Objection 2. Sciences are differentiated according to the various means through which knowledge is obtained. The astronomer and the physicist both may prove the same conclusion—that the earth, for instance, is round: the astronomer by means of mathematics (i.e. abstracting from matter), but the physicist by means of matter itself. Hence there is no reason why those things which may be learnt from philosophical science, so far as they can be known by natural reason, may not also be taught us by another science so far as they fall within revelation. Hence theology included in Sacred Doctrine differs in kind from that theology which is part of philosophy.

Article II: Whether Sacred Doctrine is a Science?

Objection 1. It seems that Sacred Doctrine is not Science. For every science proceeds from self-evident principles. But Sacred Doctrine proceeds from articles of Faith which are not self-evident, since their truth is not admitted by all. 'For all men have not faith' (II *Thessalonians* 3. 2). Therefore Sacred Doctrine is not a Science.

Objection 2. Further, no science deals with individual facts. But this Sacred Science treats of individual facts, such as the deeds of Abraham, Isaac and Jacob. Therefore Sacred Doctrine is not a science.

On the contrary, Augustine says, 'to this science alone belongs that whereby saving faith is begotten, nourished, protected, and strengthened' But this can be said of no science except Sacred Doctrine. Therefore Sacred Doctrine is a science.

I answer that, Sacred Doctrine is a science. We must bear in mind that there are two kinds of sciences. There are some which proceed from a principle known by the light of the natural intelligence, such as arithmetic and geometry. There are some which proceed from principles known by the light of higher science: thus the science of perspective proceeds from principles established by geometry, and music from principles established by arithmetic. So it is that Sacred Doctrine is a science, because it proceeds from principles established by the light of a higher science, namely, the science of God and the blessed. Hence, just as the musician accepts on authority the principles taught him by the mathematician; so sacred science is established on principles revealed by God.

Reply Objection 1. The principles of any science are either in themselves self-evident, or reducible to the conclusions of a higher science; and such, as we have said, are the principles of Sacred Doctrine.

Reply Objection 2. Individual facts are treated of in Sacred Doctrine, not because it is concerned with them principally; but they are rather introduced both as examples to be followed in our lives (as in moral sciences), and in order to establish the authority of those men through whom the Divine Revelation, on which this sacred Scripture or Doctrine is based, has come down to us.

Article V: Whether Sacred Doctrine is Nobler than other Sciences?

Objection 1. It seems that Sacred Doctrine is not nobler than other sciences; for the nobility of a science depends on the certitude it establishes. But other sciences, the principles of which cannot be doubted, seem to be more certain than Sacred Doctrine; for its principles—namely, articles of faith—can be doubted. Therefore other sciences seem to be nobler.

Objection 2. Further, it is the sign of a lower science to depend upon a higher; as music depends upon arithmetic. But Sacred Doctrine does in a sense depend upon the philosophical sciences; for Jerome observes, in his Epistle to Magnus, that 'the ancient doctors so enriched their books with the ideas and phrases of the philosophers, that thou knowest not what more to admire in them, their profane erudition or their scriptural learning'. Therefore Sacred Doctrine is inferior to other sciences.

On the contrary, Other sciences are called handmaidens of this one: 'Wisdom sent her handmaidens to call them to her citadel' (*Proverbs* 9. 3).

I answer that, Since this science is partly speculative and partly practical, it transcends all others speculative and practical. One speculative science is said to be nobler than another, either by reason of its greater certitude, or by reason of the higher worth of its subject-matter. In both these respects this science surpasses other speculative sciences; in point of greater certitude, because other sciences derive their certitude from the natural light of human reason, which can err; whereas this derives its certitude from the light of the Divine knowledge, which cannot be misled; in point of the higher worth of its subject-matter, because this science treats chiefly of those things which by their sublimity transcend human reason;

while other sciences consider only those things which are within reason's grasp. Of the practical sciences, that one is nobler which is ordained to the further purpose. Political science is nobler than military science; for the good of the army is ordained to the good of the State. But the purpose of this science, in so far as it is practical, is eternal bliss; to which as to an ultimate end the purposes of every practical science are ordained. Hence it is clear that from every standpoint it is nobler than other sciences.

Reply Objection 1. It may well happen that what is in itself the more certain may seem to us the less certain on account of the weakness of our intelligence, which is dazzled by the clearest objects of nature; as the owl is dazzled by the light of the sun. Hence the fact that some happen to doubt about articles of faith is not due to the uncertain nature of the truths, but to the weakness of human intelligence; yet the slenderest knowledge that may be obtained of the highest things is more desirable than the most certain knowledge obtained of lesser things.

Reply Objection 2. This science can in a sense depend upon the philosophical sciences, not as if it stood in need of them, but only in order to make its teaching clearer. For it does not accept its principles from other sciences; but immediately from God, by Revelation. Therefore it does not depend upon other scienes as upon the higher, but makes use of them as of the lesser, and as handmaidens; just as the master sciences make use of the sciences that supply their materials, as political of military science. That it thus uses them is not due to its own defect or insufficiency, but to the defect of our intelligence, which is more easily led by what is known through natural reason (from which proceed the other sciences), to that which is above reason, such as is taught in this science.

Article VIII: Whether Sacred Science is a Matter of Argument?

Objection 1. It seems this science is not a matter of argument. For Ambrose says 'Put arguments aside where faith is sought'. But in this science faith is especially sought: 'But these things are written that you may believe' (*John* 20. 31). Therefore Sacred Doctrine is not a matter of argument.

Objection 2. Further, if it is a matter of argument, the argument is either from authority or from reason. If it is from authority, it seems unbefitting its dignity, for the proof from authority is the weakest form of proof. But if from reason, this is unbefitting its end, because, according to Gregory, 'faith has no merit in those things of which human reason brings its own experience'. Therefore Sacred Doctrine is not a matter of argument.

On the contrary, The Scripture says that a Bishop should 'embrace that faithful word which is according to doctrine, that he may be able to exhort in sound doctrine and to convince the gainsayers' (*Titus* 1. 9).

I answer that, As other sciences do not argue in proof of their principles, but argue from their principles to demonstrate other truths in these sciences: so this doctrine does not argue in proof of its principles, which are the articles of faith, but from them it goes on to prove something else; as the Apostle from the Resurrection of Christ argues in proof of the general resurrection (I *Corinthians* 15). However, it is to be borne in mind, in regard to the philosophical sciences, that the inferior sciences neither prove their principles nor dispute with those that deny them, but leave this to a higher science; whereas the highest of them can dispute with one who denies its principles, if only the opponent will make some concessions of metaphysical principles; but if he concedes nothing, it can have no dispute with him, though it can answer his objections. Hence sacred science, since it has no science above itself, can dispute with one who denies its principles only if the opponent admits some at least of the truths obtained through divine revelation; as we can argue with heretics from texts in Holy Writ, and against those that deny one article of faith we can argue from another. If our opponent believes nothing of divine revelation, there is no longer any means of proving the articles of faith by reasoning, but only of answering his objections—if he has any—against faith. Since faith rests upon infallible truth, and since the contrary of a truth can never be demonstrated, it is clear that the arguments brought against faith cannot be strict demonstrations; but difficulties that can be answered.

Reply Objection 1. Although arguments from human reason cannot avail to prove what must be received on faith, nevertheless sacred science argues from admitted articles of faith to other truths.

Reply Objection 2. This doctrine is especially based upon arguments from authority, inasmuch as its principles are obtained by revelation: thus we ought to believe on the authority of those to whom the revelation has been given. Nor does this take away from the dignity of this doctrine, for although the argument from authority based on human reason is the weakest, yet the argument from authority based on divine revelation is the most effective. But sacred doctrine makes use even of human reason, not, indeed, to prove faith (for thereby the merit of faith would come to an end), but to make clear other things that are put forward in this doctrine. Since grace does not destroy nature, but perfects it, natural reason should minister to faith as the natural bent of the will ministers to charity. Hence the Apostle says: 'Bringing into captivity every understanding unto the obedience of faith' (II *Corinthians* 10. 5). Hence sacred doctrine makes use also of the authority of philosophers in those questions in which they were able to know the truth by natural reason, as Paul quotes a saying of Aratus: 'As some also of your own poets said, "For we are also his offspring" ' (*Acts* 17. 28). Nevertheless, sacred doctrine makes use of these authorities as extrinsic and probable arguments; but appositely uses the authority of the canonical Scriptures as an incontrovertible proof, and the authority of the Doctors of the church as one that may properly be used, yet merely as probable. For our faith rests upon the revelation made to the apostles and prophets, who wrote the canonical books and not on the revelations (if any such there are) made to other doctors. Hence Augustine says: 'Only those books of Scripture which are called canonical have I learnt to hold in such honour as to believe their authors have not erred in any way in writing them. But others I so read as not to deem anything in them to be true, merely on account of their having thought and written; whatever may have been their holiness and learning.'

Article X: Whether in Holy Scripture the Word has Several Interpretations?

Objection 1. It seems that in Holy Writ the word cannot have several interpretations, historical or literal, allegorical, tropological or moral, and anagogical. For many different interpretations in one text produce confusion and deception and destroy all force of argument. Hence no argument, but only logical fallacies, can be deduced from a multiplicity of unrelated propositions. But Holy Writ ought to be able to state the truth without any fallacy. Therefore in it there cannot be several interpretations of the word.

Objection 2. Further, Augustine says that 'the Old Testament has a fourfold division as to history, etiology, analogy and allegory'. These four seem altogether different from the four divisions mentioned in the first objection. Therefore it does not seem fitting to explain the same word of Holy Writ according to the four different interpretations mentioned above.

Objection 3. Further, besides these interpretations, there is the parabolical, which is not one of these four.

On the contrary, Gregory says: 'Holy Writ by the manner of its speech transcends every science, because in one and the same sentence, while it describes a fact, it reveals a mystery.'

I answer that, The author of Holy Writ is God, in whose power it is to signify his meaning, not by words only (as man also can do), but also by things themselves. So, whereas in every other science things are signified by words, this science has the property, that the things signified by the words have themselves also a signification. Therefore that first signification whereby words signify things belongs to the first interpretation, the historical or literal. That signification whereby things signified by words have themselves also a signification is called the spiritual interpretation, which is based on the literal interpretation, and presupposes it. This spiritual interpretation has a threefold division. As the Apostle says (*Hebrews* 7) the Old Law is a figure of the New Law, and 'the New Law itself (Dionysius says) is figure of future glory'. In the New Law, whatever our Head has done is a type of what we ought to do. Therefore, so far as the things of the Old Law signify things of the New Law, there is the allegorical interpretation; so far as the things done in Christ, or so far as the things which signify Christ, are types of what we ought to do, there is the moral interpretation. So far as they signify what relates to eternal glory, there is the anagogical interpretation. Since the literal sense is that which the author intends, and since the author of Holy Writ is God, who by one act comprehends all things by his intellect, it is not unfitting (as Augustine says) if, even according to the literal sense, one word of Holy Writ should have several interpretations.

Reply Objection 1. The multiplicity of these interpretations does not produce ambiguity or any kind of equivocation, seeing that these interpretations are not multiplied because one word signifies several things; but because the things signified by the words can be themselves types of other things. Thus in Holy Writ no confusion results, for all the interpretations are founded on one—the literal—from which alone can any argument be drawn, and not from those intended in allegory, as Augustine says. Nevertheless, nothing of Holy Scripture perishes on account of this, since nothing necessary to faith is contained under the spiritual interpretation which may not be elsewhere put forward by the Scriptures in its literal interpretation.

Reply Objection 2. These three—history, etiology, analogy—are grouped under one literal interpretation. For it is called history, as Augustine expounds, whenever anything is simply related; it is called etiology when its cause is assigned, as when Our Lord gave the reason why Moses allowed the putting away of wives—namely, on account of the hardness of men's hearts; it is called analogy whenever the truth of one text of Scripture is shown not to contradict the truth of another. Of these four, allegory alone stands for the three spiritual interpretations. Thus Hugh of S. Victor includes the anagogical under the allegorical interpretations, laying down three interpretations only—the historical, the allegorical and the tropological.

Reply Objection 3. The parabolical interpretation is contained in the literal, for by words things are signified properly and figuratively. Nor is the figure itself, but that which is figured, the literal sense. When Scripture speaks of God's arm, the literal sense is not that God has such a member, but only what is signified by this member, namely, operative power. Hence it is plain that nothing false can ever underlie the literal sense of Holy Writ.

Part I, Question 22

The Providence of God

Article II: Whether everything is subject to the Providence of God?

Objection 1. It seems that everything is not subject to Divine Providence. Nothing provided for can happen by chance. If everything was provided for by God, nothing would happen by chance. And thus hazard and luck would disappear; which is against common opinion.

Objection 2. Further, a wise provider excludes any defect or evil, as far as he can, from those over whom he has a care. But we see many evils existing. Either, then, God cannot hinder these, and thus is not omnipotent; or else he does not have care for everything.

Objection 3. Further, whatever happens of necessity does not require providence or prudence. Hence, according to the Philosopher: 'Prudence is the right reason of things contingent concerning which there is counsel and choice.' Since, then, many things happen from necessity, everything cannot be subject to Providence.

Objection 4. Further, whatsoever is left to itself cannot be subject to the providence of a governor. But men are left to themselves by God, in accordance with the words: 'God made man from the beginning, and left him in the hand of his own counsel' (*Ecclesiasticus* 15. 14). And particularly in reference to the wicked: 'I let them go according to the desires of their own heart' (*Psalm* 80. 13). Everything, therefore, cannot be subject to the Divine Providence.

Objection 5. Further, the Apostle says: 'God doth not care for oxen' (I *Corinthians* 9. 9). And we may say the same of other irrational creatures. Thus everything cannot be under the care of Divine Providence.

On the contrary, It is said of Divine Wisdom: 'She reacheth from end to end mightily, and ordereth all things sweetly' (*Wisdom* 8. 1).

I answer that, Certain persons totally denied the existence of Providence, as Democritus and the Epicureans; laying it down that the world was made by chance. Others taught that incorruptible things only were subject to Providence, but corruptible things not in their individual selves, but only according to their species; for in this respect they are incorruptible. Their views are thus expressed in the Book of Job (22. 14): 'The clouds are his covert; and he doth not consider our things; and he walketh about the poles of heaven.' Rabbi Moses, however, excluded men from amongst things corruptible, on account of the excellence of the intellect which they possess, but in reference to all else that suffers corruption he adhered to the opinion of the others.

We must say, however, that all things are subject to Divine Providence; not only in general, but even in their own individual selves. This is clear; for since every agent acts for an end, the arrangement of effects towards that end extends as far as the causality of the first agent extends. Whence it happens that in the effects of an agent something takes place which has no reference towards the end, because the effect comes from a cause other than, and outside, the intention of the agent. But the causality of God, who is the first agent, extends to all being, not only as to the constituent principles of species, but also as to the individualizing principles; not only of things subject to corruption, but also of things not so subject. Hence all things that exist in whatsoever manner are necessarily directed by God towards some end; as the Apostle says: 'Those that are, are ordained of God' (*Romans* 13. 1). Since, therefore, as the Providence of God is nothing less than the reason of the order of things towards an end, as we have said; it necessarily follows that all things, inasmuch as they participate existence, must likewise be subject to Divine Providence. It has also been shown (Q. XIV) that God knows all things; both universal and particular. Since his knowledge may be compared to the things themselves, as the knowledge of art to the objects of art, all things must of necessity come under his plan; as all things wrought by art are subject to the rule of that art.

Reply Objection. 1. There is a difference between universal and particular causes. For an event can happen which escapes the order of a particular cause; but no such thing could possibly take place in reference to a universal cause. Nothing escapes the order of a particular cause, except through the intervention and hindrance of some other particular cause; as, for instance, wood may be prevented from burning by the action of water. Since, then, all particular causes are included under the universal cause, it could not be that any effect should take place outside the range of that universal cause. So far as an effect escapes the order of a particular cause, it is said to be casual or fortuitous in respect to that cause; but if we regard the universal cause, outside whose range no effect can happen, it is said to be foreseen. As, for instance, the meeting of two servants, although to them it appears a chance circumstance, has been fully foreseen by their master, who has purposely sent them to meet at the one place, whilst they remain ignorant of this fact.

Reply Objection 2. We must speak in different terms of one who has care of a particular thing, and of one whose providence is universal, because a particular provider excludes all defects from what is subject to his care as far as he can; but one who is universal allows some little defect to remain, lest in removing it the whole plan should suffer. Hence, corruption and defects in the things of Nature around us are said to be contrary to some particular nature; but they are in keeping with the plan of universal nature; inasmuch as the defect in one thing yields to the good of another, or even to the universal good. For 'the corruption of one is the generation of another', and through this it is that a *species* is kept in existence. Since God, then, provides universally for all being, it belongs to his Providence to permit certain defects in particular effects, that the perfect good of the universe may not be hindered. If all evil were prevented, much good would be absent from the universe. A lion would cease to live, if there were no slaying of animals; and there would be no patience of martyrs if there were no tyrannical persecution. Thus Augustine says: 'Almighty God would in no wise permit evil to exist in his works, unless he were so almighty and so good as to produce good even from evil.' It would appear that it was on account of these two reasons, which we have just given, that some were persuaded to consider corruptible things, e.g. casual and evil things, as removed from the care of Divine Providence.

Reply Objection 3. Man did not make Nature; but he uses in the performance of art and virtue the things of Nature. Hence human providence does not reach to that which takes place in nature from necessity; but divine providence extends thus far, since God is the author of nature. From a motive of this kind those seemed to be moved who withdrew the course of nature from the care of divine providence, attributing it rather to the necessity of matter, as Democritus, and others of the ancients.

Reply Objection 4. When it is said that God left man to himself, this does not mean that man is exempt from divine providence; but merely that there is not given him an operating force determined to only the one effect; as in the case of things in nature, which are made to act as though directed towards an end by a higher agent: and do not act of themselves, as if they knew and directed their action towards an end, like rational creatures, through the possession of free will, by which these are able to take counsel and make a choice. Hence it is significantly said: 'In the hand of his own counsel.' But since the very act of free will is traced to God as to a cause, it necessarily follows that everything happening from the exercise of free will must be subject to divine providence. For human providence is included under the providence of God, as a particular under a universal cause. God, however, extends his providence over the just in a certain more excellent way than over the wicked; inasmuch as he prevents anything happening which would impede their final salvation. For 'to those who love God, all things conspire unto good' (*Romans* 8. 28). But from the fact that he does not restrain the wicked from the evil of guilt, he is said to abandon them; not that he altogether withdraws his providence from them; otherwise they would return to nothing, if they were not preserved in existence by his providence. This was the reason that had weight with Tully, who subtracted from the care of divine providence all those things concerning which we take counsel.

Reply Objection 5. Since a rational creature has, through the possession of free will, control over its actions, as was said above (Q. XIX), it is subject to divine providence in an especial manner, so that something is imputed to it as a fault, or as a merit; and there is given it accordingly something by way of punishment or reward. In this way the Apostle withdraws oxen from the care of God; not, however, that individual irrational creatures escape the care of divine providence; as was the opinion of Rabbi Moses.

SIN, GRACE AND MERIT

Part II (First Part), Question 82

Of Original Sin, as to its Essence

Article 1: Whether Original Sin is a Habit?

Objection 1. It seems that original sin is not a habit. For original sin is the absence of original justice, as Anselm states (*De Concep. Virg.* ii, iii, xvii), so that original sin is a privation. But privation is opposed to habit. Therefore original sin is not a habit.

Objection 2. Further, actual sin has the nature of fault more than original sin, in so far as it is more voluntary. Now the habit of actual sin has not the nature of a fault, else it would follow that a man while asleep, would be guilty of sin. Therefore no original habit has the nature of a fault.

Objection 3. Further, in wickedness act always precedes habit, because evil habits are not infused, but acquired. Now original sin is not preceded by an act. Therefore original sin is not a habit.

On the contrary, Augustine says in his book on Baptism of infants (*De Pecc. Merit. et Remiss.* i) that on account of original sin little children have the aptitude of concupiscence though they have not the act. Now aptitude denotes some kind of habit. Therefore original sin is a habit.

I answer that, As stated above (Q. XLIX, A. 4; Q. L, A. 1), habit is twofold. The first is a habit whereby power is inclined to act: thus science and virtue are called habits. In this way original sin is not a habit. The second kind of habit is the disposition of a complex nature, whereby that nature is well or ill disposed to something, chiefly when such a disposition has become like a second nature, as in the case of sickness or health. In this sense original sin is a habit. For it is an inordinate disposition, arising from the destruction of the harmony which was essential to original justice, even as bodily sickness is an inordinate disposition of the body, by reason of the destruction of that equilibrium which is essential to health. Hence it is that original sin is called the *langour of nature* (cf. Augustine, *In Psalm* 118, *serm.* iii).

Reply Objection 1. As bodily sickness is partly a privation, in so far as it denotes the destruction of the equilibrium of health, and partly something positive, viz. the very humours that are inordinately disposed, so too original sin denotes the privation of original justice, and besides this, the inordinate disposition of the parts of the soul. Consequently it is not a pure privation, but a corrupt habit.

Reply Objection 2. Actual sin is an inordinateness of an act: whereas original sin, being the sin of nature, is an inordinate disposition of nature, and has the character of fault, through being transmitted from our first parent, as stated above (Q. LXXXI, A. 1). Now this inordinate disposition of nature is a kind of habit, whereas the inordinate disposition of an act is not: and for this reason original sin can be a habit, whereas actual sin cannot.

Reply Objection 3. This objection considers the habit which inclines a power to an act: but original sin is not this kind of habit. Nevertheless a certain inclination to an inordinate act does follow from original sin, not directly, but indirectly, viz. by the removal of the obstacle, i.e. original justice, which hindered inordinate movements: just as an inclination to inordinate bodily movements results indirectly from bodily sickness. Nor is it necessary to say that original sin is a habit *infused*, or a habit acquired (except by the act of our first parent, but not by our own act); but it is a habit *inborn* due to our corrupt origin.

Article IV: Whether Original Sin is Equally in All?

Objection 1. It seems that original sin is not equally in all. Because original sin is inordinate concupiscence, as stated above (A. 3). Now all are not equally prone to acts of concupiscence. Therefore original sin is not equally in all.

Objection 2. Further, original sin is an inordinate disposition of the soul, just as sickness is an inordinate disposition of the body. But sickness is subject to degrees. Therefore original sin is subject to degrees.

Objection 3. Further, Augustine says (*De Nup. et Concup.* i) that 'lust transmits original sin to the child'. But the act of generation may be more lustful in one than in another. Therefore original sin may be greater in one than in another.

On the contrary, Original sin is the sin of nature, as stated above (Q. LXXXI, A. 1). But nature is equally in all. Therefore original sin is too.

I answer that, There are two things in original sin: one is the privation of original justice; the other is the relation of this privation to the sin of our first parent, from whom it is transmitted to man through his corrupt origin. As to the first, original sin has no degrees, since the gift of original justice is taken away entirely; and privations that remove something entirely, such as death and darkness, cannot be more or less, as stated above (Q. LXXIII, A. 2). In like manner, neither is this possible, as to the second: since all are related equally to the first principle of our corrupt origin, from which principle original sin takes the nature of guilt; for relations cannot be more or less. Consequently it is evident that original sin cannot be more in one than in another.

Reply Objection 1. Through the bond of original justice being broken, which held together all the powers of the soul in a certain order, each power of the soul tends to its own proper movement, and the more impetuously, as it is stronger. Now it happens that some of the soul's powers are stronger in one man than in another, on account of the different bodily temperaments. Consequently if one man is more prone than another to acts of concupiscence, this is not due to original sin, because the bond of original justice is equally broken in all, and the lower parts of the soul are, in all, left to themselves equally; but it is due to the various dispositions of the powers, as stated.

Reply Objection 2. Sickness of the body, even sickness of the same species, has not an equal cause in all; for instance if a fever be caused by corruption of the bile, the corruption may be greater or lesser, and nearer to, or further from a vital principle. But the cause of original sin is equal in all, so that there is no comparison.

Reply Objection 3. It is not the actual lust that transmits original sin: for, supposing God were to grant to a man to feel no inordinate lust in the act of generation, he would still transmit original sin; we must understand this to be habitual lust, whereby the sensitive appetite is not kept subject to reason by the bonds of original justice. This lust is equally in all.

Part II (*First Part*), *Question* 85

Of the Effects of Sin and, first, of the Corruption of the Good of Nature.

Article 1: *Whether sin diminishes the good of Nature?*

Objection 1. It seems that sin does not diminish the good of nature. For man's sin is no worse than the devil's. But natural good remains unimpaired in devils after sin, as Dionysius states (*Div. Nom.* iv). Therefore neither does sin diminish the good of human nature.

Objection 2 Further, when that which follows is changed, that which precedes remains unchanged, since substance remains the same when its accidents are changed. But nature exists before the voluntary action. Therefore, when sin has caused a disorder in a voluntary act, nature is not changed on that account, so that the good of nature be diminished.

Objection 3. Further, sin is an action, while diminution is a passion. Now no agent is passive by the very reason of its acting, although it is possible for it to act on one thing, and to be passive as regards another. Therefore he who sins, does not, by his sin, diminish the good of his nature.

Objection 4. Further, no accident acts on its subject; because that which is patient is a potential being, while that which is subjected to an accident, is already an actual being as regards that accident. But sin is in the good of nature as an accident in a subject. Therefore sin does not diminish the good of nature, since to diminish is to act.

On the contrary, 'A certain man going down from Jerusalem to Jericho (*Luke* 10. 30), i.e. to the corruption of sin, was stripped of his gifts, and wounded in his nature', as Bede expounds the passage. Therefore sin diminishes the good of nature.

I answer that, The good of human nature is threefold. First, there are the principles of which nature is constituted, and the properties that flow from them, such as the powers of the soul, and so forth. Secondly, since man has from nature an inclination to virtue, as stated above (Q. LX, A. 1; Q. LXIII, A. 1), this inclination to virtue is a good of nature. Thirdly, the gift of original justice, conferred on the whole human nature in the person of the first man, may be called a good of nature.

Accordingly, the first-mentioned good of nature is neither destroyed nor diminished by sin. The third good of nature was entirely destroyed through the sin of our first parent, but the second good of nature, viz. the natural inclination to virtue, is diminished by sin. Because human acts produce an inclination to like acts, as stated above (Q. L, A. 1). Now from the very fact that a thing becomes inclined to one of two contraries, its inclination to the other contrary must needs be diminished. Wherefore as sin is opposed to virtue, from the very fact that a man sins, there results a diminution of that good of nature, which is the inclination to virtue.

Reply Objection 1. Dionysius is speaking of the first-mentioned good of nature, which consists in *being, living and understanding*, as anyone may see who reads the context.

Reply Objection 2. Although nature precedes the voluntary action, it has an inclination to a certain voluntary action. Wherefore nature is not changed in itself, through a change in the voluntary action: it is the inclination that is changed in so far as it is directed to its term.

Reply Objection 3. A voluntary action proceeds from various powers, active and passive. The result is that through voluntary actions something is caused or taken away in the man who acts, as we stated when treating of the production of habits (Q. LI, A. 2).

Reply Objection 4. An accident does not act effectively on its subject, but it acts on it formally, in the same sense as when we say that whiteness makes a thing white. In this way there is nothing to hinder sin from diminishing the good of nature; but only in so far as sin is itself a diminution of the good of nature, through being an inordinateness of action. But as regards the inordinateness of the agent, we must say that suchlike inordinateness is caused by the fact that in the acts of the soul, there is an active, and a passive element: thus the sensible object moves the sensitive appetite, and the sensitive appetite inclines the reason and will, as stated above (Q. LXXVII, AA. 1, 2). The result of this is the inordinateness, not as though an accident acted on its own subject, but in so far as the object acts on the power, and one power acts on another and puts it out of order.

Article II: Whether the Entire Good of Human Nature can be destroyed by Sin?

Objection 1. It seems that the entire good of human nature can be destroyed by sin. For the good of human nature is finite, since *human nature itself is finite*. Now any finite thing is entirely taken away, if the subtraction be continuous. Since therefore the good of nature can be continually diminished by sin, it seems that in the end it can be entirely taken away.

Objection 2. Further, in a thing of one nature, the whole and the parts are uniform, as is evidently the case with air, water, flesh and all bodies with similar parts. But the good of nature is wholly uniform. Since therefore a part thereof can be taken away by sin, it seems that the whole can also be taken away by sin.

Objection 3. Further, the good of nature, that is weakened by sin, is aptitude for virtue. Now this aptitude is destroyed entirely in some on account of sin: thus the lost cannot be restored to virtue any more than the blind can to sight. Therefore sin can take away the good of nature entirely.

On the contrary, Augustine says (*Enchirid.* xiv) that 'evil does not exist except in some good'. But the evil of sin cannot be in the good of virtue or of grace, because they are contrary to it. Therefore it must be in the good of nature, and consequently it does not destroy it entirely.

I answer that, As stated above (A. 1), the good of nature, that is diminished by sin, is the natural inclination to virtue, which is befitting to man from the very fact that he is a rational being; for it is due to this that he performs actions in accord with reason, which is to act virtuously. Now sin cannot entirely take away from man the fact that he is a rational being, for then, he would no longer be capable of sin. Wherefore it is not possible for this good of nature to be destroyed entirely.

Since, however, this same good of nature may be continually diminished by sin, some, in order to illustrate this, have made use of the example of a finite thing being diminished indefinitely, without being entirely destroyed. For the Philosopher says (*Phys.* iii) that if from a finite magnitude a continual subtraction be made in the same quantity, it will at last be entirely destroyed, for instance if from any finite length I continue to subtract the length of a span. If, however, the subtraction be made each time in the same proportion, and not in the same quantity, it may go on indefinitely: as, for instance, if a quantity be halved, and one half be diminished by half, it will be possible to go on thus indefinitely, provided that what is subtracted in each case be less than what was subtracted before. But this does not apply to the question at issue, since a subsequent sin does not diminish the good of nature less than a previous sin, but perhaps more, if it be a more grievous sin.

We must, therefore, explain the matter otherwise by saying that the aforesaid inclination is to be considered as a middle term between two others: for it is based on the rational nature as on its root, and tends to the good of virtue, as to its term and end. Consequently its diminution may be understood in two ways: first, on the part of its root, secondly on the part of its term. In the first way, it is not diminished by sin, because sin does not diminish nature, as stated above (A. 1). But it is diminished in the second way, in so far as an obstacle is placed against its attaining its term. Now if it were diminished in the first way, it would needs be entirely destroyed at last by the rational nature being entirely destroyed. Since, however, it is diminished on the part of the obstacle which is placed against its attaining its term, it is evident that it can be diminished indefinitely, because obstacles can be placed indefinitely, inasmuch as man can go on indefinitely adding sin to sin: and yet it cannot be destroyed entirely, because the root of this inclination always remains. An example of this may be seen in a transparent body, which has an inclination to receive light, from the very fact that it is transparent; yet this inclination or aptitude is diminished on the part of supervening clouds, although it always remains rooted in the nature of the body.

Reply Objection 1. This objection avails when diminution is made by subtraction. But here the diminution is made by raising obstacles, and this neither diminishes nor destroys the root of the inclination, as stated above.

Reply Objection 2. The natural inclination is indeed wholly uniform:

nevertheless it stands in relation both to its principle and to its term, in respect of which diversity of relation, it is diminished on the one hand, and not on the other.

Reply Objection 3. Even in the lost the natural inclination to virtue remains, else they would have no remorse of conscience. That it is not reduced to act is owing to their being deprived of grace by Divine justice. Thus even in a blind man the aptitude to see remains in the very root of his nature, inasmuch as he is an animal naturally endowed with sight: yet this aptitude is not reduced to act, for the lack of a cause capable of reducing it, by forming the organ requisite for sight.

Part II (First Part), Question 109

Of the Necessity of Grace.

Article 1: Whether Without Grace Man Can Know Any Truth?

Objection 1. It seems that without grace man can know no truth. For, on I *Corinthians* 12. 3: 'No man can say, the Lord Jesus, but by the Holy Ghost', the gloss says: 'Every truth, by whomsoever spoken is from the Holy Ghost.' Now the Holy Ghost dwells in us by grace. Therefore we cannot know truth without grace.

Objection 2. Further, Augustine says (*Solil.* i) that 'the most certain sciences are like things lit up by the sun so as to be seen. Now God himself is he who sheds the light. And reason is in the mind as sight is in the eye. And the eyes of the mind are the senses of the soul.' Now the bodily senses, however pure, cannot see any visible object, without the sun's light. Therefore the human mind, however perfect, cannot, by reasoning, know any truth without divine light: and this pertains to the aid of grace.

Objection 3. Further, the human mind can only understand truth by thinking, as is clear from Augustine (*De Trin.* xiv). But the Apostle says (II *Corinthians* 3. 5): 'Not that we are sufficient to think anything of outselves, as of ourselves; but our sufficiency is from God.' Therefore man cannot, of himself, know truth without the help of grace.

On the contrary, Augustine says (*Retract.* i): 'I do not approve having said in the prayer, "O God, who dost wish the sinless alone to know the truth"; for it may be answered that many who are not sinless know many truths.' Now man is cleansed from sin by grace, according to *Psalm* 50. 12: 'Create a clean heart in me, O God, and renew a right spirit within my bowels.' Therefore without grace man of himself can know truth.

I answer that, To know truth is a use or act of intellectual light, since, according to the Apostle (*Ephesians* 5. 13): 'All that is made manifest is light.' Now every use implies movement, taking movement broadly, so as to call thinking and willling movements, as is clear from the Philosopher (*De Anima* iii). Now in corporeal things we see that for movement there is required not merely the form which is the principle of the movement or action, but there is also required the motion of the first mover. Now the first mover in the order of corporeal things is the heavenly body. Hence no matter how perfectly fire has heat, it would not bring about alteration, except by the motion of the heavenly body. But it is clear that as all corporeal movements are reduced to the motion of the heavenly body as to the first corporeal mover, so all movements, both corporeal and spiritual, are reduced to the simple First Mover, who is God. And hence no matter how perfect a corporeal or spiritual nature is supposed to be, it cannot proceed to its act unless it be moved by God; but this motion is according to the plan of his providence, and not by a necessity of nature, as the motion of the heavenly body. Now not only is every motion from God as from the First Mover, but all formal perfection is from him as from the First Act. And thus the act of the intellect or of any created being whatsoever depends upon God in two ways: first, inasmuch as it is from him that it has the form whereby it acts; secondly, inasmuch as it is moved by him to act.

Now every form bestowed on created things by God has power for a determined act, which it can bring about in proportion to its own proper endowment; and beyond which it is powerless, except by a superadded form, as water can only heat when heated by the fire. And thus the human understanding has a form, viz., intelligible light, which of itself is sufficient for knowing certain intelligible things, viz., those we can come to know through the senses. Higher intelligible things the human intellect cannot know, unless it be perfected by a stronger light, viz, the light of faith or prophecy which is called the 'light of grace', inasmuch as it is added to nature.

Hence we must say that for the knowledge of any truth whatsoever man needs divine help, that the intellect may be moved by God to its act. But he does not need a new light added to his natural light, in order to know the truth in all things, but only in some that surpass his natural knowledge. And yet at times God miraculously instructs some by his grace in things that can be known by natural reason, even as he sometimes brings about miraculously what nature can do.

Reply Objection 1. Every truth by whomsoever spoken is from the Holy Ghost as bestowing the natural light, and moving us to understand and speak the truth, but not as dwelling in us by sanctifying grace, or as bestowing any habitual gift superadded to nature. For this only takes place with regard to certain truths that are known and spoken, and especially in regard to such as pertain to faith, of which the Apostle speaks.

Reply Objection 2. The material sun sheds its light outside us; but the intelligible Sun, who is God, shines within us. Hence the natural light bestowed upon the soul is God's enlightenment, whereby we are enlightened to see what pertains to natural knowledge; and for this there is required no further knowledge, but only for such things as surpass natural knowledge.

Reply Objection 3. We always need God's help for every thought, inasmuch as he moves the understanding to act; for actually to understand anything is to think, as is clear from Augustine (*De Trin.* xiv).

Article II: Whether Man Can Wish or Do any Good without Grace?

Objection 1. It seems that man can wish and do good without grace. For that is in man's power, whereof he is master. Now man is master of his acts, and especially of his willing, as stated above (Q. I, A. 1; Q. XIII, A. 6). Hence man, of himself, can wish and do good without the help of grace.

Objection 2. Further, man has more power over what is according to his nature than over what is beyond his nature. Now sin is against nature, as Damascene says (*De Fide Orthod.* ii); whereas deeds of virtue are according to his nature as stated above (Q. LXXI, A. 1). Therefore since man can sin of himself, much more would it seem that of himself he can wish and do good.

Objection 3. Further, the understanding's good is truth, as the Philosopher says (*Ethic.* vi). Now the intellect can of itself know truth, even as every other thing can work its own operation of itself. Therefore, much more can man, of himself, do and wish good.

On the contrary, The Apostle says (*Romans* 9. 16): 'It is not of him that willeth' (i.e., to will), 'nor of him that runneth' (i.e., to run), 'but of God that showeth mercy'. And Augustine says (*De Corrept. et Gratia,* ii) that 'without grace men do nothing good when they either think or wish or love or act'.

I answer that, Man's nature may be looked at in two ways: first, in its integrity, as it was in our first parent before sin; secondly, as it is corrupted in us after the sin of our first parent. Now in both states human nature needs the help of God as First Mover, to do or wish any good whatsoever, as stated above (A. 1). But in the state of integrity, as regards the sufficiency of the operative power, man by his natural endowments could wish and do the good proportionate to his nature, such as the good of acquired virtue; but not surpassing good, as the good of infused virtue. But in the state of corrupt nature, man falls short of what he could do by his nature, so that he is unable to fulfil it by his own natural powers. Yet because human nature is not altogether corrupted by sin, so as to be shorn of every natural good, even in the state of corrupted nature it can, by virtue of its natural endowments, work some particular good, as to build dwellings, plant vineyards, and the like; yet it cannot do all the good natural to it, so as to fall short in nothing; just as a sick man can of himself make some movements, yet he cannot be perfectly moved with the movements of one in health, unless by the help of medicine he be cured.

And thus in the state of perfect nature man needs a gratuitous strength superadded to natural strength for one reason, viz., in order to do and wish supernatural good; but for two reasons, in the state of corrupt nature, viz., in order to be healed, and furthermore in order to carry out works of supernatural virtue, which are meritorious. Beyond this, in both states man needs the divine help, that he may be moved to act well.

Reply Objection 1. Man is master of his acts and of his willing or not willing, because of his deliberate reason, which can be bent to one side or another. And although he is master of his deliberating or not deliberating, yet this can only be by a previous deliberation; and since it cannot go on to infinity, we must come at length to this, that man's free-will is moved by an extrinsic principle, which is above the human mind, to wit by God, as the Philosopher proves in a chapter on *Good Fortune* (*Ethic. Eudem.* vii). Hence the mind of man still unweakened is not so much master of its act that it does not need to be moved by God; and much more the free-will of man weakened by sin, whereby it is hindered from good by the corruption of the nature.

Reply Objection 2. To sin is nothing else than to fail in the good which belongs to any being according to its nature. Now as every created thing has its being from another, and, considered in itself, is nothing, so does it need to be preserved by another in the good which pertains to its nature. For it can of itself fail in good, even as of itself it can fall into non-existence, unless it is upheld by God.

Reply Objection 3. Man cannot even know truth without divine help, as stated above (A. 1). And yet human nature is more corrupt by sin in regard to the desire for good, than in regard to the knowledge of truth.

Article III: Whether by His Own Natural Powers and Without Grace Man Can Love God above All Things?

Objection 1. It seems that without grace man cannot love God above all things by his own natural powers. For to love God above all things is the proper and principal act of charity. Now man cannot of himself possess charity, since the 'charity of God is poured forth in our hearts by the Holy Ghost who is given to us', as is said in *Romans* 5. 5. Therefore man by his natural powers alone cannot love God above all things.

Objection 2. Further, no nature can rise above itself. But to love God above all things is to tend above oneself. Therefore without the help of grace no created nature can love God above itself.

Objection 3. Further, to God, who is the Highest Good, is due the best love, which is that he be loved above all things. Now without grace man is not capable of giving God the best love, which is his due; otherwise it would be useless to add grace. Hence man, without grace and with his natural powers alone, cannot love God above all things.

On the contrary, As some maintain, man was first made with only natural endowments; and in this state it is manifest that he loved God to some extent. But he did not love God equally with himself, or less than himself, otherwise he would have sinned. Therefore he loved God above himself. Therefore man, by his natural powers alone, can love God more than himself and above all things.

I answer that, As was said above (P.I., Q. LX, A. 5), where the various opinions concerning the natural love of the angels were set forth, man in a state of perfect nature, could by his natural power, do the good natural to him without the addition of any gratuitous gift, though not without the help of God moving him. Now to love God above all things is natural to man and to every nature, not only rational, but irrational, and even to inanimate nature according to the manner of love which can belong to each creature. And the reason of this is that it is natural to all to seek and love things according as they are naturally fit (to be sought and loved) since 'all things act according as they are naturally fit' as stated in *Phys.* ii. Now it is manifest that the good of the part is for the good of the whole; hence everything, by its natural appetite and love, loves its own proper good on account of the common good of the whole universe, which is God. Hence Dionysius says (*Div. Nom.* iv) that 'God leads everything to love of himself'. Hence in the state of perfect nature man referred the love of himself and of all other things to the love of God as to its end; and thus he loved God more than himself and above all things. But in the state of corrupt nature man falls short of this in the appetite of his rational will, which, unless it is cured by God's grace, follows its private good, on account of the corruption of nature. And hence we must say that in the state of perfect nature man did not need the gift of grace added to his natural endowments, in order to love God above all things naturally, although he needed God's help to move him to it; but in the state of corrupt nature man needs, even for this, the help of grace to heal his nature.

Reply Objection 1. Charity loves God above all things in a higher way than nature does. For nature loves God above all things inasmuch as he is the beginning and the end of natural good; whereas charity loves him, as he is the object of beatitude, and inasmuch as man has a spiritual fellowship with God. Moreover charity adds to natural love of God a certain quickness and joy, in the same way that every habit of virtue adds to the good act which is done merely by the natural reason of a man who has not the habit of virtue.

Reply Objection 2. When it is said that nature cannot rise above itself, we must not understand this as if it could not be drawn to any object above itself, for it is clear that our intellect by its natural knowledge can know things above itself, as is shown in our natural knowledge of God. But we are to understand that nature cannot rise to an act exceeding the proportion of its strength. Now to love God above all things is not such an act; for it is natural to every creature, as was said above.

Reply Objection 3. Love is said to be best, both with respect to the degree of love, and with regard to the motive of loving, and the mode of love. And thus the highest degree of love is that whereby charity loves God as the giver of beatitude, as was said above.

Article IV: Whether Man Without Grace and by His Own Natural Powers Can Fulfil the Commandments of the Law?

Objection 1. It seems that man without grace, and by his own natural powers, can fulfil the commandments of the law. For the Apostle says (*Romans* 2. 14) that 'the Gentiles who have not the law, do by nature those things that are of the law'. Now what a man does naturally he can do of himself without grace. Hence a man can fulfil the commandments of the law without grace.

Objection 2. Further, Jerome (Pelagius) says in his Exposition of the Catholic Faith that 'they are anathema who say God has laid impossibilities upon man'. Now what a man cannot fulfil by himself is impossible to him. Therefore a man can fulfil all the commandments of himself.

Objection 3. Further of all the commandments of the law, the greatest is this, 'Thou shalt love the Lord thy God with thy whole heart' (*Matthew* 22. 37). Now man with his natural endowments can fulfil this command by loving God above all things, as stated above (A. 3). Therefore man can fulfil all the commandments of the law without grace.

On the contrary, Augustine says (*De Haeres.* lxxxviii) that it is part of the Pelagian heresy that 'they believe that without grace man can fulfil all the divine commandments'.

I answer that, There are two ways of fulfilling the commandments of the Law. The first regards the substance of the works, as when a man does works of justice, fortitude and of other virtues. And in this way man in the state of perfect nature could fulfil all the commandments of the law; otherwise he would have been unable to sin in that state, since to sin is nothing else than to transgress the divine commandments. But in the state of corrupted nature man cannot fulfil all the divine commandments without healing grace. Secondly, the commandments of the law can be fulfilled not merely as regards the substance of the act, but also as regards the mode of acting, i.e., their being done out of charity. And in this way, neither in the state of perfect nature, nor in the state of corrupt nature can man fulfil the commandments of the law without grace. Hence, Augustine (*De Corrept. et Grat.* ii) having stated that 'without grace men do no good whatever', adds: 'Not only do they know by its light what to do, but by its help they do lovingly what they know.' Beyond this, in both states they need the help of God's motion in order to fulfil the commandments, as stated above (AA. 2. 3).

Reply Objection 1. As Augustine says (*De Spir. et Lit.* xxvii) 'do not be disturbed at his saying that they do by nature those things that are of the law; for the Spirit of grace works this, in order to restore in us the image of God, after which we were naturally made'.

Reply Objection 2. What we can do with the divine assistance is not altogether impossible to us; according to the Philosopher (*Ethic* iii): 'What we can do through our friends, we can do in some sense by ourselves.' Hence Jerome (Pelagius) concedes (ibid.) that 'our will is in such a way free that we must confess we still require God's help.'

Reply Objection 3. Man cannot, with his purely natural endowments, fulfil the precept of the love of God, as stated above (A. 3).

Article V: Whether Man Can Merit Everlasting Life Without Grace?

Objection 1. It seems that man can merit everlasting life without grace. For Our Lord says (*Matthew* 19. 17): 'If thou wilt enter into life, keep the commandments'; from which it would seem that to enter into everlasting life rests with man's will. But what rests with our will, we can do of ourselves. Hence it seems that man can merit everlasting life of himself.

Objection 2. Further, eternal life is the wage or reward bestowed by God on men, according to *Matthew* 5. 12: 'Your reward is very great in heaven.' But wage or reward is meted by God to everyone according to his works, according to *Psalm* 59. 12: 'Thou wilt render to every man according to his works.' Hence, since man is master of his works, it seems that it is within his power to reach everlasting life'.

Objection 3. Further, everlasting life is the last end of human life. Now every natural thing by its natural endowments can attain its end. Much more, therefore, may man attain to everlasting life by his natural endowments, without grace.

On the contrary, The Apostle says (*Romans* 6. 23): 'The grace of God is life everlasting.' And as a gloss says, this is said 'that we may understand that God, of his own mercy, leads us to everlasting life'.

I answer that, Acts conducing to an end must be proportioned to the end. But no act exceeds the proportion of its active principle; and hence we see in natural things, that nothing can by its operation bring about an effect which exceeds its active force, but only such as is proportionate to its power. Now everlasting life is an end exceeding the proportion of human nature, as is clear from what we have said above (Q. V, A. 5). Hence man, by his natural endowments, cannot produce meritorious works proportionate to everlasting life; and for this a higher force is needed, viz., the force of grace. And thus without grace man cannot merit everlasting life; yet he can perform works conducing to good which is natural to man, as 'to toil in the fields, to drink, to eat, or to have friends' and the like, as Augustine says (*Resp. contra Pelag.* iii, Cf. *Hypognostic* iii).

Reply Objection 1. Man, by his will, does works meritorious of everlasting life; but as Augustine says, in the same book, for this it is necessary that the will of man should be prepared with grace by God.

Reply Objection 2. As the gloss upon *Romans* 6. 23, 'The grace of God is life everlasting', says, 'It is certain that everlasting life is meted to good works; but the works to which it is meted, belong to God's grace'. And it has been said (A. 4), that to fulfil the commandments of the law, in their due way, whereby their fulfilment may be meritorious, requires grace.

Reply Objection 3. This objection has to do with the natural end of man. Now human nature, since it is nobler, can be raised by the help of grace to a higher end, which lower natures can nowise reach; even as a man who can recover his health by the help of medicines is better disposed to health than one who can nowise recover it, as the Philosopher observes (*De Coelo* ii).

Question 114

Of Merit

Article I: Whether a Man may Merit Anything from God?

Objection 1. It seems that a man can merit nothing from God. For no one, it would seem, merits by giving another his due. But 'by all the good we do, we cannot make sufficient return to God, since yet more is his due', as also the Philosopher says (*Ethic.* viii). Hence it is written (*Luke*

17. 10): 'When you have done all these things that are commanded you, say: "We are unprofitable servants; we have done that which we ought to do".' Hence a man can merit nothing from God.

Objection 2. Further, it would seem that a man merits nothing from God, by what profits himself only, and profits God nothing. Now by acting well, a man profits himself or another man, but not God, for it is written (*Job* 35. 7): 'If thou do justly, what shalt thou give him, or what shall he receive of thy hand.' Hence a man can merit nothing from God.

Objection 3. Further, whoever merits anything from another makes him his debtor; for a man's wage is a debt due to him. Now God is no one's debtor; hence it is written (*Romans* 11. 35): 'Who hath first given to him, and recompense shall be made him?' Hence no one can merit anything from God.

On the contrary, It is written (*Jeremiah* 31. 16): 'There is a reward for thy work.' Now a reward means something bestowed by reason of merit. Hence it would seem that a man may merit from God.

I answer that, Merit and reward refer to the same, for a reward means something given anyone in return for work or toil as a price for it. Hence, as it is an act of justice to give a just price for anything received from another, so also is it an act of justice to make a return for work or toil. Now justice is a kind of equality, as is clear from the Philosopher (*Ethic.* v), and hence justice is simply between those that are simply equal; but where there is no simple equality between them, neither is there simple justice, but there may be a certain manner of justice, as when we say, 'right of parents or lords', as the Philosopher says, in the same book. And hence where there is justice simply, there is the character of merit and reward simply. But where there is no simple right, but only relative, there is no character of merit simply, but only relatively, in so far as the character of justice is found there; since the child merits something from his father and the slave from his lord.

Now it is clear that between God and man there is the greatest inequality: for they are infinitely apart, and all man's good is from God. Hence there can be no justice of absolute equality between man and God, but only of a certain proportion, inasmuch as both operate after their own manner. Now the manner and measure of human virtue is in man from God. Hence man's merit with God only exists on the presupposition of the divine ordination, so that man obtains from God, as a reward of his operation, what God gave him the power of operation for, even as natural things by their proper movements and operations obtain that to which they were ordained by God; differently, indeed, since the rational creature moves itself to act by its free-will, hence its action has the character of merit, which is not so in other creatures.

Reply Objection 1. Man merits, inasmuch as he does what he ought, by his free-will; otherwise the act of justice whereby anyone discharges a debt would not be meritorious.

Reply Objection 2. God seeks from our goods not profit, but glory, i.e., the manifestation of his goodness; even as he seeks it also in his own works. Now nothing accrues to him, but only to ourselves, by our worship of him. Hence we merit from God, not that by our works anything accrues to him, but inasmuch as we work for his glory.

Reply Objection 3. Since our action has the character of merit, only on the presupposition of the divine ordination, it does not follow that God is made our debtor simply, but his own, inasmuch as it is right that his will should be carried out.

Article II: Whether Anyone Without Grace Can Merit Eternal Life?

Objection 1. It seems that without grace anyone can merit eternal life. For man merits from God what he is divinely ordained to, as is stated above (A. 1). Now man by his nature is ordained to beatitude as his end; hence, too, he naturally wishes to be blessed. Hence man by his natural endowments and without grace can merit beatitude which is eternal life.

Objection 2. Further, the less a work is due, the more meritorious it is. Now, less due is that work which is done by one who has received fewer benefits. Hence, since he who has only natural endowments has received fewer gifts from God, than he who has gratuitous gifts as well as nature, it would seem that his works are more meritorious with God. And thus if he who has grace can merit eternal life to some extent, much more may he who has no grace.

Objection 3. Further, God's mercy and liberality infinitely surpass human mercy and liberality. Now a man may merit from another, even though he has not hitherto had his grace. Much more, therefore, would it seem that a man without grace may merit eternal life.

On the contrary, The Apostle says (*Romans* 6. 23): 'The grace of God, life everlasting.'

I answer that, Man without grace may be looked at in two states, as was said above (Q. CIX, A. 2); the first, a state of perfect nature, in which Adam was before his sin; the second, a state of corrupt nature, in which we are before being restored by grace. Therefore, if we speak of man in the first state, there is only one reason why man cannot merit eternal life without grace, by his purely natural endowments, viz., because man's merit depends on the divine pre-ordination. Now no act of anything whatsoever is divinely ordained to anything exceeding the proportion of the powers which are the principles of its act; for it is a law of divine providence that nothing shall act beyond its powers. Now everlasting life is a good exceeding the proportion of created nature; since it exceeds its knowledge and desire, according to I *Corinthians* 2. 9: 'Eye hath not seen, nor ear heard, neither hath it entered into the heart of man.' And hence it is that no created nature is a sufficient principle of an act meritorious of eternal life, unless there is added a supernatural gift, which we call grace. But if we speak of man as existing in sin, a second reason is added to this, viz., the impediment of sin. For since sin is an offence against God, excluding us from eternal life, as is clear from what has been said above (Q. LXXI, A. 6; Q. CXIII, A. 2), no one existing in a state of mortal sin can merit eternal life unless first he be reconciled to God, through his sin being forgiven, which is brought about by grace. For the sinner deserves not life, but death, according to *Romans* 6. 23: 'The wages of sin is death.'

Reply Objection 1. God ordained human nature to attain the end of eternal life, not by its own strength, but by the help of grace; and in this way its act can be meritorious of eternal life.

Reply Objection 2. Without grace a man cannot have a work equal to a work proceeding from grace, since the more perfect the principle, the more perfect the action. But the objection would hold good, if we supposed the operations equal in both cases.

Reply Objection 3. With regard to the first reason adduced, the case is different in God and in man. For a man receives all his power of well-doing from God, and not from man. Hence a man can merit nothing from God except by his gift, which the Apostle expresses aptly as saying (*Romans* 11. 35): 'Who hath first given to him, and recompense shall be made to him?' But man may merit from man, before he has received anything from him, by what he has received from God.

But as regards the second proof taken from the impediment of sin, the case is similar with man and God, since one man cannot merit from another whom he has offended, unless he makes satisfaction to him and is reconciled.

Article III: Whether A Man In Grace Can Merit Eternal Life Condignly?

Objection 1. It seems that a man in grace cannot merit eternal life condignly, for the Apostle says (*Romans* 8. 18): 'The sufferings of this time are not worthy (*condignae*) to be compared with the glory to come, that shall be revealed in us.' But of all meritorious works, the sufferings of the saints would seem the most meritorious. Therefore no works of men are meritorious of eternal life condignly.

Objection 2. Further, on *Romans* 6. 23, 'The grace of God, life everlasting', a gloss says: 'He might have truly said: "The wages of justice, life everlasting"; but he preferred to say "The grace of God, life everlasting", that we may know that God leads us to life everlasting of his own mercy and not by our merits.' Now when anyone merits something condignly he receives it not from mercy, but from merit. Hence it would seem that a man with grace cannot merit life everlasting condignly.

Objection 3. Further, merit that equals the reward, would seem to be condign. Now no act of the present life can equal everlasting life, which surpasses our knowledge and our desire, and moreover, surpasses the charity or love of the wayfarer, even as it exceeds nature. Therefore with grace a man cannot merit eternal life condignly.

On the contrary, What is granted in accordance with a fair judgment, would seem a condign reward. But life everlasting is granted by God, in accordance with the judgment of justice, according to II *Timothy* 4. 8: 'As to the rest, there is laid up for me a crown of justice, which the Lord, the just judge, will render to me in that day.' Therefore man merits everlasting life condignly.

I answer that, Man's meritorious work may be considered in two ways: First, as it proceeds from free-will; secondly, as it proceeds from the grace of the Holy Ghost. If it is considered as regards the substance of the work, and inasmuch as it springs from free-will, there can be no condignity because of the very great inequality. But there is congruity, on account of an equality of proportion: for it would seem congruous that, if a man does what he can, God should reward him according to the excellence of his power.

If, however, we speak of a meritorious work, inasmuch as it proceeds from the grace of the Holy Ghost moving us to life everlasting, it is meritorious of life everlasting condignly. For thus the value of its merit depends upon the power of the Holy Ghost moving us to life everlasting according to *John* 4. 14: 'Shall become in him a fount of water springing up into life everlasting.' And the worth of the work depends on the dignity of grace, whereby a man, being made a partaker of the divine nature, is adopted as a son of God, to whom the inheritance is due by right of adoption, according to *Romans* 8. 17: 'If sons, heirs also.'

Reply Objection 1. The Apostle is speaking of the substance of these sufferings.

Reply Objection 2. This saying is to be understood of the first cause of our reaching everlasting life, viz., God's mercy. But our merit is a subsequent cause.

Reply Objection 3. The grace of the Holy Ghost which we have at present, although unequal to glory in act, is equal to it virtually as the seed of a tree, wherein the whole tree is virtually. So likewise by grace the Holy Ghost dwells in man; and he is a sufficient cause of life everlasting; hence, II *Corinthians* 1. 22, he is called the pledge of our inheritance.

THE REFORMATION PERIOD

IX

LUTHER

Martin Luther (1483–1546) lived a life so fateful and controversial in its consequences that any brief account of it must be less than adequate. His parents were of the free peasant class, living in Eisleben, Germany. After early schooling, during which he suffered a good deal from poverty, he entered the University of Erfurt. Soon after graduating he entered the Augustinian monastery in his university town. He was ordained priest in 1507 and shortly afterwards became a university lecturer and then professor of biblical literature. The bulk of his lecture notes have been preserved and are an invaluable record of the development of his thought in this early period. Although he had devoted himself throughout this period with scrupulous diligence to the rigorous, ascetic discipline of his order, he failed to find the peace of mind and assurance of salvation which he sought.

Then in 1512, while meditating on *Romans* 1. 16–17, he reached a new understanding of the doctrine of salvation. This was the doctrine of justification by faith alone, which remained the centre of his theology throughout his life. It was this principle that finally led him to post his famous ninety-five theses, protesting against abuses in the sale of indulgences, on the doors of Wittenburg church. The resulting controversy led him to repudiate not only the whole doctrine of indulgences but to reject papal and episcopal authority along with the whole sacramental, doctrinal and disciplinary system of the Catholic church. He held that the Bible alone was finally authoritative and normative for Christian belief and practice. This inevitably led to his excommunication, but with the support of some of the German princes he maintained his position and secured a large following. His later association with these same German princes in their ruthless suppression of the peasant revolt is one of the most controversial aspects of his altogether controversial life.

The theological issues which divided Luther from co-reformers such as Bucer, Zwingli and Calvin cannot be fairly expounded here. Though he never met Calvin, he had more sympathy with his position than that of any of the others.

The humanist exponents of the 'new learning' were initially close tactical allies of the Reformation movement. But as Luther's doctrine took more positive shape, Erasmus, the most distinguished of the humanists, became critical. This criticism was expressed in *De Libero Arbitrio* (*On the Freedom of the Will*) (1524), which attacked what he took to be the philosophical and ethical implications of Luther's thoroughgoing doctrine of justification by faith alone. Luther replied in *De Servo Arbitrio* (*On the Bondage of the Will*) (1525), showing the rigorous self-consistency and biblical fidelity of his own position. It is part of this work that is reproduced below in the translation of J. I. Packer and O. R. Johnston (James Clarke, London, 1957).

Until very recently surprisingly little of Luther's massive literary output had been translated into English. This situation is now being put right, however. Three useful volumes in the Library of Christian Classics are: Vol. XV, *Luther, Lectures on Romans*, ed. Wilhelm Pauk (S.C.M. 1961); Vol. XVI, *Luther: Early Theological Works*, ed. T. F. Torrance (S.C.M. 1962); Vol. XVIII, *Luther: Letters of Spiritual Counsel*, ed. T. G. Tappert (S.C.M. 1955). There is also an exhaustive English edition of his complete *Works* (55 vols.) at present being produced in U.S.A. (Concordia, Muhlenburg Press, 1958 *et. seq.*).

THE ENSLAVED WILL

The outline of Christianity which you [Erasmus] have drawn up contains, among other things, this: 'We should strive with all our might, resort to the healing balm of penitence, and try by all means to compass the mercy of God, without which man's will and endeavour is ineffective.' And this: 'Nobody should despair of pardon from a God who by nature is kindness itself.' These Christ-less, Spirit-less words of yours are chillier than very ice; indeed, they spoil the beauty of your eloquence. Perhaps they are reluctant admissions dragged out of you (poor fellow) by fear of a tyrannical hierarchy, lest you should seem an utter atheist! Anyway, this is what your words assert: that there is strength within us; there is such a thing as striving with all one's strength; there is mercy in God; there are ways of compassing that mercy; there is a God who is by nature just, and kindness itself; and so on. But if one does not know what this 'strength' is—what men can do, and what is done to them—what this 'striving' is, what is the extent and limit of its effectiveness—then what should he do? What will you tell him to do? Let us see.

'It is irreligious, idle and superfluous', you say, 'to want to know whether our will effects anything in matters pertaining to eternal salvation, or whether it is wholly passive under the work of grace.' But here you speak to the contrary, saying that Christian piety consists in 'striving with all our might', and that 'apart from the mercy of God our will is ineffective'. Here you plainly assert that the will is in some respect active in matters pertaining to eternal salvation, for you represent it as striving; and, again, you represent it as the object of Divine action when you say that without God's mercy it is ineffective. But you do not define the limits within which we should think of the will as acting and as acted upon; you take pains to engender ignorance as to what God's mercy and man's will *can* effect by your very teaching as to what man's will and God's mercy *do* effect! Thus that caution of yours sends you round in circles; it has made you resolve to side with neither party, to emerge from between Scylla and Charybdis unscathed—so that if the waves in the open sea upset and overwhelm you, you can then assert all that you now deny, and deny all that you now assert!

I will set your theology before your eyes by a few analogies. Suppose a would-be poet or speech-maker never thought to ask what ability he had, what he could and could not do, and what the subject he was tackling demanded of him—never considered Horace's adage about 'What the shoulders can sustain, and what they will not bear'—but went straight to work, thinking: 'I must strive to get it done; it is *idle* and *superfluous* to ask whether I have enough learning and eloquence and ability'—what would you think of him? And if someone who wanted a rich crop from his land was not *idle* enough to perform the *superfluous* task of investigating the nature of the soil (as Virgil in the Georgics so *idly* and *pointlessly* advises), but rushed precipitately into action, thinking of nothing but the work, and ploughed the seashore and cast his seed wherever there was room, whether in the sand or in the mud—what would you think of him? And what if a man who purposed war, and wanted a glorious victory, or carried responsibility for some other piece of public service, was not so *idle* as to reflect upon what was in his power, whether the treasury could finance him, whether the soldiers were fit, whether there was opportunity for action; but disregarded the historian's advice ('Before acting, deliberate, and when you have deliberated, act speedily.'), and charged ahead with eyes shut and ears stopped, shouting nothing but 'War! War!'—pressing on with the work? Tell me, Erasmus, what would you think of such poets, farmers, generals and statesmen? I will add a text from the Gospel: 'If anyone, intending to build a tower, does not first sit down and count the cost, whether he has sufficient to finish it'—well, what is Christ's judgment on that man? (cf. *Luke* 14. 28).

In just this way, you prescribe for us nothing but things to do, and yet you forbid us to examine, measure and take knowledge of the limits of our ability, as if this were an idle, superfluous and irreligious enquiry. In this, for all that horror of imprudence and that ostentatious sobriety to which your vast caution prompts you, we find you teaching imprudence at its worst. The Sophists are fools and madmen, in fact, to pursue their idle enquiries; yet they sin less than you, who actually instruct men to cultivate madness and give themselves over to folly. And your madness is greater still, in that you assure us that this folly is the loveliest Christian piety, gravity, serious godliness—and salvation! And if we do not do as you tell us, you *assert* (you, the sworn foe of assertions!) that we are irreligious, idle and empty!—and thus you admirably dodge Scylla and escape Charybdis too! Confidence in your own ability drives you along here; you think that by your eloquence you can so dupe the public that nobody will realize what you cherish in your heart and what you are trying to achieve by these slippery writings of yours. But God is not mocked, and it is not good policy to run against him!

Furthermore: were it with reference to writing poetry, or preparing for harvest, or military or public service, or building houses, that you taught us such folly, it would still be outrageous, particularly in so great a man as yourself, yet it could have been forgiven you—at any rate, by Christians, who pay no regard to these temporal things. But when you tell Christian people to let this folly guide them in their labours, and charge them that in their pursuit of eternal salvation they should not concern themselves to know what is in their power and what is not—why, this is plainly the sin that is really unpardonable. For as long as they do not know the limits of their ability, they will not know what they should do; and as long as they do not know what they should do, they cannot repent when they err; and impenitence is the unpardonable sin. This is where your moderate, sceptical theology leads us!

So it is not irreligious, idle, or superfluous, but in the highest degree wholesome and necessary, for a Christian to know whether or not his will has anything to do in matters pertaining to salvation. Indeed, let me tell you, this is the hinge on which our discussion turns, the crucial issue between us; our aim is, simply, to investigate what ability 'free-will' has, in what respect it is the subject of Divine action and how it stands related to the grace of God. If we know nothing of these things, we shall know nothing whatsoever of Christianity, and shall be in worse case than any people on earth! He who dissents from that statement should acknowledge that he is no Christian; and he who ridicules or derides it should realize that he is the Christian's chief foe. For if I am ignorant of the nature, extent and limits of what I can and must do with reference to God, I shall be equally ignorant and uncertain of the nature, extent and limits of what God can and will do in me—though God, in fact, works all in all (cf. I *Corinthians* 12. 6). Now, if I am ignorant of God's works and power, I am ignorant of God himself; and if I do not know God, I cannot worship, praise, give thanks or serve him, for I do not know how much I should attribute to myself and how much to him. We need, therefore, to have in mind a clear-cut distinction between God's power and ours, and God's work and ours, if we would live a godly life.

So, you see, this point is a further item in any complete summary of Christianity. Self-knowledge, and the knowledge and glory of God, are bound up with it, which means, my dear Erasmus, that it is simply intolerable of you to call the knowledge of it irreligious, idle, and vain. Your claims upon us are many, but the fear of God claims of us everything. Indeed, you yourself see that all good in us is to be ascribed to God, and assert as much in your outline of Christianity; and this assertion certainly involves a second, namely, that God's mercy alone works everything, and our will works nothing, but is rather the object of Divine working, else all will not be ascribed to God. And yet a little further on you deny that it is religious, godly, or wholesome, to assert or know these things! But an inconsistent thinker, unsure and inexperienced in the things of God, cannot help talking in this fashion.

Of the necessitating foreknowledge of God

Another item in the summary of Christianity is knowing whether God foresees anything contingently, or whether we do all things of necessity. This knowledge also you represent as something irreligious, idle, and vain, just as all the ungodly do—indeed, the devils and the damned also represent it as hateful and abhorrent! You are wise to keep clear of such questions as far as you can; but you are a very poor rhetorician and theologian if you venture to open your mouth and instruct us about 'free-will' without any reference to these matters. I will act as your whetstone; though I am no rhetorician myself, I will dare to tell an excellent rhetorician his business. Suppose that Quintilian, having chosen to write on Oratory, were to say, 'In my judgment, all that superfluous nonsense about invention, arrangement, elocution, memory and pronunciation, should be left out; it is enough to know that Oratory is the ability to speak well'—would you not laugh at such an author? Yet, in just the same way, you first choose to write on 'free-will' and then exclude from consideration the entire substance and all the constituent parts of the topic you are going to write about! For you cannot know what 'free-will' is without knowing what ability man's will has, and what God does, and whether He foreknows of necessity.

Surely your rhetoricians teach that he who would speak about a subject should first say whether it exists, then what it is, what its parts are, what is contrary to it, allied to it, like it, and so on? But you deprive poor 'free-will' of all these advantages, and settle no single question relating to it save the first, i.e. whether it exists (and we shall see how worthless your arguments on *that* point are)—so that a more incompetent book on 'free-will' (apart from the elegance of its language) I never saw! In fact, the Sophists argue on this subject better than you, innocent though they are of rhetorical skill; for, when they tackle 'free-will', they do try to settle all the questions concerning it (whether it exists, what it is, what it does, how it exists, etc.)—even though they too fail to achieve their object. In this book of mine, therefore, I shall harry you and all the Sophists till you tell me exactly what 'free-will' can and does do; and I hope so to harry you (Christ helping me) as to make you repent of ever publishing your Diatribe.

It is, then, fundamentally necessary and wholesome for Christians to know that God foreknows nothing contingently, but that he foresees, purposes, and does all things according to his own immutable, eternal and infallible will. This bombshell knocks 'free-will' flat, and utterly shatters it; so that those who want to assert it must either deny my bombshell, or pretend not to notice it, or find some other way of dodging it. Before I establish this point by my own arguments and Scriptural authority, I shall first state it with the aid of *your* words.

Surely it was you, my good Erasmus, who a moment ago asserted that God is by nature just, and kindness itself? If this is true, does it not follow that he is *immutably* just and kind? that, as his nature remains unchanged to all eternity, so do his justice and kindness? And what is said of his justice and kindness must be said also of his knowledge, his wisdom, his goodness, his will, and other Divine attributes. But if it is religious, godly and wholesome, to affirm these things of God, as you do, what has come over you, that now you should contradict yourself by affirming that it is irreligious, idle and vain to say that God foreknows by necessity? You insist that we should learn the immutability of God's will, while forbidding us to know the immutability of his foreknowledge! Do you suppose that he does not will what he foreknows, or that he does not foreknow what he wills? If he wills what he foreknows, his will is eternal and changeless, because his nature is so. From which it follows, by resistless logic, that all we do, however it may appear to us to be done mutably and contingently, is in reality done necessarily and immutably in respect of God's will. For the will of God is effective and cannot be impeded, since power belongs to God's nature; and his wisdom is such that he cannot be deceived. Since, then, his will is not impeded, what is done cannot but be done where, when, how, as far as, and by whom, he foresees and wills. If the will of God were such that, when the work had been done and while it yet remained in being, the will ceased (as is the case with the will of a man, who, when he has built, say, the house he wants, ceases to will just as really as he does in death), then it could truly be said that things happen contingently and mutably. But the contrary is in fact true: the work ceases to be and the will remains in being—so far beyond the bounds of possibility is it that the production and continued existence of anything can be contingent. Lest we be deceived over our terms, let me explain that *being done contingently* does not, in Latin, signify that the thing done is itself contingent, but that it is done by a contingent and mutable will—such as is *not* to be found in God! And a deed cannot be called *contingent* unless we do it 'contingently', i.e. by chance (as it were) and without premeditation; that is, when our will or hand fastens on something presented to us as if by chance, without our having previously thought or planned anything about it.

I could wish, indeed, that a better term was available for our discussion than the accepted one, *necessity*, which cannot accurately be used of either man's will or God's. Its meaning is too harsh, and foreign to the subject; for it suggests some sort of compulsion, and something that is against one's will, which is no part of the view under debate. The will, whether it be God's or man's, does what it does, good or bad, under no compulsion, but just as it wants or pleases, as if totally free. Yet the will of God, which rules over our mutable will, is changeless and sure—as Boetius sings, 'Immovable Thyself, Thou movement giv'st to all'; and our will, principally because of its corruption, can do no good of itself. The reader's understanding, therefore, must supply what the word itself fails to convey, from his knowledge of the intended signification—the immutable will of God on the one hand, and the impotence of our corrupt will on the other. Some have called it *necessity of immutability*, but the phrase is both grammatically and theologically defective.

This is a point over which the Sophists have toiled for many years now (and have been defeated at last, and forced to give in): they maintained that *all things take place necessarily, but by necessity of consequence* (as they put it) *and not by necessity of the thing consequent*. By this distinction they eluded the force of their own admission—or, rather, *de*luded themselves! I shall not find it hard to show how unreal the distinction is. By *necessity of consequence*, they mean, roughly speaking, this: If God wills something, then it must needs be; but that which thus comes to be is something which of itself need not be; for only God exists necessarily, and everything else can cease to be, if God so wills. This is to say that God's action is necessary, if He wills it, but the thing done is not in itself necessary. But what do they establish by this play on words? This, I suppose—the thing done is not necessary; that is, it has no necessity in its own essential nature: which is just to say, that the thing done is not God Himself! Nonetheless, it remains true that each thing *does* happen necessarily, if God's action is necessary or there is a necessity of consequence, however true it may be that it does *not* happen necessarily, in the sense that it is not God and has no necessity of its own essential nature. If I come to exist of necessity, it does not much worry me that my existence and being are in themselves mutable; contingent and mutable as I am (and I am not God, the necessary Being), yet I still come to exist!

So their absurd formula, *all things take place by necessity of consequence, but not by necessity of the thing consequent*, amounts merely to this: everything takes place by necessity, but the things that take place are not God himself. But what need was there to tell us that?—as though there were any fear of our claiming that things which happen are God, or possess a divine and necessarily existent nature! So our original proposition still stands and remains unshaken: all things take place by necessity. There is no obscurity or ambiguity about it. In Isaiah, it says 'My counsel shall stand, and my will shall be done' (46. 10); and any schoolboy knows the meaning of 'counsel', 'will', 'shall be done', 'shall stand'!

And why should these matters be thought so recondite for us Christians that it is irreligious, idle, and vain to study and know them, when they are on the lips of heathen poets and ordinary people so frequently? How often does Vergil, for one, mention Fate? 'All things stand fixed by law immutable.' Again, 'Fixed is the day of every man'. Again, 'If the Fates summon you'. Again, 'If thou shalt break the binding cord of Fate'.[1] The poet simply seeks to show that in the destruction of Troy and the beginning of the Roman empire Fate did more than all the efforts of men. Indeed, he makes even his immortal gods subject to fate. Jupiter and Juno themselves needs must yield to it. Hence the poets represented the three Fates as immutable, implacable and irrevocable in their decrees. Those wise men knew, what experience of life proves, that no man's purposes ever go forward as planned, but events overtake all men contrary to their expectation. 'Could Troy have stood by human arm, it should have stood by mine', says Vergil's Hector.[2] Hence that commonest of all remarks, which is on everyone's lips—'God's will be done'; and 'If God will, we will do it'; and: 'God so willed', 'such was the will of those above'. 'Such was your will', says Vergil. Whence we see that the knowledge of predestination and of God's prescience has been left in the world no less certainly than the notion of the Godhead itself. But those who wished to seem wise argued themselves out of it till their hearts grew dark and they became fools, as *Romans* 1 says (vv. 21–2),

[1] Vergil, *Aeneid*, 2. 324, 6. 883, 7. 314, 10. 465.

[2] *Aeneid*, 2. 291 f.

and denied, or pretended not to know, things which the poets, and the common people, and even their own consciences held as being most familiar, most certain, and most true.

Of the importance of knowing that God necessitates all things

I would also point out, not only how true these things are (I shall discuss that more fully from Scripture on a later page), but also how godly, reverent and necessary it is to know them. For where they are not known, there can be no faith, nor any worship of God. To lack this knowledge is really to be ignorant of God—and salvation is notoriously incompatible with such ignorance. For if you hesitate to believe, or are too proud to acknowledge, that God foreknows and wills all things, not contingently, but necessarily and immutably, how can you believe, trust and rely on his promises? When he makes promises, you ought to be out of doubt that he knows, and can and will perform, what he promises; otherwise, you will be accounting him neither true nor faithful, which is unbelief, and the height of irreverence, and a denial of the most high God! And how can you be thus sure and certain, unless you know that certainly, infallibly, immutably and necessarily, he knows, wills and will perform what he promises? Not only should we be sure that God wills, and will execute his will, necessarily and immutably; we should glory in the fact, as Paul does in *Romans* 3—'Let God be true, but every man a liar' (v. 4), and again, 'Not that the word of God has failed' (*Romans* 9. 6), and in another place, 'The foundation of God standeth sure, having his seal, the Lord knoweth them that are his' (II *Timothy* 2. 19). In *Titus* 1 he says: 'Which God, that cannot lie, promised before the world began' (v. 2). And *Hebrew* 11 says: 'He that cometh, must believe that God is, and that he is a rewarder of them that hope in him' (v. 6).

If, then, we are taught and believe that we ought to be ignorant of the necessary foreknowledge of God and the necessity of events, Christian faith is utterly destroyed, and the promises of God and the whole gospel fall to the ground completely; for the Christian's chief and only comfort in every adversity lies in knowing that God does not lie, but brings all things to pass immutably, and that his will cannot be resisted, altered or impeded.

Observe now, my good Erasmus, where that cautious, peace-loving theology of yours leads us! You call us back, and prohibit our endeavours to learn about God's foreknowledge and the necessity which lies on men and things, and advise us to leave behind, and avoid, and look down on such enquiries; and in so doing you teach us your own ill-advised principles—that we should seek after ignorance of God (which comes to us without our seeking, and indeed is born in us), and so should spurn faith, abandon God's promises, and discount all the consolations of the Spirit and convictions of our consciences. Epicurus himself would hardly give such advice! Moreover, not content with this, you call those who are concerned to acquire the knowledge in question godless, idle and empty, and those who care nothing for it you call godly, pious and sober. What do you imply by these words, but that Christians are idle, empty and godless fellows? and that Christianity is a trivial, empty, stupid and downright godless thing? So here again, in your desire to discourage us from anything rash, you allow yourself to be carried to the contrary extreme (as fools do) and teach the very quintessence of godless, suicidal folly. Do you see, now, that at this point your book is so godless, blasphemous and sacrilegious, that its like cannot be found anywhere? (pp. 75–85) . . .

Of the alleged disadvantages of proclaiming that God necessitates all things

In the last part of your Preface, where you earnestly dissuade us from our kind of doctrine, you think victory is almost won. 'What' (you say) 'can be more useless than to publish to the world the paradox that all we do is done, not by "free-will", but of mere necessity, and Augustine's view that God works in us both good and evil; that he rewards his own good works in us, and punishes his own evil works in us?' (You are copious here in giving reasons, or, rather, in demanding that we give them.) 'What a flood-gate of iniquity' (you say) 'would the spread of such news open to people! What wicked man would amend his life? Who would believe that God loved him? Who would fight against his flesh?' (I wonder that in this furious outburst you did not remember the matter in hand, and say: 'where then will free-will be found?' !)

My good Erasmus! I reply as before. If you think these paradoxes are inventions of men, why do you oppose them? why get so heated? against whom are you speaking? Is there any man in the world today who has attacked the doctrines of men more strongly than Luther? Your lecture is wasted on me! If, however, you believe these paradoxes to be words of God, then where is your conscience, where is your shame, where is, I will not say your famous moderation, but the fear and reverence which you owe to the true God?—for what you are saying is that there is no information more useless than God's Word! So your Creator must learn from you, his creature, what may usefully be preached and what not? God was stupid and thoughtless, was he, that he did not know what should be taught till you came along to tell him how to be wise, and what to command?—as if without your pointing it out he would not have realized that this paradox involves the consequence you draw? No; if God has willed that these things should be openly proclaimed and published, who are you to forbid it? The apostle Paul, in his epistle to the Romans, frankly discusses these very matters, not in a corner, but openly, publicly, before the whole world, and in harsher terms than those you quote. 'Whom he will he hardeneth', he says; and again, 'God, willing to show forth his wrath', etc. (*Romans* 9. 18, 22). What is harder (to the flesh, at any rate) than Christ's saying, 'Many are called, but few chosen'? (*Matthew* 22. 14). And again, 'I know whom I have chosen'? (*John* 13. 18). On your view, of course, there is no information more useless than all this—your reason being, presumably, that it might drive the ungodly to despair, hatred and blasphemy!

Here, I see, you are taking the view that the truth and usefulness of Scripture should be measured and decided according to the feeling of men—to be precise, of the ungodliest of men; so that nothing henceforth will be true, Divine and wholesome but what these persons find pleasing and acceptable; and what is not so will at once become useless, untrue and harmful. What else do you here plead for, but that the words of God may thus depend on, and stand or fall by, the will and authority of men? But Scripture says the opposite, that all things stand or fall by the will and authority of God, and that all the earth keeps silence before the face of the Lord (cf. *Habakkuk* 2. 20). One who talks as you do must imagine that the living God is no more than a wild inconsequent ranter shouting from a soap-box,[1] whose words you may interpret, receive or refute as you please, according to their observed effect on the ungodly. Here you make plain, my dear Erasmus, just how little sincerity lay behind your advice, given earlier, that we should revere the majesty of the judgments of God. Then, dealing with the doctrines of Scripture (where there is no need to revere hidden mysteries, since no doctrines in fact are such), you warned us in the most pious language against any inquisitive invasion of the Corycian caverns, and well-nigh frightened us off reading the Bible altogether—though Bible-reading is something to which Christ and the apostles urgently exhort us, as elsewhere you do yourself. But now that we have actually come, not just to the doctrines of Scripture or the Corycian cavern, but to the awful secret of God's Majesty—that is, as was said, the question, why does he work as he does—here you break down the barriers and burst in, all but blaspheming! What indignation against God do you not display, because you may not see the reason and design of his counsel! Why do you not invoke obscurities and ambiguities here? Why do you not restrain yourself, and discourage others, from prying into matters which God wills to keep hidden from us, and has not made known in the Scriptures? Here we should lay our hand on our mouth; here we should revere what lies concealed, and adore the secret decrees of the Divine Majesty, and cry

[1] *levem et imprudentem rabulam in aliquo suggesto declamantem.*

with Paul: 'Who art thou, O man, that contendest with God?' (*Romans* 9. 20).

'Who' (you say) 'will try and reform his life?' I reply, Nobody! Nobody can! God has no time for your practitioners of self-reformation, for they are hypocrites. The elect, who fear God, will be reformed by the Holy Spirit; the rest will perish unreformed. Note that Augustine does not say that a reward awaits *nobody's* works, or *everybody's* works, but *some men's* works. So there will be some who reform their lives.

'Who will believe' (you say) 'that God loves him?' I reply, Nobody! Nobody can! But the elect shall believe it; and the rest shall perish without believing it, raging and blaspheming, as you describe them. So there will be some who believe it.

You say that a flood-gate of iniquity is opened by our doctrines. So be it. Ungodly men are part of that evil leprosy aforementioned, which we must endure. Nevertheless, these are the very doctrines which throw open to the elect, who fear God, a gateway to righteousness, an entrance into heaven, and a road to God! (pp. 97–99) . . .

Of the spontaneity of necessitated acts

As for the other paradox, 'all we do is done, not by free-will, but of mere necessity'—let us take a brief look at it, for we must not let such a mischievous remark go unchallenged. My comment is simply this: if it be proved that our salvation is not of our own strength or counsel, but depends on the working of God alone (which is something I hope to demonstrate later in the main discussion), does it not clearly follow that when God is not present to work in us, all is evil, and of necessity we act in a way that contributes nothing towards our salvation? For if it is not we, but God alone, who works salvation in us, it follows that willy-nilly, nothing we do has any saving significance prior to his working in us.

I said 'of necessity'; I did not say 'of compulsion'; I meant, by a necessity not of *compulsion*, but of what they call *immutability*. That is to say: a man without the Spirit of God does not do evil against his will, under pressure, as though he were taken by the scruff of the neck and dragged into it, like a thief or footpad being dragged off against his will to punishment; but he does it spontaneously and voluntarily. And this willingness or volition is something which he cannot in his own strength eliminate, restrain or alter. He goes on willing and desiring to do evil; and if external pressure forces him to act otherwise, nevertheless his will within remains averse to so doing and chafes under such constraint and opposition. But it would not thus chafe were it being changed, and were it yielding to constraint willingly. This is what we mean by *necessity of immut-*

ability: that the will cannot change itself, nor give itself another bent, but, rather, is the more provoked to crave the more it is opposed, as its chafing proves; for this would not occur, were it free or had 'free-will'. Ask experience how impervious to dissuasion are those those hearts are set on anything! If they abandon their quest of it, they only do so under pressure, or because of some counter-attraction, never freely—whereas, when their hearts are not thus engaged, they spare their labour, and let events take their course.

On the other hand: when God works in us, the will is changed under the sweet influence of the Spirit of God. Once more it desires and acts, not of compulsion, but of its own desire and spontaneous inclination. Its bent still cannot be altered by any opposition; it cannot be mastered or prevailed upon even by the gates of hell; but it goes on willing, desiring and loving good, just as once it willed, desired and loved evil. Experience proves this too. How firm and invincible are holy men, who, when forcibly constrained to sin, are the more provoked thereby to desire good—even as flames are fanned, rather than quenched, by the wind. Here, too, there is no freedom, no 'free-will', to turn elsewhere, or to desire anything else, as long as the Spirit and grace of God remain in a man.

In a word: if we are under the God of this world, strangers to the work of God's Spirit, we are led captive by him at his will, as Paul said to Timothy (II *Timothy* 2. 26), so that we cannot will anything but what he wills. For he is a 'strong man armed', who keeps his palace to such good effect that those he holds are at peace, and raise no stir or feeling against him—otherwise, Satan's kingdom would be divided against itself, and could not stand; but Christ says it does stand. And we acquiesce in his rule willingly and readily, according to the nature of willingness, which, if constrained, is not 'willingness'; for constraint means rather, as one would say, 'unwillingness'. But if a stronger appears, and overcomes Satan, we are once more servants and captives, but now desiring and willingly doing what *He* wills—which is royal freedom (cf. *Luke* 11.18–22).

So man's will is like a beast standing between two riders. If God rides, it wills and goes where God wills: as the Psalm says, 'I am become as a beast before thee, and I am ever with thee' (*Psalm* 73. 22–3). If Satan rides, it wills and goes where Satan wills. Nor may it choose to which rider it will run, or which it will seek; but the riders themselves fight to decide who shall have and hold it. (pp. 102–4) . . .

Romans 4. 2–3*: the total irrelevance of works to man's righteousness before God*

Let us cite the example that Paul goes on to cite, that of Abraham. He says: 'If Abraham were justified by works he hath whereof to glory;

but not before God. For what saith the Scripture? Abraham believed God, and it was reckoned unto him for righteousness' (*Romans* 4. 2–3). Here, too, please take note of Paul's distinction as he recounts Abraham's twofold righteousness. The one is of works; that is, moral and civil. But Paul says that this did not justify Abraham in the sight of God, even though it made him righteous in the eyes of men. He has glory before men by reason of that righteousness, but is yet without the glory of God. None can say that it is the works of the law, or ceremonial works, that are here condemned, for Abraham lived many years before the law. Paul simply speaks of Abraham's works, and those his best works; for it would be absurd to argue as to whether a man is justified by evil works. If, now, Abraham is righteous by none of his works, so that, unless he puts on another righteousness (that of faith), both he and all his works are left under the power of ungodliness, it is apparent that no man can make any advance towards righteousness by his works; and it is further apparent that no works, efforts or endeavours of 'free-will' are of any avail in God's sight, but that they are all adjudged ungodly, unrighteous, and evil. For if a man himself is not righteous, neither are his works and endeavours righteous; and if they are not righteous, they merit damnation and wrath.

The other righteousness is that of faith, and consists, not in any works, but in the gracious favour and reckoning of God. See how Paul stresses the word 'reckoned'; how he insists on it, and repeats it, and enforces it. 'To him that worketh', he says, 'the reward is *reckoned*, not of grace, but of debt. But to him that worketh not, but believeth on him that justifieth the ungodly, his faith is *reckoned* for righteousness', according to the purpose of God's grace. Then he quotes David as saying the same about the reckoning of grace. 'Blessed is the man to whom the Lord has not imputed sin', etc. (vv. 4 ff.). He repeats the word 'reckon' in this chapter about ten times.

In short, Paul sets 'him that worketh' and 'him that worketh not' side by side, and leaves none in the middle between them. He declares that righteousness is not reckoned to him that worketh, but is reckoned to him that worketh not, if only be believes. There is no way by which 'free-will', with its effort and endeavour, can dodge or escape; it must either be numbered with 'him that worketh', or with 'him that worketh not'. If with 'him that worketh', you have heard Paul say that righteousness is not reckoned to it. If with 'him that worketh not, but believeth' on God, righteousness is reckoned to it. But then it will not be the power of 'free-will', but a new creation by faith. And if righteousness is not reckoned to 'him that worketh', it becomes clear that his works are nothing but sins, evil and ungodly in God's sight.

No impudent Sophist can here object that, though man be evil, yet his work need not be evil. For Paul specifies not 'man' simply, but 'him that worketh', his intention being to declare in the plainest words that man's actual works and efforts are condemned, whatever they are and by whatever name or appearance they go. It is of good works that he speaks, for he is arguing about justification and merit. And when he speaks of 'him that worketh', he speaks comprehensively of all who work and of all the works that they do, but especially of their good and upright works. Otherwise, his distinction between 'him that worketh' and 'him that worketh not' would not hold water.

Of other arguments against 'free-will', not here developed

I here pass by arguments of great strength drawn from the purpose of grace, from the promise, from the power of the law, from original sin, and from God's election; every one of which by itself could utterly overthrow 'free-will', thus:

If the source of grace is the predestinating purpose of God, then it comes by necessity, and not by any effort or endeavour on our part, as I showed above.

Again: If God promised grace before the law, as Paul argues here and in Galatians, then it does not come by works or by law, else the promise would come to nothing; and faith also (by which Abraham was justified before the law was given) would come to nothing, should works avail.

Again: since the law is the strength of sin, displaying it without removing it, it makes the conscience guilty before God and threatens wrath. This is Paul's meaning when he says: 'the law worketh wrath' (*Romans* 4. 15). How then could righteousness be procured by the law? And if we get no help from the law, how can we get help from the power of our will alone?

Again: since by the single offence of the one man, Adam, we all lie under sin and condemnation, how can we set our hand to anything that is not sinful and damnable? When he says 'all', he excepts none; not the power of 'free-will', nor any worker, whether he works and endeavours or not; he is of necessity included with the rest among the 'all'. Neither should we sin or be condemned by reason of the single offence of Adam, if that offence were not our own; who could be condemned for another's offence, especially in the sight of God? But his offence becomes ours; not by imitation, nor by any act on our part (for then it would not be the single offence of Adam, since we should have committed it, not he), but it becomes ours by birth. (We must, however, discuss this elsewhere.) Original sin itself, then, does not allow 'free-will' any power at all except to sin and incur condemnation.

These arguments, I repeat, I pass by; both because they are so very plain and powerful, and also because I have said something of them above. If, indeed, I wanted to review all the passages in Paul alone that overthrow 'free-will', I could do nothing better than give a running commentary on his entire writings, showing that the boasted power of 'free-will' is refuted by almost every word—as I have done already in the case of these third and fourth chapters of Romans. I chose to deal with them particularly, because I wanted to show up the sleepy-headedness of all those friends of ours who read Paul in such a fashion that the last things they see in these perfectly plain passages are the mighty arguments against 'free-will' to which I have referred; and I wished also to expose the folly of their confidence in the authority and writings of the ancient doctors, and to leave them to think over what force the aforementioned clear arguments would have, if handled with care and judgment.

Of Paul's cogency against 'free-will'

Speaking for myself, I am astounded that, when Paul so often uses these comprehensive terms, 'all', 'none', 'not', 'never', 'without', as in 'they are *all* gone out of the way, there is *none* righteous, *none* that doeth good, no, not one'; '*all* are sinners condemned by the offence of one'; 'we are justified by faith *without* the law, *without* works' (so that he who would alter Paul's language could not thereby increase the clarity and plainness of his speech)—I am amazed, I repeat, how it has happened that in face of these comprehensive terms and statements, others that are contrary, yes, contradictory to them should have won acceptance, such as: 'Some are not gone out of the way, are not unrighteous, are not evil, are not sinners, are not condemned; there is something in man that is good and strives after good'; as though he who strives after good, whoever he may be, is not covered by the terms: 'all', 'none', and 'not'! Personally, I could find nothing, even if I wished, to advance in reply against Paul, but would be forced to include the power of my own 'free-will', and its endeavour with it, among the 'all' and 'none' of which Paul speaks—unless we are to introduce a new grammar, and a new mode of speech! Had Paul used such an expression once, or in one place only, it might have been permissible to suspect a figure of speech and to isolate and strain the words. But as it is, he uses such expressions constantly, in both affirmative and negative sentences, and everywhere expresses his views by categorical statement and comprehensive contrast; so that not only the natural force of words and the actual flow of speech, but also that which comes before and after, the whole surrounding context, and the scope and contents of his entire argument, unite to prove what his meaning is: Paul intends to say that apart from faith in Christ there is nothing but sin and condemnation.

I promised to refute 'free-will' in such a way that none of my opponents would be able to resist, and this, I think, I have done; even if they will not own themselves beaten and come over to my view, or be silent. That, after all, it is not in my power to bring about; it is the gift of the Spirit of God.

Romans 8. 5: *the state of man without the Spirit*

Before we hear the evangelist John, let me add a crowning testimony from Paul (and if this does not suffice, I am ready to marshal the whole of Paul against 'free-will' by means of a running commentary on all he wrote!) In *Romans* 8, dividing the human race into two, 'flesh' and 'spirit', as Christ does in *John* 3 (v. 6), he says: 'They that are after the flesh do mind the things of the flesh, but they that are after the Spirit do mind the things of the Spirit' (v. 5). That Paul here calls all 'carnal' that are not 'spiritual' is plain, both from the opposition of 'spirit' and 'flesh' in the division itself, and from Paul's own next words: 'But ye are not in the flesh, but in the Spirit, if so be that the Spirit of God dwell in you. Now if any man have not the Spirit of Christ, he is none of his' (v. 9). What is the meaning of: 'Ye are not in the flesh, if the Spirit is in you', but those who have not the Spirit are of necessity in the flesh? And he that is not Christ's, whose else is he but Satan's? It stands good then, that those who lack the Spirit are in the flesh, and under Satan.

Now let us see that Paul thinks about endeavour and the power of 'free-will' in carnal men. 'They that are in the flesh cannot please God.' Again: 'The carnal mind is death.' Again: 'The carnal mind is enmity against God.' Once more: 'It is not subject to the law of God, neither indeed can be' (vv. 5–8). How can endeavours towards good be made by that which is death, and displeases God, and is enmity against God, and disobeys God, and cannot obey him? Paul did not mean to say that the carnal mind is *dead*, and *at enmity* with God, but that it is *death itself* and *enmity itself*, which cannot possibly be subject to the law of God or please God; as he had said a little before ('For what the law *could not do*, in that it was weak through the flesh, God did', etc. (v. 3)).

I, too, know of Origen's fancy about the 'threefold affection', one called 'flesh', another 'soul', and the other 'spirit', the soul being in the middle between the other two, and able to turn either flesh-wards or spirit-wards. But these are just his own dreams; he retails them, but does not prove them. Paul here calls everything without the Spirit 'flesh', as I have shown. Therefore, the highest virtues of the best men are 'in the flesh'; that is, they are dead, and at enmity with God, not subject to God's law nor able to be so, and not pleasing God. Paul does not say merely that they are not subject, but that they cannot be subject. So also Christ says in *Matthew* 7: 'An evil tree cannot bring forth good fruit' (v. 18). And in *Matthew* 12: 'How can ye, being evil, speak that which is good?' (v. 34). Here you see that not only do we speak evil, but we cannot speak good. And though He says elsewhere that we, though evil, know how to give good things to our children (cf. *Matthew* 7. 11), yet he denies that we do good, even by our giving of good things, because the good things which we give are God's creatures, and we, being evil, cannot give those good things in good fashion. He addresses this word to all men, even to his own disciples. So that this pair of statements by Paul, that 'the righteous lives by faith' (*Romans* 1. 17), and that 'whatsoever is not of faith, is sin' (*Romans* 14. 23), stand confirmed. The latter follows from the former; for if it is only by faith that we are justified, it is evident that they who are without faith are not yet justified; and those who are not justified are sinners; and sinners are evil trees, and can only sin and bear evil fruit. Wherefore, 'free-will' is nothing but the slave of sin, death and Satan, not doing anything, nor able to do or attempt anything, but evil!

Romans 10. 20, 9. 30–31*: salvation by grace has no reference to previous endeavour*

Add to this the instance quoted in the tenth chapter of Romans from Isaiah: 'I was found of them that sought me not, I manifested myself to them that asked not after me' (v. 20; *Isaiah* 65. 1). Paul says this of the Gentiles—that it was given to them to hear and know Christ when previously they could not even think of him, much less seek him or prepare themselves for him by the power of 'free-will'. From this instance it is clear enough that grace comes so freely, that no thought of it, and certainly no endeavour or desire after it, precedes its coming. And take the case of Paul, when he was Saul—what did he do with all the power of his 'free-will'? Certainly, if his state of mind be regarded, his heart was set on what was best and highest. But look at the endeavour whereby he found grace! Not only did he not seek grace, but he received it through his own mad fury against it!

Of the Jews, on the other hand, Paul says in chapter 9: 'The Gentiles, which followed not after righteousness, have attained unto the righteousness which is by faith. But Israel, which followed after the law of righteousness, hath not attained unto the law of righteousness' (vv. 30–1). What word can any defender of 'free-will' breathe against this? The Gentiles, when filled with ungodliness and every vice, receive righteousness freely by the mercy of God; the Jews, who follow after righteousness with the greatest effort and endeavour, do so in vain. Is not this just to say that the endeavours of 'free-will' after the highest are vain, and that by them it rather grows worse and is carried away backwards? None can say that the Jews' efforts were not made with the highest power of 'free-will'. Paul himself bears record of them in the tenth chapter, that 'they have a zeal of God, but not according to knowledge' (v. 2). So nothing that is assigned to 'free-will' was lacking to the Jews; yet nothing resulted—indeed, the reverse of what they sought resulted! In the Gentiles, nothing that is assigned to 'free-will' was present; yet for them the righteousness of God resulted. What is this but proof positive, by the very clear example of the two nations and the very plain testimony of Paul, that grace is given freely to the undeserving and utterly unworthy, and is not attained by any of the efforts, endeavours, or works, small or great, of even the best and most upright men who seek and follow after righteousness with flaming zeal?

John 1. 5, 10–13, 16*: salvation for a sinful world is by the grace of Christ through faith alone*

Now let us come to John, who is also an eloquent and powerful scourge of 'free-will'.

Right at the outset, he assigns to 'free-will' such blindness that it does not even see the light of truth, so far it is from being able to strive after it. He says: 'The light shineth in darkness, but the darkness comprehendeth it not' (*John* 1. 5). And straight after: 'He was in the world, and the world knew him not; he came unto his own, and his own knew him not' (vv. 10–11). What do you think he means by 'world'? will you exempt any man from being so called, save him that is new created by the Holy Ghost? The use of this term, 'world', is characteristic of this Apostle; and by it he simply means, the whole human race. So whatever he says of the 'world' must be understood of 'free-will', as being the most excellent thing in man. According to this apostle, then, the 'world' does not know the light of truth; the 'world' hates Christ and his; the 'world' neither knows nor sees the Holy Spirit; the whole 'world' is set in wickedness; all that is in the 'world' is the lust of the flesh and of the eyes, and the pride of life. 'Love not the world.' 'Ye are of the world' says Christ; 'the world cannot hate you, but me it hateth, because I testify that its works are evil' (cf. *John* 15. 19, 14. 17; I *John* 5. 19, 2. 16, 2. 15; *John* 8. 23, 7. 7). All these and many similar passages are proclamations of what 'free-will' is—the principal part of the 'world', ruling under Satan's command! John himself speaks of the 'world' antithetically, so that the 'world' means whatever is not taken out of the world to be under the Spirit. Thus Christ says to his apostles: 'I have taken you out of the world, and set you', etc. (*John* 15. 19). If, now, there were any in the world who endeavoured after good by the power of 'free-will' (as there should be, if 'free-will' had any power), then, out of respect for them, John should have modified his statement, so as not, by generalizing, to implicate them in all the evil deeds with which he charges the world. But this he does not do: from which it is clear that he is making 'free-will' guilty of all that is charged against the world. And his reason is, that the world does all that it does by the power of 'free-will', that is, by will and reason, its own most excellent parts.

He goes on: 'But as many as received him, to them gave he power to become the sons of God, even to them that believe on his name: which were born, not of blood nor of the will of the flesh, nor of the will of man, but of God' (1. 12–13). By this exhaustive division he rejects from the kingdom of Christ 'blood', 'the will of the flesh', and 'the will of man'. 'Blood' means, I think, the Jews; that is, those who expected to be the children of the kingdom because they were the children of Abraham and the fathers, and so gloried in their 'blood'. 'The will of the flesh' I understand as the efforts which the people exerted in the works of the law; for 'flesh' here means carnal men without the Spirit, who were certainly possessed of will and endeavour, but who, because the Spirit was not in them, possessed them in a carnal manner only. 'The will of man' I understand in a general sense, of the efforts of all men, that is, the nations, or any man whatsoever, whether in the law or without the law. So the sense is: the sons of God became such, not by carnal birth, nor by zeal for the law, nor by any other human effort, but only by being born of God. Now, if they are not born of the flesh, nor trained by the law, nor prepared by any human discipline, but are born again of God, it is apparent that 'free-will' avails nothing here. 'Man', I think, is used in the Hebrew way, to mean 'any man', or 'all men', just as 'flesh' is used antithetically to mean 'people without the Spirit'. 'Will', I think, is used to denote the highest power in man—that is, the principal part, 'free-will'. But even supposing that I do not hit the precise meaning of the individual words, the substance of the matter is still perfectly plain—that John by this division is rejecting everything that is not 'born of God'; which, as he himself explains, is something that results from 'believing on his name'. 'The will of man', or 'free-will', which is neither new birth from God nor yet faith, is therefore necessarily included in this rejection. If 'free-will' could avail anything, John ought not to reject 'the will of man', nor should he draw men away from it and direct them to faith and new birth alone, lest the words of Isaiah 5 should be pronounced against him: 'Woe unto you that call good evil!' (v. 20). But as it is, seeing that he rejects alike 'blood', 'the will of the flesh', and 'the will of man', it is certain that the will of man is of no more avail to make men the sons of God than 'blood' or carnal birth. And none doubts that carnal birth does not make sons of God; for Paul says: 'They which are the children of the flesh, these are not the children of God' (*Romans* 9. 8), and proves it by the cases of Ishmael and Esau.

The same John introduces the Baptist speaking of Christ thus: 'And of his fulness have we all received, and grace for grace' (1. 16). He says that we receive grace out of the fullness of Christ—but for what merit or effort? 'For grace', he says; that is, the grace of Christ; as Paul says: 'The grace of God, and the gift of grace, which is by one man, Jesus Christ, hath abounded unto many' (*Romans* 5. 15). Where now is the endeavour of 'free-will' that secures grace? John is here saying, not only that grace is not received by any effort of our own, but that it comes by the grace of another, that is 'one man, Jesus Christ'. So, either it is false that we receive our grace for the grace of another, or else it is apparent that 'free-will' is nothing; for these two positions cannot stand together, that the grace of God is *both* so cheap that it may be gained anywhere and everywhere by a little endeavour on the part of any man, *and* so dear that it is given to us only in and through the grace of this one great man!

And I could wish that the guardians of 'free-will' would be taught by this passage to recognize that when they assert 'free-will' they are denying Christ. For if I obtain the grace of God by my own endeavour, what need have I of the grace of Christ for the receiving of my grace? When I have the grace of God, what do I need besides? The Diatribe said, and all the Sophists say, that we obtain the grace of God by our own endeavour, and are thereby made ready to receive it, not, indeed, as of *condignity*, but as of *congruity*.[1] This is plainly to deny Christ. It is for his grace, the Baptist says here, that we receive grace. Earlier on, I confuted their fabrication about 'condignity' and 'congruity' showing that these are empty words, but that what they really believe in is condign merit, and that their view involves greater impiety than that of the Pelagians; as I said. Thus it is that the ungodly Sophists, together with the Diatribe, deny the Lord Christ, who bought us, more than ever the Pelagians or any heretics did! So utterly does grace refuse to allow any particle or power of 'free-will' to stand beside it! (pp. 295–305) . . .

Of the comfort of knowing that salvation does not depend on 'free-will'

I frankly confess that, for myself, even if it could be, I should not want 'free-will' to be given me, nor anything to be left in my own hands to enable me to endeavour after salvation; not merely because in face of so many dangers, and adversities, and assaults of devils, I could not stand

[1] *licet non de condigno, sed de congruo.*

my ground and hold fast my 'free-will' (for one devil is stronger than all men, and on these terms no man could be saved); but because, even were there no dangers, adversities, or devils, I should still be forced to labour with no guarantee of success, and to beat my fists at the air. If I lived and worked to all eternity, my conscience would never reach comfortable certainty as to how much it must do to satisfy God. Whatever work I had done, there would still be a nagging doubt[1] as to whether it pleased God, or whether he required something more. The experience of all who seek righteousness by works proves that; and I learned it well enough myself over a period of many years, to my own great hurt. But now that God has taken my salvation out of the control of my own will, and put it under the control of his, and promised to save me, not according to my working or running, but according to his own grace and mercy, I have the comfortable certainty that he is faithful and will not lie to me, and that he is also great and powerful, so that no devils or opposition can break him or pluck me from him. 'No one', he says, 'shall pluck them out of my hand, because my Father which gave them me is greater than all' (*John* 10. 28–9). Thus it is that, if not all, yet some, indeed many, are saved; whereas, by the power of 'free-will' none at all could be saved, but every one of us would perish.

Furthermore, I have the comfortable certainty that I please God, not by reason of the merit of my works, but by reason of his merciful favour promised to me; so that, if I work too little, or badly, he does not impute it to me, but with fatherly compassion pardons me and makes me better. This is the glorying of all the saints in their God.

Of faith in the justice of God in his dealings with men

You may be worried that it is hard to defend the mercy and equity of God in damning the undeserving, that is, ungodly persons, who, being born in ungodliness, can by no means avoid being ungodly, and staying so, and being damned, but are compelled by natural necessity to sin and perish; as Paul says: 'We were all the children of wrath, even as others' (*Ephesians* 2. 3), created such by God himself from a seed that had been corrupted by the sin of the one man, Adam. But here God must be reverenced and held in awe, as being most merciful to those whom he justifies and saves in their own utter unworthiness; and we must show some measure of deference to his Divine wisdom by believing him just when to us he seems unjust. If his justice were such as could be adjudged just by human reckoning, it clearly would not be Divine; it would in no way differ from human justice. But inasmuch as he is the one true God, wholly incomprehensible and inaccessible to man's understanding,

[1] *scrupulus.*

it is reasonable, indeed inevitable, that his justice also should be incomprehensible; as Paul cries, saying: 'O the depth of the riches both of the wisdom and knowledge of God! How unsearchable are his judgments, and his ways past finding out! (*Romans* 11. 33). They would not, however, be 'unsearchable' if we could at every point grasp the grounds on which they are just. What is man compared with God? How much can our power achieve compared with his power? What is our strength compared with his strength? What is our knowledge compared with his wisdom? What is our substance compared with his substance? In a word, what is all that we are compared with all that he is? If, now, even nature teaches us to acknowledge that human power, strength, wisdom, knowledge and substance, and all that is ours, is as nothing compared with the Divine power, strength, wisdom, knowledge and substance, what perversity is it on our part to worry at the justice and the judgment of the only God, and to arrogate so much to our own judgment as to presume to comprehend, judge and evaluate God's judgment! Why do we not in like manner say at this point: 'Our judgment is nothing compared with God's judgment'? Ask reason whether force of conviction does not compel her to acknowledge herself foolish and rash for not allowing God's judgment to be incomprehensible, when she confesses that all the other things of God are incomprehensible! In everything else, we allow God his Divine Majesty; in the single case of his judgment, we are ready to deny it! To think that we cannot for a little while *believe* that he is just, when he has actually promised us that when he reveals his glory we shall all clearly *see* that he both was and is just!

I will give a parallel case, in order to strengthen our faith in God's justice, and to reassure that 'evil eye' which holds him under suspicion of injustice. Behold! God governs the external affairs of the world in such a way that, if you regard and follow the judgment of human reason, you are forced to say, either that there is no God, or that God is unjust; as the poet said: 'I am often tempted to think there are no gods.' See the great prosperity of the wicked, and by contrast the great adversity of the good. Proverbs, and experience, the parent of proverbs, bear record that the more abandoned men are, the more successful they are. 'The tabernacles of robbers prosper,' says Job (12. 6), and *Psalm* 73 complains that sinners in the world are full of riches (*Psalm* 73. 12). Is it not, pray, universally held to be most unjust that bad men should prosper, and good men be afflicted? Yet that is the way of the world. Hereupon some of the greatest minds have fallen into denying the existence of God, and imagining that Chance governs all things at random. Such were the Epicureans, and Pliny. And Aristotle, wishing to set his 'prime Being' free from misery, holds that he sees nothing but himself; for Aristotle supposes that it would be very irksome to such a Being to behold so many evils and injustices! And the Prophets, who believed in God's existence, were still more tempted concerning the injustice of God. Jeremiah, Job, David, Asaph and others are cases in point. What do you suppose Demosthenes and Cicero thought, when, having done all they could, they received as their reward an unhappy death? Yet all this, which looks so much like injustice in God, and is traduced as such by arguments which no reason or light of nature can resist, is most easily cleared up by the light of the gospel and the knowledge of grace, which teaches us that though the wicked flourish in their bodies, yet they perish in their souls. And a summary explanation of this whole inexplicable problem is found in a single little word: *There is a life after this life; and all that is not punished and repaid here will be punished and repaid there; for this life is nothing more than a precursor, or, rather, a beginning, of the life that is to come.*

If, now, this problem, which was debated in every age but never solved, is swept away and settled so easily by the light of the gospel, which shines only in the Word and to faith, how do you think it will be when the light of the Word and faith shall cease, and the real facts, and the Majesty of God, shall be revealed as they are? Do you not think that the light of glory will be able with the greatest ease to solve problems that are insoluble in the light of the word and grace, now that the light of grace has so easily solved this problem, which was insoluble by the light of nature?

Keep in view three lights: the light of nature, the light of grace, and the light of glory (this is a common and a good distinction). By the light of nature, it is inexplicable that it should be just for the good to be afflicted and the bad to prosper; but the light of grace explains it. By the light of grace, it is inexplicable how God can damn him who by his own strength can do nothing but sin and become guilty. Both the light of nature and the light of grace here insist that the fault lies not in the wretchedness of man, but in the injustice of God; nor can they judge otherwise of a God who crowns the ungodly freely, without merit, and does not crown, but damns another, who is perhaps less, and certainly not more, ungodly. But the light of glory insists otherwise, and will one day reveal God, to whom alone belongs a judgment whose justice is incomprehensible, as a God whose justice is most righteous and evident—provided only that in the meanwhile we *believe* it, as we are instructed and encouraged to do by the example of the light of grace explaining what was a puzzle of the same order to the light of nature.

I shall here end this book, ready though I am to pursue the matter further, if need be; but I think that abundant satisfaction has here been afforded for the godly man who is willing to yield to truth without stubborn resistance. For if we believe it to be true that God foreknows and foreordains all things; that he cannot be deceived or obstructed in his foreknowledge and predestination; and that nothing happens but at his will (which reason itself is compelled to grant); then, on reason's own testimony, there can be no 'free-will' in man, or angel or in any creature.

So, if we believe that Satan is the prince of this world, ever ensnaring and opposing the kingdom of Christ with all his strength, and that he does not let his prisoners go unless he is driven out by the power of the Divine Spirit, it is again apparent that there can be no 'free-will'.

So, if we believe that original sin has ruined us to such an extent that even in the godly, who are led by the Spirit, it causes abundance of trouble by striving against good, it is clear that in a man who lacks the Spirit nothing is left that can turn itself to good, but only to evil.

Again, if the Jews, who followed after righteousness with all their powers, fell into unrighteousness instead, while the Gentiles, who followed after unrighteousness, attained to an unhoped-for righteousness, by God's free gift, it is equally apparent from their very works and experience that man without grace can will nothing but evil.

And, finally, if we believe that Christ redeemed men by his blood, we are forced to confess that all of man was lost; otherwise, we make Christ either wholly superfluous, or else the redeemer of the least valuable part of man only; which is blasphemy, and sacrilege (pp. 313–18) . . .

X

CALVIN

John Calvin (1509–64) was born in France. Surprisingly little is known of his early years. He was the son of a civil servant. After giving early evidence of his brilliance as a scholar, he trained for the priesthood in Paris, but turned to law and classical studies in Orleans and Bruges. He returned to Paris in 1531 and added the study of Hebrew to his other interests. The so-called New Learning which had emerged from the Renaissance captivated him and at the same time the disturbing Lutheran theology was just beginning to break through the conservatism of Paris. Shortly after his return to Paris, Calvin experienced a profound religious conversion. His critical attitude to the Roman Catholic authorities began to involve him in trouble. He fled to Angoulême. In 1534 he resigned the chaplaincy which he held in Paris and celebrated communion in the new Evangelical Church of France. This was a decisive act. He emigrated to Basle in Switzerland, where he joined a group of distinguished Reformed theologians. He began work on the most comprehensive and systematic of his books, *Institutes of the Christian Religion*, the Latin version of which was published in 1536. A French edition appeared in 1540.

In 1536 Calvin was called to the leadership of the Reformed community in Geneva. The reformation in Geneva had been as much a political as a religious manœuvre. Calvin expelled the Anabaptists and secured some measure of civil and ecclesiastical discipline. The ascendancy of other factions in Geneva forced him to leave the city in 1538. He lived for three years in Strassburg, devoting himself to study and writing. In 1541 he returned to the leadership of Geneva and established there the theocratic community which became the model not only for the Reformed communities in Switzerland, but also in France and Scotland.

He wrote voluminously on nearly every aspect of Reformed doctrine and commentaries on nearly every book of Scripture as well as leaving behind him a permanent record of a great many sermons and meditations. His theology clearly owed much to the other Reformers—especially Luther and Bucer—but he formulated the system with a quite new brilliance and clarity.

So much of Calvin's writing has been seminal for Protestant theology that it is difficult to know by which aspects of his thought he should be represented. In view of his normative influence on large areas of Protestant church order, I have chosen to represent him by extracts from the *Institutes* on the authority of Scriptures, the church, and the Sacraments.

Nearly all of Calvin's works have been published in English by the Calvin Translation Society (48 vols., Edinburgh, 1863–1900). A more manageable and generously representative selection of his work will be found in the *Library of Christian Classics* (S.C.M. Press): Vols. XX and XXI, *Institutes of the Christian Religion*, ed. John T. Hunt (1961); Vol. XXII, *Theological Treatises*, ed. J. K. S. Reid (1954); Vol. XXIII, *Commentaries and Letters*, ed. Joseph Haroutunian (1958). The translation of the *Institutes* used below is that of Henry Beveridge published by James Clarke, Edinburgh, as reprinted in 1949.

INSTITUTES OF THE CHRISTIAN RELIGION

BOOK I, CHAPTER 7

The Word of God

1. Before proceeding farther, it seems proper to make some observations on the authority of Scripture, in order that our minds may not only be prepared to receive it with reverence, but be divested of all doubt.

When that which professes to be the Word of God is acknowledged to be so, no person, unless devoid of common sense and the feelings of a man, will have the desperate hardihood to refuse credit to the speaker. But since no daily responses are given from heaven, and the Scriptures are the only records in which God has been pleased to consign his truth to perpetual remembrance, the full authority which they ought to possess with the faithful is not recognized, unless they are believed to have come from heaven, as directly as if God had been heard giving utterance to them. This subject well deserves to be treated more at large, and pondered more accurately. But my readers will pardon me for having more regard to what my plan admits than to what the extent of this topic requires.

A most pernicious error has very generally prevailed—viz. that Scripture is of importance only in so far as conceded to it by the suffrage of the church; as if the eternal and inviolable truth of God could depend on the will of men. With great insult to the Holy Spirit, it is asked, Who can assure us that the Scriptures proceeded from God; who guarantee that they have come down safe and unimpaired to our times; who persuade us that *this* book is to be received with reverence, and *that one* expunged from the list, did not the church regulate all these things with certainty? On the determination of the church, therefore, it is said, depend both the reverence which is due to Scripture and the books which are to be admitted into the canon. Thus profane men, seeking, under the pretext of the church, to introduce unbridled tyranny, care not in what absurdities they entangle themselves and others, provided they extort from the simple this one acknowledgment—viz. that there is nothing which the church cannot do. But what is to become of miserable consciences in quest of some solid assurance of eternal life, if all the promises with regard to it have no better support than man's judgment? On being told so, will they cease to doubt and tremble? On the other hand, to what jeers of the wicked is our faith subjected—into how great suspicion is it brought with all, if believed to have only a precarious authority lent to it by the good-will of men?

2. These ravings are admirably refuted by a single expression of an apostle. Paul testifies that the church is 'built on the foundation of the apostles and prophets' (*Ephesians* 2. 20). If the doctrine of the apostles and prophets is the foundation of the church, the former must have had its certainty before the latter began to exist. Nor is there any room for the cavil, that though the church derives her first beginning from thence, it still remains doubtful what writings are to be attributed to the apostles and prophets, until her judgment is interposed. For if the Christian church was founded at first on the writings of the prophets, and the preaching of the apostles, that doctrine, wheresoever it may be found, was certainly ascertained and sanctioned antecedently to the church, since, but for this, the church herself never could have existed. Nothing, therefore, can be more absurd than the fiction, that the power of judging Scripture is in the church, and that on her nod its certainty depends. When the church receives it, and gives it the stamp of her authority, she does not make that authentic which was otherwise doubtful or controverted, but, acknowledging it as the truth of God, she, as in duty bound, shows her reverence by an unhesitating assent. As to the question, How shall we be persuaded that it came from God without recurring to a decree of the church? it is just the same as if it were asked, How shall we learn to distinguish light from darkness, white from black, sweet from bitter? Scripture bears upon the face of it as clear evidence of its truth, as white and black do of their colour, sweet and bitter of their taste.

3. I am aware it is usual to quote a sentence of Augustine, in which he says that he would not believe the gospel, were he not moved by the authority of the church (Aug. *Cont. Epist. Fundament.* c.v.). But it is easy to discover from the context, how inaccurate and unfair it is to

give it such a meaning. He was reasoning against the Manichees, who insisted on being implicitly believed, alleging that they had the truth, though they did not show they had. But as they pretended to appeal to the gospel in support of Manes, he asks what they would do if they fell in with a man who did not even believe the gospel—what kind of argument they would use to bring him over to their opinion. He afterwards adds, 'But I would not believe the gospel', etc.; meaning, that were he a stranger to the faith, the only thing which could induce him to embrace the gospel would be the authority of the church. And is it anything wonderful, that one who does not know Christ should pay respect to men?

Augustine, therefore, does not here say that the faith of the godly is founded on the authority of the church; nor does he mean that the certainty of the gospel depends upon it; he merely says that unbelievers would have no certainty of the gospel, so as thereby to win Christ, were they not influenced by the consent of the church. And he clearly shows this to be his meaning, by thus expressing himself a little before: 'When I have praised my own creed, and ridiculed yours, who do you suppose is to judge between us; or what more is to be done than to quit those who, inviting us to certainty, afterwards command us to believe uncertainty, and follow those who invite us, in the first instance, to believe what we are not yet able to comprehend, that waxing stronger through faith itself, we may become able to understand what we believe—no longer men, but God himself internally strengthening and illuminating our minds?' These unquestionably are the words of Augustine (August. *Cont. Epist. Fundament.* cap. iv); and the obvious inference from them is, that this holy man had no intention to suspend our faith in Scripture on the nod or decision of the church, but only to intimate (what we too admit to be true) that those who are not yet enlightened by the Spirit of God, become teachable by reverence for the church, and thus submit to learn the faith of Christ from the gospel. In this way, though the authority of the church leads us on, and prepares us to believe in the gospel, it is plain that Augustine would have the certainty of the godly to rest on a very different foundation.

At the same time, I deny not that he often presses the Manichees with the consent of the whole church, while arguing in support of the Scriptures, which they rejected. Hence he upbraids Faustus (Lib. xxxii) for not submitting to evangelical truth—truth so well founded, so firmly established, so gloriously renowned, and handed down by sure succession from the days of the apostles. But he nowhere insinuates that the authority which we give to the Scriptures depends on the definitions or devices of men. He only brings forward the universal judgment of the church, as a point most pertinent to the cause, and one, moreover, in which he had the advantage of his opponents. Any one who desires to see this more fully proved may read his short treatise, *De Utilitate Credendi* (The Advantages of Believing), where it will be found that the only facility of believing which he recommends is that which affords an introduction, and forms a fit commencement to inquiry; while he declares that we ought not to be satisfied with opinion, but to strive after substantial truth.

4. It is necessary to attend to what I lately said, that our faith in doctrine is not established until we have a perfect conviction that God is its author. Hence, the highest proof of Scripture is uniformly taken from the character of him whose word it is. The prophets and apostles boast not their own acuteness, or any qualities which win credit to speakers, nor do they dwell on reasons; but they appeal to the sacred name of God, in order that the whole world may be compelled to submission. The next thing to be considered is, how it appears not probable merely, but certain, that the name of God is neither rashly nor cunningly pretended. If, then, we would consult most effectually for our consciences, and save them from being driven about in a whirl of uncertainty, from wavering, and even stumbling at the smallest obstacle, our conviction of the truth of Scripture must be derived from a higher source than human conjectures, judgments, or reasons; namely, the secret testimony of the Spirit. It is true, indeed, that if we choose to proceed in the way of argument, it is easy to establish, by evidence of various kinds, that if there is a God in heaven, the Law, the Prophecies, and the Gospel, proceeded from him. Nay, although learned men, and men of the greatest talent, should take the opposite side, summoning and ostentatiously displaying all the powers of their genius in the discussion; if they are not possessed of shameless effrontery, they will be compelled to confess that the Scripture exhibits clear evidence of its being spoken by God, and, consequently, of its containing his heavenly doctrine. We shall see a little farther on, that the volume of sacred Scripture very far surpasses all other writings. Nay, if we look at it with clear eyes and unbiased judgment, it will forthwith present itself with a divine majesty which will subdue our presumptuous opposition, and force us to do it homage.

Still, however, it is preposterous to attempt, by discussion, to rear up a full faith in Scripture. True, were I called to contend with the craftiest despisers of God, I trust, though I am not possessed of the highest ability or eloquence, I should not find it difficult to stop their obstreperous mouths; I could, without much ado, put down the boastings which they mutter in corners, were anything to be gained by refuting their cavils. But although we may maintain the sacred Word of God against gainsayers, it does not follow that we shall forthwith implant the certainty which faith requires in their hearts. Profane men think that religion rests only on opinion, and, therefore, that they may not believe foolishly, or on slight grounds desire and insist to have it proved by reason that Moses and the prophets were divinely inspired. But I answer, that the testimony of the Spirit is superior to reason. For as God alone can properly bear witness to his own words, so these words will not obtain full credit in the hearts of men, until they are sealed by the inward testimony of the Spirit. The same Spirit, therefore, who spoke by the mouth of the prophets, must penetrate our hearts, in order to convince us that they faithfully delivered the message with which they were divinely intrusted. This connection is most aptly expressed by Isaiah in these words, 'My Spirit that is upon thee, and my words which I have put in thy mouth, shall not depart out of thy mouth, nor out of the mouth of thy seed, nor out of the mouth of thy seed's seed, saith the Lord, from henceforth and for ever' (*Isaiah* 59. 21). Some worthy persons feel disconcerted, because, while the wicked murmur with impunity at the word of God, they have not a clear proof at hand to silence them, forgetting that the Spirit is called an earnest and seal to confirm the faith of the godly, for this very reason, that, until he enlightens their minds, they are tossed to and fro in a sea of doubts.

5. Let it therefore be held as fixed, that those who are inwardly taught by the Holy Spirit acquiesce implicity in Scripture; that Scripture, carrying its own evidence along with it, deigns not to submit to proofs and arguments, but owes the full conviction with which we ought to receive it to the testimony of the Spirit. Enlightened by him, we no longer believe, either on our own judgment or that of others, that the Scriptures are from God; but, in a way superior to human judgment, feel perfectly assured—as much so as if we beheld the divine image visibly impressed on it—that it came to us, by the instrumentality of men, from the very mouth of God. We ask not for proofs or probabilities on which to rest our judgment, but we subject our intellect and judgment to it as too transcendent for us to estimate. This, however, we do, not in the manner in which some are wont to fasten on an unknown object, which, as soon as known, displeases, but because we have a thorough conviction that, in holding it, we hold unassailable truth; not like miserable men, whose minds are enslaved by superstition, but because we feel a divine energy living and breathing in it—an energy by which we are drawn and animated to obey it, willingly indeed, and knowingly, but more vividly and effectually than could be done by human will or knowledge. Hence, God most justly exclaims by the mouth of Isaiah, 'Ye are my witnesses, saith the Lord, and my servant whom I have chosen, that ye may know and believe me, and understand that I am he' (*Isaiah* 43. 10).

Such, then, is a conviction which asks not for reasons; such, a knowledge which accords with the highest reason, namely, knowledge in which the mind rests more firmly and securely than in any reasons; such, in fine, the conviction which revelation from heaven alone can produce. I say nothing more than every believer experiences in himself, though my words fall far short of the reality. I do not dwell on this subject at present, because we will return to it again: only let us now understand that the only true faith is that which the Spirit of God seals on our hearts. Nay, the modest and teachable reader will find a sufficient reason in the promise contained in Isaiah, that all the children of the renovated Church 'shall be taught of the Lord' (*Isaiah* 54. 13). This singular privilege God bestows on his elect only, whom he separates from the rest of mankind. For what is the beginning of true doctrine but prompt alacrity to hear the word of God? And God, by the mouth of Moses, thus demands to be heard: 'It is not in heaven, that thou shouldst say, Who shall go up for us to heaven, and bring it unto us, that we may hear and do it? But the word is very nigh unto thee, in thy mouth and in thy heart' (*Deuteronomy* 30. 12, 14). God having been pleased to reserve the treasure of intelligence for his children, no wonder that so much ignorance and stupidity is seen in the generality of mankind. In the *generality*, I include even those specially chosen, until they are ingrafted into the body of the church. Isaiah, moreover, while reminding us that the prophetical doctrine would prove incredible not only to strangers, but also to the Jews, who were desirous to be thought of the household of God, subjoins the reason, when he asks, 'To whom hath the arm of the Lord been revealed?' (*Isaiah* 53. 1). If at any time, then, we are troubled at the small number of those who believe, let us, on the other hand, call to mind, that none comprehend the mysteries of God save those to whom it is given.

BOOK III, CHAPTER 2

Faith

6. The true knowledge of Christ consists in receiving him as he is offered by the Father—namely, as invested with his Gospel. For, as he is appointed as the end of our faith, so we cannot directly tend towards him except under the guidance of the Gospel. Therein are certainly unfolded to us treasures of grace. Did these continue shut, Christ would profit us little. Hence Paul makes faith the inseparable attendant of doctrine in these words, 'Ye have not so learned Christ; if so be that ye have heard him, and have been taught by him, as the truth is in Jesus' (*Ephesians*

4. 20, 21). Still I do not confine faith to the Gospel in such a sense as not to admit that enough was delivered to Moses and the Prophets to form a foundation of faith; but as the Gospel exhibits a fuller manifestation of Christ, Paul justly terms it the doctrine of faith (I *Timothy* 4. 6). For which reason, also, he elsewhere says, that, by the coming of faith, the Law was abolished (*Romans* 10. 4), including under the expression a new and unwonted mode of teaching, by which Christ, from the period of his appearance as the great Master, gave a fuller illustration of the Father's mercy, and testified more surely of our salvation. But an easier and more appropriate method will be to descend from the general to the particular. First, we must remember, that there is an inseparable relation between faith and the word, and that these can no more be disconnected from each other than rays of light from the sun. Hence in Isaiah the Lord explains, 'Hear, and your soul shall live' (*Isaiah* 55. 3). And John points to this same fountain of faith, in the following words, 'These are written that ye might believe' (*John* 20. 31). The Psalmist also, exhorting the people to faith, says, 'Today, if ye will hear his voice' (*Psalm* 95. 7), to *hear* being uniformly taken for to *believe*. In fine, in Isaiah the Lord distinguishes the members of the church from strangers by this mark, 'All thy children shall be taught of the Lord' (*Isaiah* 54. 13); for if the benefit was indiscriminate, why should he address his words only to a few? Corresponding with this, the Evangelists uniformly employ the terms *believers* and *disciples* as synonymous. This is done especially by Luke in several passages of the Acts. He even applies the term *disciple* to a woman (*Acts* 9. 36). Wherefore, if faith declines in the least degree from the mark at which it ought to aim, it does not retain its nature, but becomes uncertain credulity and vague wandering of mind. The same word is the basis on which it rests and is sustained. Declining from it, it falls. Take away the word, therefore, and no faith will remain. We are not here discussing whether, in order to propagate the word of God by which faith is engendered, the ministry of man is necessary (this will be considered elsewhere); but we say that the word itself, whatever be the way in which it is conveyed to us, is a kind of mirror in which faith beholds God. In this, therefore, whether God uses the agency of man, or works immediately by his own power, it is always by his word that he manifests himself to those whom he designs to draw to himself. Hence Paul designates faith as the obedience which is given to the Gospel (*Romans* 1. 5); and writing to the Philippians, he commends them for the obedience of faith (*Philippians* 2. 17). For faith includes not merely the knowledge that God is, but also, nay chiefly, a perception of his will towards us. It concerns us to know not only what he is in himself, but also in what character he is pleased to manifest himself to us. We now see, therefore, that faith is the knowledge of the

divine will in regard to us, as ascertained from his word. And the foundation of it is a previous persuasion of the truth of God. So long as your mind entertains any misgivings as to the certainty of the word, its authority will be weak and dubious, or rather it will have no authority at all. Nor is it sufficient to believe that God is true, and cannot lie or deceive, unless you feel firmly persuaded that every word which proceeds from him is sacred, inviolable truth.

7. But since the heart of man is not brought to faith by every word of God, we must still consider what it is that faith properly has respect to in the word. The declaration of God to Adam was, 'Thou shalt surely die' (*Genesis* 2. 17); and to Cain, 'The voice of thy brother's blood crieth unto me from the ground' (*Genesis* 4. 10); but these, so far from being fitted to establish faith, tend only to shake it. At the same time, we deny not that it is the office of faith to assent to the truth of God whenever, whatever, and in whatever way he speaks: we are only inquiring what faith can find in the word of God to lean and rest upon. When conscience sees only wrath and indignation, how can it but tremble and be afraid? and how can it avoid shunning the God whom it thus dreads? But faith ought to seek God, not shun him. It is evident, therefore, that we have not yet obtained a full definition of faith, it being impossible to give the name to every kind of knowledge of the divine will. Shall we, then, for *will*, which is often the messenger of bad news and the herald of terror, substitute the benevolence or mercy of God? In this way, doubtless, we make a nearer approach to the nature of faith. For we are allured to seek God when told that our safety is treasured up in him; and we are confirmed in this when he declares that he studies and takes an interest in our welfare. Hence there is need of the gracious promise, in which he testifies that he is a propitious Father; since there is no other way in which we can approach to him, the promise being the only thing on which the heart of man can recline. For this reason, the two things, mercy and truth, are uniformly conjoined in the Psalms as having a mutual connexion with each other. For it were of no avail to us to know that God is true, did he not in mercy allure us to himself; nor could we of ourselves embrace his mercy did not he expressly offer it. 'I have declared thy faithfulness and thy salvation: I have not concealed thy loving-kindness and thy truth. Withhold not thy tender mercies from me, O Lord: let thy loving-kindness and thy truth continually preserve me' (*Psalm* 40. 10, 11). 'Thy mercy, O Lord, is in the heavens; and thy faithfulness reacheth unto the clouds' (*Psalm* 36. 5). 'All the paths of the Lord are mercy and truth unto such as keep his covenant and his testimonies' (*Psalm* 25. 10). 'His merciful kindness is great towards us: and the truth of the Lord endureth for ever' (*Psalm* 117. 2). 'I will praise thy name for thy loving-

kindness and thy truth' (*Psalm* 138. 2). I need not quote what is said in the Prophets, to the effect that God is merciful and faithful in his promises. It were presumptuous in us to hold that God is propitious to us, had we not his own testimony, and did he not prevent us by his invitation, which leaves no doubt or uncertainty as to his will. It has already been seen that Christ is the only pledge of love, for without him all things, both above and below, speak of hatred and wrath. We have also seen, that since the knowledge of the divine goodness cannot be of much importance unless it leads us to confide in it, we must exclude a knowledge mingled with doubt—a knowledge which, so far from being firm, is continually wavering. But the human mind, when blinded and darkened, is very far from being able to rise to a proper knowledge of the divine will; nor can the heart, fluctuating with perpetual doubt, rest secure in such knowledge. Hence, in order that the word of God may gain full credit, the mind must be enlightened, and the heart confirmed, from some other quarter. We shall now have a full definition of faith if we say that it is a firm and sure knowledge of the divine favour toward us, founded on the truth of a free promise in Christ, and revealed to our minds, and sealed on our hearts, by the Holy Spirit. . . .

16. The principal hinge on which faith turns is this: We must not suppose that any promises of mercy which the Lord offers are only true out of us, and not at all in us: we should rather make them ours by inwardly embracing them. In this way only is engendered that confidence which he elsewhere terms peace (*Romans* 5. 1); though perhaps he rather means to make peace follow from it. This is the security which quiets and calms the conscience in the view of the judgment of God, and without which it is necessarily vexed and almost torn with tumultuous dread, unless when it happens to slumber for a moment, forgetful both of God and of itself. And verily it is but for a moment. It never long enjoys that miserable obliviousness, for the memory of the divine judgment, ever and anon recurring, stings it to the quick. In one word, he only is a true believer who, firmly persuaded that God is reconciled, and is a kind Father to him, hopes everything from his kindness, who, trusting to the promises of the divine favour, with undoubting confidence anticipates salvation; . . .

19. The whole, then, comes to this: As soon as the minutest particle of faith is instilled into our minds, we begin to behold the face of God placid, serene, and propitious; far off, indeed, but still so distinctly as to assure us that there is no delusion in it. In proportion to the progress we afterwards make (and the progress ought to be uninterrupted), we obtain a nearer and surer view, the very continuance making it more familiar to us. Thus we see that a mind illumined with the knowledge of God is

at first involved in much ignorance—ignorance, however, which is gradually removed. Still this partial ignorance or obscure discernment does not prevent that clear knowledge of the divine favour which holds the first and principal part in faith. For as one shut up in a prison, where from a narrow opening he receives the rays of the sun indirectly and in a manner divided, though deprived of a full view of the sun, has no doubt of the source from which the light comes, and is benefited by it; so believers, while bound with the fetters of an earthly body, though surrounded on all sides with much obscurity, are so far illumined by any slender light which beams upon them and displays the divine mercy as to feel secure.

20. The Apostle elegantly adverts to both in different passages. When he says, 'We know in part, and we prophecy in part'; and 'Now we see through a glass darkly' (I *Corinthians* 13. 9, 12), he intimates how very minute a portion of divine wisdom is given to us in the present life. For although those expressions do not simply indicate that faith is imperfect so long as we groan under a weight of flesh, but that the necessity of being constantly engaged in learning is owing to our imperfection, he at the same time reminds us, that a subject which is of boundless extent cannot be comprehended by our feeble and narrow capacities. This Paul affirms of the whole church, each individual being retarded and impeded by his own ignorance from making so near an approach as were to be wished. But that the fore-taste which we obtain from any minute portion of faith is certain, and by no means fallacious, he elsewhere shows, when he affirms that 'We all, with open face beholding as in a glass the glory of the Lord, are changed into the same image, from glory to glory, even as by the Spirit of the Lord' (II *Corinthians* 3. 18). In such degrees of ignorance much doubt and trembling is necessarily implied, especially seeing that our heart is by its own natural bias prone to unbelief. To this we must add the temptations which, various in kind and infinite in number are ever and anon violently assailing us. In particular, conscience itself, burdened with an incumbent load of sins, at one time complains and groans, at another openly rebels. Therefore, whether adverse circumstances betoken the wrath of God, or conscience finds the subject and matter within itself, unbelief thence draws weapons and engines to put faith to flight, the aim of all its efforts being to make us think that God is adverse and hostile to us, and thus, instead of hoping for any assistance from him, to make us dread him as a deadly foe.

21. To withstand these assaults, faith arms and fortifies itself with the word of God. . . .

31. Hence again we infer, as has already been explained, that faith has no less need of the word than the fruit of a tree has of a living root;

because, as David testifies, none can hope in God but those who know his name (*Psalm* 9. 10). This knowledge, however, is not left to every man's imagination, but depends on the testimony which God himself gives to his goodness. This the same Psalmist confirms in another passage, 'Thy salvation according to thy word' (*Psalm* 119. 41). Again, 'Save me', 'I hoped in thy word' (*Psalm* 119. 146, 147). Here we must attend to the relation of faith to the word, and to salvation as its consequence. Still, however, we exclude not the power of God. If faith cannot support itself in the view of this power, it never will give him the honour which is due. Paul seems to relate a trivial or very ordinary circumstance with regard to Abraham, when he says, that he believed that God, who had given him the promise of a blessed seed, was able also to perform it (*Romans* 4. 21). And in like manner, in another passage, he says of himself, 'I know whom I have believed, and am persuaded that he is able to keep that which I have committed unto him against that day' (II *Timothy* 1. 12). But let any one consider with himself, how he is ever and anon assailed with doubts in regard to the power of God, and he will readily perceive, that those who duly magnify it have made no small progress in faith. We all acknowledge that God can do whatsoever he pleases; but while every temptation, even the most trivial, fills us with fear and dread, it is plain that we derogate from the power of God, by attaching less importance to his promises than to Satan's threatenings against them. . . .

35. Having elsewhere shown more fully, when treating of the corruption of our nature, how little able men are to believe (Book II, c. ii, iii), I will not fatigue the reader by again repeating it. Let it suffice to observe, that the spirit of faith is used by Paul as synonymous with the very faith which we receive from the Spirit, but which we have not naturally (II *Corinthians* 4. 13). Accordingly, he prays for the Thessalonians, 'that our God would count you worthy of this calling, and fulfil all the good pleasure of his goodness, and the work of faith with power' (II *Thessalonians* 1. 2). Here, by designating faith the *work* of God, and distinguishing it by way of epithet, appropriately calling it his *good pleasure*, he declares that it is not of man's own nature; and not contented with this, he adds, that it is an illustration of divine power. In addressing the Corinthians, when he tells them that faith stands not 'in the wisdom of man, but in the power of God' (I *Corinthians* 2. 4), he is no doubt speaking of external miracles; but as the reprobate are blinded when they behold them, he also includes that internal seal of which he elsewhere makes mention. And the better to display his liberality in this most excellent gift, God does not bestow it upon all promiscuously, but, by special privilege, imparts it to whom he will. To this effect we have already

quoted passages of Scripture, as to which Augustine, their faithful expositor, exclaims (*De Verbo Apost. Serm.* ii), 'Our Saviour, to teach that faith in him is a gift, not a merit, says, "No man can come to me, except the Father, which hath sent me, draw him" (*John* 6. 44). It is strange when two persons hear, the one despises, the other ascends. Let him who despises impute it to himself; let him who ascends not arrogate it to himself.' In another passage, he asks, 'Wherefore is it given to the one, and not to the other? I am not ashamed to say, This is one of the deep things of the cross. From some unknown depth of the judgments of God, which we cannot scrutinize, all our ability proceeds. I see that I am able; but how I am able I see not:—this far only I see, that it is of God. But why the one, and not the other? This is too great for me: it is an abyss, a depth of the cross. I can cry out with wonder; not discuss and demonstrate.' The whole comes to this, that Christ, when he produces faith in us by the agency of his Spirit, at the same time ingrafts us into his body, that we may become partakers of all blessings. . . .

BOOK IV, CHAPTER 1

The Visible Church

7. The judgment which ought to be formed concerning the visible Church which comes under our observation, must, I think, be sufficiently clear from what has been said. I have observed that the Scriptures speak of the church in two ways. Sometimes when they speak of the church they mean the church as it really is before God—the church into which none are admitted but those who by the gift of adoption are sons of God, and by the sanctification of the Spirit true members of Christ. In this case it not only comprehends the saints who dwell on the earth, but all the elect who have existed from the beginning of the world. Often, too, by the name of church is designated the whole body of mankind scattered throughout the world, who profess to worship one God and Christ, who by baptism are initiated into the faith; by partaking of the Lord's Supper profess unity in true doctrine and charity, agree in holding the word of the Lord, and observe the ministry which Christ has appointed for the preaching of it. In this church there is a very large mixture of hypocrites, who have nothing of Christ but the name and outward appearance: of ambitious, avaricious, envious, evil-speaking men, some also of impurer lives, who are tolerated for a time, either because their guilt cannot be legally established, or because due strictness of discipline is not always observed. Hence, as it is necessary to believe the invisible church, which is manifest to the eye of God only, so we are also enjoined to

regard this Church which is so called with reference to man, and to cultivate its communion.

8. Accordingly, inasmuch as it was of importance to us to recognize it, the Lord has distinguished it by certain marks, and as it were symbols. It is, indeed, the special prerogative of God to know those who are his, as Paul declares in the passage already quoted (II *Timothy* 2. 19). And doubtless it has been so provided as a check on human rashness, the experience of every day reminding us how far his secret judgments surpass our apprehension. For even those who seemed most abandoned, and who had been completely despaired of, are by his goodness recalled to life, while those who seemed most stable often fall. Hence, as Augustine says, 'In regard to the secret pre-destination of God, there are very many sheep without, and very many wolves within' (August. *Hom. in Joann.* 45). For he knows, and has his mark on those who know neither him nor themselves. Of those again who openly bear his badge, his eyes alone see who of them are unfeignedly holy, and will persevere even to the end, which alone is the completion of salvation. On the other hand, foreseeing that it was in some degree expedient for us to know who are to be regarded by us as his sons, he has in this matter accommodated himself to our capacity. But as here full certainty was not necessary, he has in its place substituted the judgment of charity, by which we acknowledge all as members of the Church who by confession of faith, regularity of conduct, and participation in the sacraments, unite with us in acknowledging the same God and Christ. The knowledge of his body, inasmuch as he knew it to be more necessary for our salvation, he has made known to us by surer marks.

9. Hence the form of the Church appears and stands forth conspicuous to our view. Wherever we see the word of God sincerely preached and heard, wherever we see the sacraments administered according to the institution of Christ, there we cannot have any doubt that the Church of God has some existence, since his promise cannot fail, 'Where two or three are gathered together in my name, there am I in the midst of them' (*Matthew* 18. 20). But that we may have a clear summary of this subject, we must proceed by the following steps:—The church universal is the multitude collected out of all nations, who, though dispersed and far distant from each other, agree in one truth of divine doctrine, and are bound together by the tie of a common religion. In this way it comprehends single churches, which exist in different towns and villages, according to the wants of human society, so that each of them justly obtains the name and authority of the church; and also comprehends single individuals, who by a religious profession are accounted to belong to such churches, although they are in fact aliens

from the church, but have not been cut off by a public decision. There is, however, a slight difference in the mode of judging of individuals and of churches. For it may happen in practice that those whom we deem not altogether worthy of the fellowship of believers, we yet ought to treat as brethren, and regard as believers, on account of the common consent of the church in tolerating and bearing with them in the body of Christ. Such persons we do not approve by our suffrage as members of the church, but we leave them the place which they hold among the people of God, until they are legitimately deprived of it. With regard to the general body we must feel differently; if they have the ministry of the word, and honour the administration of the sacraments, they are undoubtedly entitled to be ranked with the church, because it is certain that these things are not without a beneficial result. Thus we both maintain the church universal in its unity, which malignant minds have always been eager to dissever, and deny not due authority to lawful assemblies distributed as circumstances require.

10. We have said that the symbols by which the church is discerned are the preaching of the word and the observance of the sacraments, for these cannot anywhere exist without producing fruit and prospering by the blessing of God. I say not that wherever the word is preached fruit immediately appears; but that in every place where it is received, and has a fixed abode, it uniformly displays its efficacy. Be this as it may, when the preaching of the gospel is reverently heard, and the sacraments are not neglected, there for the time the face of the church appears without deception or ambiguity and no man may with impunity spurn her authority, or reject her admonitions, or resist her counsels, or make sport of her censures, far less revolt from her, and violate her unity. For such is the value which the Lord sets on the communion of his church, that all who contumaciously alienate themselves from any Christian society, in which the true ministry of his word and sacraments is maintained, he regards as deserters of religion. So highly does he recommend her authority, that when it is violated he considers that his own authority is impaired. For there is no small weight in the designation given to her, 'the house of God', 'the pillar and ground of truth' (I *Timothy* 3. 15). By these words Paul intimates, that to prevent the truth from perishing in the world, the Church is its faithful guardian, because God has been pleased to preserve the pure preaching of his word by her instrumentality, and to exhibit himself to us as a parent while he feeds us with spiritual nourishment, and provides whatever is conducive to our salvation. Moreover, no mean praise is conferred on the church when she is said to have been chosen and set apart by Christ as his spouse, 'not having spot or wrinkle, or any such thing' (*Ephesians* 5. 27), as 'his body, the

fulness of him that filleth all in all' (*Ephesians* 1. 23). Whence it follows, that revolt from the church is denial of God and Christ. Wherefore there is the more necessity to beware of a dissent so iniquitous; for seeing by it we aim as far as in us lies at the destruction of God's truth, we deserve to be crushed by the full thunder of his anger. No crime can be imagined more atrocious than that of sacrilegiously and perfidiously violating the sacred marriage which the only-begotten Son of God has condescended to contract with us.

BOOK IV, CHAPTER 14

The Sacraments

1. Akin to the preaching of the gospel, we have another help to our faith in the sacraments, in regard to which, it greatly concerns us that some sure doctrine should be delivered, informing us both of the end for which they were instituted, and of their present use. First, we must attend to what a sacrament is. It seems to me, then, a simple and appropriate definition to say, that it is an external sign, by which the Lord seals on our consciences his promises of good-will toward us, in order to sustain the weakness of our faith, and we in our turn testify our piety towards him, both before himself, and before angels as well as men. We may also define more briefly by calling it a testimony of the divine favour toward us, confirmed by an external sign, with a corresponding attestation of our faith towards him, You may make your choice of these definitions, which in meaning differ not from that of Augustine, which defines a sacrament to be a visible sign of a sacred thing, or a visible form of an invisible grace, but does not contain a better or surer explanation. As its brevity makes it somewhat obscure, and thereby misleads the more illiterate, I wished to remove all doubt, and make the definition fuller by stating it at greater length.

2. The reason why the ancients used the term in this sense is not obscure. The old interpreter, whenever he wished to render the Greek term μυστήριον into Latin, especially when it was used with reference to divine things, used the word *sacramentum*. Thus, in Ephesians, 'Having made known unto us the mystery (*sacramentum*) of his will'; and again, 'If ye have heard of the dispensation of the grace of God, which is given me to you-wards, how that by revelation he made known unto me the mystery' (*sacramentum*) (*Ephesians* 1. 9; 3. 2). In the Colossians, 'Even the mystery which hath been his from ages and from generations, but is now made manifest to his saints, to whom God would make known what is the riches of the glory of this mystery' (*sacramentum*) (*Colossians* 1. 26).

Also in the First Epistle to Timothy, 'Without controversy, great is the mystery (*sacramentum*) of godliness: God was manifest in the flesh' (I *Timothy* 3. 16). He was unwilling to use the word *arcanum* (secret), lest the word should seem beneath the magnitude of the thing meant. When the thing, therefore, was sacred and secret, he used the term *sacramentum*. In this sense it frequently occurs in ecclesiastical writers. And it is well known, that what the Latins call *Sacramenta*, the Greeks call *μυστήρια* (mysteries). The sameness of meaning removes all dispute. Hence it is that the term was applied to those signs which gave an august representation of things spiritual and sublime. This is also observed by Augustine, 'It were tedious to discourse of the variety of signs; those which relate to divine things are called sacraments' (August. *Ep.* 5, *ad Marcell.*).

3. From the definition which we have given, we perceive that there never is a sacrament without an antecedent promise, the sacrament being added as a kind of appendix, with the view of confirming and sealing the promise, and giving a better attestation, or rather, in a manner, confirming it. In this way God provides first for our ignorance and sluggishness, and, secondly, for our infirmity; and yet, properly speaking, it does not so much confirm his word as establish us in the faith of it. For the truth of God is in itself sufficiently stable and certain, and cannot receive a better confirmation from any other quarter than from itself. But as our faith is slender and weak, so if it be not propped up on every side, and supported by all kinds of means, it is forthwith shaken and tossed to and fro, wavers, and even falls. And here, indeed, our merciful Lord, with boundless condescension, so accommodates himself to our capacity, that seeing how from our animal nature we are always creeping on the ground, and cleaving to the flesh, having no thought of what is spiritual, and not even forming an idea of it, he declines not by means of these earthly elements to lead us to himself, and even in the flesh to exhibit a mirror of spiritual blessings. For, as Chrysostom says (*Hom.* 60, *ad Popul.*). 'Were we incorporeal, he would give us these things in a naked and incorporeal form. Now because our souls are implanted in bodies, he delivers spiritual things under things visible. Not that the qualities which are set before us in the sacraments are inherent in the nature of the things, but God gives them this signification.'

4. This is commonly expressed by saying that a sacrament consists of the word and the external sign. By the word we ought to understand not one which, muttered without meaning and without faith, by its sound merely, as by a magical incantation, has the effect of consecrating the element, but one which, preached, makes us understand what the visible sign means. The thing, therefore, which was frequently done, under the tyranny of the Pope, was not free from great profanation of

the mystery, for they deemed it sufficient if the priest muttered the formula of consecration, while the people, without understanding, looked stupidly on. Nay, this was done for the express purpose of preventing any instruction from thereby reaching the people: for all was said in Latin to illiterate hearers. Superstition afterwards was carried to such a height, that the consecration was thought not to be duly performed except in a low grumble, which few could hear. Very different is the doctrine of Augustine concerning the sacramental word. 'Let the word be added to the element, and it will become a sacrament. For whence can there be so much virtue in water as to touch the body and cleanse the heart, unless by the agency of the word, and this not because it is said, but because it is believed? For even in the word the transient sound is one thing, the permanent power another. This is the word of faith which we preach says the Apostle (*Romans* 10. 8). Hence, in the Acts of the Apostles, we have the expression, "Purify their hearts by faith" (*Acts* 15. 9). And the Apostle Peter says, "The like figure whereunto even baptism doth now save us (not the putting away of the filth of the flesh, but the answer of a good conscience)" (I *Peter* 3. 21). This is the word of faith which we preach: by which word doubtless baptism also, in order that it may be able to cleanse, is consecrated' (August. *Hom. in Joann.* 13). You see how he requires preaching to the production of faith. And we need not labour to prove this, since there is not the least room for doubt as to what Christ did, and commanded us to do, as to what the apostles followed, and a purer church observed. Nay, it is known that, from the very beginning of the world, whenever God offered any sign to the holy Patriarchs, it was inseparably attached to doctrine, without which our senses would gaze bewildered on an unmeaning object. Therefore, when we hear mention made of the sacramental word, let us understand the promise which, proclaimed aloud by the minister, leads the people by the hand to that to which the sign tends and directs us.

5. Nor are those to be listened to who oppose this view with a more subtle than solid dilemma. They argue thus: We either know that the word of God which precedes the sacrament is the true will of God, or we do not know it. If we know it, we learn nothing new from the sacrament which succeeds. If we do not know it, we cannot learn it from the sacrament, whose whole efficacy depends on the word. Our brief reply is: The seals which are affixed to diplomas, and other public deeds, are nothing considered in themselves, and would be affixed to no purpose if nothing was written on the parchment, and yet this does not prevent them from sealing and confirming when they are appended to writings. It cannot be alleged that this comparison is a recent fiction of our own, since Paul himself used it, terming *circumcision a seal* (*Romans*

4. 11), where he expressly maintains that the circumcision of Abraham was not for justification, but was an attestation to the covenant, by the faith of which he had been previously justified. And how, pray, can any one be greatly offended when we teach that the promise is sealed by the sacrament, since it is plain, from the promises themselves, that one promise confirms another? The clearer any evidence is, the fitter is it to support our faith. But sacraments bring with them the clearest promises, and, when compared with the word, have this peculiarity, that they represent promises to the life, as if painted in a picture. Nor ought we to be moved by an objection founded on the distinction between sacraments and the seals of documents—viz. that since both consist of the carnal elements of this world, the former cannot be sufficient or adequate to seal the promises of God, which are spiritual and eternal, though the latter may be employed to seal the edicts of princes concerning fleeting and fading things. But the believer, when the sacraments are presented to his eye, does not stop short at the carnal spectacle, but by the steps of analogy which I have indicated, rises with pious consideration to the sublime mysteries which lie hidden in the sacraments.

6. As the Lord calls his promises covenants (*Genesis* 6. 18; 9. 9; 17. 2), and sacraments signs of the covenants, so something similar may be inferred from human covenants. What could the slaughter of a hog effect, unless words were interposed or rather preceded? Swine are often killed without any interior or occult mystery. What could be gained by pledging the right hand, since hands are not unfrequently joined in giving battle? But when words have preceded, then by such symbols of covenant sanction is given to laws, though previously conceived, digested, and enacted by words. Sacraments, therefore, are exercises which confirm our faith in the word of God; and because we are carnal, they are exhibited under carnal objects, that thus they may train us in accommodation to our sluggish capacity, just as nurses lead children by the hand. And hence Augustine calls a sacrament a *visible word* (August. *in Joann. Hom.* 89), because it represents the promises of God as in a picture, and places them in our view in a graphic bodily form (August. *cont. Faust. Lib.* xix). We might refer to other similitudes, by which sacraments are more plainly designated, as when they are called the pillars of our faith. For just as a building stands and leans on its foundation, and yet is rendered more stable when supported by pillars, so faith leans on the word of God as its proper foundation, and yet when sacraments are added leans more firmly, as if resting on pillars. Or we may call them mirrors, in which we may contemplate the riches of the grace which God bestows upon us. For then, as has been said, he manifests himself to us in as far as our

dullness can enable us to recognize him, and testifies his love and kindness to us more expressly than by word.

7. It is irrational to contend that sacraments are not manifestations of divine grace toward us, because they are held forth to the ungodly also, who, however, so far from experiencing God to be more propitious to them, only incur greater condemnation. By the same reasoning, the gospel will be no manifestation of the grace of God, because it is spurned by many who hear it; nor will Christ himself be a manifestation of grace, because of the many by whom he was seen and known, very few received him. Something similar may be seen in public enactments. A great part of the body of the people deride and evade the authenticating seal, though they know it was employed by their sovereign to confirm his will; others trample it under foot, as a matter by no means appertaining to them; while others even execrate it: so that, seeing the condition of the two things to be alike, the appropriateness of the comparison which I made above ought to be more readily allowed. It is certain, therefore, that the Lord offers us his mercy, and a pledge of his grace, both in his sacred word and in the sacraments; but it is not apprehended save by those who receive the word and sacraments with firm faith; in like manner as Christ, though offered and held forth for salvation to all, is not, however, acknowledged and received by all. Augustine, when intending to intimate this, said that the efficacy of the word is produced in the sacrament, *not because it is spoken, but because it is believed*. Hence Paul, addressing believers, includes communion with Christ, in the sacraments, as when he says, 'As many of you as have been baptized into Christ have put on Christ' (*Galatians* 3. 27). Again, 'For by one Spirit we are all baptized into one body' (I *Corinthians* 12. 13). But when he speaks of a preposterous use of the sacraments, he attributes nothing more to them than to frigid, empty figures; thereby intimating, that however the ungodly and hypocrites may, by their perverseness, either suppress, or obscure, or impede the effect of divine grace in the sacraments, that does not prevent them, where and whenever God is so pleased, from giving a true evidence of communion with Christ, or prevent them from exhibiting, and the Spirit of God from performing, the very thing which they promise. We conclude, therefore, that the sacraments are truly termed evidences of divine grace, and as it were, seals of the good-will which he entertains toward us. They, by sealing it to us, sustain, nourish, confirm, and increase our faith. The objections usually urged against this view are frivolous and weak. They say that our faith, if it is good, cannot be made better; for there is no faith save that which leans unshakingly, firmly, and undividedly, on the mercy of God. It had been better for the objectors to pray, with the apostles, 'Lord, increase our faith' (*Luke* 17. 5),

than confidently to maintain a perfection of faith which none of the sons of men ever attained, none ever shall attain, in this life. Let them explain what kind of faith his was who said, 'Lord, I believe; help thou mine unbelief' (*Mark* 9. 24). That faith, though only commenced, was good, and might, by the removal of the unbelief, be made better. But there is no better argument to refute them than their own consciousness. For if they confess themselves sinners (This, whether they will or not, they cannot deny), then they must of necessity impute this very quality to the imperfection of their faith. . . .

14. On the other hand, it is to be observed, that as these objectors impair the force, and altogether overthrow the use of the sacraments, so there are others who ascribe to the sacraments a kind of secret virtue, which is nowhere said to have been implanted in them by God. By this error the more simple and unwary are perilously deceived, while they are taught to seek the gifts of God where they cannot possibly be found, and are insensibly withdrawn from God, so as to embrace instead of his truth mere vanity. For the schools of the Sophists have taught with general consent that the sacraments of the new law, in other words, those now in use in the Christian Church, justify, and confer grace, provided only that we do not interpose the obstacle of mortal sin. It is impossible to describe how fatal and pestilential this sentiment is, and the more so, that for many ages it has, to the great loss of the Church, prevailed over a considerable part of the world. It is plainly of the devil: for, first, in promising a righteousness without faith, it drives souls headlong on destruction; secondly, in deriving a cause of righteousness from the sacraments, it entangles miserable minds, already of their own accord too much inclined to the earth, in a superstitious idea, which makes them acquiesce in the spectacle of a corporeal object rather than in God himself. I wish we had not such experience of both evils as to make it altogether unnecessary to give a lengthened proof of them. For what is a sacrament received without faith, but most certain destruction to the Church? For, seeing that nothing is to be expected beyond the promise, and the promise no less denounces wrath to the unbeliever than offers grace to the believer, it is an error to suppose that anything more is conferred by the sacraments than is offered by the word of God, and obtained by true faith. From this another thing follows—viz. that assurance of salvation does not depend on participation in the sacraments, as if justification consisted in it. This, which is treasured up in Christ alone, we know to be communicated, not less by the preaching of the Gospel than by the seal of the sacrament, and may be completely enjoyed without this seal. So true is it, as Augustine declares, that there may be invisible sanctification without a visible sign, and, on the other hand, a

visible sign without true sanctification (August. *de Quaest. Vet. Test. Lib.* iii). For, as he elsewhere says, 'Men put on Christ, sometimes to the extent of partaking in the sacrament, and sometimes to the extent of holiness of life' (August. *de Bapt. Cont. Donat.* cap. xxiv). The former may be common to the good and the bad, the latter is peculiar to the good. . . .

17. Wherefore, let it be a fixed point, that the office of the sacraments differs not from the word of God; and this is to hold forth and offer Christ to us, and, in him, the treasures of heavenly grace. They confer nothing, and avail nothing, if not received in faith, just as wine and oil, or any other liquor, however large the quantity which you pour out, will run away and perish unless there be an open vessel to receive it. When the vessel is not open, though it may be sprinkled all over, it will nevertheless remain entirely empty. We must be aware of being led into a kindred error by the terms, somewhat too extravagant, which ancient Christian writers have employed in extolling the dignity of the sacraments. We must not suppose that there is some latent virtue inherent in the sacraments by which they, in themselves, confer the gifts of the Holy Spirit upon us, in the same way in which wine is drunk out of a cup, since the only office divinely assigned them is to attest and ratify the benevolence of the Lord towards us; and they avail no farther than accompanied by the Holy Spirit to open our minds and hearts, and make us capable of receiving this testimony, in which various distinguished graces are clearly manifested. For the sacraments, as we lately observed, are to us what messengers of good news are to men, or earnests in ratifying pactions. They do not of themselves bestow any grace, but they announce and manifest it, and like earnests and badges, give a ratification of the gifts which the divine liberality has bestowed upon us. The Holy Spirit, whom the sacraments do not bring promiscuously to all, but whom the Lord specially confers on his people, brings the gifts of God along with him, makes way for the sacraments, and causes them to bear fruit. But though we deny not that God, by the immediate agency of his Spirit, countenances his own ordinance, preventing the administration of the sacraments which he has instituted from being fruitless and vain, still we maintain that the internal grace of the Spirit, as it is distinct from the external ministration, ought to be viewed and considered separately. God, therefore, truly performs whatever he promises and figures by signs; nor are the signs without effect, for they prove that he is their true and faithful author. The only question here is, whether the Lord works by proper and intrinsic virtue (as it is called), or resigns his office to external symbols? We maintain, that whatever organs he employs detract nothing from his primary operation. In this doctrine of the sacraments, their

dignity is highly extolled, their use plainly shown, their utility sufficiently proclaimed, and moderation in all things duly maintained; so that nothing is attributed to them which ought not to be attributed, and nothing denied them which they ought to possess. Meanwhile, we get rid of that fiction by which the cause of justification and the power of the Holy Spirit are included in elements as vessels and vehicles, and the special power which was overlooked is distinctly explained. Here, also, we ought to observe, that what the minister figures and attests by outward action, God performs inwardly, lest that which God claims for himself alone should be ascribed to mortal man. This Augustine is careful to observe: 'How does both God and Moses sanctify? Not Moses for God, but Moses by visible sacraments through his ministry, God by invisible grace through the Holy Spirit. Herein is the whole fruit of visible sacraments; for what do these visible sacraments avail without that sanctification of invisible grace?' . . .

XI
HOOKER

Richard Hooker (1553–1600) is one of the formative theologians of the Anglican tradition. His life is well known from Isaac Walton's famous biography—though in spite of its literary excellence, this account is apparently not to be trusted in every particular. Richard Hooker went up to Oxford as a penurious but able scholar. After graduating, he lectured on Logic and also, for a time, on Hebrew. He was appointed Master of the Temple in London—an appointment which involved him in much bitter public controversy. His chief opponents were Walter Travers and Thomas Cartwright, who favoured Calvinist doctrine and polity for the English Church. Hooker became increasingly the theologian and in some measure the architect of the more moderate type of conservative reform which is so characteristic of the Anglican tradition. But the hasty utterances of such public controversy and manœuvre were little to Hooker's taste. At his own request he demitted the Mastership in 1591 and was appointed to the parish of Boscombe and made sub-dean of Salisbury Cathedral. This gave him opportunity to approach the crucial problems of the character that reformed religion should take in England with the academic calm and systematic deliberation that suited his bent. The outcome was his great work, *Of the Laws of Ecclesiastical Polity, Eight Books*. The first four books appeared in 1594. In 1595 he was appointed to the living of Bishopsbourne near Canterbury and remained there until his death.

Whenever the first instalment of *Ecclesiastical Polity* appeared, it was evident that the controversy between the Puritan and conservative elements in the Church had been elevated to an entirely new level. Hallam says of him that he 'mingled in these vulgar controversies like a knight of romance among caitiff brawlers'. Only five books of the *Ecclesiastical Polity* were published before his death. The remaining three were published posthumously in a regrettably garbled version. The first book, from which the extracts below are taken, formulates a general philosophy of law and places those principles which are normative for church order and belief within this wider context. The second book counters the Puritan assertion that the Bible provides the only rule by which men should live. The third book attacks the notion 'that in Scripture there must be of necessity contained a form of Church polity, the laws whereof may in nowise be altered'. The fourth book deals with the accusation that the conservative party in the Church of England are 'corrupted by popery'. The fifth book reviews, expounds and defends the forms and doctrines of the Elizabethan Book of Common Prayer.

The references below are to Keble's fourth (1863) edition.

LAW ETERNAL

I am not ignorant that by 'law eternal' the learned for the most part do understand the order, not which God hath eternally purposed himself in all his works to observe, but rather that which with himself he hath set down as expedient to be kept by all his creatures according to the several conditions wherewith he hath endued them. They who thus are accustomed to speak apply the name of Law unto that only rule of working which superior authority imposeth; whereas we somewhat more enlarging the sense thereof term any kind of rule or canon, whereby actions are framed, a law. Now that law which, as it is laid up in the bosom of God, they call eternal, receiveth according unto the different kinds of things which are subject unto it different and sundry kinds of names. That part of it which ordereth natural agents we call usually Nature's law; that which Angels do clearly behold and without any swerving observe is a law Celestial and heavenly; the law of Reason, that which bindeth creatures reasonable in this world, and with which by reason they may most plainly perceive themselves bound; that which bindeth them, and is not known but by special revelation from God, Divine law; Human law, that which out of the law either of reason or of God men probably gathering to be expedient, they make it a law. All things therefore, which are as they ought to be, are conformed unto *this second law eternal*; and even those things which to this eternal law are not conformable are notwithstanding in some sort ordered by *the first eternal law*. For what good or evil is there under the sun, what action correspondent or repugnant unto the law which God hath imposed upon his creatures, but in or upon it God doth work according to the law which himself hath eternally purposed to keep; that is to say, the *first law eternal*? So that a twofold law eternal being thus made, it is not hard to conceive how they both take place in all things (pp. 204–5)....

God alone excepted, who actually and everlastingly is whatsoever he may be, and which cannot hereafter be that which now he is not; all other things besides are somewhat in possibility, which as yet they are not in act. And for this cause there is in all things an appetite or desire, whereby they incline to something which they may be; and when they are it, they shall be perfecter than they are now. All which perfections are contained under the general name of Goodness. And because there is not in the world any thing whereby another may not some way be made the perfecter, therefore all things that are, are good.

Again, sith there can be no goodness desired which proceedeth not from God himself, as from the supreme cause of all things; and every effect doth after a sort contain, at leastwise resemble, the cause from which it proceedeth: all things in the world are said in some sort to seek the highest, and to covet more or less the participation of God himself. Yet this doth no where so much appear as it doth in man, because there are so many kinds of perfections which man seeketh. The first degree of goodness is that general perfection which all things do seek, in desiring the continuance of their being. All things therefore coveting as much as may be to be like unto God in being ever, that which cannot hereunto attain personally doth seek to continue itself another way, that is by offspring and propagation. The next degree of goodness is that which each thing coveteth by affecting resemblance with God in the constancy and excellency of those operations which belong unto their kind. The immutability of God they strive unto, by working either always or for the most part after one and the same manner; his absolute exactness they imitate, by tending unto that which is most exquisite in every particular (pp. 215–16)....

Man doth seek a triple perfection: first a sensual, consisting in those things which very life itself requireth either as necessary supplements, or as beauties and ornaments thereof; then an intellectual, consisting in those things which none underneath man is either capable of or acquainted with; lastly a spiritual and divine, consisting in those things whereunto we tend by supernatural means here, but cannot here attain unto them. They who make the first of these three the scope of their whole life, are said by the Apostle[1] to have no god but only their belly, to be earthly-minded men. Unto the second they bend themselves, who seek especially to excel in all such knowledge and virtue as doth most commend men. To this branch belongeth the law of moral and civil perfection. That there is somewhat higher than either of these two, no other proof doth need than the very process of man's desire, which being natural should be frustrate, if there were not some farther thing wherein it might rest at the length contented, which in the former it cannot do. For man doth not seem to rest satisfied, either with fruition of that wherewith his life is preserved, or with performance of such actions as advance him most deservedly in estimation; but doth further covet, yea oftentimes manifestly pursue with great sedulity and earnestness, that which cannot stand

[1] *Philippians* 3. 19.

him in any stead for vital use; that which exceedeth the reach of sense; yea somewhat above capacity of reason, somewhat divine and heavenly, which with hidden exultation it rather surmiseth than conceiveth; somewhat it seeketh, and what that is directly it knoweth not, yet very intentive desire thereof doth so incite it, that all other known delights and pleasures are laid aside, they give place to the search of this but only suspected desire. If the soul of man did serve only to give him being in this life, then things appertaining unto this life would content him, as we see they do other creatures; which creatures enjoying what they live by seek no further, but in this contention do shew a kind of acknowledgment that there is no higher good which doth any way belong unto them. With us it is otherwise. For although the beauties, riches, honours, sciences, virtues, and perfections of all men living, were in the present possession of one; yet somewhat beyond and above all this would still be sought and earnestly thirsted for. So that Nature even in this life doth plainly claim and call for a more divine perfection than either of these two that have been mentioned.

This last and highest estate of perfection whereof we speak is received of men in the nature of a Reward. Rewards do always presuppose such duties performed as are rewardable. Our natural means therefore unto blessedness are our works; nor is it possible that Nature should ever find any other way to salvation than only this. But examine the works which we do, and since the first foundation of the world what one can say, My ways are pure? Seeing then all flesh is guilty of that for which God hath threatened eternally to punish, what possibility is there this way to be saved? There resteth therefore either no way unto salvation, or if any, then surely a way which is supernatural, a way which could never have entered into the heart of man as much as once to conceive or imagine, if God himself had not revealed it extraordinarily. For which cause we term it the Mystery or secret way of salvation (pp. 257–8). . . .

From salvation therefore and life all flesh being excluded this way, behold how the wisdom of God hath revealed a way mystical and supernatural, a way directing unto the same end of life by a course which groundeth itself upon the guiltiness of sin, and through sin desert of condemnation and death. For in this way the first thing is the tender compassion of God respecting us drowned and swallowed up in misery; the next is redemption out of the same by the precious death and merit of a mighty Saviour, which hath witnessed of himself, saying, 'I am the way', the way that leadeth us from misery into bliss. This supernatural way had God in himself prepared before all worlds. The way of supernatural duty which to us he hath prescribed, our Saviour in the Gospel of St John doth note, terming it by an excellency, the Work of God,

'This is the work of God that ye believe in him whom he hath sent'. Not that God doth require nothing unto happiness at the hands of men saving only a naked belief (for hope and charity we may not exclude); but that without belief all other things are as nothing, and it the ground of those other divine virtues.

Concerning Faith, the principal object whereof is that eternal Verity which hath discovered the treasures of hidden wisdom in Christ; concerning Hope, the highest object whereof is that everlasting Goodness which in Christ doth quicken the dead; concerning Charity, the final object whereof is that incomprehensible Beauty which shineth in the countenance of Christ the Son of the living God: concerning these virtues, the first of which beginning here with a weak apprehension of things not seen, endeth with the intuitive vision of God in the world to come; the second beginning here with a trembling expectation of things far removed and as yet but only heard of, endeth with real and actual fruition of that which no tongue can express; the third beginning here with a weak inclination of heart towards him unto whom we are not able to approach, endeth with endless union, the mystery whereof is higher than the reach of the thoughts of men; concerning that Faith, Hope, and Charity, without which there can be no salvation, was there ever any mention made saving only in that law which God himself hath from heaven revealed? There is not in the world a syllable muttered with certain truth concerning any of these three, more than hath been supernaturally received from the mouth of the eternal God.

Laws therefore concerning these things are supernatural, both in respect of the manner of delivering them, which is divine; and also in regard of the things delivered, which are such as have not in nature any cause from which they flow, but were by the voluntary appointment of God ordained besides the course of nature, to rectify nature's obliquity withal (pp. 260–2)....

Laws that concern supernatural duties are all positive, and either concern men supernaturally as men, or else as parts of a supernatural society, which society we call the church. To concern men as men supernaturally is to concern them as duties which belong of necessity to all, and yet could not have been known by any to belong unto them, unless God had opened them himself, inasmuch as they do not depend upon any natural ground at all out of which they may be deduced, but are appointed of God to supply the defect of those natural ways of salvation, by which we are not now able to attain thereunto. The church being a supernatural society doth differ from natural societies in this, that the persons unto whom we associate ourselves, in the one are men simply considered as men, but they to whom we be joined in the other, are

God, Angels, and holy men. Again the church being both a society and a society supernatural, although as it is a society it have the selfsame original grounds which other politic societies have, namely, the natural inclination which all men have unto sociable life, and consent to some certain bond of association, which bond is the law that appointeth what kind of order they shall be associated in: yet unto the church as it is a society supernatural this is peculiar, that part of the bond of their association which belongs to the Church of God must be a law supernatural, which God himself hath revealed concerning that kind of worship which his people shall do unto him. The substance of the service of God therefore so far forth as it hath in it any thing more than the Law of Reason doth teach, may not be invented of men, as it is amongst the heathens, but must be received from God himself, as always it hath been in the church, saving only when the church hath been forgetful of her duty.

Wherefore to end with a general rule concerning all the laws which God hath tied men unto: those laws divine that belong, whether naturally or supernaturally, either to men as men, or to men as they live in politic society, or to men as they are of that politic society which is the church, without any further respect had unto any such variable accident as the state of men and of societies of men and of the church itself in this world is subject unto; all laws that so belong unto men, they belong for ever, yea although they be Positive Laws, unless being positive God himself which made them alter them. The reason is, because the subject or matter of laws in general is thus far forth constant: which matter is that for the ordering whereof laws were instituted, and being instituted are not changeable without cause, neither can they have cause of change, when that which gave them their first institution remaineth for ever one and the same. On the other side, laws that were made for men or societies or churches, in regard of their being such as they do not always continue, but may perhaps be clean otherwise a while after, and so may require to be otherwise ordered than before; the laws of God himself which are of this nature, no man endued with common sense will ever deny to be of a different constitution from the former, in respect of the one's constancy and the mutability of the other. And this doth seem to have been the very cause why St John doth so peculiarly term the doctrine that teacheth salvation by Jesus Christ,[1] *Evangelium aeternum*, 'an eternal Gospel'; because there can be no reason wherefore the publishing thereof should be taken away, and any other instead of it proclaimed, as long as the world doth continue: whereas the whole law of rites and ceremonies, although delivered with so great solemnity, is notwith-

[1] *Apocalypse* 14. 6.

standing clean abrogated, inasmuch as it had but temporary cause of God's ordaining it (pp. 273–5)....

Easier a great deal it is for men by law to be taught what they ought to do, than instructed how to judge as they should do of law: the one being a thing which belongeth generally unto all, the other such as none but the wiser and more judicious sort can perform. Yea, the wisest are always touching this point the readiest to acknowledge, that soundly to judge of a law is the weightiest thing which any man can take upon him. But if we will give judgment of the laws under which we live; first let that law eternal be always before our eyes, as being of principal force and moment to breed in religious minds a dutiful estimation of all laws, the use and benefit whereof we see; because there can be no doubt but that laws apparently good are (as it were) things copied out of the very tables of that high everlasting law; even as the book of that law hath said concerning itself, 'By me kings reign', and by me 'princes decree justice'.[1] Not as if men did behold that book and accordingly frame their laws; but because it worketh in them, because it discovereth and (as it were) readeth itself to the world by them, when the laws which they make are righteous. Furthermore, although we perceive not the goodness of laws made, nevertheless sith things in themselves may have that which we peradventure discern not, should not this breed a fear in our hearts, how we speak or judge in the worse part concerning that, the unadvised disgrace whereof may be no mean dishonour to him, towards whom we profess all submission and awe? Surely there must be very manifest iniquity in laws, against which we shall be able to justify our contumelious invectives. The chiefest root whereof, when we use them without cause, is ignorance how laws inferior are derived from that supreme or highest law.

The first that receive impression from thence are natural agents. The law of whose operations might be haply thought less pertinent, when the question is about laws for human actions, but that in those very actions which most spiritually and supernaturally concern men, the rules and axioms of natural operations have their force. What can be more immediate to our salvation than our persuasion concerning the law of Christ towards his church? What greater assurance of love towards his church, than the knowledge of that mystical union, whereby the church is become as near unto Christ as any one part of his flesh is unto other? That the church being in such sort his he must needs protect it, what proof more strong than if a manifest law so require, which law it is not possible for Christ to violate? And what other law doth the Apostle for this allege, but such as is both common unto Christ with us, and unto

[1] *Proverbs* 8. 15.

us with other things natural; 'No man hateth his own flesh, but doth love and cherish it'?[1] The axioms of that law therefore, whereby natural agents are guided, have their use in the moral, yea, even in the spiritual actions of men, and consequently in all laws belonging unto men howsoever.

Neither are the Angels themselves so far severed from us in their kind and manner of working, but that between the law of their heavenly operations and the actions of men in this our state of mortality such correspondence there is, as maketh it expedient to know in some sort the one for the other's more perfect direction. Would Angels acknowledge themselves 'fellow-servants'[2] with the sons of men, but that both having one Lord, there must be some kind of law which is one and the same to both, whereunto their obedience being perfecter is to our weaker both a pattern and a spur? Or would the Apostles, speaking of that which belongeth unto saints as they are linked together in the bond of spiritual society,[3] so often make mention how Angels therewith are delighted, if in things publicly done by the church we are not somewhat to respect what the Angels of heaven do? Yea, so far hath the Apostle Saint Paul proceeded, as to signify[4] that even about the outward orders of the church which serve but for comeliness, some regard is to be had of Angels, who best like us when we are most like unto them in all parts of decent demeanour. So that the law of Angels we cannot judge altogether impertinent unto the affairs of the church of God.

Our largeness of speech how men do find out what things reason bindeth them of necessity to observe, and what it guideth them to choose in things which are left as arbitrary; the care we have had to declare the different nature of laws which severally concern all men, from such as belong unto men either civilly or spiritually associated, such as pertain to the fellowship which nations, or which Christian nations, have amongst themselves, and in the last place such as concerning every or any of these God himself hath revealed by his Holy Word: all serveth but to make manifest, that as the actions of men are of sundry distinct kinds, so the laws thereof must accordingly be distinguished. There are in men operations, some natural, some rational, some supernatural, some politic, some finally ecclesiastical: which if we measure not each by his own proper law, whereas the things themselves are so different, there will be in our understanding and judgment of them confusion.

As that first error sheweth, whereon our opposites in this cause have grounded themselves. For as they rightly maintain that God must be glorified in all things, and that the actions of men cannot tend unto his

[1] *Ephesians* 5. 29. [2] *Apocalypse* 19. 10.

[3] I *Peter* 1. 12; *Ephesians* 3. 10; I *Timothy* 5. 21. [4] I *Corinthians* 11. 10.

glory unless they be framed after his law; so it is their error to think that the only law which God hath appointed unto men in that behalf is the sacred Scripture. By that which we work naturally, as when we breathe, sleep, move, we set forth the glory of God as natural agents do,[1] albeit we have no express purpose to make that our end, nor any advised determination therein to follow a law, but do that we do (for the most part) not as much as thinking thereon. In reasonable and moral actions another law taketh place; a law by the observation whereof[2] we glorify God in such sort, as no creature else under man is able to do; because other creatures have not judgment to examine the quality of that which is done by them, and therefore in that they do they neither can accuse nor approve themselves. Men do both, as the Apostle teacheth; yea, those men which have no written law of God to shew what is good or evil, carry written in their hearts the universal law of mankind, the Law of Reason, whereby they judge as by a rule which God hath given unto all men for that purpose.[3] The law of reason doth somewhat direct men how to honour God as their Creator; but how to glorify God in such sort as is required, to the end he may be an everlasting Saviour, this we are taught by divine law, which law both ascertaineth the truth and supplieth unto us the want of that other law. So that in moral actions, divine law helpeth exceedingly the law of reason to guide man's life; but in supernatural it alone guideth.

Proceed we further; let us place man in some public society with others, whether civil or spiritual; and in this case there is no remedy but we must add yet a further law. For although even here likewise the laws of nature and reason be of necessary use, yet somewhat over and besides them is necessary, namely human and positive law, together with that law which is of commerce between grand societies, the law of nations, and of nations Christian. For which cause the law of God hath likewise said, 'Let every soul be subject to the higher powers'.[4] The public power of all societies is above every soul contained in the same societies. And the principal use of that power is to give laws unto all that are under it; which laws in such case we must obey, unless there be reason shewed which may necessarily enforce that the law of Reason or of God doth enjoin the contrary. Because except our own private and but probable resolutions be by the law of public determinations overruled, we take away all possibility of sociable life in the world. A plainer example whereof than ourselves we cannot have. How cometh it to pass that we are at this present day so rent with mutual contentions, and that the church is so much troubled about the polity of the church? No doubt if men had been willing to learn how many laws their actions in this

[1] *Psalm* 148. 7–9. [2] *Romans* 1. 21. [3] Ibid. 2. 15. [4] Ibid. 13. 1.

life are subject unto, and what the true force of each law is, all these controversies might have died the very day they were first brought forth.

It is both commonly said, and truly, that the best men otherwise are not always the best in regard of society. The reason whereof is, for that the law of men's actions is one, if they be respected only as men; and another, when they are considered as parts of a politic body. Many men there are, than whom nothing is more commendable when they are singled; and yet in society with others none less fit to answer the duties which are looked for at their hands. Yea, I am persuaded, that of them with whom in this cause we strive, there are whose betters amongst men would be hardly found, if they did not live amongst men, but in some wilderness by themselves. The cause of which their disposition so unframable unto societies wherein they live, is, for that they discern not aright what place and force these several kinds of laws ought to have in all their actions. Is there question either concerning the regiment of the church in general, or about conformity between one church and another, or of ceremonies, offices, powers, jurisdictions in our own church? Of all these things they judge by that rule which they frame to themselves with some show of probability, and what seemeth in that sort convenient, the same they think themselves bound to practise; the same by all means they labour mightily to uphold; whatsoever any law of man to the contrary hath determined they weigh it not. Thus by following the law of private reason, where the law of public should take place, they breed disturbance.

For the better inuring therefore of men's minds with the true distinction of laws, and of their several force according to the different kind and quality of our actions, it shall not peradventure be amiss to shew in some example how they all take place. To seek no further, let but that be considered, than which there is not any thing more familiar unto us, our food.

What things are food and what are not we judge naturally by sense[1]; neither need we any other law to be our director in that behalf than the selfsame which is common unto us with beasts.

But when we come to consider food, as of a benefit which God of his bounteous goodness hath provided for all things living[2]; the law of Reason doth here require the duty of thankfulness at our hands, towards him at whose hands we have it. And lest appetite in the use of food should lead us beyond that which is meet, we owe in this case obedience to that law of Reason, which teacheth mediocrity in meats and drinks. The same things divine law teacheth also, as at large we have showed it doth all parts of moral duty, whereunto we all of necessity stand bound, in regard of the life to come.

[1] *Job* 34. 3. [2] *Psalm* 145. 15–16.

But of certain kinds of food the Jews sometimes had, and we ourselves likewise have, a mystical, religious, and supernatural use, they of their paschal lamb and oblations, we of our bread and wine in the Eucharist; which use none but divine law could institute.

Now as we live in civil society, the state of the commonwealth wherein we live both may and doth require certain laws concerning food; which laws, saving only that we are members of the commonwealth where they are of force, we should not need to respect as rules of action, whereas now in their place and kind they must be respected and obeyed.

Yea, the selfsame matter is also a subject wherein sometime ecclesiastical laws have place; so that unless we will be authors of confusion in the church, our private discretion, which otherwise might guide us a contrary way, must here submit itself to be that way guided, which the public judgment of the church hath thought better. In which case that of Zonaras concerning fasts may be remembered. 'Fastings are good, but let good things be done in good and convenient manner. He that transgresseth in fasting the orders of the holy fathers', the positive laws of the church of Christ, must be plainly told, 'that good things do lose the grace of their goodness, when in good sort they are not performed'.[1]

And as here man's private fancies must give place to the higher judgment of that church which is in authority a mother over them; so the very actions of whole churches have in regard of commerce and fellowship with other churches been subject to laws concerning food, the contrary unto which laws had else been thought more convenient for them to observe; as by that order of abstinence from strangled and blood may appear; an order grounded upon that fellowship which the churches of the Gentiles had with the Jews.

Thus we see how even one and the selfsame thing is under divers considerations conveyed through many laws; and that to measure by any one kind of law all the actions of men were to confound the admirable order, wherein God hath disposed all laws, each as in nature, so in degree, distinct from other.

Wherefore that here we may briefly end: of Law there can be no less acknowledged, than that her seat is the bosom of God, her voice the harmony of the world: all things in heaven and earth do her homage, the very least as feeling her care, and the greatest as not exempted from her power: both Angels and men and creatures of what condition soever, though each in different sort and manner, yet all with uniform consent, admiring her as the mother of their peace and joy (pp. 278–85).

[1] *Zonar. in Can. Apost.* 66. p. 34.

THE PERIOD OF EXPERIMENTAL THEOLOGY

XII

JONATHAN EDWARDS

Jonathan Edwards (1703–58) was the son of a New England pastor. He was a serious and precocious child. In 1720 he graduated at Yale and proceeded to study divinity at Newhaven. He was for a short time a pastor in New York, then a tutor at Yale. In 1727 he became the colleague of his grandfather, Solomon Stoddart, as pastor of the Northampton congregation. He was a notable and effective preacher, but in 1750 he became estranged from his congregation, chiefly over his insistence upon evidence of conversion of the heart as well as profession of faith as a qualification for admission to communion. He left and became a missionary to the Indians in Massachusetts. In 1757 he was appointed president of Princeton College (later Princeton University), but died tragically of smallpox a few months later.

In an impressively comprehensive system he interpreted the type of Calvinist theology prevalent in New England in terms of the philosophy and science of his day (e.g. Locke and Newton). This intellectual sophistication was combined with a simplicity and intensity of religious sentiment, reacting strongly against the formalism which had become characteristic of the Reformed and Puritan traditions. Strong expressions of 'evangelical' emotions were taking place in the early 1740's throughout the American Colonies in 'The Great Awakening' (usually without the restraints of Edwards' intellect). Edwards stoutly defended these manifestations, but placed them within the context of a balanced theology. His *Treatise Concerning Religious Affections* (1746)—from which the selections below have been made—is the most important and systematic expression of this aspect of his thought. Perhaps the most important academically of all his writings was his *Freedom of the Will* (1754), in which he defended a version of the Reformed doctrine against libertarian views. It has attained the status of a classic for philosophy as well as theology.

A new American critical edition of *The Works of Jonathan Edwards*, ed. Perry Miller (1957 *et seq.*), is now nearing completion. See also Perry Miller, *Jonathan Edwards*, for a general account of his thought; also Clarence H. Faust and Thomas H. Johnson (eds.), *Jonathan Edwards, Representative Selections* (1935). The references below are to the edition

The Works of President Edwards (8 vols.) published by James Black and Son, London, 1817.

ON RELIGIOUS AFFECTIONS

God has endued the soul with two principal faculties: The one, that by which it is capable of *perception* and speculation, or by which it discerns, and judges of things; which is called the understanding. The other, that by which the soul is some way inclined with respect to the things it views or considers: or it is the faculty by which the soul beholds things—not as an indifferent unaffected spectator, but—either as liking or disliking, pleased or displeased, approving or rejecting. This faculty is called by various names: it is sometimes called the *inclination*; and, as it respects the actions determined and governed by it, the *will*: and the mind, with regard to the exercise of this faculty, is often called the *heart*.

The exercises of this faculty are of two sorts; either, those by which the soul is carried out towards the things in view in approving them, being pleased with, and inclined to them; or, those in which the soul opposes the things in view, in disapproving them; and in being displeased with, averse from, and rejecting them.—And as the exercises of the inclination are various in their kinds, so they are much more various in their degrees. There are some exercises of pleasedness or displeasedness, inclination or disinclination, wherein the soul is carried but a little beyond a state of perfect indifference. And there are other degrees, wherein the approbation or dislike, pleasedness or aversion, are stronger; wherein we may rise higher and higher, till the soul comes to act vigorously and sensibly, and its actings are with that strength, that (through the laws of union which the Creator has fixed between soul and body) the motion of the blood and animal spirits begins to be sensibly altered; whence oftentimes arises some bodily sensation, especially about the heart and vitals, which are the fountain of the fluids of the body. Whence it comes to pass, that the mind, with regard to the exercises of this faculty, perhaps in all nations and ages, is called the heart. And it is to be noted, that they are these more vigorous and sensible exercises of this faculty, which are called the affections.

The will, and the affections of the soul, are not two faculties; the affections are not essentially distinct from the will, nor do they differ from the mere actings of the will and inclination, but only in the liveliness and sensibility of exercise.—It must be confessed, that language is here somewhat imperfect, the meaning of words in a considerable measure loose and unfixed, and not precisely limited by custom which governs the use of language. In some sense, the affection of the soul differs nothing at all from the will and inclination, and the will never is in any exercise further than it is affected; it is not moved out of a state of perfect indifference, any otherwise than as it is affected one way or other. But yet there are many actings of the will and inclination, that are not so commonly called affections. In every thing we do, wherein we act voluntarily, there is an exercise of the will and inclination. It is our inclination that governs us in our actions; but all the actings of the inclination and will, are not ordinarily called affections. Yet, what are commonly called affections are not essentially different from them, but only in the degree and manner of exercise. In every act of the will whatsoever, the soul either likes or dislikes, is either inclined or disinclined to what is in view. These are not essentially different from the affections of love and hatred. A liking or inclination of the soul to a thing, if it be in a high degree, vigorous and lively, is the very same thing with the affection of love: and a disliking and disinclining, if in a great degree, is the very same with hatred. In every act of the will for, or towards something not present, the soul is in some degree inclined to that thing; and that inclination, if in a considerable degree, is the very same with the affection of desire. And in every degree of an act of the will, wherein the soul approves of something present, there is a degree of pleasedness; and that pleasedness, if it be in a considerable degree, is the very same with the affection of joy and delight. And if the will disapproves of what is present, the soul is in some degree displeased, and if that displeasedness be great, it is the very same with the affection of grief or sorrow.

. . . (Works, Vol. 4, pp. 10–11)

True religion, in great part, consists in the affections. What has been said of the nature of the affections makes this evident; and may be sufficient, without adding anything further, to put this matter out of doubt: for who will deny that true religion consists, in a great measure, in vigorous and lively actings of the inclination and will of the soul, or the fervent exercises of the heart? That religion which God requires, and will accept, does not consist in weak, dull, and lifeless wishes, raising us but a little above a state of indifference. God, in his word, greatly insists upon it, that we be in good earnest, fervent in spirit, and our hearts vigorously engaged in religion: *Romans* 12. 11. 'Be ye fervent in spirit, serving the Lord.' *Deuteronomy* 10. 12. 'And now Israel, what doth the Lord thy God require of thee, but to fear the Lord thy God, and to walk in all his ways, and to love him, and to serve the Lord thy God with all thy heart, and with all thy soul?' And Chapter 6. 4, 5. 'Hear, O Israel, the Lord our God is one Lord: and thou shalt love the Lord thy God with all thy heart, and with all thy soul, and with all thy might.' It is such a fervent, vigorous engagedness of the heart in religion, that is the fruit of a real circumcision of the heart, or true regeneration, and that has the promises of life; *Deuteronomy* 30. 6. 'And the Lord thy God will circumcise thine heart, and the heart of thy seed, to love the Lord thy God with all thy heart, and with all thy soul, that thou mayest live.'

. . . (p. 13)

Such is man's nature, that he is very inactive, any otherwise than he is influenced by either love or hatred, desire, hope, fear, or some other affection. These affections we see to be the moving springs in all the affairs of life, which engage men in all their pursuits; and especially in all affairs wherein they are earnestly engaged, and which they pursue with vigour. We see the world of mankind exceedingly busy and active; and their affections are the springs of motion: take away all love and hatred, all hope and fear, all anger, zeal, and affectionate desire, and the world would be, in a great measure, motionless and dead: there would be no such thing as activity amongst mankind, or any earnest pursuit whatsoever. It is affection that engages the covetous man, and him that is greedy of wordly profits; it is by the affections that the ambitious man is put forward in his pursuit of wordly glory; and the affections also actuate the voluptuous man, in his pleasure and sensual delights. The world continues, from age to age, in a continual commotion and agitation, in pursuit of these things; but take away affection, and the spring of all this motion would be gone; the motion itself would cease. And as in worldly things, worldly affections are very much the spring of men's motion and action; so in religious matters, the spring of their actions are very much religious affections: he that has doctrinal knowledge and speculation only, without affection, never is *engaged* in the business of religion.

. . . (pp. 14–15)

The Spirit of God so dwells in the hearts of the saints, that he there, as a seed or spring of life, exerts and communicates himself, in this his sweet and divine nature. He makes the soul a partaker of God's beauty and Christ's joy, so that the saint has truly fellowship with the Father, and with his Son Jesus Christ, in thus having communion or participation of the Holy Ghost. The grace which is in the hearts of the saints, is of the same nature with the divine holiness, though infinitely less in degree; as the brightness in a diamond which the sun shines upon, is of the same nature with the brightness of the sun, but only that it is as nothing to it in degree. Therefore Christ says, *John* 3. 6, 'That which is born of the Spirit, is spirit'; i.e. the grace that is begotten in the hearts of the saints, is something of the same nature with that Spirit, and so is properly called a spiritual nature; after the same manner as that which is born of the flesh is flesh, or that which is born of corrupt nature is corrupt nature.

. . . (pp. 105–6)

True saints *only* have that which is spiritual; others not only have not these communications of the Spirit in so high a degree as the saints, but have nothing of that nature or kind. For the Apostle James tells us, that natural men have not the Spirit; and Christ teaches the necessity of a new birth, or a being born of the Spirit, from this, that he that is born of the flesh, has only flesh and no spirit (*John* 3. 6). They have not the Spirit of God dwelling in them in any degree; for the Apostle teaches, that all who have the Spirit of God dwelling in them are his (*Romans* 8. 9–11). And, having the Spirit of God is spoken of as a certain sign, that persons shall have the eternal inheritance; for it is the earnest of it (II *Corinthians* 1. 22 and 5. 5; *Ephesians* 1. 14); and having any thing of the Spirit is mentioned as a sure sign of being in Christ, I *John* 4. 13: 'Hereby know we that we dwell in him, because he hath given us of his Spirit.' Ungodly men, not only have not so much of the divine nature as the saints, but they are not partakers of it; which implies that they have nothing of it; for being partaker of the divine nature is spoken of as the peculiar privilege of the true saints (II *Peter* 1. 4). Ungodly men are not partakers of God's holiness (*Hebrews* 12. 10). A natural man has no experience of those things that are spiritual: he is so far from it, that he knows nothing about them, and is a perfect stranger to them. To talk about such things is all foolishness to him, he knows not what it means, I *Corinthians* 2. 14: 'The natural man receiveth not the things of the Spirit of God; for they are foolishness to him: neither can he know them, because they are spiritually discerned.' And to the like purpose Christ teaches us that the world is wholly unacquainted with the Spirit of God, *John* 14. 17: 'Even the Spirit of truth, whom the world cannot receive, because it seeth him not, neither knoweth him.' And it is further evident, that natural men have nothing in them of the same nature with the true grace of the saints, because the Apostle teaches us, that those of them who go farthest in religion, have no charity, or true Christian love (I *Corinthians* 13). So Christ elsewhere reproves the Pharisees, those high pretenders to religion, that they 'had not the love of God in them' (*John* 5. 42). Hence natural men have no communion or fellowship with Christ, or participation in him, as these words signify, for this is spoken of as the peculiar privilege of the saints (I *John* 1. 3, 6, 7; I *Corinthians* 1. 8, 9). And the Scripture speaks of the actual existence of a gracious principle in the soul, though in its first beginning, like a seed planted there, as inconsistent with a man's being a sinner (I *John* 3. 9). And natural men are represented in Scripture, as having no spiritual light, no spiritual life, and no spiritual being; and therefore conversion is often compared with opening the eyes of the blind, raising the dead, and a work of creation, wherein creatures are made entirely new, and becoming new-born children.

From these things it is evident, that those gracious influences of the saints, and the effects of God's Spirit which they experience, are entirely above nature, and altogether of a different kind from anything that men find in themselves by the exercise of natural principles. No improvement of those principles that are natural, no advancing or exalting of them to higher degrees, and no kind of composition will ever bring men to them; because they not only differ from what is natural, and from every thing that natural men experience, in degree and circumstances, but also in kind; and are of a nature vastly more excellent. And this is what I mean by 'supernatural' when I say that *gracious affections are from those influences that are supernatural.*

From hence it follows, that in those gracious exercises and affections which are wrought in the saints, through the saving influences of the Spirit of God, there is a new inward perception or sensation of their minds, entirely different in its nature and kind, from anything that ever their minds were the subjects of before they were sanctified. For, if God by his mighty power produces something that is new, not only in degree and circumstances, but in its whole nature—and that which could be produced by no exalting, varying or compounding of what was there before, or by adding any thing of the like kind—then, doubtless, something entirely new is felt, or perceived. There is what some metaphysicians call a new simple idea. If grace be, in the sense above described, an entirely new kind of principle; then the exercises of it are also new. And if there be in the soul a new sort of conscious exercises, which the soul knew nothing of before, and which no improvement, composition, or management of what it was before could produce; then it follows that the mind has an entirely new kind of perception or sensation. Here is, as it were, a new spiritual sense, or a principle of a new kind of perception or spiritual sensation, which is in its whole nature different from any former kinds of sensation of the mind, as tasting is diverse from any of the other senses. And something is perceived by a true saint, in the exercise of this new sense of mind, in spiritual and divine things, as entirely diverse from any thing that is perceived in them, by natural men, as the sweet taste of honey is diverse from the ideas men get of honey by looking on and feeling it. So that the spiritual perceptions which a sanctified and spiritual person has, are not only diverse from all that natural men have, as the perceptions of the same sense may differ one from another, but rather as the ideas and sensations of different senses differ. Hence the work of the Spirit of God in regeneration is often in Scripture compared to the giving of a new sense, eyes to see, ears to hear, unstopping the ears of the deaf, opening the eyes of them that were born blind, and turning from darkness unto light. And because this spiritual sense is immensely the most noble and excellent, and that without which all other principles of perception, and all our faculties are useless and vain; therefore the giving of this new sense, with the blessed fruits and effects of it in the soul, is compared to raising the dead, and to a new creation.

. . . (pp. 107–9)

Another thing wherein those affections that are truly gracious and holy, differ from those that are false, is beautiful symmetry and proportion. Not that the symmetry of the virtues and gracious affections of the saints, in this life, is perfect; it oftentimes is in many things defective, through the imperfection of grace, want of proper instructions, errors in judgment, some particular unhappiness of natural temper, defects in education, and many other disadvantages that might be mentioned. But yet there is in no wise that monstrous disproportion in gracious affections, and the various parts of true religion in the saints, that is very commonly to be observed in the false religion and counterfeit graces of hypocrites.

In the truly holy affections of the saints is found that proportion, which is the natural consequence of the universality of their sanctification. They have the whole image of Christ upon them: they have put off the old man, and have put on the new man entire in all his parts and members. 'It hath pleased the Father that in Christ all the fulness should dwell': there is in him every grace: 'he is full of grace and truth': and they that are Christ's 'of his fulness receive, and grace for grace' (*John* I. 14, 16). There is every grace in them which is in Christ: 'grace for grace': that is, grace answerable to grace: there is no grace in Christ, but there is its image in believers to answer it. The image is a true image; and there is something of the same beautiful proportion in the image, which is in the original; there is feature for feature, and member for member. There is symmetry and beauty in God's workmanship. The natural body which God hath made, consists of many members; and all are in a beautiful proportion: so the new man consists of various graces and affections. The body of one that was born a perfect child, may fail of exact proportion through distemper, weakness, or injury of some of its members; yet the disproportion is in no measure like that of those who are born monsters.

. . . (pp. 257–8)

Not only is there often in hypocrites, an essential deficiency, as to the various kinds of religious affections; but also a strange partiality and disproportion, in the same affections, with regard to different objects.—Thus as to the affection of love, some make high pretences, and a great shew of love to God and Christ, and it may be have been greatly affected with what they have heard or thought concerning them: but they have not a spirit of love and benevolence towards men, but are disposed to contention, envy, revenge, and evil-speaking; and will, it may be, suffer an old grudge to rest in their bosoms towards a neighbour for seven years together, if not twice seven years; living in real ill-will and bitterness of spirit towards him. And it may be in their dealings with their neighbours, they are not very strict and conscientious in observing the rule of 'doing to others, as they would that they should do to them': I *John* 4. 20. 'If a man say, I love God, and hateth his brother, he is a liar: for he that loveth not his brother whom he hath seen, how can he love God whom he hath not seen?' On the other hand, there are others who appear as if they had a great deal of benevolence to men, who are very good-natured and generous in their way; but have no love to God.

. . . (p. 260)

What has been observed of the affections of love, is applicable also to other religious affections. Those that are true, extend in some proportion to their due and proper objects: but the false, are commonly strangely disproportionate. So it is with religious desires and longings; these in the saints, are towards those things that are spiritual and excellent in general, and in some proportion to their excellency, importance or necessity, or the near concern they have in them: but in false longings, it is often far otherwise. They will strangely run, with impatient vehemence, after something of less importance, when other things of greater importance are neglected. Thus, for instance, some persons are attended with a vehement inclination, an accountably violent pressure, to declare to others what they experience, and to exhort them; when there is at the same time no inclination, in any proportionable measure, to other things, to which true Christianity has a great, yea, a greater tendency; as pouring out the soul before God in secret, earnest prayer and praise to him, more conformity to him, living more to his glory, etc. We read in Scripture of 'groanings that cannot be uttered', and 'soul-breakings for the longing it hath'; and longings, thirstings, and pantings, much more frequently to these latter things than the former.

. . . (p. 263)

Gracious and holy affections have their exercise and fruit in Christian practice. I mean, they have that influence and power upon him who is the subject of them, that they cause that a practice, which is universally conformed to, and directed by Christian rules, should be the practice and business of his life.

. . . (p. 275)

The reason why the gracious affections have such a tendency and effect, appears from many things that have already been observed in the preceding parts of this discourse.

The reason of it appears particularly from this, that gracious affections arise from those operations and influences which are spiritual, and that the inward principle from whence they flow, is something divine, a communication of God, a participation of the divine nature, Christ living in the heart, the holy Spirit dwelling there, in union with the faculties of the soul, as an internal vital principle, exerting his own proper nature in the exercise of those faculties. This is sufficient to shew us why true grace should have such activity, power and efficacy. No wonder that what is divine, is powerful and effectual; for it has omnipotence on its side. If God dwells in the heart, and be vitally united to it, he will shew that he is a God by the efficacy of his operation. Christ is not in the heart of a saint as in a sepulchre, as a dead saviour that does nothing; but as in his temple, one that is alive from the dead. For in the heart where Christ savingly is, there he lives, and exerts himself after the power of that endless life, that he received at his resurrection. Thus every saint who is the subject of the benefit of Christ's suffering, is made to know and experience the power of his resurrection. The Spirit of Christ, which is the immediate spring of grace in the heart, is all life, all power, all act; II *Corinthians* 2. 4: 'In demonstration of the Spirit, and of power.' I *Thessalonians* 1. 5: 'Our gospel came not unto you in word only, but also in power, and in the Holy Spirit.'—I *Corinthians* 4. 20: 'The kingdom of God is not in word, but in power.' Hence saving affections, though oftentimes they do not make so great a noise and show as others; yet have in them a secret solidity, life and strength, whereby they take hold of, and carry away the heart, leading it into a kind of captivity, II *Corinthians* 10. 5, gaining a full and steadfast determination of the will for God and holiness, *Psalm* 110. 3: 'Thy people shall be willing in the day of thy power.' And thus it is that holy affections have a governing power in the course of a man's life. A statue may look very much like a real man, and a beautiful man; yea it may have, in its appearance to the eye, the resemblance of a very lively, strong and active man: but yet an inward principle of life and strength is wanting; and therefore it does nothing, it brings nothing to pass, there is no action or operation to answer the shew. False discoveries and affections do not go deep enough, to reach and govern the spring of men's actions and practice. The seed in the stony ground had not deepness of earth; the root did not go deep enough to bring forth fruit. But gracious affections go to the very bottom of the heart, and take hold of the very inmost springs of life and activity. Herein chiefly appears the power of true godliness, viz. in its being effectual in practice. And the efficacy of godliness in this respect, is what the Apostle respects, when he speaks of the power of godliness, II *Timothy* 3. 5, for he there is particularly declaring, how some professors of religion would notoriously fail in the practice of it, and then in the fifth verse observes, that in being thus of an unholy practice, they deny the *power* of godliness, though they have the *form* of it. Indeed the power of godliness is exerted in the first place within the soul; in the sensible, lively exercise of gracious affections there. Yet the principal *evidence* of this power is in those exercises of holy affections that are practical; conquering the will, the lusts, and corruptions of men, and carrying them on in the way of holiness, through all temptation, difficulty and opposition.

. . . (pp. 284–5)

XIII

JOHN WESLEY

John Wesley (1703–91) scarcely needs an introduction. As the founder of Methodism and a great evangelical preacher he is well known. It is typical of Wesley that his theology is usually expressed in homiletic or devotional form. One aspect of his teaching, however, which did receive a more formal theological treatment was his doctrine of Christian perfection. It is by this that I have chosen to represent him.

He was born at Epworth, being the son of an Anglican rector and his fifteenth child. In his strongly religious upbringing he was much influenced by his mother's piety. He was educated at Charterhouse and Oxford, ordained deacon in 1725 and priested in 1728. For a time he lectured on Greek language and literature at Oxford. After the death of his father, he and his brother Charles went to Georgia to conduct a mission among the American Indians. The mission was not a great success. He remained at this time a very formal high churchman, but was much impressed by his encounters during these travels with various types of less formal piety—particularly that of the Moravians.

After his return to England he underwent a profound conversion while listening to a reading from Luther's *Preface to the Epistle to the Romans*. From this point onwards his liturgical and doctrinal formalism was left behind and he went far in the other direction. He organized the Methodist movement with incredible energy and inspired it with his devotional fervour. There can be no doubt that he did not initially intend a breach with the Anglican Communion, but when he ordained his assistant, Dr Coke, superintendent (or bishop) in 1784 and instructed him to ordain others, separate denominational status became inevitable.

He was a very prolific writer and publisher. His main literary legacy is his *Journal*, edited by N. Curnock (8 vols., 1909–16) and his *Standard Sermons*, edited by E. H. Sugden (1921). The passage reproduced below is taken from the third edition of *The Works of the Rev. John Wesley, M.A.*, published by John Mason, London, 1830.

CHRISTIAN PERFECTION

Question. What is Christian perfection?

Answer. The loving God with all our heart, mind, soul, and strength. This implies, that no wrong temper, none contrary to love, remains in the soul; and that all the thoughts, words, and actions, are governed by pure love.

Question. Do you affirm, that this perfection excludes all infirmities, ignorance, and mistake?

Answer. I continually affirm quite the contrary, and always have done so.

Question. But how can every thought, word, and work, be governed by pure love, and the man be subject at the same time to ignorance and mistake?

Answer. I see no contradiction here: 'A man may be filled with pure love, and still be liable to mistake.' Indeed I do not expect to be freed from actual mistakes, till this mortal puts on immortality. I believe this to be a natural consequence of the soul's dwelling in flesh and blood. For we cannot now think at all, but by the mediation of those bodily organs which have suffered equally with the rest of our frame. And hence we cannot avoid sometimes thinking wrong, till this corruptible shall have put on incorruption.

But we may carry this thought farther yet. A mistake in judgment may possibly occasion a mistake in practice. For instance: Mr De Renty's mistake touching the nature of mortification, arising from prejudice of education, occasioned that practical mistake, his wearing an iron girdle. And a thousand such instances there may be, even in those who are in the highest state of grace. Yet, where every word and action springs from love, such a mistake is not properly a sin. However, it cannot bear the rigour of God's justice, but needs the atoning blood.

Question. What was the judgment of all our brethren who met at Bristol in August 1758, on this head?

Answer. It was expressed in these words: (1) Every one may mistake as long as he lives. (2) A mistake in opinion may occasion a mistake in practice. (3) Every such mistake is a transgression of the perfect law. Therefore, (4) Every such mistake, were it not for the blood of atonement, would expose to eternal damnation. (5) It follows, that the most perfect have continual need of the merits of Christ, even for their actual transgressions, and may say for themselves, as well as for their brethren, 'Forgive us our trespasses'.

This easily accounts for what might otherwise seem to be utterly unaccountable; namely, that those who are not offended when we speak of the highest degree of love, yet will not hear of living without sin. The reason is, they know all men are liable to mistake, and that in practice as well as in judgment. But they do not know, or do not observe, that this is not sin, if love is the sole principle of action.

Question. But still, if they live without sin, does not this exclude the necessity of a Mediator? At least, is it not plain that they stand no longer in need of Christ in his priestly office?

Answer. Far from it. None feel their need of Christ like these; none so entirely depend upon him. For Christ does not give life to the soul separate from, but in and with, himself. Hence his words are equally true of all men, in whatsoever state of grace they are: 'As the branch cannot bear fruit of itself, except it abide in the vine; no more can ye, except ye abide in me: Without (or separate from) me ye can do nothing.'

In every state we need Christ in the following respects, (1) Whatever grace we receive, it is a free gift from him. (2) We receive it as his purchase, merely in consideration of the price he paid. (3) We have this grace, not only from Christ, but in him. For our perfection is not like that of a tree, which flourishes by the sap derived from its own root, but, as was said before, like that of a branch which, united to the vine, bears fruit; but severed from it, is dried up and withered. (4) All our blessings, temporal, spiritual, and eternal, depend on his intercession for us, which is one branch of his priestly office, whereof therefore we have always equal need. (5) The best of men still need Christ in his priestly office, to atone for their omissions, their short-comings (as some not improperly speak), their mistakes in judgment and practice, and their defects of various kinds. For these are all deviations from the perfect law, and consequently need an atonement. Yet that they are not properly sins, we apprehend may appear from the words of St Paul, 'He that loveth, hath fulfilled the law; for love is the fulfilling of the law'. (*Romans* 13. 10.) Now, mistakes, and whatever infirmities necessarily flow from the corruptible state of the body, are no way contrary to love; nor therefore, in the Scripture sense, sin.

To explain myself a little farther on this head: (1) Not only sin, properly so called (that is, a voluntary transgression of a known law), but sin, improperly so called (that is, an involuntary transgression of the law, known or unknown), needs the atoning blood. (2) I believe there is no such perfection in this life as excludes these involuntary transgressions which I apprehend to be naturally consequent on the ignorance and mistakes inseparable from morality. (3) Therefore *sinless perfection* is a phrase I never use, lest I should seem to contradict myself. (4) I believe, a person filled with the love of God is still liable to these involuntary transgressions. (5) Such transgressions you may call sins, if you please: I do not, for the reasons above-mentioned.

Question. What advice would you give to those that do, and those that do not, call them so?

Answer. Let those that do not call them sins, never think that themselves or any other persons are in such a state as that they can stand before infinite justice without a Mediator. This must argue either the deepest ignorance, or the highest arrogance and presumption.

Let those who do call them so, beware how they confound these defects with sins, properly so called.

But how will they avoid it? How will these be distinguished from those, if they are all promiscuously called sins? I am much afraid, if we should allow any sins to be consistent with perfection, few would confine the idea to those defects concerning which only the assertion could be true.

Question. But how can a liableness to mistake consist with perfect love? Is not a person who is perfected in love every moment under its influence? And can any mistake flow from pure love?

Answer. I answer, (1) Many mistakes may consist with pure love; (2) Some may accidentally flow from it: I mean, love itself may incline us to mistake. The pure love of our neighbour, springing from the love of God, thinketh no evil, believeth and hopeth all things. Now, this very temper, unsuspicious, ready to believe and hope the best of all men, may occasion our thinking some men better than they really are. Here then is a manifest mistake, accidentally flowing from pure love.

Question. How shall we avoid setting perfection too high or too low?

Answer. By keeping to the Bible, and setting it just as high as the Scripture does. It is nothing higher and nothing lower than this—the pure love of God and man; the loving God with all our heart and soul, and our neighbour as ourselves. It is love governing the heart and life, running through all our tempers, words, and actions.

Question. Suppose one had attained to this, would you advise him to speak of it?

Answer. At first perhaps he would scarce be able to refrain, the fire would be so hot within him; his desire to declare the loving-kindness of the Lord carrying him away like a torrent. But afterwards he might; and then it would be advisable, not to speak of it to them that know not God (it is most likely, it would only provoke them to contradict and blaspheme); nor to others, without some particular reason, without some good in view. And then he should have especial care to avoid all appearance of boasting; to speak with the deepest humility and reverence, giving all the glory to God.

Question. But would it not be better to be entirely silent, not to speak of it at all?

Answer. By silence, he might avoid many crosses, which will naturally and necessarily ensue, if he simply declare, even among believers, what God has wrought in his soul. If, therefore, such a one were to confer with flesh and blood, he would be entirely silent. But this could not be done with a clear conscience; for undoubtedly he ought to speak. Men do not light a candle to put it under a bushel; much less does the all-wise God. He does not raise such a monument of his power and love, to hide it from all mankind. Rather, he intends it as a general blessing to those who are simple of heart. He designs thereby, not barely the happiness of that individual person, but the animating and encouraging others to follow after the same blessing. His will is, 'that many shall see it' and rejoice, 'and put their trust in the Lord'. Nor does anything under heaven more quicken the desires of those who are justified, than to converse with those whom they believe to have experienced a still higher salvation. This places that salvation full in their view, and increases their hunger and thirst after it; an advantage which must have been entirely lost, had the person so saved buried himself in silence.

Question. But is there no way to prevent these crosses which usually fall on those who speak of being thus saved?

Answer. It seems they cannot be prevented altogether, while so much of nature remains even in believers. But something might be done, if the Preacher in every place would, (1) Talk freely with all who speak thus; and, (2) Labour to prevent the unjust or unkind treatment of those in favour of whom there is reasonable proof.

Question. What is reasonable proof? How may we certainly know one that is saved from all sin?

Answer. We cannot infallibly know one that is thus saved (no, nor even one that is justified), unless it should please God to endow us with the miraculous discernment of spirits. But we apprehend those would be sufficient proofs to any reasonable man, and such as would leave little room to doubt either the truth or depth of the work: (1) If we had clear evidence of his exemplary behaviour for some time before this supposed change. This would give us reason to believe, he would not 'lie for God', but speak neither more nor less than he felt; (2) If he gave a distinct account of the time and manner wherein the change was wrought, with sound speech which could not be reproved; and, (3) If it appeared that all his subsequent words and actions were holy and unblamable.

The short of the matter is this: (1) I have abundant reason to believe, this person will not lie; (2) He testifies before God, 'I feel no sin, but all love; I pray, rejoice, and give thanks without ceasing; and I have as clear an inward witness, that I am fully renewed, as that I am justified'. Now, if I have nothing to oppose to this plain testimony, I ought in reason to believe it.

It avails nothing to object, 'But I know several things wherein he is quite mistaken'. For it has been allowed, that all who are in the body are liable to mistake; and that a mistake in judgment may sometimes occasion a mistake in practice; though great care is to be taken that no ill use be made of this concession. For instance: Even one that is perfected in love may mistake with regard to another person, and may think him, in a particular case, to be more or less faulty than he really is. And hence he may speak to him with more or less severity than the truth requires. And in this sense (though that be not the primary meaning of St James), 'in many things we offend all'. This therefore is no proof at all, that the person so speaking is not perfect.

Question. But is it not a proof, if he is surprised or fluttered by a noise, a fall, or some sudden danger?

Answer. It is not; for one may start, tremble, change colour, or be otherwise disordered in body, while the soul is calmly stayed on God, and remains in perfect peace. Nay, the mind itself may be deeply distressed, may be exceeding sorrowful, may be perplexed and pressed down by heaviness and anguish, even to agony, while the heart cleaves to God by perfect love, and the will is wholly resigned to him. Was it not so with the Son of God himself? Does any child of man endure the distress, the anguish, the agony, which he sustained? And yet he knew no sin.

Question. But can any one who has a pure heart prefer pleasing to unpleasing food; or use any pleasure of sense which is not strictly necessary? If so, how do they differ from others?

Answer. The difference between these and others in taking pleasant food is, (1) They need none of these things to make them happy; for they have a spring of happiness within. They see and love God. Hence they rejoice evermore, and in everything give thanks. (2) They may use them, but they do not seek them. (3) They use them sparingly, and not for the sake of the thing itself. This being premised, we answer directly—Such a one may use pleasing food, without the danger which attends those who are not saved from sin. He may prefer it to unpleasing, though equally wholesome, food, as a means of increasing thankfulness, with a single eye to God, who giveth us all things richly to enjoy; On the same principle, he may smell to a flower, or eat a bunch of grapes, or take any other pleasure which does not lessen but increase his delight in God. Therefore, neither can we say that one perfected in love would be incapable of marriage, and of worldly business: If he were called thereto, he would be more capable than ever; as being able to do all things without hurry or carefulness, without any distraction of spirit.

Question. But if two perfect Christians had children, how could they be born in sin, since there was none in the parents?

Answer. It is a possible, but not a probable, case; I doubt whether it ever was or ever will be. But waving this, I answer, Sin is entailed upon me, not by immediate generation, but by my first parent. 'In Adam all died: by the disobedience of one, all men were made sinners'; all men, without exception, who were in his loins when he ate the forbidden fruit.

We have a remarkable illustration of this in gardening: Grafts on a crab-stock bear excellent fruit; but sow the kernels of this fruit, and what will be the event? They produce as mere crabs as ever were eaten.

Question. But what does the perfect one do more than others? more than the common believers?

Answer. Perhaps nothing; so may the providence of God have hedged him in by outward circumstances. Perhaps not so much; though he desires and longs to spend and be spent for God; at least, not externally: he neither speaks so many words, nor does so many works. As neither did our Lord himself speak so many words, or do so many, no, nor so great works, as some of his Apostles (*John* 14. 12). But what then? This is no proof that he has not more grace; and by this God measures the outward work. Hear ye him: 'Verily, I say unto you, this poor widow has cast in more than them all.' Verily, this poor man, with his few broken words, hath spoken more than them all. Verily, this poor woman, that hath given a cup of cold water, hath done more than them all. O cease to 'judge according to appearance', and learn to 'judge righteous judgment!'

Question. But is not this a proof against him—I feel no power either in his words or prayer?

Answer. It is not; for perhaps that is your own fault. You are not likely to feel any power therein, if any of these hindrances lie in the way: (1) Your own deadness of soul. The dead Pharisees felt no power even in his words who 'spake as never man spake'. (2) The guilt of some unrepented sin lying upon the conscience. (3) Prejudice toward him of any kind. (4) Your not believing that state to be attainable wherein he professes to be. (5) Unreadiness to think or own he has attained it. (6) Overvaluing or idolizing him. (7) Overvaluing yourself and your own judgment. If any of these is the case, what wonder is it that you feel no power in anything he says? But do not others feel it? If they do, your argument falls to the ground. And if they do not, do none of these hindrances lie in their way too? You must be certain of this before you can build any argument thereon; and even then your argument will prove no more than that grace and gifts do not always go together.

'But he does not come up to my idea of a perfect Christian.' And perhaps no one ever did, or ever will. For your idea may go beyond, or at least beside, the scriptural account. It may include more than the Bible includes therein, or, however, something which that does not include. Scripture perfection is, pure love filling the heart, and governing all the words and actions. If your idea includes anything more or anything else, it is not scriptural; and then no wonder, that a scripturally perfect Christian does not come up to it.

I fear many stumble on this stumbling-block. They include as many ingredients as they please, not according to Scripture, but their own imagination, in their idea of one that is perfect; and then readily deny any one to be such, who does not answer that imaginary idea.

The more care should we take to keep the simple, scriptural account continually in our eye. Pure love reigning alone in the heart and life—this is the whole of scriptural perfection.

Question. When may a person judge himself to have attained this?

Answer. When, after having been fully convinced of inbred sin, by a far deeper and clearer conviction than that he experienced before justification, and after having experienced a gradual mortification of it, he experiences a total death to sin, and an entire renewal in the love and image of God, so as to rejoice evermore, to pray without ceasing, and in everything to give thanks. Not that 'to feel all love and no sin' is a sufficient proof. Several have experienced this for a time, before their souls were fully renewed. None therefore ought to believe that the work is done, till there is added the testimony of the Spirit, witnessing his entire sanctification, as clearly as his justification.

Question. But whence is it, that some imagine they are thus sanctified, when in reality they are not?

Answer. It is hence; they do not judge by all the preceding marks, but either by part of them, or by others that are ambiguous. But I know no instance of a person attending to them all, and yet deceived in this matter. I believe, there can be none in the world. If a man be deeply and fully convinced, after justification, of inbred sin; if he then experience a gradual mortification of sin, and afterwards an entire renewal in the image of God; if to this change, immensely greater than that wrought when he was justified, be added a clear, direct witness of the renewal; I judge it as impossible this man should be deceived herein, as that God should lie. And if one whom I know to be a man of veracity testify these things to me, I ought not, without some sufficient reason, to reject his testimony.

Question. Is this death to sin, and renewal in love, gradual or instantaneous?

Answer. A man may be dying for some time; yet he does not, properly speaking, die, till the instant the soul is separated from the body; and in that instant he lives the life of eternity. In like manner, he may be dying to sin for some time; yet he is not dead to sin, till sin is separated from his soul; and in that instant he lives the full life of love. And as the change undergone, when the body dies, is of a different kind, and infinitely greater than any we had known before, yea, such as till then it is impossible to conceive; so the change wrought, when the soul dies to sin, is of a different kind, and infinitely greater than any before, and than any can conceive till he experiences it. Yet he still grows in grace, in the knowledge of Christ, in the love and image of God; and will do so, not only till death, but to all eternity.

Question. How are we to wait for this change?

Answer. Not in carless indifference, or indolent inactivity; but in vigorous, universal obedience, in a zealous keeping of all the commandments, in watchfulness and painfulness, in denying ourselves, and taking up our cross daily; as well as in earnest prayer and fasting, and a close attendance on all the ordinances of God. And if any man dream of attaining it any other way (yea, or of keeping it when it is attained, when he has received it even in the largest measure) he deceiveth his own soul. It is true, we receive it by simple faith: but God does not, will not, give that faith, unless we seek it with all diligence, in the way which he hath ordained.

This consideration may satisfy those who inquire, why so few have received the blessing. Inquire, how many are seeking it in this way; and you have a sufficient answer.

Prayer especially is wanting. Who continues instant therein? Who wrestles with God for this very thing? So, 'ye have not, because ye ask not; or because ye ask amiss', namely, that you may be renewed before you die. *Before you die*? Will that content you? Nay, but ask that it may be done now; today, while it is called today. Do not call this 'setting God a time'. Certainly, today is his time as well as tomorrow. Make haste, man, make haste! Let

> Thy soul break out in strong desire
> The perfect bliss to prove;
> Thy longing heart be all on fire
> To be dissolved in love!

Question. But may we not continue in peace and joy till we are perfected in love?

Answer. Certainly we may; for the kingdom of God is not divided against itself; therefore, let not believers be discouraged from 'rejoicing in the Lord always'. And yet we may be sensibly pained at the sinful nature that still remains in us. It is good for us to have a piercing sense of this, and a vehement desire to be delivered from it. But this should only incite us the more zealously to fly every moment to our strong Helper the more earnestly to 'press forward to the mark, the prize of our high calling in Christ Jesus'. And when the sense of our sin most abounds, the sense of his love should much more abound.

Question. How should we treat those who think they have attained?

Answer. Examine them candidly, and exhort them to pray fervently, that God would show them all that is in their hearts. The most earnest exhortations to abound in every grace, and the strongest cautions to avoid all evil, are given throughout the New Testament, to those who are in the highest state of grace. But this should be done with the utmost tenderness; and without any harshness, sternness, or sourness. We should carefully avoid the very appearance of anger, unkindness, or contempt. Leave it to Satan thus to tempt, and to his children to cry out, 'Let us examine him with despitefullness and torture, that we may know his meekness and prove his patience'. If they are faithful to the grace given, they are in no danger of perishing thereby; no, not if they remain in that mistake till their spirit is returning to God.

Question. But what hurt can it do to deal harshly with them?

Answer. Either they are mistaken, or they are not. If they are, it may destroy their souls. This is nothing impossible, no, nor improbable. It may so enrage or so discourage them, that they will sink and rise no more. If they are not mistaken, it may grieve those whom God has not grieved, and do much hurt unto our own souls. For undoubtedly he that toucheth them, toucheth, as it were, the apple of God's eye. If they are indeed full of his Spirit, to behave unkindly or contemptuously to them is doing no little despite to the Spirit of grace. Hereby, likewise, we feed and increase in ourselves evil surmising, and many wrong tempers. To instance only in one: What self-sufficiency is this, to set ourselves up for inquisitors-general, for peremptory judges in these deep things of God? Are we qualified for the office? Can we pronounce, in all cases, how far infirmity reaches? what may, and may not, be resolved into it? what may in all circumstances, and what may not, consist with perfect love? Can we precisely determine, how it will influence the look, the gesture, the tone of voice? If we can, doubtless we are 'the men, and wisdom shall die with us'.

Question. But if they are displeased at our not believing them, is not this a full proof against them?

Answer. According as that displeasure is: If they are angry, it is a proof against them; if they are grieved, it is not. They ought to be grieved, if we disbelieve a real work of God, and thereby deprive ourselves of the advantage we might have received from it. And we may easily mistake this grief for anger, as the outward expressions of both are much alike.

Question. But is it not well to find out those who fancy they have attained when they have not?

Answer. It is well to do it by mild, loving examination. But it is not well to triumph even over these. It is extremely wrong, if we find such an instance, to rejoice as if we had found great spoils. Ought we not rather to grieve, to be deeply concerned, to let our eyes run down with tears? Here is one who seemed to be a living proof of God's power to save to the uttermost; but, alas! it is not as we hoped. He is weighed in the balance, and found wanting! And is this matter of joy? Ought we not to rejoice a thousand times more, if we can find nothing but pure love?

'But he is deceived.' What then? It is a harmless mistake, while he feels nothing but love in his heart. It is a mistake which generally argues great grace, an high degree both of holiness and happiness. This should be a matter of real joy to all that are simple of heart; not the mistake itself, but the height of grace which for a time occasions it. I rejoice that this soul is always happy in Christ, always full of prayer and thanksgiving. I rejoice that he feels no unholy temper, but the pure love of God continually. And I will rejoice, if sin is suspended till it is totally destroyed.

Question. Is there no danger then in a man's being thus deceived?

Answer: Not at the time that he feels no sin. There was danger before, and there will be again when he comes into fresh trials. But so long as he feels nothing but love animating all his thoughts, and words, and actions, he is in no danger; he is not only happy, but safe, 'under the shadow of the Almighty'; and, for God's sake, let him continue in that love as long as he can. Meantime, you may do well to warn him of the danger that will be, if his love grow cold and sin revive; even the danger of casting away hope, and supposing, that, because he hath not attained yet, therefore he never shall.

Question. But what, if none have attained it yet? What, if all who think so are deceived?

Answer. Convince me of this, and I will preach it no more. But understand me right; I do not build any doctrine on this or that person. This or any other man may be deceived, and I am not moved. But, if there are none made perfect yet, God has not sent me to preach perfection.

Put a parallel case: For many years I have preached, 'There is a peace of God which passeth all understanding'. Convince me that this word has fallen to the ground; that in all these years none have attained this peace; that there is no living witness of it at this day; and I will preach it no more.

'O, but several persons have died in that peace.' Perhaps so; but I want living witnesses. I cannot indeed be infallibly certain that this or that person is a witness; but if I were certain there are none such, I must have done with this doctrine.

'You misunderstand me. I believe some who died in this love, enjoyed it long before their death. But I was not certain that their former testimony was true till some hours before they died.'

You had not an infallible certainty then: And a reasonable certainty you might have had before; such a certainty as might have quickened and comforted your own soul, and answered all other Christian purposes. Such a certainty as this any candid person may have, suppose there be any living witness, by talking one hour with that person in the love and fear of God.

Question. But what does it signify, whether any have attained it or no, seeing so many Scriptures witness for it?

Answer. If I were convinced that none in England had attained what has been so clearly and strongly preached by such a number of Preachers, in so many places, and for so long a time, I should be clearly convinced that we had all mistaken the meaning of those Scriptures; and therefore, for the time to come, I too must teach that 'sin will remain till death'.

(*Works*, Vol. XI, pp. 394–406.)

XIV

HEGEL

Georg Wilhelm Friedrich Hegel (1770–1831), born in Stuttgart, attended the Theological Institute of Tübingen University where he formed important friendships with young Schelling and the poet Hölderlin. He reacted strongly against the dry rationalism of the post-Enlightenment theology. He was later associated with the University of Jena, then of Heidelberg where he held the chair of philosophy from 1816 to 1818, and finally the University of Berlin where he enjoyed a popularity quite outstanding even in those days of great lecturing. His philosophical endeavour has had incalculable repercussions in political theory (e.g. Karl Marx), in theory of culture and history, and in metaphysics and philosophy. From his death until the turn of the century his writings dominated the thought of Europe.

In general, philosophers have been excluded from this volume in favour of positive theology. But Hegel must be an exception in that his philosophy is by far the most impressive modern attempt to unite philosophy and positive Christian doctrine in a single system. His early theological writings, recently made available (*On Christianity:* Early Theological Writings by Friedrich Hegel; tr. T. M. Knox and Richard Kroner; University of Chicago Press, 1948; Harper Torchbooks, 1961), show to what extent his whole philosophy arose out of his struggles to come to terms with the Christian religion. The extracts below are taken from his first major work, *The Phenomenology of Mind*, tr. J. B. Baillie; Allen and Unwin, revised ed. 1931. Some of his other main works are *The Science of Logic, Encyclopedia of the Philosophical Sciences, Outlines of the Philosophy of Right*. Other works, put together partly from student notes, are: *Philosophy of Religion, Philosophy of History, Philosophy of Fine Art, History of Philosophy*.

Unfortunately Hegel is the most difficult of all the European Philosophers and his theological thought is the most difficult aspect of his system. It is only by reading a good deal of Hegel that we can get the hang of his obscure language. The following rather over-simplified summary of *The Phenomenology of Mind* may facilitate comprehension of the extract.

(1) We are aware of two opposing elements (or moments) in conscious-

ness—the self (our bare consciousness) on the one hand and the objects of which we are conscious on the other. (2) These two opposing principles create an unhappy contradiction in consciousness. (3) This tension is the driving force of all culture, which is the continuous struggle of finite reason to overcome this unhappy diremption of consciousness into self and not-self. (4) This process reaches fulfilment only when the ultimate unity of the subjective and objective elements of consciousness is realized. (5) In Christian Trinitarian doctrine we understand this in a figurative way. God the Father, as Absolute Spirit, is Absolute Self-consciousness. He sets up the antithesis to his own perfect subjectivity in creating the world. His self-alienation in this object reaches fulfilment in the Incarnation. This is also the beginning of the At-one-ment. In the Holy Spirit the synthesis and ultimate unity are realized. (6) But so long as we rest in this purely pictorial understanding, we have not fully arrived at the ultimate fulfilment of rational consciousness. We must pass beyond it to philosophical understanding.

The passages reproduced below illustrate something of his way of interpreting Trinitarian doctrine.

THE ABSOLUTE AS TRINITY

That Absolute Spirit has taken on the shape of self-consciousness inherently, and therefore also consciously to itself—this appears now as the belief of the world, the belief that spirit exists *in fact* as a definite self-consciousness, i.e. as an actual human being; that spirit is an object for immediate experience; that the believing mind *sees*, *feels*, and *hears* this divinity.[1] Taken thus it is not imagination, not a fancy; it is actual in the believer. Consciousness in that case does not set out from its own inner life, does not start from thought, and in itself combine the thought of God with existence; rather it sets out from immediate present existence, and recognizes God in it.

The moment of immediate existence is present in the content of the notion, and present in such a way that the religious spirit, on the return of all ultimate reality into consciousness, has become simple positive self, just as the actual spirit as such, in the case of the 'unhappy consciousness', was just this simple self-conscious negativity. The self of the existent spirit has in that way the form of complete immediacy. It is neither set up as something thought, or imaginatively represented, nor as something produced, as is the case with the immediate self in natural religion, or again in religion as art. Rather, this concrete God is beheld sensuously and immediately as a self, as a real individual human being; only so is it a self-consciousness.

[1] e.g. in Christianity.

This incarnation of the Divine Being, its having essentially and directly the shape of self-consciousness, is the simple content of Absolute Religion. Here the Divine Being is known as Spirit; this religion is the Divine Being's consciousness concerning itself that it is Spirit. For spirit is knowledge of self in a state of alienation of self: spirit is the Being which is the process of retaining identity with itself in its otherness. This, however, is Substance, so far as in its accidents substance at the same time is turned back into itself; and is so, not as being indifferent towards something unessential and, consequently, as finding itself in some alien element, but as being there within itself, i.e. so far as it is subject or self.

In this form of religion the Divine Being is, on that account, *revealed.* Its being revealed obviously consists in this, that what it is, is known. It is, however, known just in its being known as spirit, as a Being which is essentially self-consciousness.

There is something in its object concealed from consciousness if the object is for consciousness an 'other', or something alien, and if consciousness does not know the object as its self. This concealment, this secrecy, ceases when the Absolute Being *qua* spirit is object of consciousness. For here in its relation to consciousness the object is in the form of self; i.e. consciousness immediately knows itself there, or is manifest, revealed, to itself in the object. Itself is manifest to itself only in its own certainty of self; the object it has is the self; self, however, is nothing alien and extraneous, but inseparable unity with itself, the *immediately universal.* It is the pure notion, pure thought, or self-existence (being-for-self), which is immediately *being*, and, therewith, being-for-another, and, *qua* this being-for-another, is immediately turned back into itself and is at home with itself (*bei sich*). It is thus the truly and solely revealed. The Good, the Righteous, the Holy, Creator of Heaven and Earth, etc.—all these are predicates of a subject, universal moments, which have their support on this central point, and only *are* when consciousness goes back into thought.

As long as it is *they* that are known, their ground and essential being, the Subject itself, is not yet revealed; and in the same way the specific determinations of the universal are not this universal itself. The Subject itself, and consequently this pure universal too, is, however, revealed as self; for this self is just this inner being reflected into itself, the inner being which is immediately given and is the proper certainty of that self, for which it is given. To be in its notion that which reveals and is revealed —this is, then, the true shape of spirit; and moreover, this shape, its notion, is alone its very essence and its substance. Spirit is known as self-consciousness, and to this self-consciousness it is directly revealed, for it is this self-consciousness itself. The divine nature is the same as the human, and it is this unity which is intuitively apprehended (*angeschaut*).

Here, then, we find as a fact consciousness, or the general form in which Being is aware of Being—the shape which Being adopts—to be identical with its self-consciousness. This shape is itself a self-consciousness; it is thus at the same time an existent object; and this existence possesses equally directly the significance of pure thought, of Absolute Being.

The absolute Being existing as a concrete actual self-consciousness, seems to have descended from its eternal pure simplicity; but in fact it has, in so doing, attained for the first time its highest nature, its supreme reach of being. For only when the notion of Being has reached its simple purity of nature, is it *both* the absolute abstraction, which is pure thought and hence the pure singleness of self, *and* immediacy or objective being, on account of its simplicity.

What is called sense-consciousness is just this pure abstraction; it is this kind of thought for which being is the immediate. The lowest is thus at the same time the highest; the revealed which has come forth entirely to the surface is just therein the deepest reality. That the Supreme Being is seen, heard, etc., as an existent self-consciousness—this is, in very truth, the culmination and consummation of its notion. And through this consummation, the Divine Being is given and exists immediately in its character as Divine Being.

This immediate existence is at the same time not solely and simply immediate consciousness; it is *religious* consciousness. This immediacy means not only an existent self-consciousness, but also the purely thought-constituted or Absolute Being; and these meanings are inseparable. What we [the philosophers] are conscious of in our conception—that objective being is ultimate essence—is the same as what the religious consciousness is aware of. This unity of being and essence, of thought which is immediately existence, is immediate knowledge on the part of this religious consciousness just as it is the inner thought or the mediated reflective knowledge of this consciousness. For this unity of being and thought is self-consciousness and actually exists; in other words, the thought-constituted unity has at the same time this concrete shape and form of what it is. God, then, is here revealed, as he is; he actually exists as he is in himself; he is real as Spirit. God is attainable in pure speculative knowledge alone, and only *is* in that knowledge, and is merely that knowledge itself, for he is spirit; and this speculative knowledge is the knowledge furnished by revealed religion. That knowledge knows God to be thought, or pure Essence; and knows this thought as actual being and as a real existence, and existence as the negativity of itself, hence as Self, an individual 'this' and a universal self. It is just this that revealed religion knows.

The hopes and expectations of preceding ages pressed forward to, and were solely directed towards this revelation, the vision of what Absolute Being is, and the discovery of themselves therein. This joy, the joy of seeing itself in Absolute Being, becomes realized in self-consciousness, and seizes the whole world. For the Absolute is Spirit, it is the simple movement of those pure abstract moments, which express just this—that Ultimate Reality is then, and not till then, known as Spirit when it is seen and beheld as immediate self-consciousness.

This conception of spirit knowing itself to be spirit, is still the immediate notion; it is not yet developed. The ultimate Being is spirit; in other words, it has appeared, it is revealed. This first revelation is itself immediate; but the immediacy is likewise thought, or pure mediation, and must therefore exhibit and set forth this moment in the sphere of immediacy as such.

Looking at this more precisely, spirit, when self-consciousness is immediate, is 'this' individual self-consciousness set up in contrast to the universal self-consciousness. It is a one, an excluding unit, which appears to that consciousness, for which it exists, in the as yet impervious form of a sensuous other, an unresolved entity in the sphere of sense. This other does not yet know spirit to be its own; in other words, spirit, in its form as an individual self, does not yet exist as equally universal self, as *all* self. Or again, the shape it assumes has not as yet the form of the notion, i.e. of the universal self, of the self which in its immediate actual reality is at once transcended, is thought, universality, without losing its reality in this universality.

The preliminary and similarly immediate form of this universality is, however, not at once the form of thought itself, of the notion as notion; it is the universality of actual reality, it is the 'allness', the collective totality, of the selves, and is the elevation of existence into the sphere of figurative thought (*Vorstellung*); just as in general, to take a concrete example, the 'this' of sense, when transcended, is first of all the 'thing' of 'perception', and is not yet the 'universal' of 'understanding'.

This individual human being, then, which Absolute Being is revealed to be, goes through in its own case as an individual the process found in sense existence. He is the *immediately* present God; in consequence, his being passes over into his *having been*. Consciousness, for which God is thus sensuously present, ceases to see him, to hear him: it *has* seen him, it *has* heard him. And it is because it only *has* seen and heard him, that it first becomes itself spiritual consciousness;[1] or, in other words, he has now arisen in Spirit, as he formerly rose before consciousness as an object visiting in the sphere of sense. For, a consciousness which sees and

[1] Cp. 'He that hath seen me hath seen the Father' (*John* 14). 'If I go not away the Comforter will not come unto you' (ibid., 16).

hears him by sense, is one which is itself merely an immediate consciousness, which has not cancelled and transcended the disparateness of objectivity, has not withdrawn it into pure thought, but knows this objectively presented individual, and not itself, as spirit. In the disappearance of the immediate existence of what is known to be Absolute Being, immediacy acquires its negative moment. Spirit remains the immediate self of actual reality, but in the form of the universal self-consciousness of a religious communion,[1] a self-consciousness which rests in its own proper substance, just as in it this substance is universal subject: it is not the individual subject by himself, but the individual along with the consciousness of the communion, and what he is for this communion is the complete whole of the individual spirit.

The conditions 'past' and 'distance' are, however, merely the imperfect form in which the immediateness gets mediated or made universal; this is merely dipped superficially in the element of thought, is kept there as a sensuous mode of immediacy, and not made one with the nature of thought itself. It is lifted out of sense merely into the region of pictorial presentation; for this is the synthetic [external] connexion of sensuous immediacy and its universality or thought.

Pictorial presentation constitutes the characteristic form in which spirit is conscious of itself in this its religious communion. This form is not yet the self-consciousness of spirit which has reached its notion as notion; the mediating process is still incomplete. In this connexion of being and thought, then, there is a defect; spiritual life is still cumbered with an unreconciled diremption into a 'here' and a 'beyond'. The *content* is the true content; but all its moments, when placed in the element of mere imaginative presentation, have the character, not of being conceptually comprehended, but of appearing as completely independent aspects, externally related to one another.

In order that the true content may also obtain its true form for consciousness, the latter must necessarily pass to a higher plane of mental development, where the absolute Substance is not intuitively apprehended but conceptually comprehended and where consciousness is *for itself* brought to the level of its self-consciousness;—as this has already taken place objectively or for us [who have analysed the process of experience].

We have to consider this content as it exists in its consciousness. Absolute Spirit is content; that is how it exists in the shape of its truth. But its truth consists not merely in being the substance or the inherent reality of the religious communion; nor again in coming out of this inwardness into the objectivity of imaginative thought; but in becoming concrete actual self, reflecting itself into self, and being *Subject*. This, then, is the

[1] 'Lo, I am with you alway, even unto the end of the world' (*Matthew* 28; also 18. 20).

process which spirit realizes in its communion; this is its *life*. What this self-revealing spirit is in and for itself, is therefore not brought out by the rich content of its life being, so to say, untwined and reduced to its original and primitive strands, to the ideas, for instance, presented before the minds of the first imperfect religious communion, or even to what the actual human being [incarnating the Divine Spirit] has spoken.[1] This reversion to the primitive is based on the instinct to get at the notion, the ultimate principle; but it confuses the origin, in the sense of the immediate existence of the first historical appearance, with the simplicity of the notion. By thus impoverishing the life of spirit, by clearing away the idea of the communion and its action with regard to its idea, there arises, therefore, not the notion, but bare externality and particularity, merely the historical manner in which spirit once upon a time appeared, the soulless recollection of a presumably (*gemeinten*) individual historical figure and its past.[2]

Spirit is content of its consciousness to begin with in the form of pure substance; in other words, it is content of its pure consciousness. This element of thought is the process of descending into existence, or individuality. The middle term between these two is their synthetic connexion, the consciousness of passing into otherness, the process of imaginative presentation as such. The third stage is the return from this presentation and from that otherness; in other words, it is the element of self-consciousness itself.

These three moments constitute the life of spirit. Its resolution in imaginative thought consists in its taking on a determinate mode of being; this determinateness, however, is nothing but one of its moments. Its detailed process thus consists in spreading its nature out in each of its moments as in an element in which it lives: and in so far as each of these spheres completes itself in itself, this reflexion into itself is at the same time the transition into another sphere of its being. Imaginative presentation constitutes the middle term between pure thought and self-consciousness as such, and is merely *one* of the determinate forms. At the same time however, as has been shown, the character belonging to such presentation —that of being 'synthetic connexion'—is spread over all these elements and is their common characteristic.

The content itself, which we have to consider, has partly been met with already, as the idea of the 'unhappy' and the 'believing' consciousness. In the case of the 'unhappy' consciousness, however, the content has the characteristic of being produced from consciousness and for which it yearns, a content wherein the spirit can never be satiated nor find rest because the content is not yet its own content inherently and essentially,

[1] viz. Christ.

[2] The life and work of the historical Jesus.

or in the sense of being its substance. In the case of the 'believing' consciousness, again, this content was regarded as the impersonal Being of the World, as the essentially objective content of imaginative thought—a pictorial thinking that seeks to escape the actual world altogether, and consequently has not the certainty of self-consciousness, a certainty which is cut off from it, partly as being conceit of knowledge, partly as being pure insight. The consciousness of the religious communion, on the other hand, possesses the content as its substance, just as the content is the certainty the communion has of its own spirit.

Spirit, represented at first as substance in the element of pure thought, is, thus, primarily the eternal essential Being, simple, self-identical, which does not, however, have this abstract meaning of essential Being, but the meaning of Absolute Spirit. Yet spirit consists, not in being a meaning, not in being the inner, but in being the actual, the real. 'Simple eternal essential Being' would, therefore, be spirit merely in empty phrase, if we remained at the level of pictorial thought, and went no further than the expression of 'simple eternal essential Being'. 'Simple essential Being', however, because it is abstraction, is in point of fact the inherently negative, is indeed the negativity of reflective thought, or negativity as found in Being *per se*: i.e. it is absolute distinction from itself, is pure process of becoming its other. *Qua* essential Being, it is merely implicit, or for us: but since this purity of form is just abstraction or negativity, it is *for itself*, it is the self, the notion. It is thus objective; and since pictorial thinking apprehends and expresses as an event what has just been expressed as the *necessity* of the notion, it will be said that the eternal Being begets for itself an other. But in this otherness it has likewise, *ipso facto*, returned into itself again; for the distinction is distinction in itself, i.e. the distinction is directly distinguished merely from itself, and is thus the unity returned into itself.

There are thus three moments to be distinguished: Essential Being; explicit Self-existence, which is the express otherness of essential Being, and for which that Being is object; and Self-existence or Self-knowledge *in* that other. The essential Being beholds only itself in its Self-existence, in its objective otherness. In thus emptying itself, in this kenosis, it is merely within itself: the independent Self-existence which excludes itself from essential Being is the knowledge of itself on the part of essential Being. It is the 'Word', the Logos, which when spoken empties the speaker of himself, outwardizes him, and leaves him behind emptied, but is as immediately perceived, and only this act of self-perceiving himself is the actual existence of the 'Word'. Hence, then, the distinctions which are set up are just as immediately resolved as they are made, and are just as directly made as they are resolved, and the truth and the reality consist precisely in this self-closed circular process.

This movement within itself expresses the absolute Being *qua* Spirit. Absolute Being, when not grasped as Spirit, is merely the abstract void, just as spirit which is not grasped as this process is merely an empty word. Since its moments are grasped *purely as* moments, they are notions in restless activity, which *are* merely in being inherently their own opposite, and in finding their rest in the whole. But the pictorial thought of the religious communion is not this notional thinking; it has the content without its necessity; and instead of the form of the notion it brings into the realm of pure consciousness the natural relations of Father and Son. Since it thus, even when thinking, proceeds by way of figurative ideas, absolute Being is indeed revealed to it, but the moments of this Being, owing to this [externally] synthetic pictorial thinking, partly fall of themselves apart from one another, so that they are not related to each other through their own very notion, while, partly again, this figurative thinking retreats from the pure object it deals with, and takes up a merely external relation towards it. The object is externally revealed to it from an alien source, and in this thought of Spirit it does not recognize its own self, does not recognize the nature of pure self-consciousness. In so far as the form of figurative thinking and that way of thinking by means of relationships derived from nature have to be transcended, and especially the method of taking the moments of the process, which Spirit is, as isolated immovable substances or subjects, instead of transient moments —this transcendence is to be looked at as a compulsion on the part of the notion, in the way we formerly pointed out when dealing with another aspect. But since it is only an instinct, it mistakes its own real character, rejects the content along with the form, and, what comes to the same thing, degrades the content into a historical imaginative idea and an heirloom handed down by tradition. In this way there is retained and preserved only what is purely external in belief, and the retention of it as something dead and devoid of knowledge; while the inner element in belief has passed away, because this would be the notion knowing itself as notion.

(pp. 757–68) . . .

If we further consider the kind of prodecure that pictorial thinking adopts as it goes along, we find in the first place the expression that the Divine Being 'takes on' human nature. Here it is *eo ipso* asserted that implicitly and inherently the two are not separate: just as in the statement, that the Divine Being from the beginning empties Itself of Itself, that its objective existence becomes concentrated in Itself and becomes evil, it is not asserted but implied that *per se* this evil existence is *not* something alien to the Divine nature. Absolute Being would be merely an empty name if in very truth there were any other being external to it, if there were a 'fall' from it. The aspect of self-concentration really constitutes the essential moment of the self of Spirit.

That this self-centredness, whence primarily comes its reality, belongs to the Divine Being—while this is for *us* a notion, and so as far as it *is* a notion—appears to pictorial thinking as an inconceivable happening. The inherent and essential nature assumes for figurative thought the form of an indifferent objective fact. The thought, however, that those apparently mutually repugnant moments, absolute Being and self-existent Self, are not inseparable, comes also before this figurative way of thinking (since it does possess the real content), but that thought appears *afterwards*, in the form that the Divine Being empties Itself of Itself and is made flesh. This figurative idea, which in this manner is still immediate and hence not spiritual, i.e. it knows the human form assumed by the Divine as merely a particular form, not yet as a universal form—becomes spiritual for this consciousness in the process whereby God, who has assumed shape and form, surrenders again his immediate existence, and returns to his essential Being. The essential Being is then Spirit only when it is reflected into itself.

The reconciliation of the Divine Being with its other as a whole, and, specifically, with the *thought* of this other—evil—is thus presented here in a figurative way. If this reconciliation is expressed *conceptually*, by saying it consists in the fact that evil is inherently the same as what goodness is, or again that the Divine Being is the same as nature in its entire extent, just as nature separated from God is simply nothingness—then this must be looked at as an unspiritual mode of expression which is bound to give rise to misunderstandings. When evil is the *same* as goodness, then evil is just *not* evil nor goodness good; on the contrary, both are really done away with—evil in general, self-centred self-existence, and goodness, self-less simplicity. Since in this way they are both expressed in terms of their notion, the unity of the two is at once apparent; for self-centred self-existence is simple knowledge; and what is self-less simplicity is similarly pure self-existence, centred within itself. Hence, if it must be said that good and evil in this their conception, i.e. so far as they are *not* good and evil, are the same, just as certainly it must be said that they are not the same, but absolutely different; for simple self-existence, or again pure knowledge, are equally pure negativity or *per se* absolute distinction. It is only these two propositions that make the whole complete; and when the first is asserted and asseverated, it must be met and opposed by insisting on the other with immovable obstinacy. Since both are equally right, they are both equally wrong, and their wrong consists in taking such abstract forms as 'the same' and 'not the same', 'identity' and 'non-identity', to be something true, fixed and real and in resting on them.

Neither the one nor the other has truth; their truth is just in their movement, the process in which simple sameness is abstraction and thus absolute distinction, while this again, being distinction *per se*, is distinguished from itself and so is self-identity. Precisely this is what we have in the sameness of the Divine Being and Nature in general and human nature in particular: the former is Nature so far as it is not essential Being; Nature is Divine in its essential Being. But it is in Spirit that we find both abstract aspects affirmed as they truly are, viz. as cancelled and preserved at once: and this way of affirming them cannot be expressed by the judgment, by the soulless word 'is', the copula of the judgment. In the same way Nature is nothing outside its essential Being [God]; but this nothing itself *is* all the same; it is absolute abstraction, therefore pure thought or self-centredness, and with its moment of opposition to spiritual unity it is the principle of Evil. The difficulty people find in these conceptions is due solely to sticking to the term 'is', and forgetting the character of thought, where the moments as much *are* as they *are not*—are only the process which is Spirit. It is this spiritual unity—unity where the distinctions are merely in the form of moments, or as transcended—which became known to pictorial thinking in that atoning reconciliation spoken of above. And since this unity is the universality of self-consciousness, self-consciousness has ceased to be figurative or pictorial in its thinking; the process has turned back into it.

Spirit thus takes up its position in the third element, in universal self-consciousness: Spirit is its own community. The movement of this community being that of self-consciousness, which distinguishes itself from its figurative idea, consists in explicitly bringing out what has implicitly become established. The dead Divine Man, or Human God, is implicitly universal self-consciousness. Or, since this self-consciousness constitutes one side of the opposition involved in figurative thought, viz. the side of evil, which takes natural existence and individual self-existence to be the essential reality—this aspect, which is pictured as independent, and not yet as a moment, has, on account of its independence, to raise itself in and for itself to the level of spirit; it has to reveal the process of Spirit in its self.

(pp. 775–8) . . .

In this way, then, Spirit is Spirit knowing its own self. It knows itself; that, which is for it object, exists, or, in other words, its figurative idea is the true absolute content. As we saw, the content expresses just Spirit itself. It is at the same time not merely content of self-consciousness, and not merely object *for* self-consciousness; it is also actual Spirit. It is this by the fact of its passing through the three elements of its nature: this movement through its whole self constitutes its actual reality. What moves itself, that is Spirit; it is the subject of the movement, and it is likewise the moving process itself, or the substance through which the subject passes. We saw how the notion of spirit arose when we entered the sphere of religion: it was the process of spirit certain of its self, which forgives evil, and in so doing puts aside its own simplicity and rigid unchangeableness: it was, to state it otherwise, the process, in which what is absolutely in opposition recognizes itself as the same as its opposite, and this knowledge breaks out into the 'yea, yea', with which one extreme meets the other. The religious consciousness, to which the Absolute Being is revealed, beholds this notion, and does away with the distinction of its self from what it beholds; and as it is Subject, so it is also Substance; and is thus itself Spirit just because and in so far as it is this process.

This religious communion, however, is not yet fulfilled in this its self-consciousness. Its content, in general, is put before it in the form of a pictorial idea; so that this disruption still attaches even to the actual spiritual character of the communion—to its return out of its figurative thinking; just as the element of pure thought itself was also hampered with that opposition.[1] This spiritual communion is not also consciously aware what it is; it is spiritual self-consciousness, which is not object to itself as this self-consciousness, or does not develop into clear consciousness of itself. Rather, so far as it is consciousness, it has before it those picture-thoughts which were considered.

We see self-consciousness at its last turning point become inward to itself and attain to knowledge of its inner being, of its self-centredness. We see it relinquish its natural existence, and reach pure negativity. But the positive significance—viz. that this negativity, or pure inwardness of knowledge is just as much the self-identical essential Being: put otherwise, that Substance has here attained to being absolute self-consciousness—this is, for the devotional consciousness, an external other. It grasps this aspect—that the knowledge which becomes purely inward is inherently absolute simplicity, or Substance—as the pictorial idea of something which is not thus by its very conception, but as the act of satisfaction obtained from an (alien) other. In other words, it is not really aware as a fact that this depth of pure self is the power by which the abstract essential Being is drawn down from its abstractness and raised to the level of self by the force of this pure devotion. The action of the self hence retains towards it this negative significance, because the relinquishment of itself on the part of substance is for the self something *per se*; the self does not at once grasp and comprehend it, or does not find it in its *own* action as such.

Since this unity of Essential Being and Self has been inherently brought

[1] i.e. between spiritual consciousness and objective idea.

about, consciousness has this idea also of its reconciliation, but in the form of an imaginative idea. It obtains satisfaction by attaching, in an external way, to its pure negativity the positive significance of the unity of itself with essential Being. Its satisfaction thus itself remains hampered with the opposition of a beyond. Its own peculiar reconciliation therefore enters its consciousness as something remote, something far away in the future, just as the reconciliation, which the other self achieved, appears as away in the distance of the past. Just as the individual divine man[1] has an implied (essential, *an sich*) father and only an actual mother, in like manner the universal divine man, the spiritual communion, has as its father its own proper action and knowledge, while its mother is eternal Love, which it merely *feels*, but does not behold in its consciousness as an actual immediate object. Its reconciliation, therefore, is in its heart, but still with its conscious life sundered in twain and its actual reality shattered. What falls within its consciousness as the immanent essential element, the aspect of pure mediation, is the reconciliation that lies beyond: while what appears as actually present, as the aspect of immediacy and of existence, is the world which has yet to await transfiguration. The world is no doubt implicitly reconciled with the essential Being; and that Being no doubt knows that it no longer regards the object as alienated from itself, but as one with itself in its Love. But for self-consciousness this immediate presence has not yet the form and shape of spiritual reality. Thus the spirit of the communion is, in its immediate consciousness, separated from its religious consciousness, which declares indeed that these two modes of consciousness inherently are *not* separated; but this is an implicitness which is not realized, or has not yet become an equally absolute explicit self-existence.

(pp. 782–5)

[1] The historical Christ.

XV
McLEOD CAMPBELL

John McLeod Campbell (1800–72) read divinity at both Glasgow and Edinburgh Universities. He was ordained minister of the parish of Rhu in Scotland in 1825. It is characteristic of his theology that he sought persistently to understand and interpret formal ecclesiastical doctrine in the light of living spiritual experience. 'The internal evidence of the atonement within us ought to be the surest stronghold of Christianity', he maintained. The centre of his theological preoccupation was the doctrine of the atonement, and for him the centre of the atonement was God's active, fatherly love and the perfect Sonship of the Christ.

In 1830 he was charged with heresy before the General Assembly of the Church of Scotland for preaching the universal efficacy of the atonement. The case was carried against him and he was deprived of his parish. His followers built a church in Glasgow. Though he was careful never to attempt to form a sect, he preached there until failing health forced him into retirement.

The passage below is taken from *The Nature of the Atonement* (Macmillan, 1878)—a work whose importance lies in its presentation of a quite distinctive interpretation of the Atonement.

THE NATURE OF THE ATONEMENT

That due repentance for sin, could such repentance indeed be, would expiate guilt, there is a strong testimony in the human heart, and so the first attempt at peace with God is an attempt at repentance—which attempt, indeed, becomes less and less hopeful, the longer, and the more earnestly and honestly it is persevered in—but this not because it comes to be felt that a true repentance would be rejected even if attained, but because its attainment is despaired of—all attempts at it being found, when taken to the divine light, and honestly judged in the sight of God, to be mere selfish attempts at something that promises safety—not evil indeed, in so far as they are instinctive efforts at self-preservation, but having nothing in them of the nature of a true repentance, or a godly sorrow for sin or pure condemnation of it because of its own evil; nothing, in short, that is a judging sin and a confessing it in true sympathy with the divine judgment upon it. So that the words of Whitfield come to be deeply sympathized in, 'our repentance needeth to be repented of, and our very tears to be washed in the blood of Christ'.

That we may fully realize what manner of an equivalent to the dishonour done to the law and name of God by sin, an adequate repentance and sorrow for sin must be, and how far more truly than any penal infliction such repentance and confession must satisfy divine justice, let us suppose that all the sin of humanity has been committed by one human spirit, on whom is accumulated this immeasurable amount of guilt, and let us suppose this spirit loaded with all this guilt to pass out of sin into holiness, and to become filled with the light of God, becoming perfectly righteous with God's own righteousness—such a change, were such a change possible, would imply in the spirit so changed, a perfect condemnation of the past of its own existence, and an absolute and perfect repentance, a confession of its sin commensurate with its evil. If the sense of personal identity remained, it must be so. Now, let us contemplate this repentance with reference to the guilt of such a spirit, and the question of pardon for its past sin, and admission now to the light of God's favour. Shall this repentance be accepted as an atonement and the past sin being thus confessed, shall the divine favour flow out on that present perfect righteousness which thus condemns the past? or, shall that repentance be declared inadequate? shall the present perfect righteousness be rejected on account of the past sin, so absolutely and perfectly repented of? and shall divine justice still demand adequate punishment for the past sin, and refuse to the present righteousness adequate acknowledgement—the favour which, in respect of its own nature, belongs to it? It appears to me impossible to give any but one answer to these questions. We feel that such a repentance as we are supposing would, in such a case, be the true and proper satisfaction to offended justice, and that there would be more atoning worth in one tear of the true and perfect sorrow which the memory of the past would awaken in this now holy spirit, than in endless ages of penal woe. Now, with the difference of personal identity, the case I have supposed is the actual case of Christ, the holy one of God, bearing the sins of all men on his spirit—in Luther's words, 'the one sinner'—and meeting the cry of these sins for judgment, and the wrath due to them, absorbing and exhausing that divine wrath in that adequate confession and perfect response on the part of man, which was possible only to the infinite and eternal righteousness in humanity.

I have said that my hypothetical, and indeed impossible case, and that case which the history of our redemption actually presents, differ only in respect of the *personal identity* of the guilty and the righteous. And, to one looking at the subject with a hasty superficial glance, this difference may seem to involve all the difficulties connected with imputation of guilt and substituted punishment. Yet it can only so appear to a hasty and superficial glance. For, independent of the higher character of the moral atonement supposed, as compared with the enduring as a substitute a penal infliction, this adequate sorrow for the sin of man, and adequate confession of its evil implies no fiction—no imputation to the sufferer of the guilt of the sin for which he suffers; but only that he has taken the nature, and become the brother of those whose sin he confesses before the Father, and that he feels concerning their sins what, as the holy one of God, and as perfectly loving God and man, he must feel.

In contemplating our Lord as yielding up his soul to be filled with the sense of the Father's righteous condemnation of our sin, and as responding with a perfect Amen to that condemnation, we are tracing what was a necessary step in his path as dealing with the Father on our behalf. His intercession presupposes this expiatory confession, and cannot be conceived of apart from it. Not only so—but it is also certain that we cannot rightly conceive of this confession, to be in the light in which it was made, without seeing that the intercession that accompanied it was necessary to its completeness, as a full response to the mind of the Father towards us and our sins.

I have endeavoured to present Christ's expiatory confession of our sins to the mind of the reader as much as possible by itself, and as a distinct object of thought, because it most directly corresponds, in the place it occupies, to the penal suffering which has been assumed; and I have desired to place these two ways of meeting the divine wrath against sin, as ascribed to the mediator, in contrast. But the intercession by which that confession was followed up, must be taken into account as a part of the full response of the mind of the Son to the mind of the Father—a part of that utterance in humanity which propitiated the divine mercy by the righteous way in which it laid hold of the hope for man which was in God. 'He bare the sins of many, and made intercession for the transgressors.' In the light of that true knowledge of the heart of the Father in which the Son responded to the Father's condemnation of our sins, the nature of that condemnation was so understood that his love was at liberty, and was encouraged to accompany confession by intercession: —not an intercession which contemplated effecting a change in the heart of the Father, but a confession which combined with acknowledgement of the righteousness of the divine wrath against sin, hope for man from that love in God which is deeper than that wrath—in truth originating it—determining also its nature, and justifying the confidence that, its righteousness being responded to, and the mind which it expresses shared in, that wrath must be appeased.

Therefore, when we would conceive to ourselves, that Amen to the mind of the Father in its aspect toward us and our sins, which, pervading the humanity of the Son of God, made his soul a fit offering for sin, and when we would understand how this sacrifice was to God a sweet-smelling savour, we must consider not only the response which was in that Amen to the divine condemnation of sin, but also the *response which was in it to the divine love in its yearnings over us sinners*. In itself the intercession of Christ was the perfected expression of that forgiveness which he cherished toward those who were returning hatred for his love. But it was also the form his love must take if he would obtain redemption for us. Made under the pressure of the perfect sense of the evil of our state, this intercession was full of the Saviour's peculiar sorrow and suffering—a part of the sacrifice of Christ: its power as an *element of atonement* we must see, if we consider that it was the voice of the divine love coming from humanity, offering for man a pure intercession according to the will of God, offering that prayer for man which was the utterance alike of love to God and love to man—that prayer which accorded with our need and the Father's glory as seen and felt in the light of the Eternal love by the Son of God and our Brother.

We do not understand the divine wrath against sin, unless such confession of its evil as we are now contemplating is felt to be the true and right meeting of that wrath on the part of humanity. We do not understand the forgiveness that is in God, unless such intercession as we are now contemplating is felt to be that which will lay hold of that forgiveness, and draw it forth. It was not in us so to confess our own sins; neither was there in us such knowledge of the heart of the Father. But, if another could in this act for us—if there might be a mediator, an intercessor—one at once sufficiently one with us, and yet sufficiently separated from our sin to feel in sinless humanity what our sinful humanity, could it in sinlessness look back on its sins, would feel of Godly condemnation of them and sorrow for them, so confessing them before God—one coming sufficiently near to our need of mercy to be able to plead for mercy for us according to that need, and at the same time, so abiding in the *bosom of the Father*, and in the light of his love and secret of his heart, as, in interceding for us to take full and perfect advantage of all that is *there* that is on our side, and wills our salvation—if the Son of God has, in the power of love, come into the capacity of such mediation in taking our nature and becoming our brother, and in that same power of love has been contented to suffer all that such mediation, accomplished in suffering flesh implied—is not in the suitableness and the acceptableness of the sacrifice of Christ, when his soul was made an offering for sin, what we can understand? In truth, we cannot realize the life of Christ as he moved on this earth in the sight of men, and contemplate his witness-bearing against sin, and his forgiveness towards sinners, and hear the Father say of him, 'This is my beloved Son in whom I am well pleased', and yet doubt that that mind towards sin and sinners which he thus manifested, and the Father thus acknowledged, would be altogether acceptable, and a sacrifice to God of a sweet-smelling savour, in its atoning confession of sin and intercession for sinners.

I know that the adequacy of the atonement to be a foundation for the remission of sins cannot be fully apprehended, or the righteousness of God in accepting it as a sacrifice for sin, be fully justified, apart from its prospective reference to the divine purpose of making us through Christ partakers in eternal life. Yet I will, even at this point, express the hope, that the purpose of God to extend mercy to sinners being realized, and the considerations connected with the name of God and the honour of his law, which had to be taken into account, being present to the mind, it will be felt, that the atonement, as now set forth, was the suitable preparation for that contemplated manifestation of mercy; and I venture to express this hope here, and thus early, because, I am not unwilling that the atonement as now represented, and while considered only in its retrospective reference, should be compared with the conception of the atonement as Christ's bearing, as our substitute, the punishment of our sins—the rather, that that is a retrospective conception exclusively. But, I repeat it, I feel that it is placing the atonement, as now set forth, under a disadvantage as to its power to commend itself to the conscience, to look at its retrospective adequacy thus apart from its prospective reference; to the consideration of which I now proceed.

(pp. 124–9)

When we consider humanity in the light shed upon it by the life of Christ in humanity, we see together revealed to us the great evil of its condition as possessed by us sinners, and its great capacity of good as that capacity is brought out by the Son of God. Now, this is not the same thing with seeing the same person first sinful and then righteous; nor is the problem which it presents the same exactly, as in that hypothetical case—but, still, what we are thus contemplating involves a closely analogous question for the determination of the righteous Lord who loveth righteousness. As the dishonour done to God in humanity cries out against it, so does the honour done to God plead in its favour—not in the way, certainly, of an off-set in respect of which the honour may cover over, gild over, the dishonour, and so humanity be regarded with acceptance as one whole; not thus—although the honour be divine as well as human, while the dishonour is simply human—but as the revelation of an inestimable preciousness that was hidden in humanity, hidden from the inheritors of humanity themselves, but not hid from God, and now brought forth into manifestation by the Son of God. For the revealer of the Father is also the revealer of man, who was made in God's image.

This high capacity of good pertaining to humanity is not indeed to be contemplated as belonging to us apart from our relation to the Son of God. For although in one sense it is quite correct to speak of the righteousness of Christ as the revelation of the capacity of righteousness that was in humanity, a capacity that remained to man although hidden under sin—in truth, humanity had this capacity only relatively, that is, as dwelt in by the Son of God; and therefore, there was in the righteousness of Christ in humanity no promise for humanity apart from the Son of God's having power over all flesh to impart eternal life. We cannot, therefore, see hope for man in the righteousness of Christ, apart from the contemplation of this power as possessed by Christ. Therefore, there must be a relation between the Son of God and the sons of men, not according to the flesh only, but also according to the spirit—the second Adam must be a quickening spirit, and the head of every man be Christ. But if we see this double relation as subsisting between Christ and men, if we see him as the Lord of their spirits, as well as a partaker in their flesh, that air of legal fiction, which, in contemplating the atonement, attaches to our identification with Christ and Christ's identification with us, so long as this is contemplated as matter of external arrangement, will pass away, and the depth and reality of the bonds which connect the Saviour and the saved will bear the weight of this identification, and fully justify to the enlightened conscience that constitution of things in which Christ's confession of our sins expiates them, and Christ's righteousness in humanity clothes us with its own interest in the sight of God: for thus, that divine righteousness of the Son of God is seen as necessarily shedding to the mind of the Father its own glory and its own preciousness over all humanity—but in a way as remote from the imputation of righteousness as Christ's bearing our sins, as this has now been illustrated, and confessing them, is from imputation to him of our sins.

(pp. 137–9) . . .

I have said above that we are to understand that he who is the revealer of God to man is also the revealer of man to himself. Apart from Christ we know not our God, and apart from Christ we know not ourselves: as, indeed, it is also true, that we are as slow to apprehend and to welcome the one revelation as the other—as slow to see man in Christ, as to see God in Christ. We have seen how much loss even earnest and deep thinking and holy men have suffered through not looking upon the life of love in Christ as the revelation of the Father—how it has thus come to pass that, looking upon Christ's love to men merely as the fulfilment for man of the law under which man was, they have dwelt on that fulfilment, and enlarged on the circumstances which prove how perfect it was, and yet have not read the heart of God—the love of God to all men, in that record of the life of Christ which they were studying. And so, also, these same men, through the assumption that in the life of Christ they were contemplating the working out of a legal righteousness for man, to be his by imputation, as they were turned away from seeing God in Christ, so have also been turned away from seeing man in Christ, seeing themselves in Christ, seeing the capacities of their own being in Christ. Not for his own sake but for our sakes did the Son of God reveal the hidden capacity of good that is in man by putting forth in humanity the power of the law of the Spirit of his own life—the life of sonship. 'For what the law could not do, in that it was weak through the flesh, God sending his own Son in the likeness of sinful flesh, and as a sacrifice for sin, condemned sin in the flesh, that the righteousness of the law might be fulfilled in us who walk not after the flesh, but after the spirit.' We, then, for whose sake this has been, must learn to see in this revelation of what humanity is when pervaded with the life of sonship that redemption of which we were capable, and which we have in Christ, and set ourselves to the study of the twofold discovery of God and of man in Christ, with the conviction that in it are hid for us all the treasures of wisdom and knowledge.

(pp. 144–5) . . .

Let us in this light regard Christ's being delivered for our offences, and raised again for our justification. The offences for which he made expiation were ours—that expiation being the due atonement for the sin of man—accepted on behalf of all men. His righteousness, declared in his resurrection from the dead, is ours—the proper righteousness for man, and in him given to all men: and that righteousness is NOT the *past fact of legal obligation* discharged, but the *mind of sonship towards the Father*; for in the beloved Son is the Father seen to be well pleased, and in our being through him to the Father dear children will it come to pass that the Father will be well pleased in us.

(pp. 149–50) . . .

XVI

SCHLEIERMACHER

Friedrich Daniel Ernst Schleiermacher (1768–1834) was the son of a Prussian army chaplain. He was educated in the pietistic Moravian tradition, but when he became an undergraduate in the University of Halle, he came up against the new spirit of rationalism which had dominated the religious thought of Europe in the eighteenth century. But although this caused Schleiermacher to break with the Moravians, the intensity of religious feeling which he had acquired among them remained with him. He served in various parishes and chaplaincies and also as Professor of Theology, firstly in the University of Halle (1804–7), then at Berlin University (1810–34). It is characteristic of him that he absorbed every cultural influence that came to bear upon him. This does not mean that his philosophy and theology were merely eclectic. His work represents one of the most powerful attempts to forge all the vigorous cultural developments of the early nineteenth century into a unified theological system. He fell strongly under the influence of Kant's critical philosophy, but at the same time had a sensitive appreciation of the Romantic movement. In metaphysics he was influenced by Plato and Spinoza.

His theology is dominated by two main aims. Firstly, he seeks to show that religious awareness is *sui generis* and cannot be exhaustively analysed into merely ethical and metaphysical beliefs. But secondly, an understanding of man's religious awareness provides the key to ethical and metaphysical understanding. This religious awareness consists of an intuition of our own finitude and of the complete dependence of all finite being upon the infinite. This immediate perception is called the 'feeling of absolute dependence'. This is the 'God-consciousness' which constitutes the central and distinctive element in all religion. But it is more than mere feeling (emotion), for it is the foundation of all true knowledge and understanding.

The Christian religion as revealed and exemplified in Jesus Christ is the completion and perfection of all religion. It also opens the possibility of the ideal completion and perfection of all the values of human culture. The central and essential factor is the religious consciousness of Jesus.

He is the religious genius whose perfect 'God-consciousness' opens up the possibility of fulfilment for all mankind.

Though over-shadowed as a philosopher by Hegel, he dominated evangelical theology throughout the whole of the nineteenth century. His writings are voluminous, though only a part of them is available in English. His two most important theological works are, without question, *On Religion, Speeches to its Cultured Despisers*, tr. John Oman (Kegan Paul, London, 1893) and *The Christian Faith*, tr. and ed. H. R. Mackintosh and J. S. Stewart (T. and T. Clark, Edinburgh, 1928). The first of these works is the easier of the two, but is more important for the philosophy of religion than for doctrinal theology. For this reason I have preferred passages from *The Christian Faith*, illustrating his interpretation of the divinity of the Christ in terms of his unique God-consciousness. This work, which is his systematic and comprehensive account of Christian doctrine, was first published by Schleiermacher in 1821, and then in an extensively revised edition in 1830.

CHRISTIAN GOD-CONSCIOUSNESS

§ 32. *The immediate feeling of absolute dependence is presupposed and actually contained in every religious and Christian self-consciousness as the only way in which, in general, our own being and the infinite Being of God can be one in self-consciousness.*

1. The fact that the whole Christian religious consciousness is here presupposed is entirely legitimate, for here we abstract entirely from the specific content of the particular Christian experiences, and what we have stated is in no way affected by these differences. Hence nothing can be deduced from the above proposition either for or against any dogmatic formulation of such specific content. But if anyone would maintain that there might be a Christian religious experience in which the Being of God was not involved in such a manner, i.e. experiences which contained absolutely no consciousness of God, our proposition would certainly exclude him from the domain of that Christian belief which we are going to describe. Our proposition appeals, therefore, against such a person to the religious self-consciousness as it appears and is recognized everywhere in the Evangelical (Protestant) Church: that is, we assert that in every religious affection, however much its special contents may predominate, the God-consciousness must be present and cannot be neutralized by anything else, so that there can be no relation to Christ which does not contain also a relation to God. At the same time, we also assert that this God-consciousness, as it is here described, does not constitute by itself alone an actual moment in religious experience, but always in connexion

with other particular determinations; so that this God-consciousness maintains its identity through its particular moments in all manifestations of Christian piety, just as in life generally the self-consciousness of an individual does in the different moments of his existence. Hence the view that in every Christian affection there must be a relation to Christ does not in the least contradict our proposition. Much more is this the case when the pious feeling comes to expression as an actual moment in the form of pleasure or pain. For the Christian faith, however, the incapacity implied in religious pain must be ascribed to lack of fellowship with the Redeemer, while, on the other hand, the ease in evoking pious feeling which goes along with religious pleasure is regarded as a possession which comes to us from this fellowship. Thus it is evident that, within the Christian communion, there can be no religious experience which does not involve a relation to Christ.

2. It is possible to give a non-religious explanation of this sense of absolute dependence; it might be said that it only means the dependence of finite particulars on the whole and on the system of all finite things, and that what is implied and made the centre of reference is not God but the world. But we can only regard this explanation as a misunderstanding. For we recognize in our self-consciousness an awareness of the world, but it is different from the awareness of God in the same self-consciousness. For the world, if we assume it to be a unity, is nevertheless in itself a divided and disjointed unity which is at the same time the totality of all contrasts and differences and of all the resulting manifold determinations, of which every man is one, partaking in all the contrasts. To be one with the world in self-consciousness is nothing else than being conscious that we are a living part of this whole; and this cannot possibly be a consciousness of absolute dependence; the more so that all living parts stand in reciprocal interaction with each other. This oneness with the whole in each several part is essentially twofold: a feeling of dependence, indeed, so far as the other parts act spontaneously upon it, but also a feeling of freedom in so far as it likewise reacts spontaneously on the other parts. The one is not to be separated from the other.

The feeling of absolute dependence, accordingly, is not to be explained as an awareness of the world's existence, but only as an awareness of the existence of God, as the absolute undivided unity. For neither is there in relation to God an immediate feeling of freedom, nor can the feeling of dependence in relation to him be such that a feeling of freedom can be its counterpart. On the contrary, at the highest point of Christian devotion and with the clearest consciousness of the most unimpeded self-activity, the absoluteness of the feeling of dependence remains undiminished. This is what is indicated by the statement that the realization of oneself as absolutely dependent is the only way in which God and the ego can co-exist in self-consciousness. If we abolish this distinction and mistake the self-consciousness which refers to God as referring only to the world, then we must dispute in the latter the reality of this feeling of freedom and, indeed, consequently entirely reject it, since there is no moment in self-consciousness in which we do not think of ourselves as one with the world. This non-religious explanation, which casts aside what we hold to be the characteristic of the religious consciousness as a deception, comes sometimes from those who explain all feeling of freedom as illusion and sometimes even from those who, maintaining that there is nothing upon which we could feel ourselves absolutely dependent, reject all distinction between the ideas of God and the world.

3. It is obvious that, as we are no longer moving outside the province of Christian piety, we do not here concern ourselves with the only partially developed and differentiated religious feeling which constitutes polytheistic types of belief; the Christian feeling can only exist side by side with monotheism. On the other hand, it may be objected that the foregoing statement is not pertinent to our subject, because it is not so much peculiarly Christian as characteristic of monotheism in general. The answer is that there is no purely monotheistic piety in which the God-consciousness alone and by itself forms the content of religious experiences. Just as there is always present in Christian piety a relation to Christ in conjunction with the God-consciousness, so in Judaism there is always a relation to the Lawgiver, and in Mohammedanism to the revelation given through the Prophet. In our Holy Scriptures for this reason God is constantly referred to by the name of the Father of our Lord Jesus Christ. The saying of Christ also (*John* 14. 7-9) implies that every relation to Christ includes also the God-consciousness.

§ 33. *This feeling of absolute dependence, in which our self-consciousness in general represents the finitude of our being, is therefore not an accidental element, or a thing which varies from person to person, but is a universal element of life; and the recognition of this fact entirely takes the place, for the system of doctrine, of all the so-called proofs of the existence of God.*

. . . [Omitting supporting quotations from Melanchthon, Zwingli and Clement.]

1. One cannot concede the postulated self-consciousness with the content we have already described, and yet maintain that it is something unessential, i.e. that it may or may not be present in a man's life according to whether, in the course of his life, he meets with this or that experience. For its emergence does not depend at all upon the fact that something

definite and objective is given in the experience of a partially developed subject, but only on the fact that in some way or other the sensory consciousness has been stimulated from without. But what is presupposed on the subjective side is only that which is common to all—the intelligence in its subjective function, in which the disposition towards God-consciousness is a constituent element.

That the feeling of absolute dependence as such is the same in all, and not different in different persons, follows from the fact that it does not rest upon any particular modification of human nature but upon the absolutely general nature of man, which contains in itself the potentiality of all those differences by which the particular content of the individual personality is determined.

Further, if a difference is admitted between perfection and imperfection as measured by greater or less development, this arises from the fact that the emergence of this feeling depends upon a contrast having been apprehended in consciousness; the lack of development is simply the lack of differentiation of functions. For when the objective consciousness and self-consciousness are not yet clearly differentiated in such a way as nevertheless to be distinctly connected together, in that case the consciousness as a whole has not yet become genuinely human. And if sensuous self-consciousness and the higher self-consciousness are not thus differentiated from one another and related to one another, development is incomplete.

2. We may conclude then that godlessness within the Christian community has its cause simply in defective or arrested development. Should it occur however in spite of a complete development, we can only regard this as illusion and appearance. It is nevertheless possible to distinguish in the main three types of godlessness.

The first is the childish complete lack of God-consciousness, which as a rule disappears in the course of the natural development of the individual, and only in exceptional cases degenerates into brutal godlessness in such as bitterly resist their own wider development. Both things are to be met with outside the Christian community for the most part among peoples that innocently or voluntarily remain on the lowest grade of development. The existence of this type, however, is hardly to be proved historically.

The second type of godlessness is the sensual. This occurs when a feeling of absolute dependence actually appears, but intimately associated with awareness of that on which there can be no absolute dependence; since what is conceived as capable of passion can give no absolute dependence, for it implies the possibility of self-initiated activity upon it. Face to face with this contradiction, it may be doubted whether the disposition towards God-consciousness has really been operative, the appearance merely being obscured by perverted reflexion, or whether the inner reflexion corresponds to the original, inner fact, so that the latter does not really belong to the province of piety. But a comparison of the way in which in childhood the God-consciousness at first manifests itself shows that here certainly the disposition to God-consciousness is already effective; it is only on account of the imperfect development of self-consciousness that the process cannot fully be carried to its conclusion. This condition is obviously akin to Polytheism, for the same germ of multiplicity is there also, only it is restrained by opposing influences; further, this anthropomorphic conception is sometimes of a more pure and spiritual kind and sometimes verges of Fetishism.

Finally, the third type of godlessness is the so-called definite denial of God—Atheism, which is propounded as a speculative theory in the midst of a Christian society, in a condition of full development and even in the highest stage of culture. This again is twofold. In part it is a wicked fear of the sternness of the God-consciousness, and hence, though moments of enlightenment intervene, clearly a product of licentiousness and thus a sickness of the soul usually accompanied by contempt of everything intellectual; and of this (godlessness) it can be said that it is naught because it entirely lacks inner truth. And in part it is simply a reasoned opposition to the current and more or less inadequate representations of the religious consciousness. Moreover, the atheism of the eighteenth century was, for the most part, a struggle against petrified, anthropomorphic presentations of doctrine, a struggle provoked by the tyranny of the church. But when, over and above the defects of representation, the inner facts of self-consciousness themselves are thus wholly misconstrued, this serious misunderstanding is none the less merely a disease of the understanding which may revive sporadically and from time to time, but never produces anything that is historically permanent. This fact cannot therefore be pled against our assertion that the feeling of absolute dependence, as here expounded, and the God-consciousness contained in it are a fundamental moment of human life.

3. But even supposing its universality could be disputed, still no obligation would arise for the system of doctrine to prove the existence of God; that would be an entirely superfluous task. For since in the Christian church the God-consciousness should be developed in youth, proofs, even if youth were capable of understanding them, could only produce an objective consciousness, which is not the aim here, nor would it in any way generate piety. We are not concerned here with the question whether there are such proofs, and whether, if we have no immediate certitude of God, then that of which we do have immediate certitude, and by which God could be proved, must not itself be God. Our point simply is that

these proofs can never be a component part of the system of doctrine; for that is only for those who have the inner certainty of God, as we have already described it, and of that they can be directly conscious at every moment. On our interpretation of Christian doctrine it would be quite unnecessary to enlarge on this point did it not seem essential to protest against the general custom of furnishing Dogmatics at this point with such proofs, or at least of referring to them as already familiar from other sciences. It is obvious that for the purpose of Dogmatics this reference is quite useless: for neither in catechetical nor in homiletical nor in missionary work can such proofs be of any value. Experience, too, shows how little can be accomplished by such a polemic against theoretical atheism as above described. Dogmatics must therefore presuppose intuitive certainty or faith; and thus, as far as the God-consciousness in general is concerned, what it has to do is not to effect its recognition but to explicate its content. That such proofs are not the concern of Dogmatics is obvious also from the fact that it is impossible to give them dogmatic form; for we cannot go back to Scripture and symbolical books, since they themselves do not prove, but simply assert. Moreover, he for whom such assertion is authoritative needs no further proof.

The prevalent method of inflating Christian doctrine with rational proofs and criticism had its origin in the confusion of Dogmatics and philosophy in the old Patristic times. Closely related to this, and therefore to be named here, is the equally erroneous view that Christian theology, to which Dogmatics also belongs, is differentiated from Christian religion by its sources of knowledge. Religion, for instance, it is argued, draws from Scripture only, but theology draws also from the Fathers, reason and philosophy. But as theology itself draws from Scripture, and the Scriptures themselves have arisen out of the Christian religion, what originates in reason and philosophy cannot be Christian theology. It is certainly a great gain here, and elsewhere, to banish all material of this kind from the Christian system of doctrine, for only thus is a uniformity of method to be established. Such a difficult choice as that between moral proofs, geometrical proofs, and probable proofs is not a task for any dogmatic theologian to take up, even if it be only for his own personal satisfaction.

§ 91. *We have fellowship with God only in a living fellowship with the Redeemer, such that in it his absolutely sinless perfection and blessedness represents a free spontaneous activity, while the recipient's need of redempton represents a free assimilative receptivity.*

1. This is the basic consciousness that each Christian has of his own state of grace, even where the most dissimilar views of Christianity prevail.

The consciousness of one who in no degree relates the potency of the God-consciousness which he finds in himself to Jesus is not Christian at all; while, if he does so relate it, but without in any degree recognizing the contrast noted in our proposition, then, since he finds in himself, not merely no sin, but not even imperfection, and is altogether spontaneous and independent in his activity, he must have left the state of grace behind him, and have himself become a Christ. If, on the other hand, a man relates his state, as touching fellowship with God, to Jesus, but without finding in himself any living receptivity for him, then he certainly believes in Christ in so far as he assumes him to possess a saving influence, but as yet he does not find himself a recipient of grace, for he cannot have experienced any change through Christ. For there can be no change in a living being without his own activity; hence, without such activity—that is, in a purely passive way—no influence exerted by another can really be received. Or again, if a man's own activity were one of opposition, if it were simply resistance, then the grace would necessarily have been imparted against his will, that is by compulsion, and so would not be blessedness. Thus all real vital fellowship with Christ, in which he is in any sense taken as Redeemer, depends on the fact that living receptivity for his influence is *already* present, and *continues* to be present. And this holds true equally for every moment and degree; for, once arrived at the limit, the connexion would necessarily break off of itself. . . .

§ 93. *If the spontaneity of the new corporate life is original in the Redeemer and proceeds from him alone, then as an historical individual he must have been at the same time ideal (i.e. the ideal must have become completely historical in him), and each historical moment of his experience must at the same time have borne within it the ideal.*

1. If the peculiar dignity of the Redeemer can be measured only by his total activity as resting upon that dignity, while this activity can be seen in its completeness only in the corporate life he founded; if, further, on the one hand, all other religious communities are destined to pass over into this one, so that all religious life existing apart from this is imperfect, whereas in this there is perfection; if, on the other hand, this life itself, at all times and even in its highest development, has no other relation to the Redeemer than that which has been indicated above,[1] so that it can be all that it is only in virtue of its susceptibility to his influence: then the dignity of the Redeemer must be thought of in such a way that he is capable of achieving this. But inasmuch as his activity, so far as we can relate it directly and exclusively to his person, is to be considered in the first place

[1] § 91.

in his public life, but in this life there are no conspicuous isolated acts which definitely stood out in separation from the rest of it, the true manifestation of his dignity, which is identical with his activity in founding a community, lies not in isolated moments, but in the whole course of his life. These are the two truths which, in our proposition, are not simply laid down but are also fully and at every point related to each other.

2. Now, if we live in the Christian fellowship, with the conviction which is common to all Christians, that no more perfect form of the God-consciousness lies in front of the human race, and that any new form would simply be a retrograde step; and, further, that every increase in the activity of the God-consciousness within the Christian fellowship proceeds, not from any newly-added power, but always and only from an ever-active susceptibility to his influence, clearly every given state of this corporate life must remain no more than an approximation to that which exists in the Redeemer himself; and just this is what we understand by his ideal dignity. But this corporate life is not concerned with the multifarious relationships of human life—as though Christ must have been ideal for all knowledge or all art and skill which have been developed in human society—but only with the capacity of the God-consciousness to give the impulse to all life's experiences and to determine them. Hence we do not make the ideality of the Redeemer cover more than this. To this, it is true, it might still be objected that, since the potency of the God-consciousness in the corporate life itself remains always imperfect at best, we must certainly attribute an *exemplary* (*vorbildliche*) dignity to the Redeemer, but ideality (*Urbildlichkeit*) (which properly, asserts the existence of the concept itself), that is absolute perfection, is not necessarily to be attributed to him, not even according to the principle laid down above, for it is not necessary to explain the result, which always remains imperfect. Rather, it might be argued, this is the fundamental exaggeration into which believers fall when they regard Christ in the mirror of their own imperfection; and this exaggeration continually perpetuates itself in the same manner, since believers in all ages read into Jesus whatever they are able to conceive as ideal in this sphere. But in this connexion there are two things to be observed. First, that on this view (if clearly realized) there must be developed at least a wish—for the absolutely perfect is always at least an object of aspiration—the more the individual subordinates his personal consciousness to the God-consciousness, even a hope, that some day the human race, if only in its noblest and best, will pass beyond Christ and leave him behind. But this clearly marks the end of the Christian faith, which on the contrary knows no other way to a pure conception of the ideal than an ever-deepening understanding of

Christ. If, on the other hand, this consequence is not consciously realized, or is definitely rejected, then this limitation of the ideal to the merely exemplary can only be a misunderstood rule of prudence, the apparent ground for which will reveal itself later. Second, we must reflect, on the one hand, that as soon as we grant the possibility of a continued progress in the potency of the God-consciousness, while denying that its perfection exists anywhere, we can also no longer maintain that the creation of man has been or will be completed, since undoubtedly in progress thus continual perfection remains always only a bare possibility. And this would be to assert less of man than of other creatures—for it may be said of all more limited kinds of being that their concept is perfectly realized in the totality of individuals, which complete each other. But this cannot hold of a species which develops itself freely, if the perfection of an essential vital function be posited in the concept but actually found in no individual; for perfection cannot be obtained by adding together things that are imperfect. And, on the other hand, it is to be considered how difficult it would necessarily be to indicate a difference between a true ideal and such an example in which there at the same time resides the power to produce every possible advance in the totality. For productivity belongs only to the concept of the ideal and not to that of the exemplary. We must conclude, then, that ideality is the only appropriate expression for the exclusive personal dignity of Christ.

With regard to the above statement, however, that the thought either of desire or of ability to go beyond Christ marks the end of the Christian faith, here, too, it is not easy to distinguish, among the various conceptions of it which leave room for the perfectibility of Christianity, between those which, although they do not seem so, nevertheless are still Christian, and those which are not, yet wish to pass as such. Everyone recognizes that there is a great difference between two classes. There are those who say it is not only possible but our duty to go beyond much of what Christ taught his disciples, because he himself (since human thought is impossible without words) was seriously hindered by the imperfection of language from giving real expression to the innermost content of his spiritual being in clearly defined thoughts; and the same, it may be held, is true in another sense of his actions also, in which the relations by which they were determined, and therefore imperfection, are always reflected. This, however, does not prevent us from attributing to him absolute ideality in his inner being, in the sense that that inner being may always transcend its manifestation, and what is manifested be only an ever more perfect presentation of it. But there is another class: those who are of opinion that Christ is no more even in his inner being than could be manifested of it, while the fellowship of doctrine and life which takes its origin from

Christ, with the testimonies to him which it preserves, has in virtue of special divine guidance so fortunate an organization that both doctrine and life can easily be re-modelled in accordance with any more perfect ideal which later generations might conceive, without the fellowship needing to lose its historical identity, so that the necessity of founding new religious fellowships has been for all time done away. A single step more, and even the first presuppositions of the Christian faith will be removed; and that step may quite consistently be taken. For if Christ was so much under the constraint of what was necessarily involved in his appearance in history, then both he himself, and his whole achievement as well, must be capable of being explained simply by what was historically given him. That is, Christianity in its entirety can be explained by Judaism at the stage of development which it had then reached—the stage at which it was possible for a man like Jesus to be born of it. Accordingly, Christianity was nothing but a new development of Judaism, though a development saturated with foreign philosophies then current, and Jesus was nothing but a more or less original and revolutionary reformer of the Jewish law.

3. But however certain it may be that the source of such a corporate life, continually advancing in the power of its God-consciousness, can lie only in the ideal, it is not on that account any easier to understand just how the ideal can have been revealed and manifested in a truly historically-conditioned individual. Even generally considered, we are compelled to keep the two ideas separate, and, whether we are speaking of works of art or of the forms of nature, we regard each separate one only as a complement of the rest and as requiring completion by them. But if sin is posited as a corporate act of the human race, what possibility then remains that an ideal individual could have developed out of this corporate life? The way of escape, which suggests that the ideal might be produced by human thought and transferred more or less arbitrarily to Jesus, is already cut off. In that case Christianity would be founded upon an imperfect ideal; it would therefore have to give up its claim to take up into itself all forms of faith and to develop out of itself more and more perfection and blessedness. But if our aim is to make room in human nature before Christ, and apart from him, for the power of producing within itself a pure and perfect ideal—then human nature, since there is a natural connexion between reason and will, cannot have been in a condition of universal sinfulness. Hence, if the man Jesus was really ideal, or if the ideal became historical and actual in him—the one expression means the same as the other—in order to establish a new corporate life within the old and out of it, then certainly he must have entered into the corporate life of sinfulness, but he cannot have come out of it, but must

be recognized in it as a miraculous fact (*eine wunderbare Erscheinung*), and yet (in harmony with the analogies established above) only in the meaning of the word 'miracle' which has here once for all been determined. His peculiar spiritual content, that is, cannot be explained by the content of the human environment to which he belonged, but only by the universal source of spiritual life in virtue of a creative divine act in which, as an absolute maximum, the conception of man as the subject of the God-consciousness comes to completion. But since we can never properly understand the beginnings of life, full justice is done to the demand for the perfect historicity of this perfect ideal, if, from then on, he developed in the same way as all others, so that from birth on his powers gradually unfolded, and, from the zero point of his appearance onwards, were developed to completeness in the order natural to the human race. This applies also to his God-consciousness, with which we are here specially concerned; which certainly, in the case of others as little as in his, is infused by education—the germ of it is found originally in all—but which in him too, as in all, had to develop gradually in human fashion into a really manifest consciousness, and antecedently was only present as a germ, although in a certain sense always present as an active power. So even during this period of development, after it had actually become a consciousness, it could exert its influence over the sensuous self-consciousness only in the measure in which the various functions of the latter had already emerged, and thus, even regarded from this side, it appeared as itself something that was only gradually unfolding to its full extent. If we make the mistake of thinking that, on account of his ideal nature, we must deny this and assume that from the very beginnings of his life he carried the God-consciousness as such within himself—then from the very outset he must have been conscious of himself as an Ego; indeed (the deduction is very simple), he must have been master of language from the first, at least so far as its more abstract part is concerned, and before he ever spoke; thus his whole earliest childhood must have been mere appearance. This excludes the thought of a true human life and quite definitely adopts the error of Docetism; and on these terms we should have to separate in time that in which Christ is like all men from what in him is ideal, allotting to the former the whole period of development up to the beginning of mature manhood, and only then allowing the ideal to come in over and above. But this latter is then inconceivable without an absolute miracle. Nay more, sin too would then, at that earlier stage, be at least possible in him, and therefore also certainly actually present, even if only in the faintest degree; and thus Jesus would be Redeemer and redeemed in one person—with all the further consequences of that.

The pure historicity of the person of the Redeemer, however, involves also this fact, that he could develop only in a certain similarity with his surroundings, that is, in general after the manner of his people. For since mind and understanding drew their nourishment solely from this surrounding world, and his free self-activity too had in this world its determined place, even his God-consciousness, however original its higher powers, could only express or communicate itself in ideas which he had appropriated from this sphere, and in actions which as to their possibility were predetermined in it.[1] If we wished to deny this dependence of the development upon surroundings, we should logically have to assume an empirical omniscience in Christ, in virtue of which all human forms of thought, as well as languages, would have been equally familiar to him, so that he would have lived in whatever is true and right in each of these just as much as in that of his native land. We should also have to add the same omniscience relatively to the various human relationships and their management. And this, too, would mean the loss of true humanity.

4. Further, whatever is involved in the ideality of the contents of his personal spiritual life must also be compatible with this purely human conception of his historical existence. Thus, in the first place, his development must be thought of as wholly free from everything which we have to conceive as conflict. For it is not possible that, where an inner conflict has ever at any time taken place, the traces of it should ever disappear completely. Just as little could the ideal have been recognized as present where even the slightest traces of this conflict betrayed themselves. The power with which the God-consciousness, so far as it was developed at each particular moment, determined that moment, could never have been in doubt, or disturbed by the memory of an earlier conflict. Nor could he ever have found himself in a condition through which a conflict could have been occasioned in the future, that is, there could have been in him, even from the beginning, no inequality in the relation of the various functions of sensuous human nature to the God-consciousness. Thus at every moment even of his period of development he must have been free from everything by which the rise of sin in the individual is conditioned. Two things, further, are quite well possible together: first, that all powers, both the lower ones which were to be mastered and the controlling higher ones, emerged only in gradual development, so that the latter were able to dominate the former only in the measure of their development; and, secondly, that the domination itself was nevertheless at each moment complete in the sense that nothing was ever able to find a place in the sense-nature which did not instantly take its place as an

[1] It will doubtless be generally recognized that this is implied in the statement in *Galatians* 4. 4, that Christ was made under the law.

instrument of the spirit, so that no impression was taken up merely sensuously into the innermost consciousness and elaborated apart from God-consciousness into an element of life, nor did any action, that can really be regarded as such, and as a real whole, ever proceed solely from the sense-nature and not from the God-consciousness. What we could lay down above only as a possibility, namely, a sinless development of a human individual life, must have become actual in the person of the Redeemer in virtue of this undisturbed identity of the relationship, so that we can represent the growth of his personality from earliest childhood on to the fullness of manhood as a continuous transition from the condition of purest innocence to one of purely spiritual fullness of power, which is far removed from anything which we call virtue. For in the condition of innocence there is an activity of the God-consciousness, but only an indirect one, which, though still latently, restrains every movement in the sense-experience which must develop into opposition. The nearest approximation to this, which not seldom occurs in our experience, we usually call 'a happy child-like nature'. The adult fullness of power, on the other hand, although its growth is gradual and the result of practice, is distinguished from virtue in this respect, that it is not the result of a conflict, inasmuch as it does not need to be worked out either through error or through sin, nor even through an inclination to either. And this purity must on no account be regarded as a consequence of outward protection, but must have its ground in the Man himself, that is, in the higher God-consciousness implanted in him originally. Otherwise, since such outward protection depends upon the action of others, the ideal in him would be produced rather than productive, and he himself would be just as much the first from the totality redeemed, as afterwards himself the Redeemer.

Secondly, so far as what is conditioned by race in his person is concerned, Christ could hardly be a complete man if his personality were not determined by this factor; but such determination in no way concerns the real principle of his life but only the organism. Racial peculiarity is in no way the type of his self-activity; it is only the type of his receptivity for the self-activity of the spirit; nor can it have been like a repelling or exclusive principle in him, but must have been united with the freest and most unclouded appreciation of everything human, and with the recognition of the identity of nature and also of spirit in all human forms; also it must have been without any effort to extend what in him was racial beyond its appointed limits. And it is only when we have guarded ourselves thus that we can say that the racial too in him is ideally determined, both in itself and in its relation to the whole of human nature.

5. Here we can only call attention in passing and by anticipation to the

influence which this conception of the ideality of the Redeemer in the perfectly natural historicity of his career exercises on all the Christian doctrines current in the church, all of which must be formulated differently if that conception more or less is given up. To begin with, the fact that all doctrines and precepts developed in the Christian church have universal authority only through their being traced back to Christ, has no other ground than his perfect ideality in everything connected with the power of the God-consciousness. In so far as this is set aside, there must be conceded a possibility of doctrines and precepts arising in the sphere of piety which go beyond the utterances of Christ. Similarly, the preaching of the written word, in so far as it contains only glorification of Christ, and the sacrament of the altar, can be regarded as permanent institutions in the Christian church only if we premise that the whole development and maintenance of Christian piety must always proceed from vital fellowship with Christ. Nor would Christ be presented as a universal example unless his relation to all original differences in individuals were uniform—for otherwise he would necessarily be more of an example for some than others. This only becomes possible through his ideality. But just as little could he be a universal example, unless every moment of his life were ideal. Otherwise it would be necessary first to distinguish the ideal from the non-ideal, which could only be done according to an external law, which (it follows) would be superior to him. That law would come in, unless (as his ideality implies) what is racially determined in him had been limited; otherwise we should have to consent to adopt into the Christian norm of life all that is simply Jewish in his life. Moreover, these points, cardinal for the Christian fellowship, are not doctrines which became current only through later developments; they are the original doctrines of his disciples, closely bound up with the way in which they applied to Jesus the idea of the Messiah, and such as are easily brought into connexion with his own utterances, so far as these are accessible to us.

94. *The Redeemer, then, is like all men in virtue of the identity of human nature, but distinguished from them all by the constant potency of his God-consciousness, which was a veritable existence of God in him.*

1. That the Redeemer should be entirely free from all sinfulness is no objection at all to the complete identity of human nature in him and others, for we have already laid down that sin is so little an essential part of the being of man that we can never regard it as anything else than a disturbance of nature. It follows that the possibility of a sinless development is in itself not incongruous with the idea of human nature; indeed, this possibility is involved, and recognized, in the consciousness of sin as

guilt, as that is universally understood. This likeness, however, is to be understood in such a general sense that even the first man before the first sin stood no nearer the Redeemer, and was like him in no higher sense, than all other men. For if even in the life of the first man we must assume a time when sin had not yet appeared, yet every first appearance of sin leads back to a sinful preparation. But the Redeemer too shared in the same vicissitudes of life, without which we can hardly imagine the entrance of sin at a definite moment even in Adam, for they are essential to human nature. Furthermore, the first man was originally free from all the contagious influences of a sinful society, while the Redeemer had to enter into the corporate life when it had already advanced far in deterioration, so that it would hardly be possible to attribute his sinlessness to external protection—which we certainly must somehow admit in the case of the first man, if we would not involve ourselves in contradictions. Of the Redeemer, on the contary, we must hold that the ground of his sinlessness was not external to himself, but that it was a sinlessness essentially grounded in himself, if he was to take away, through what he was in himself, the sinfulness of the corporate life. Therefore, so far as sin is concerned, Christ differs no less from the first man than from all others.

The identity of human nature further involves this, that the manner in which Christ differs from all others also has its place in this identity. This would not be the case if it were not involved in human nature that individuals, so far as the measure of the different functions is concerned, are originally different from each other, so that to every separate corporate life (regarded in space as well as in time) there belong those who are more and less gifted; and we only arrive at the truth of life when we thus correlate those who differ from each other. In the same way, therefore, all those who in any respect give character to an age or district are bound up with those over whom (as being defective in that particular respect) they extend an educative influence, even as Christ is bound up with those whom his preponderatingly powerful God-consciousness links to the corporate life thus indicated. The greater the difference, and the more specific the activity, the more must these also have established themselves against the hindering influences of a worthless environment, and they can be understood only by reference to this self-differentiating quality of human nature, not by reference to the group in which they stand; although by divine right they belong to it, as the Redeemer does to the whole race.

2. But in admitting that what is peculiar in the Redeemer's kind of activity belongs to a general aspect of human nature, we by no means wish to reduce this activity, and the personal dignity by which it is conditioned, to the same measure as that of others. The simple fact that

faith in Christ postulates a relation on his part to the whole race, while everything analogous is valid only for definite individual times and places, is sufficient to prove this. For no one has yet succeeded, in any sphere of science or art, and no one will ever succeed, in establishing himself as head, universally animating and sufficient for the whole human race.

For this peculiar dignity of Christ, however, in the sense in which we have already referred back the ideality of his person to this spiritual function of the God-consciousness implanted in the self-consciousness, the terms of our proposition alone are adequate; for to ascribe to Christ an absolutely powerful God-consciousness, and to attribute to him an existence of God in him are exactly the same thing. The expression, 'the existence of God in anyone', can only express the relation of the omnipresence of God to this one. Now since God's existence can only be apprehended as pure activity, while every individualized existence is merely an intermingling of activity and passivity—the activity being always found apportioned to this passivity in every other individualized existence—there is, so far no existence of God in any individual thing, but only an existence of God in the world. And only if the passive conditions are not purely passive, but mediated through vital receptivity, and this receptivity confronts the totality of finite existence (so far, i.e. as we can say of the individual as a living creature that, in virtue of the universal reciprocity, it in itself represents the world), could we suppose an existence of God in it. Hence this clearly does not hold of what is individualized as an unconscious thing; for since an unconscious thing brings no living receptivity to meet all the forces of consciousness it cannot represent these forces in itself. But just as little and for the same reason can what is conscious but not intelligent represent them, so that it is only in the rational individual that an existence of God can be admitted. How far this is also true similarly and without distinction if we regard reason as functioning in objective consciousness lies outside our investigation. But so far as the rational self-consciousness is concerned, it is certain that the God-consciousness which (along with the self-consciousness) belongs to human nature originally, before the Redeemer and apart from all connexion with him, cannot fittingly be called an existence of God in us, not only because it was not a pure God-consciousness (either in polytheism or even in Jewish monotheism, which was everywhere tinctured with materialistic conceptions, whether cruder or finer), but also because, such as it was, it did not assert itself as activity, but in these religions was always dominated by the sensuous self-consciousness. If, then, it was able neither to portray God purely and with real adequacy in thought, nor yet to exhibit itself as pure activity, it cannot be represented as an existence of God in us. But just as the unconscious forces of nature and non-rational life became a revelation of God to us only so far as we bring that conception with us, so also that darkened and imperfect God-consciousness by itself is not an existence of God in human nature, but only in so far as we bring Christ with us in thought and relate it to him. So that originally it is found nowhere but in him, and he is the only 'other' in which there is an existence of God in the proper sense, so far, that is, as we posit the God-consciousness in his self-consciousness as continually and exclusively determining every moment, and consequently also this perfect indwelling of the Supreme Being as his peculiar being and his inmost self. Indeed, working backwards we must now say, if it is only through him that the human God-consciousness becomes an existence of God in human nature, and only through the rational nature that the totality of finite powers can become an existence of God in the world, that in truth he mediates all existence of God in the world and all revelation of God through the world, in so far as he bears within himself the whole new creation which contains and develops the potency of the God-consciousness.

3. But if as a person of this kind he needs to have the whole human development in common with us, so that even this existence of God must in him have had a development in time, and as the most spiritual element in his personality could only emerge into manifestation after the lower functions; yet he cannot have entered life as one for whom the foundations of sin had already been laid before his being began to be manifested. We have envisaged this earlier establishment of sin for all of us, without entering upon natural-scientific investigations into the origin of the individual life, and the coming together in us (if we may use the phrase) of soul and body, but simply by holding to the general facts of experience; so here, too, we seek to combine with these facts only the relatively supernatural, which we have already admitted in general for the entrance of the Redeemer into the world.

The origin of every human life may be regarded in a twofold manner, as issuing from the narrow circle of descent and society to which it immediately belongs, and as a fact of human nature in general. The more definitely the weaknesses of that narrow circle repeat themselves in an individual, the more valid becomes the first point of view. The more the individual by the kind and degree of his gifts transcends that circle, and the more he exhibits what is new within it, the more we are thrown back upon the other explanation. This means that the beginning of Jesus' life cannot in any way be explained by the first factor, but only and exclusively by the second; so that from the beginning he must have been free from every influence from earlier generations which disseminated sin and disturbed the inner God-consciousness, and he can only be understood as an original act of human nature, i.e. as an act of human nature as not affected by sin. The beginning of his life was also a new implanting of the God-consciousness which creates receptivity in human nature; hence this content and that manner of origin are in such a close relation that they mutually condition and explain each other. That new implanting came to be through the beginning of his life, and therefore that beginning must have transcended every detrimental influence of his immediate circle; and because it was such an original and sin-free act of nature, a filling of his nature with God-consciousness became possible as its result. So that upon this relation too the fullest light is thrown if we regard the beginning of the life of Jesus as the completed creation of human nature. The appearance of the first man constituted at the same time the physical life of the human race; the appearance of the Second Adam constituted for this nature a new spiritual life, which communicates and develops itself by spiritual fecundation. And as in the former its originality (which is the condition of the appearance of human nature) and its having emerged from creative divine activity are the same thing, so also in the Redeemer both are the same—his spiritual originality, set free from every prejudicial influence of natural descent, and that existence of God in him which also proves itself creative. If the impartation of the Spirit to human nature which was made in the first Adam was insufficient, in that the spirit remained sunk in sensuousness and barely glanced forth clearly at moments as a presentiment of something better, and if the work of creation has only been completed through the second and equally original impartation to the Second Adam, yet both events go back to one undivided eternal divine decree and form, even in a higher sense, only one and the same natural system, though one unattainable by us.

XVII
RITSCHL

Albrecht Ritschl (1822–89) was the son of a Lutheran bishop. Like most of his generation he came early under the influence of Hegel, but became increasingly eclectic in his use of philosophy, being influenced also by Schleiermacher, Lotze and above all by Kant. He held the chair of theology first at Bonn then at Gottingen. Theologically he claimed to be in the tradition of both Luther and Schleiermacher. But he reacted strongly against the element of mystical pietism in Schleiermacher in favour of a more practical, ethical theology. He reacted equally against the rationalism of Hegel. This left only the moral, practical sphere in which he could find the essence of the Christian religion. Because of his rejection of direct philosophical and mystical knowledge of God, he held that we cannot know what God is in himself. We can know only his moral will and holy love as these are disclosed to us in Jesus Christ. The Christ, in turn, is disclosed to us only through the Bible and the community which he founded and in which his Spirit abides. Therefore, Ritschl maintained, the beginning as well as the end of a theological system must be the doctrine of justification and reconciliation. This doctrine, in turn, if it is to illuminate our Christian understanding, must be interpreted not merely formally and forensically, but in the light of the religious quality of the life and acts of Jesus Christ. In this emphasis he provided much of the theological inspiration behind the interest of late nineteenth and early twentieth century 'liberal' theology in the historic life of Jesus. At the same time he also foreshadowed the Christocentric character of more recent confessional theology. His treatment of the Kingdom of God as the social community in which the moral fruits of justification and reconciliation are appropriated and given concrete expression is one of the roots of the 'social gospel'. Yet the thoroughly eschatological emphasis of much contemporary theology also derives ultimately from this same aspect of Ritschl's thought.

His great work *The Christian Doctrine of Justification and Reconciliation* is in three volumes. The first deals with the history of the doctrine, beginning with Anselm and Abelard. The second volume expounds the biblical basis of the doctrine. The third, and by far the most important volume, gives his own systematic and constructive interpretation. It is this third volume which is available in translation. The passages below are taken from the English translation, edited by H. R. Mackintosh and A. B. Macaulay (T. and T. Clark, Edinburgh, 1902).

GOD AS FATHER AND AS LOVING WILL

Our task is to ascertain in general the attribute of God through which the positively Christian conception of the forgiveness of sins is to be understood. Now it is almost inconceivable that the orthodox theologians, in spite of their endeavours to reproduce the ideas of Holy Scripture, have been entirely oblivious of the fact that Jesus explicitly connected this operation of God with *his attribute as Father*. He directed his disciples to invoke God as Father when they prayed to him for forgiveness of their sins; and, to bring home to them the necessity of their forgiving their fellow-men, he promised them that their Father in heaven would also forgive them their sins (*Luke* 11. 2–4; *Mark* 11. 25; *Matthew* 6. 9–15). In so far, too, as the forgiveness of sins is mediated through the expiatory death of Christ, the Apostles recognize the love, or the grace, or the righteousness, that is, the self-consistent saving purpose, of God as the ground of that scheme (*Romans* 3. 25–6; *Hebrews* 2. 9). Moreover, the Old Testament idea of sacrifice, through which this whole circle of conceptions must be understood, contains nothing analogous to the judicial procedure of vicarious punishment; the sacrifices of the law are rather the symbols of a divinely-ordained scheme for the appropriation of the Covenant-grace. It is true that the God whom we invoke as Father, has also inherent in his nature the attribute of impartial judge (I *Peter* 1. 7); but he acts as judge only in vindicating the rights of his people. The title of judge as applied to God has therefore for Christians no real place alongside of, or over, the relation in which he stands to them as Father. It is only therefore, when the love of God, regarded as Father, is conceived as the will which works toward the destined end, that the real equivalence of forgiveness and justification, which is represented in the religious conception of things, can be made good. If, however, God be preconceived as judge in the forensic sense, the two ideas come into direct antagonism with one another, as was indeed explicitly maintained by the leading representatives of the older theology. The man who has gone through the punishment he has merited can, of course, be no more looked upon as a criminal, but he cannot by any means yet be regarded as an active and successful member of the moral community; in order to attain this place, the discharged culprit must give special evidence of his fitness for membership in the community. If, therefore, a judicial procedure on the part of God is recognized in this, that he regards sinners as free from punishment and guilt on account of the satisfaction which Christ has made, he must also, in order to judge them as positively righteous, impute to them the merit of Christ. It has been shown (p. 89) that this train of thoughts carries us beyond the limits of the conceptions derived from the analogy of the human judge. But the forgiveness extended by a father to his child combines in one act the judgment that a fault committed by the child ought to bring about no alienation between father and child, and the expression of the purpose to admit the child, as a right and gracious action, to the unfettered intercourse of love.

The attribute of father stands in relation to the peculiar moral and legal fellowship of the family. Therefore all the preceding arguments regarding the attitude of God to the forgiveness of sins, which have been derived from the analogy of the head of the State, that is, the legal and only relatively moral society of the people, are found to be incongruous with the Christian idea of God. The representation of God under the attribute of Father corresponds exactly to the transference to the whole of mankind of his relative moral and legal Lordship over the people of Israel for the bringing about of the highest moral end. Now, not only does this universal destination of the Kingdom of God exclude comparison with the form of government of any definite people, but the designation of God as our Father shows expressly that the real analogy for the Kingdom of God should be sought, not in the national state, but in the family. The consequences which this principle involves for the representation of the Christian view of the world cannot yet be brought out. One result, however, is the confirmation of a formerly established position (p. 62), namely that the forgiveness of sins by God as Father finds no real standard of comparison in the right of pardon which belongs to the head of the state. The difference between the two is seen in this, that the right of pardon is only exercised in individual instances of legal condemnation, which as such stand in no connexion with one another and always form exceptions to the recognized legal order, while the forgiveness of sins by God as Father is a universal, though not unconditioned, fundamental law, established in the interest of the community of the Kingdom of God.

If, then, justification in the Christian sense is related to God under the attribute—to use a human analogy—of Father, not of judge, the ground on which Heidegger distinguishes justification and adoption becomes untenable. The only valid distinction between the two ideas is that forgiveness, or justification, or reconciliation, refers generally to the admission of sinners to fellowship with God in spite of sin, whereas in adoption the confidential relation to God which is thereby established is specially described in terms of the normal relation of children to a father. The connexion being such, the idea of reconciliation is shown to be of equal constitutive significance for Christianity with the name of God as the Father of our Lord Jesus Christ. But the ideas of *reconciliation* and *adoption* agree with one another also in a formal respect. For adoption must also be conceived as a resolution of will in the form of a synthetic judgment. The Reformed theologians, who alone give the idea of adoption an independent place in the Christian system, occupy themselves with describing the distinctions between the notions of divine and human adoption. But we ought rather to seek to ascertain the harmony between the two. Now such harmony cannot be found in the idea of the establishment of a right of inheritance for a person of alien descent. For those persons who have in the Christian sense been adopted by God as his children, attain that rank only under the presupposition that in a certain real sense they derive their being from God, that is, that they have been created in his image. In harmony therewith, and in contrast to the alienation which sin causes between God and men, the adoption of the believing signifies their reception into that peculiar fellowship with God which is represented under the analogy of the family. Now, the moral fellowship of the human family rests not only on natural descent, but on a judgment of the value of this fellowship by the husband and wife, and on the purpose of the father to educate his children to become spiritual and moral persons. The father's moral relation to his children therefore rests in every case on an act of υἱοθεσία so that this idea is not exclusively applicable to children of alien descent. The certainty of blood-relationship is not the sufficient ground of the father's care; for there are fathers who shirk their responsibilities. Therefore the resolution to bring up one's children does not follow from the analytic judgment that one is the author of the children's life. On the contrary, this resolution, like every other resolution, is a synthetic judgment, even though it usually appears as a logical conclusion from the recognition of blood relationship. The latter, however, is the case only when the resolution to give moral education to the children is included in the resolution to form the marriage union. On the other hand, the resolution to assume charge of a natural child for the purpose of moral education is usually absent, unless the purpose of the resolution to enter upon the marriage state be combined with sexual connexion. If, therefore, the divine υἱοθεσία in the Christian sense is understood in reference to the closest conceivable spiritual fellowship between man and God, then the form of the resolution, which is a synthetic judgment, is in exact harmony with that of the analogous resolution in the relationship of the human family, which we have taken as our standard of comparison. Seeing, however, that the resolution to admit children to moral fellowship applies not only, as a general rule, to children of the blood, but also, in extraordinary cases, to alien children, and that the resolution can extend in these cases only to the transmission of property rights, the idea of the divine υἱοθεσία cannot be held to be completely harmonious in these essential respects with its human analogue. For those who are admitted to the rank of children of God are all, by virtue of their innate moral destiny, 'of divine race', but all in reality, because of sin, 'as alien children' to God. Through the paramount influence of this fact, therefore, the divine υἱοθεσία appears as most closely analogous to the human legal form of adoption. If, now, justification is an operation in which God appears under the attribute of Father, then the adoption of men as God's children is a substantially equivalent idea. The latter modifies the former only in this respect, that the fellowship with God to which sinners are admitted, is conceived to be as close as that which exists between the head and the members of a family. Therefore the functions in which the believing make manifest their justification and reconciliation must also be conceived as the functions of sonship to God. (*Justification and Reconciliation*, pp. 93–8.) . . .

Theology, in delineating the moral order of the world, must take as its starting-point that conception of God in which the relation of God to his Son our Lord is expressed, a relation which, by Christ's mediation, is extended likewise to his community. For when the Apostles, in the Epistles of the New Testament, describe God as our Father, that is an abbreviated expression for the Christian name for God, which when fully stated runs, 'the God and Father of our Lord Jesus Christ' (II *Corinthians* 1. 3; 11. 31; *Romans* 15. 6; *Colossians* 1. 3; I *Peter* 1. 3; *Ephesians* 1. 3). As the name of God is always used in Scripture as a compendious description of his revelation, it is clear that, when God reveals himself as Father through his Son Jesus Christ, the process is only completed when the community accepts the revelation by acknowledging the Mediator who brings it as its Lord. Any attempt, therefore, to construct a scientific doctrine of God must be wrong which fails to keep in view all the aspects of this name. The name God has the same sense when used of Father, Son and Holy Spirit (*Matthew* 28. 19). For the name denotes God in so far as he reveals himself, while the Holy Spirit is the power of God which enables the community to appropriate his self-revelation as Father through his Son (I *Corinthians* 2. 12). That the revelation of God through his Son, however, embraces the community which acknowledges his Son as her Lord, and how it does so, is explained by saying that God manifests himself to the Son and to the community as *loving Will*. As this conception of God is recognized as coming from the source of knowledge which is authoritative for the Christian community, it likewise follows that the goodness of God to all men, in bestowing on them the good things of nature (*Matthew* 5. 45; *Acts* 14. 17), is an inference which Christ drew from the knowledge he possessed of the love of God to him and to his community. Thus the goodness of God, as the general presupposition of everything, is embraced in the specific attribute of the divine Fatherhood; or, in other words, the truth that he has revealed himself to the Christian community as love. There is no other conception of equal worth beside this which need to be taken into account. This is especially true of the conception of the divine holiness, which, in its Old Testament sense, is for various reasons not valid in Christianity, while its use in the New Testament is obscure. Even the recognition of the personality of God does not imply independent knowledge apart from our defining him as loving Will. It only decides the form to be given to this content, for without this content of loving Will the conception of spiritual personality is not sufficient to explain the world as a connected whole. The step, therefore, which we take now in bringing forward the truly Christian view of God ought not to be understood as though in his contrast to the world God were conceived, first of all, in general, as personality, and secondly, in particular, as loving Will—and this in such a way that while consistent knowledge of the world might be drawn from the first conception, the second would yield simply more knowledge of the same sort. What I mean is rather this, that the conception of love is the only adequate conception of God, for it enables us, both to understand the revelation which comes through Christ to his community, and at the same time to solve the problem of the world. For this purpose, the merely formal conception of personality is insufficient: for it leaves us free to ascribe all possible kinds of content to the divine Will. Now, if an entirely different sort of world were just as possible for God as the world which actually exists, there is no perceptible reason why the actual world was ever raised by God above the level of possibility. And therefore, either the formal conception of the divine personality is as unserviceable as a pantheistic notion would be, or it can be successfully employed only as the form whose special content is love.

It cannot be doubted, as a historical fact, that individuality (*Besonderheit*) is everywhere a characteristic of the religious idea of God. But the Scotists on the one hand, and the Spinozists on the other, regard with distrust and aversion the suggestion that a conception of God marked by this characteristic is an appropriate expression of a scientific principle of knowledge. Both follow the maxim: *omnis determinatio est negatio*, and negation seems altogether incompatible with the idea of God. Scotism, however, fails to explain the fact that there is a real world, while Spinozism fails to explain the world as it really is. But modern Pantheism is not at all averse to the view that the Absolute forms the reality of the world by the gradual particularization of itself, so as to reach its full realization through the special organ of the human spirit and its special function of intuition and methodical knowledge. If we think God as the universal ground of all reality, we cannot avoid ascribing individuality to him in some way or other. For even in logic the particular comes under the universal only because it comes under the individual. The will, too, becomes the universal ground of particular real acts only by keeping to a definite direction and simultaneously refraining from other possible directions. On the other hand, the Spinozistic principle that every special determination implies negation, amounts to no more than the logical law that the conceptions of the individual and the *differentia* always hold good together, or that we distinguish things by their species. If, therefore, the conception of individuality is inapplicable to God, God cannot be distinguished from things, nor things from God. Either everything is God, or everything is world. Either the distinction of things from one another and from the universal substance is a delusion, or it is a self-deception to assume the existence of an intelligent Creator of the world which is distinct from him, and differentiated within itself. But this latter assumption was found necessary to explain the world, differentiated as it is into nature and spiritual life, with this further circumstance, that men regard their common moral life as the final end of the world. To eliminate individuality from the conception of God, therefore, is wrong, for it leads to absurd conclusions.

God's personal will, like any other force, can be thought as the cause of effects only when acting in a definite direction. As Will, God can be thought only as in conscious relation to the end which he himself is. Nevertheless, this formal truth is inadequate to explain anything which is not God; it is inadequate, therefore, to explain the world. Unless it can be shown that, and how the world is embraced in the personal end which God sets before himself, then even this analysis of the divine Will leads to nothing. We shall find that the conception of love, which is the key to the revelation of God in Christianity, carries us past the difficulties which accompany that analysis. Still, the preliminary question arises, whether to determine the divine Will in this specific way is not to menace the value of the conception of God. For if God, conceived under the special attribute of love, is subordinated to a generic conception of will, it might be argued that this generic idea, as the higher, might claim to be in value the equivalent of God. Here the difficulty solved above returns in another form. Nevertheless, the specific character assigned to God's Will is not such that the affirmation of it is the negation of some other specific character which in itself might possibly belong to him, nor is it such that some other being might have to be viewed, under some other category, as deserving comparison with God. The truth rather is, that only through the special attribute of love is it possible to derive the world from God; this quality of love, therefore, serves in general to discover to us in God the ground of the unity of nature and spirit, and the law of their co-existence. It cannot, therefore, be regarded as lessening the cosmic significance of God. The logical superiority of the genus to the species never implies that the genus has an existence apart from the species. The conception of God, therefore, when it is specifically determined as love, is not to be regarded as being subordinated to some hypothetical substance, called 'Will in general' or 'indeterminate Will', and thus possessed of the absoluteness which does not belong to Will when defined as love. For we have seen that indeterminate Will is incapable of explaining anything.

The word 'love' is frequently used to denote the feeling of the worth of an object for the Self. But as such feeling always sets the will in motion, either to appropriate the loved object or to enrich its existence, ordinary usage comprises these kinds of movement of the will also under the designation of love. Nor is common usage ambiguous in doing so, for the two aspects of the emotion are closely related to one another. Love, as feeling, fulfils its nature when it excites the will; and love, as will, includes the feeling of the same name. The conception of love, therefore, is completely expressed by combining both. Love is will aiming either at the appropriation of an object or at the enrichment of its existence, because moved by a feeling of its worth. But this definition needs to be supplimented by special qualifications. *First*, it is necessary that the objects which are loved should be of like nature to the subject which loves, namely, persons. When we speak of love for things or animals, the conception is degraded beneath its proper meaning. *Secondly*, love implies a will which is constant in its aim. If the objects change, we may have fancies, but we cannot love. *Thirdly*, love aims at the promotion of the other's personal end, whether known or conjectured. To render assistance in ordinary matters does not require love, but only good-feeling, a less definite thing. Love, however, is not merely interested in the loved one's affairs, which may perhaps have simply an accidental connection with him. What love does is rather to estimate everything which concerns the other, by its bearing on the character in which the loved one is precious to the lover. Whatever valuable spiritual acquirements the other may possess, or whatever is still necessary for his perfection, becomes the content of the definite ideal which the lover sets before himself. Love desires either to promote, to maintain, and through sympathetic interest to enjoy the individuality of character acquired by the other, or to assist him in securing those blessings which are necessary to ensure the attainment of his personal ideal. *Fourthly*, if love is to be a constant attitude of the will, and if the appropriation and the promotion of the other's personal end are not alternately to diverge, but to coincide in each act, then the will of the lover must take up the other's personal end and make it part of his own. That is, love continually strives to develop and to appropriate the individual self-end of the other personality, regarding this as a task necessary to the very nature of its own personal end, its own conscious individuality. This characteristic implies that the will, as love, does not give itself up for the other's sake. To take up this position is not, as some have objected, to introduce the element of egoism into the conception of love. For the will is egoistic when it sets itself in opposition to the common aims of others; but in the present case, the will is directed to the closest fellowship with another and to a common end. This conception of love may without any difficulty be tested by being applied to all sub-species of love, such as friendship, conjugal affection, paternal affection, and love for one's parents.

When, now, we apply this conception to God, it becomes clear that neither the indeterminate notion of a cosmos, nor the notion of the natural world, can be conceived as the correlate of this particular aspect of the divine will; for in them there is nothing akin to God. The proposition, that God created the world out of love, is useless to begin with, so far as it can bear the meaning that God communicates himself to mere creatures, and gives their existence realization as though it were the ultimate aim of his personal end. We can find an object which corresponds to his nature as love only in one or many personal beings. We cannot, of course, decide from the conception of love itself whether the forth-bringing of one loved person, or the forth-bringing, education, and perfecting of a world of spirits, constitutes the end which, under the conception of love, must be thought as embraced within the personal end of God. But the world also is for us a given fact, and an examination of the various aspects of the conception of God cannot but have some bearing upon the existence of the world, in which a multiplicity of persons exist as members of a race. These come into existence as a multitude of individuals, participating, as they do, in material and organic nature. For matter is the original expression of the multiplex, and the precondition of all multiplicity; while organic matter is the expression of the differentiation of a living multiplicity conditioned by the nexus of species and genus. Consideration of the world, therefore, shows that a multiplicity of persons, together composing a race, may be the object of the divine love; while, apart from this empirical observation, it is at least as conceivable that God's personal end should be bound up with that of a single kindred spirit as with that of a multiplicity of spirits.

Now, if we follow out, in the first instance, the connection given in experience between the world of spirits and nature, we find that we may draw, from the relations between the world of spirits and God's character as love, a necessary conclusion regarding the origin of the world of nature. If it be an essential part of God's personal end that he should create a multitude of spirits, formed after their own kind, and that he should bring them to perfection in order to manifest himself to them as love, then the world of nature, viewed in its separate formation as distinct from the world of men, cannot be viewed as a mere arbitrary appendix, but must rather be regarded as a means to the divine end. The rest of nature might be an arbitrary appendix to the existence of the human race, were it not called into existence by a divine Will whose character is love—were it, in other words, the creation of a purely indeterminate divine Will. But absolutely nothing definite or real can be derived from such a ground as this. Nature, therefore, must likewise be explained from the divine Will in its self-given character of love. But, owing to its lack of kinship with God, it cannot be the direct object and the last end of his loving will. And so nothing remains but to conclude, that nature is called into being to serve as a means to God's essential purpose in creating the world of spirits. In this way the statement that God has created the world out of love receives its proper limitations, and the creation of nature by God is given the value of a relative necessity, the necessity, namely, of serving as a means to God's previously chosen end of calling into being a multitude of spirits akin to himself. Granted, therefore, that the world of nature in general cannot be known directly as the creation of God, and that, on the other hand, the moral development of men as individuals, and their union through progressive fellowship in good, demand for their explanation the idea of a God, it must still be remembered that these results cannot be attained save through the means furnished by our natural endowment. For the apparatus by which the individual life and all commerce in things spiritual is carried on, presupposes for its permanent existence the whole immeasurable system of the world, mechanical, chemical, organic. Consequently, if we must conceive God as necessary to guarantee our personal morality and our moral fellowship, we must recognize that the entire universe is designed to serve this divine end; for otherwise we could not view even our moral life as an object of divine care. The whole universe, therefore, considered thus as the precondition of the moral kingdom of created spirits, is throughout God's creation for this end.

We have now provisionally recognized a multitude of spirits, together forming a race, as a possible object of the divine love. But the question may be asked whether, since multiplicity is a necessary characteristic of them, they can really be akin in nature to the one divine Will. For the human race, in virtue of its attribute of multiplicity, is involved in the conditions under which the genera and species of all organic creatures exist. *Qua* multiplicity, therefore, the human race is akin to nature and not akin to God. In order to prove its kinship with God, it would be necessary to conceive the human race as a unity in spite of its natural multiplicity, a unity which is other than its natural generic unity. The conception we are in search of is given in the idea of the Christian community, which makes the Kingdom of God its task. This idea of the moral unification of the human race, through action prompted by universal love to our neighbour, represents a unity of many which belongs to the realm of the thoroughly defined, in other words, the good will. The multitude of spirits who, for all their natural and generic affinity, may yet, in the practical expression they give to their will, be utterly at variance, attain a supernatural unity through mutual and social action prompted by love, action which is no longer limited by considerations of family, class, or nationality—and this without abrogating the multiplicity given in experience. It is an essential characteristic of the Kingdom of God that, as the final end which is being realized in the world and as the supreme good of created spirits, it transcends the world, just as God himself is supramundane. The idea of the Kingdom of God, therefore, gives a supramundane character to humanity as bound to him, i.e. it both transcends and completes all the natural and particular motives which unite men together. Consequently, the unity of the human race thus reached is so far akin to the unity of the divine Will that in it may be seen the object of the divine love. But the community, which is called on to form itself by union into the Kingdom of God, and whose activity consists in carrying out this assigned task, depends entirely for its origin on the fact that the Son of God is its Lord, to whom it renders obedience. The community, as the object to which God's love extends, cannot even be conceived apart from the presupposition that it is governed continually by its founder as its Lord, and that its members go through the experience of being transformed into that peculiar character of which their Lord is the original, and which through him, is communicated to them (II *Corinthians* 3. 18; *Romans* 8. 29). The community of Christ, therefore, is the correlative of the love of God, only because the love in which God embraces his Son and assures to him his unique position (*Mark* 1. 11, 9. 7; *John* 15. 9, 17. 24; *Colossians* 1. 13; *Ephesians* 1. 6), comes through him to act upon those likewise who belong to him as his disciples or his community. Every aspect of this relationship to Christ, however, is comprised under the principle, that the Son of God is acknowledged as the Lord of his community, and under this condition transfers to it his own relation to God. The perfect name of God, by which he reveals himself to this community, owes its interpretation, accordingly, to these progressive manifestations of his love. God is love, inasmuch as he reveals himself through his Son to the community, which he has founded, in order to form it into the Kingdom of God, so that in designing for men this supramundane destiny he realizes his own glory, or the fulfilment of his personal end. Herein is the love of God perfected that we love our brethren in the Kingdom of God (I *John* 4. 12). But as, from our point of view, this consummation always appears as one yet to be attained, our progress towards it is guided by our perception of the truth that for us the love of God, in his relation to his Son our Lord, is an assured fact. Lastly, it becomes clear in this connection that the destination of man for the Kingdom of God, in the form of the community of God's Son, is to be included in the Christian conception of man, and not to be distinguished from it as something lying above and beyond it.

If, now, the creation and government of the world are accordingly to be conceived as the means whereby created spiritual beings—men—are formed into the Kingdom of God in the community of Christ, then the view of the world given in Christianity is the key to solve the problem of the world in general. The fact that this religion, in its origin, wears a particular historical guise, is no hindrance to its being destined to become the universal faith of humanity. The conception of God, however, through which this result is reached, avoids the difficulties in which is entangled the conception of God held by the older school of theologians, and rises above the dilemma in which the orthodox and the Scotist theories circle aimlessly round one another. When God is conceived as love, through the relation of his will to his Son and the community of the Kingdom of God, he is not conceived as being anything apart from and prior to his self-determination as love. He is either conceived as love, or simply not at all. If anyone thinks it necessary, after the analogy of human personality, to conceive of God first as infinite Being, or as indeterminate Will, or as quiescent Character, which may advance within itself to self-determination as love, what he conceives under these prefatory ideas is simply not God. For they mean something that *becomes*. But God is conceived as loving Will, when we regard his Will as set upon the forth-bringing of his Son and the community of the Kingdom of God; and if we abstract from that, what we conceive is not God at all. At the same time, the eternity of God is guaranteed by the very fact that we are compelled to think God in that self-determination as love in which we actually do think him; for the content of our thought would not be really God, if we still posited something as prior in order to deduce from it his character as love. Nor is the act of thought which I am describing at all difficult. It has its analogy in the feeling of self and the judgment upon self of which we are conscious in exalted moments of moral will, and in which we discover experimentally our power of self-determination towards good, and rise above all the obstacles which are present within us and without. (*Justification and Reconciliation*, pp. 272–83). . . .

When we investigated the Kingdom of God as the correlate of the thought that God is love, it appeared that this organization of men can be construed as the object and end of God's love, only in so far as it is conformed to the type of its founder, the Son of God. The harmony with God and likeness to him which the Kingdom of God must maintain in order to be understood as the objective of God's love, attaches to the said Kingdom only in so far as it is called into being by the Son of God, and bows to him as its Lord. In other words, it is on the Son of God that in the first place the Father's love falls, and, only for his sake, on the community of which he is Lord. Moreover, if these relations are eternally involved in God's will of love, it follows from our recognition of this fact, that the special significance Christ has for us is by no means exhausted in our appreciation of him as a revelation conditioned by time. On the contrary, it is implied that, as founder and Lord of the Kingdom of God, Christ is as much the object of God's eternal knowledge and will as is the moral unification of mankind, which is made possible through him, and whose prototype he is; or rather, that, not only in time but in the eternity of the divine knowledge and will, Christ precedes his community. Of course, to this statement a certain qualification must be added. For whatever belonged to the natural and generic limitations of Christ, more especially his individual natural endowments and his Jewish nationality, cannot be taken as the object of the eternal will of God, since these things are by their very nature bound up with the world, consequently can be fore-ordered, even by God, only through a volition in time. But Christ, we know, reduced the significance of these limitations to mere means toward his own spiritual life, in particular toward the apprehension of his own religious fellowship with God, and the carrying out of the vocation he had embraced. Sharing the religious and moral customs of the Jews, he yet knows himself, as the Son of God, exalted above them; in discharging the duties of his vocation toward his countrymen, he knows his work destined to be fruitful, at the same time that he distinctly foresees its fruitlessness among the Jews; in his own life-conduct, that universal human morality of which the Kingdom of God shall be the perfect realization so markedly preponderates, that we fail to notice in him those traces of individual temperament which are wont to count for something even in the most perfect of men. Yet Christ's life was not merely an abstract presentation of universal human morality; for he gave the whole wealth of personal devotion to the universal content of his vocation. Rather is he himself the prototype of that life of love and elevation above wordly motive, which forms the distinguishing characteristic of the Kingdom of God; and this as the deliberate result of his vocation to be the founder of that Kingdom, not in any mere application of the principle of the Kingdom to the separate details of human life, which is the source from which other men derive their ethical vocations. If, therefore, the Kingdom of God as the correlate of the divine self-end is the eternal object of the love of God, this is so because Christ as the prototype and inspiring force of that union of the many in one, in other words, as the Head and Lord of that Kingdom, is the eternal object of the love of God, so that in this special form the Kingdom of God is present eternally to the divine knowledge and will, while its individual members are objects of the knowledge of God in time.

The congruity between the Son of God and God as his Father, by which the conceivability of this eternal relation must be determined, reaches, however, still further. For if the idea of love is necessarily confined to beings of a like order, then, of course, it cannot be applied to God in any such way that the thought of God must be subsumed under some higher genus. Rather must everything that is compared with God be first regarded in the light of the distinction between being and becoming. Here theological tradition comes to meet us with the thesis that no being shares in the aseity of God. Yet the distinction between God and all forms of being is specific, in so far as it can just as little be got rid of or dispensed with in actual life as can the distinction between two members of a species. On the other hand, the individual spirit is marked by every possible characteristic we think of as existing originally in God. Therefore we may use the idea of species in order to compare spiritual beings with God, provided we make the reservation, that everything we class in the same species with God comes ever from God, while God, in regard to what he is, does not become, but everlastingly is, and that nothing we compare with God ever attains the character of aseity. With this, theological tradition in so far corresponds, that in affirming the divinity of Christ, it expressly excludes aseity, and by asserting the eternal generation of the Son, applies the category of becoming, as distinct from being, to that existence which is to be denoted as the eternal object of the divine love. Under this condition, the view expounded above—that the eternally-beloved Son of God, on the ground of the like content of his personal will, and of the uniqueness of the relation he holds to the community of the Kingdom of God and to the world, is to be conceived under the attribute of Godhead—accords with the traditional theology. Of course our time-conditioned view of things cannot get rid of the antithesis between God's eternal decree and the realization of the same in the empirical phenomena of time, just as our conception of the community of the Kingdom of God is bound up with the antithesis between the calling in time and the choosing before the foundation of the world. At the same time we must premise that this relation does not mean for God that there is in him any want or need; rather is his self-sufficiency everlastingly satisfied in what to us, in the long series of preparatory stages, looks like the expression of want. For this reason the eternal Godhead of the Son, in the sense here described, is perfectly intelligible only as object of the divine mind and will, that is, only for God himself. But if at the same time we discount, in the case of God, the interval between the purpose and the accomplishment, then we get the formula that Christ exists for God eternally as that which he appears to us under the limitations of time. But only for God, since for us, as pre-existent, Christ is hidden. Inasmuch, then, as God's standpoint is impossible for us, we shall be wise if we content ourselves with this formal proof of our religious estimate of Christ. Only this, too, may be added by way of conclusion, namely, that by the same line of reasoning the Spirit of God, as the Holy Spirit, also becomes intelligible. The Spirit of God is the knowledge God has of himself, as of his own self-end. The Holy Spirit denotes in the New Testament the Spirit of God, in so far as the latter is the ground of that knowledge of God and that specific moral and religious life which exist in the Christian community. Since the community has for its conscious purpose the realization of the Kingdom of God as the divine self-end, it is correct to say, that the practical knowledge of God in this community which is dependent upon God, is identical with the knowledge which God has of himself, even as the love of God is perfected in the fact that within the community love is practised toward the brethren. But if in his Son God loves eternally the community that is like his Son, in other words, if the community is *eo ipso* the eternal object of God's will of love, then also it is God's eternal will that his Spirit should be the Holy Spirit in the community of the Kingdom of God. In the form of this eternal purpose, the Spirit of God proceeds from God, inasmuch, namely, as he is destined to enter into the community which enjoys the perfect knowledge of God. (*Justification and Reconciliation*, pp. 468–72.)

NEW BEGINNINGS

XVIII
NEWMAN

John Henry Newman (1801–90) was the son of an English banker. He experienced a conversion at the age of 15, the memory of which remained with him all his life. He went to Trinity College, Oxford, then to a fellowship at Oriel. He was ordained to the Anglican ministry in 1826. With passing years he acquired progressively firmer views on church order, liturgy and doctrine. He became the most distinguished founder of the Anglo-Catholic movement, which received the name 'Tractarian' movement from Newman's *Tracts for the Times*, published at intervals during his Anglican period. Newman, however, went further than his friends of the Tractarian movement. He came to the conviction that the logical outcome of the line of thought he was pursuing must be submission to Rome. In 1846 he was received into the Catholic Church. Thereafter he lived a mainly secluded, monastic life of considerable austerity along with a few followers. In 1854 to 1858 he was rector of the newly established catholic university of Dublin. This occasioned his famous volume *The Idea of a University*. After being in somewhat bad odour with the British public from the time of his reception into the Roman Catholic church Newman's greatness and integrity were finally recognized by the public at large in his closing years. He was made an honorary fellow of Trinity in 1878. In 1879 he was made a cardinal of the church.

Of his writings, his *Apologia pro vita sua* stands among the great spiritual autobiographies. His *Grammar of Assent* introduced a new type of Christian apologetic to the Roman Catholic tradition. His published sermons and tracts, apart from the interest of their matter, are often of great literary merit. His *Essay on the Development of Christian Doctrine*—from which passages are reproduced below—was written just before his transition from the Anglican to the Roman Catholic communion. The references are to the edition published by James Toovey, London, 1846.

AUTHORITY IN CHRISTIANITY

If the Christian doctrine, as originally taught, admits of true and important developments, as was argued in the foregoing Section, this is a strong antecedent argument in favour of a provision in the Dispensation for putting a seal of authority upon those developments. The probability of their being known to be true varies with their truth. The two ideas are certainly quite distinct of revealing and guaranteeing a truth, and they are often distinct in fact. There are various revelations all over the earth which do not carry with them the evidence of their divinity. Such are the inward suggestions and secret illuminations granted to so many individuals; such are the traditionary doctrines which are found among the heathen, that 'vague and unconnected family of religious truths, originally from God, but sojourning, without the sanction of miracle or a definite home, as pilgrims up and down the world, and discernible and separable from the corrupt legends with which they are mixed, by the spiritual mind alone'.[1] There is nothing impossible in the notion of a revelation occurring without evidences that it is a revelation; just as human sciences are a divine gift, yet are reached by our ordinary powers and have no claim on our faith. But Christianity is not of his nature: it is a revelation which comes to us as a revelation, as a whole, objectively, and with a profession of infallibility; and the only question to be determined relates to the matter of the revelation. If then there are certain great truths, or properties, or observances, naturally and legitimately resulting from the doctrines originally professed, it is but reasonable to include these true results in the idea of the revelation, to consider them parts of it, and if the revelation be not only true, but guaranteed as true, to anticipate that they will be guaranteed inclusively. Christianity, unlike other revelations of God's will, except the Jewish, of which it is a continuation, is an objective religion, or a revelation with credentials; it is natural then to view it wholly as such, and not partly *sui generis*, partly like others. Such as it begins, such let it be considered to continue: if certain large developments of it are true, they must surely be accredited as true.

An objection, however, is often made to the doctrine of infallibility *in limine*, which is too important not to be taken into consideration. It is urged that, as all religious knowledge rests on moral evidence, not on demonstration, our belief in the church's infallibility must be of this character; but what can be more absurd than a probable infallibility, or a certainty resting on doubt?—I believe, because I am sure; and I am sure because I think. Granting then that the gift of infallibility be adapted, when believed, to unite all intellects in one common confession, it is as difficult of proof as the developments which it is to prove, and nugatory therefore, and in consequence improbable in a Divine Scheme. 'The advocates of Rome', it has been urged as an *argumentum ad hominem*, yet it will serve to express the objection as used for its own sake, 'insist on the necessity of an infallible guide in religious matters, as an argument that

[1] *Arians*, Ch.5. sect.3, p. 89.

such a guide has really been accorded. Now it is obvious to inquire how individuals are to know with certainty that Rome *is* infallible . . . how any ground can be such as to bring home to the mind infallibly that she is infallible; what conceivable proof amounts to more than a probability of the fact; and what advantage is an infallible guide, if those who are to be guided have, after all, no more than an opinion, as the Romanists call it, that she is infallible?'[1]

This argument, however, except when used, as is intended in this passage, against such persons as would remove all doubt from religion, is certainly a fallacious one. For since, as all allow, the Apostles were infallible, it tells against their infallibility, or the infallibility of Scripture, as truly as against the infallibility of the church; for no one will say that the Apostles were made infallible for nothing, yet we are only morally certain that they were infallible. Further, if we have but probable grounds for the church's infallibility, we have but the like for the impossibility of certain things, the necessity of others, the truth, the certainty of others; and therefore the words *infallibility*, *necessity*, *truth*, and *certainty* ought all of them to be banished from the language. But why is it more inconsistent to speak of an uncertain infallibility than of a doubtful truth or a contingent necessity, phrases which present ideas clear and undeniable? In truth we are playing with words when we use arguments of this sort. When we say that a person is infallible, we mean no more than that what he says is always true, always to be believed, always to be done. The term is resolvable into these phrases as its equivalents; either then the phrases are inadmissible, or the idea of infallibility must be allowed. A probable infallibility is a probable gift of never erring; a reception of the doctrine of a probable infallibility is faith and obedience towards a person founded on the probability of his never erring in his declarations or commands. What is inconsistent in this idea? Whatever then be the particular means of determining infallibility, the abstract objection may be put aside.

Again, it is sometimes argued that such a dispensation would destroy our probation, as dissipating doubt, precluding the exercise of faith, and obliging us to obey whether we wish it or no; and it is urged that a Divine Voice spoke in the first age, and difficulty and darkness rest upon all subsequent ones; as if infallibility and personal judgment were incompatible; but this is to confuse the subject. We must distinguish between a revelation and the reception of it, not between its earlier and later stages. A revelation, in itself divine, and guaranteed as such, may be received, doubted, argued against, perverted, rejected, by individuals according to the state of mind of each. Ignorance, misapprehension, unbelief, and other causes, do not at once cease to operate because the revelation is in itself

[1] *Proph. Office*, p. 148.

true and in its proofs irrefragable. We have then no warrant at all for saying that an accredited revelation will exclude doubts and difficulties, or dispense with anxious diligence on our part, though it may in its own nature tend to do so. Infallibility does not interfere with moral probation; the two notions are perfectly distinct. It is no objection then to the idea of an arbitrary authority, such as I am supposing, that it lessens the task of personal inquiry, unless it be an objection to the authority of Revelation altogether. A Church, or a Council, or a Pope, or a Consent of Christendom, limits the inquiries of the individual in no other way than Scripture limits them: it does limit them; but, while it limits their range, it preserves intact their probationary character; we are tried as really, though not on so large a field. To suppose that the doctrine of a permanent authority in matters of faith interferes with our free-will and responsibility is, as before, to forget that there were infallible teachers in the first age, and heretics and schismatics in the ages subsequent. There may have been a supreme authority from first to last, and a moral judgment from first to last. Moreover, those who maintain that Christian truth must be gained solely by personal efforts are bound to show that methods, ethical and intellectual, are granted to individuals sufficient for gaining it; else the mode of probation they advocate is less, not more, perfect than that which proceeds upon external authority. On the whole, then, no argument against continuing the principle of objectiveness into the developments of Revelation is deducible from the conditions of our moral responsibility.

Perhaps it will be urged that the Analogy of Nature is against our anticipating the continuance of an external authority which has once been given; because, in the words of the profound thinker who has already been cited, 'We are wholly ignorant what degree of new knowledge it were to be expected God would give mankind by revelation, upon supposition of his affording one; or how far, and in what way, he would interpose miraculously to qualify them to whom he should originally make the revelation for communicating the knowledge given by it, and to secure their doing it to the age in which they should live, and to secure its being transmitted to posterity'; and because 'we are not in any sort able to judge whether it were to be expected that the revelation should have been committed to writing, or left to be handed down, and consequently corrupted, by verbal tradition, and at length sunk under it'.[1] But this reasoning does not here apply, as has already been observed; it contemplates only the abstract hypothesis of a revelation, not the fact of an existing revelation of a particular kind, which may of course in various ways modify our state of knowledge, by settling some of those very points on which, before it was given, we had no means of deciding. Nor

[1] *Anal.* ii. 3.

can it, as I think, be fairly denied that the argument from Analogy in one point of view tells against anticipating a revelation at all, for an innovation upon the physical order of the world is by the very force of the terms inconsistent with its ordinary course. We cannot then regulate our antecedent view of the character of a revelation by a test which, applied simply, overthrows the very notion of a revelation altogether. Anyhow, Analogy is in some sort violated by the fact of a revelation, and the question before us only relates to the extent of that violation.

I will hazard a distinction here between the facts of revelation and its principles—the argument from Analogy is more concerned with its principles than with its facts. The revealed facts are special and singular, from the nature of the case: but it is otherwise with the revealed principles; they are common to all the works of God: and if the Author of Nature be the Author of Grace, it may be expected that, while the two systems of facts are distinct and independent, the principles displayed in them will be the same, and form a connecting link between them. In this identity of principle lies the Analogy of Natural and Revealed Religion, in Butler's sense of the word. The doctrine of the Incarnation is a fact, and cannot be paralleled by anything in nature;[1] the doctrine of Mediation is a principle, and is abundantly exemplified in its provisions. Miracles are facts; inspiration is a fact; divine teaching once for all, and a continual teaching, are each a fact; probation by means of intellectual difficulties is a principle both in nature and in grace, and may be carried on in the system of grace either by a standing ordinance of teaching or by one definite act of teaching, and that with an analogy as perfect in either case to the order of nature; nor can we succeed in arguing from the analogy of that order against a standing guardianship of revelation without arguing also against its original bestowal. Supposing the order of nature once broken by the introduction of a revelation, the continuance of that revelation is but a question of degree; and the circumstance that a work has begun makes it more probable than not that it will proceed. We have no reason to suppose that there is so great a distinction of dispensation between ourselves and the first generation of Christians, as that they had a living infallible guidance, and we have not.

The case then stands thus: that Revelation has introduced a new law of divine governance over and above those laws which appear in the natural course of the world; and henceforth our argument for a standing authority in matters of faith proceeds on the analogy of Nature, and from the fact of Christianity. Preservation is involved in the idea of creation. As the Creator rested on the seventh day from the work which he had made, yet he 'worketh hitherto'; so he gave the Creed once for all in the

[1] *Univ. Serm.*, pp. 33, 34.

beginning, yet blesses its growth still, and dispenses its increase. His word 'shall not return unto him void, but accomplish' his pleasure. As creation argues continual governance, so are Apostles harbingers of Popes.

Moreover, it must be borne in mind that, as the essence of all religion is authority and obedience, so the distinction between natural religion and revealed lies in this, that the one has a subjective authority, and the other an objective. Revelation consists in the manifestation of the Invisible Divine Power, or in the substitution of the voice of a Lawgiver for the voice of conscience. The supremacy of conscience is the essence of natural religion; the supremacy of Apostle, or Pope, or Church, or Bishop, is the essence of revealed; and when such external authority is taken away, the mind falls back again upon that inward guide[1] which it possessed even before Revelation was vouchsafed. Thus, what conscience is in the system of nature, such is the voice of Scripture, or of the church, or of the Holy See, as we may determine it, in the system of Revelation. It may be objected, indeed, that conscience is not infallible; it is true, but still it is ever to be obeyed. And this is just the prerogative which controversialists assign to the See of St Peter; it is not in all cases infallible, it may err beyond its special province, but it has even in all cases a claim on our obedience. 'All Catholics and heretics', says Bellarmine, 'agree in two things: first, that it is possible for the Pope, even as Pope, and with his own assembly of councillors, or with General Council, to err in particular controversies of fact, which chiefly depend on human information and testimony; secondly, that it is possible for him to err as a private Doctor, even in universal questions of right, whether of faith or of morals, and that from ignorance, as sometimes happens to other doctors. Next, all Catholics agree in other two points, not, however, with heretics, but solely with each other: first, that the Pope with General Council cannot err, either in framing decrees of faith or general precepts of morality; secondly, that the Pope when determining anything in a doubtful matter, whether by himself or with his own particular Council, *whether it is possible for him to err or not, is to be obeyed* by all the faithful.'[2] And as obedience to conscience, even supposing conscience ill-informed, tends to the improvement of our moral nature, and ultimately of our knowledge, so obedience to our ecclesiastical superior may subserve our growth in illumination and sanctity, even though he should command what is extreme or inexpedient, or teach what is external to his legitimate province.

The common sense of mankind does but support a conclusion thus forced upon us by analogical considerations. It feels that the very idea of Revelation implies a present informant and guide, and that an infallible

[1] *Univ. Serm.*, pp. 34, 35. [2] *De Rom. Pont.* iv. 2.

one; not a mere abstract declaration of truths not known before to man, or a record of history, or the result of an antiquarian research, but a message and a lesson speaking to this man and that. This is shown by the popular notion which has prevailed among us since the Reformation, that the Bible itself is such a guide; and which succeeded in overthrowing the supremacy of Church and Pope, for the very reason that it was a rival authority, not resisting merely, but supplanting it. In proportion, then, as we find, in matter of fact, that the inspired Volume is not calculated or intended to subserve that purpose, are we forced to revert to that living and present guide, which, at the era of her rejection, had been so long recognized as the dispenser of Scripture according to times and circumstances, and the arbiter of all true doctrine and holy practice to her children. We feel a need, and she alone of all things under heaven supplies it. We are told that God has spoken. Where? In a book? We have tried it, and it disappoints; it disappoints, that most holy and blessed gift, not from fault of its own, but because it is used for a purpose for which it was not given. The Ethiopian's reply, when St Philip asked him if he understood what he was reading, is the voice of nature: 'How can I, unless some man shall guide me?' The church undertakes that office; she does what none else can do, and this is the secret of the power. 'The human mind', it has been said, 'wishes to be rid of doubt in religion; and a teacher who claims infallibility is readily believed on his simple word. We see this constantly exemplified in the case of individual pretenders among ourselves. In Romanism the church pretends to it; she rids herself of competitors by forestalling them. And probably, in the eyes of her children, this is not the least persuasive argument for her infallibility, that she alone of all churches dares claim it, as if a secret instinct and involuntary misgivings restrained those rival communions which go so far towards affecting it.'[1] These sentences, whatever be the errors of their wording, surely express a great truth. The most obvious answer, then, to the question, why we yield to the authority of the church in the questions and developments of faith, is, that some authority there must be if there is a revelation, and other authority there is none but she. In the words of St Peter to her Divine Master and Lord, 'To whom shall we go?' Nor must it be forgotten in confirmation, that Scripture expressly calls the church 'the pillar and ground of the Truth', and promises her as by covenant that 'the Spirit of the Lord that is upon her, and his words which he has put in her mouth shall not depart out of her mouth, nor out of the mouth of her seed, nor out of the mouth of her seed's seed, from henceforth and for ever'.[2]

And if the very claim to infallible arbitration in religious disputes is of so weighty importance and interest in all ages of the world, much more is

[1] *Proph. Office*, p. 141. [2] I *Timothy* 3. 16; *Isaiah* 59. 21.

it welcome at a time like the present, when the human intellect is so busy, and thought so fertile, and opinions so indefinitely divided. The absolute need of a spiritual supremacy is at present the strongest of arguments in favour of its supply. Surely, either an objective revelation has not been given, or it has been provided with means for impressing its objectiveness on the world. If Christianity be a social religion, as it certainly is, and if it be based on certain ideas acknowledged as divine, or a creed, which shall here be assumed, and if these ideas have various aspects, and make distinct impressions on different minds, and issue in consequence in a multiplicity of developments, true, or false, or mixed, as has been shown, what influence will suffice to meet and to do justice to these conflicting conditions, but a supreme authority ruling and reconciling individual judgments by a divine right and a recognized wisdom? In barbarous times the will is reached through the senses; but in an age in which reason, as it is called, is the standard of truth and right, it is abundantly evident to any one, who mixes ever so little with the world, that, if things are left to themselves, every individual will have his own view of things, and take his own course; that two or three agree together today to part tomorrow; that Scripture will be read in contrary ways, and history will be analysed into subtle but practical differences; that philosophy, taste, prejudice, passion, party, caprice, will find no common measure, unless there be some supreme power to control the mind and to compel agreement. There can be no combination on the basis of truth without an organ of truth. As cultivation brings out the colours of flowers, and domestication the hues of animals, so does education of necessity develop differences of opinion; and while it is impossible to lay down first principles in which all will unite, it is utterly unreasonable to expect that this man should yield to that, or all to one. I do not say there are no eternal truths, such as the poet speaks of,[1] which all acknowledge in private, but that there are none sufficiently commanding to be the basis of public union and action. The only general persuasive in matters of conduct is authority; that is, when truth is in question, a judgment which we consider superior to our own. If Christianity is both social and dogmatic, and intended for all ages, it must, humanly speaking, have an infallible expounder. Else you will secure unity of form at the loss of unity of doctrine, or unity of doctrine at the loss of unity of form; you will have to chose between a comprehension of opinions and a resolution into parties, between latitudinarian and sectarian error; you may be tolerant or intolerant of contrarieties of thought, but contrarieties you will have. By the Church of England a hollow uniformity is preferred to an infallible chair; and by the sects of England, an interminable division. Germany and Geneva began with

[1] *Οὐ γάρ τι νῦν γε καχθες κ.τ.λ.*

persecution, and have ended in scepticism. The doctrine of infallibility is a less violent hypothesis than this sacrifice either of faith or of charity. It secures the objects, without, to say the least, violating the letter of the revelation.

I have called the doctrine of Infallibility an hypothesis: let it be so considered for the sake of argument, that is, let it be considered to be a mere position, supported by no direct evidence, but required by the facts of the case, and reconciling them with each other. That hypothesis is indeed, in matter of fact, maintained and acted on in the largest portion of Christendom, and from time immemorial; but let this coincidence be accounted for by the need. Moreover, it is not a naked or isolated fact, but the animating principle of a large scheme of doctrine which the need itself could not simply create; but let this system be merely called its development. Yet even as an hypothesis, which has been held by one out of various communions, it may not be lightly put aside. Some hypothesis all parties, all controversialists, all historians must adopt, if they would treat of Christianity at all. Gieseler's 'Text Book' bears the profession of being a dry analysis of Christian history; yet on inspection it will be found to be written on a positive and definite theory, and to bend facts to meet it. An unbeliever, as Gibbon, assumes one hypothesis, and an Ultramontane, as Baronius, adopts another. The school of Hurd and Newton consider that Christianity slept for centuries upon centuries, except among those whom historians call heretics. Others speak as if the oath of Supremacy or the *congé d' élire* could be made the measure of St Ambrose, and they fit the Thirty-nine Articles on the fervid Tertullian. The question is, which of all these theories is the simplest, the most natural, the most persuasive. Certainly the notion of development under infallible authority is not a less grave, a less winning hypothesis, than the chance and coincidence of events, or the Oriental Philosophy, or the working of Antichrist, to account for the rise of Christianity and the formation of its theology. (pp. 117–30)

XIX

MAURICE

Frederick Denison Maurice (1805–72) was, in many respects, a man born before his time. He anticipates many of the best insights of contemporary theology in a way that was not and could not be appreciated in his own day. He was contemporary with Pusey and the rise of the 'high' church party, with Coleridge and the early development of 'broad' church theology, with Kingsley and the beginnings of religious socialism, with Darwin and the impact of evolutionary theory on church doctrine, with Bishop Colenso and the beginnings of biblical criticism. With all these movements he had some affinity and to the problems which each raises he made some contribution; yet he can be identified with none of them. His work has proved to be of more permanent interest and value than any English theologian of the period. He must be regarded as one of the men who set the stage for contemporary theology.

Maurice was the son of a Unitarian minister. He studied law at Cambridge, but did not graduate because he could not at that time regard himself as a member of the established church. (Subscription to the Thirty-nine Articles was at that time a condition of graduation.) Later, he came to embrace the doctrine of the Church of England whole-heartedly. He was ordained deacon in 1834 and soon afterwards became chaplain to Guy's Hospital in London. At this time he wrote *The Kingdom of Christ*, expressing a doctrine both of the church and of human society. In 1840 he was elected to the chair of English Literature in King's College, London. In 1846 he was appointed also to the chair of Ecclesiastical History.

His *Theological Essays*, in which he advocated a new approach to the doctrine of Atonement, appeared in 1853. This resulted in his being deprived of his chair under suspicion of unorthodoxy—though his association with left-wing political ideas was perhaps an equal motive for his dismissal. He continued in pastoral work for some time and then was appointed Professor of Moral Philosophy in Cambridge in 1866. He held this appointment till his death.

Much of his theology is contained in his sermons and addresses, of which he published a good many volumes. Some of these are, *Sermons on the*

Prayer Book, *Patriarchs and Lawgivers of the Old Testament*, *The Gospel of St John* and *The Doctrine of Sacrifice*.

A full bibliography of F. D. Maurice's writings is given in the biography by his son, Sir Frederick Maurice, *The Life of Frederick Denison Maurice, chiefly told in his own Letters*, 2 vols; fourth edition, 1885. Reference should also be made to *The Theology of F. D. Maurice*, by A. R. Vidler, 1949.

References below are to the second edition of *The Kingdom of Christ*, Rivington, London, 1842.

THE SPIRITUAL CONSTITUTION OF MAN

This fact, that men exist in families, which seems so grievously to disturb the inventors of systems, is perhaps the very one which would be most likely to suggest the thought to a plain person, that there must be a moral or spiritual constitution for mankind. We are obliged to speak of every man as being in two conditions. He is in a world of objects which offer themselves to his senses, and which his senses may be fitted to entertain. He is a son, perhaps he is a brother. These two states are equally inevitable; they are also perfectly distinct. You cannot by any artifice reduce them under the same law or name. To describe the one you must speak of what we see, or hear, or handle or smell; to describe the other, you must speak of what we are; 'I *am* a son', 'I *am* a brother'. It is impossible therefore to use the word '*circumstances*' in reference to the one state with the same strictness with which you apply it to the other. All the things which I have to do with, I naturally and rightly call, my circumstances—*they stand round me*: but that which is necessary in an account of myself, seems to be entitled to another name. We commonly call it a *relationship*. And this difference soon becomes more conspicuous. We speak of a man *having* a bad digestion or a bad hearing; we speak of his *being* a bad brother or a bad son. By both these phrases we imply that there is a want of harmony between the man and his condition. But by the one we evidently wish to signify that there need not be this want of harmony, that he is *voluntarily* acting as if he were not in a relation in which nevertheless he is, and must remain. This inconsistency we describe by the term moral evil, or whatever equivalent phrase we may have invented; for some equivalent, whether we like it or not, we must have.

It might seem to follow from these observations, that the family state is the *natural* one for man; and accordingly we speak of the affections which correspond to this state, as especially natural affections. But it should be remembered that we use another phrase which is apparently inconsistent with this; we describe the savage condition, that is to say, the one in which man is striving to be independent, as the natural state of society. And though it may be doubtful whether that should be called a *state of society*, which is the contradiction of all states and of all society, yet there seems a very considerable justification for the application of the word *natural* to it: seeing that we cannot be acquainted with a family, or be members of a family, without knowing in others—without feeling in ourselves, certain inclinations which tend to the dissolution of its bonds, and to the setting up of that separate independent life, which when exhibited on a large scale we name the savage or wild life. These inclinations are kept down by discipline, and the affections which attract us to the members of our family are called out in opposition to them; surely, therefore, it cannot be a mistake to describe them by the name which we ordinarily apply to plants that spring up in a soil, uncultivated and uncalled for.

We have here some of the indications of a spiritual constitution; that is to say, we have the marks of a state which is designed for a voluntary creature; which *is* his, whether he approve it or no; against which, he has a nature or inclination to rebel. But still, most persons would mean something more by the phrase than this; they would ask how you could call that spiritual, which had no reference to religion. Now the histories and mythologies of all the people with whom we are acquainted bear unequivocal witness to this fact, that men have connected the ideas of fathers, children, husbands, brothers, sisters, with the beings whom they worshipped. This is the first, rudest observation which we make upon them. But, when we search further, we begin to see that this simple observation has the most intimate connexion with the whole of mythology; that it is not merely *a* fact in reference to it, but the fact, without which all others which encounter us are unintelligible. You say all kinds of offices are attributed to the gods and goddesses; they rule over this town and that river, they dispense this blessing or send that curse. Be it so; but who are they who exercise these powers? The mythology tells you of relations existing between them; also of relations between them and the objects of their bounty and their enmity. In later ages, when we are studying the differences in the mythology of different nations, it is no wonder that we should notice the character of the soil, the nature of the climate, the beauty or the dreariness of the country, the rains or the inundations which watered it, as circumstances helping to determine the views which the inhabitants entertained of their unseen rulers. And then the transition is very easy to the belief, that by these observations we have accounted for their faith, and that the histories of the gods are merely accidental poetical embellishments. But, if we consider that the worshippers evidently felt that which we call accidental to be essential; that the merging the gods in the objects with which they were connected was merely an artifice of later philosophy; that the circumstances of soil and climate did indeed occasion some important *differences* between the objects reverenced in various nations, but that the circumstance of their being parents, brothers, and sisters, so far as we know, was *common* to all, or only wanting in those which were utterly savage, that is, in which the human relations were disregarded: if we observe that those who endeavour to explain mythology by the phenomena of the world, are obliged to beg what they call 'a law of nature', alleging that we are naturally inclined to inquire into the origin of any great and remarkable objects which we see; if we will notice how utterly inconsistent it is with all experience and observation to attribute such a disposition as this to men, whose feelings and faculties have not been by some means previously awakened—how very little a savage is struck by any, except the most glaring and alarming phenomena, and how much less he thinks about them: if we will reflect upon these points, we may perhaps be led to adopt the opinion that the simplest method of solving the difficulty is the best; that it is not our being surrounded with a strange world of sensible objects which leads us to think of objects with which we do not sensibly converse, but that these perceptions come to us through our family relationships; that we become more and more merely idolaters when these relationships are lost sight of, and the other facts of our condition only regarded; that a world without family relationships would have no worship, and on the other hand, that without worship all the feelings and affections of family life would have utterly perished.

But is there no meaning in that savage wish for independence? is it merely the dissolution and destruction of those family bonds which are meant for men, or is it the indication that he was meant for other bonds than these, not perhaps of necessity incompatible with them? History seems to decide the question in favour of the latter opinion. It seems to say, that as there is a worse state of society than the patriarchal, there is also a better and more advanced one; it declares that the faculties which are given to man never have had their proper development and expansion, except in a *national* community. (pp. 328–34) . . .

. . . Now, we may observe several facts, too obvious to escape the most careless student of history, except it should be from their very obviousness, which are closely connected with this. One is, that in every organized nation at its commencement, there is a high respect for family relations, that they embody themselves necessarily in the national constitution; another is, that there is a struggle between these relations and the national polity, although they form so great an element in it; the legislator feeling, that each brother, husband, father, is a citizen, and that as such, he comes directly under his cognizance.

(pp. 335–6) . . .

But a time came when thoughts were awakened in men's minds of something more comprehensive than either this family or this national constitution. The former belonged to all men; yet, in another respect it was narrow, separating men from each other. The latter was obviously exclusive; a nation was limited to a small locality; it actually treated all that lay beyond it, and whom it could not subdue to itself, as aliens, if not enemies. If this exclusion were to continue, there was certainly some nation which *ought* to reign, which had a right to make its polity universal. Great Asiatic monarchies there had been, which had swallowed all tribes and kingdoms into themselves, but these had established a rule of mere physical force.

Might not Greece, the land of intellectual force, show that it was meant to rule over all? The young hero of Macedon went forth in this hope, and in a few years accomplished his dream. In a few more his empire was broken in pieces; Greece was not to be the lord of the world: still in the Egyptian and Syrian dynasties which she sent forth, she asserted a mental supremacy. But a nation which paid no homage to art or to philosophy swallowed up all these dynasties, and with them all that remained of Greece herself. A universal polity was established in the world, and the national life, the family life of Rome, perished at the very moment in which she established it.

Was there a religion connected with this universal polity as there was with the family and the national? We find that there was. The Emperor was the great God. To him all people and nations and languages were to bow. Subject to this supreme divinity all others might be tolerated and recognized. No form of religion was to be proscribed unless it were absolutely incompatible with the worship of a Tiberius and a Vitellius. It has been suggested already, that this Roman Empire answers exactly to the idea of a universal *world*. If there is to be anything different from this—if there is to be *an universal church*, we ought to know of what elements it is to be composed, we ought to know whether it also sets aside family or national life, or whether it justifies their existence, reconciles them to itself, and interprets the problems of ancient history concerning their mysterious meaning.

(pp. 339–41) . . .

. . . Every one who reads the Old Testament, must perceive that the idea of a covenant of God with a certain people, is that which presides in it. In plain history, in lofty prayers and songs, in impassioned denunciations of existing evil, and predictions of coming misery—this idea is still at the root of all others. Take it away, and not merely is there no connexion between the different parts, but each book by itself, however simple in its language or in its details, becomes an incoherent rhapsody. A person then, who had no higher wish than to understand the character and feelings of that strange people which has preserved its identity through so many generations, would of course begin with examining into the account of this covenant. He would feel that the call of Abraham, the promise made to him and to his seed, and the seal of it which was given him, were most significant parts of this record. But, one thought would strike him above all—This covenant is said to be with a *family:* with a man doubtless in the first instance—but with a man expressly and emphatically as the head of a family. The very terms of the covenant, and every promise that it held forth, was inseparably associated with the hope of a posterity. It is impossible to look upon the patriarchal character of Abraham, as something accidental to his character as the chosen witness and servant of the Most High. These two positions are absolutely inseparable. The fact of his relationship to God is interpreted to him by the feeling of his human relations, and his capacity of fulfilling them arose from his acknowledgement of the higher relation. (pp. 344–5) . . .

. . . That there is a God *related* to men and made known to men through their human relations, this was the faith of Abraham, the beginner of the church on earth. But this truth could not be exhibited in one individual faithful man; it must be exhibited through a family. (p. 346) . . .

The national polity of the Jews was in its essence exclusive. We dwell upon this fact, as if it destroyed all connexion between this polity and that of the Pagans, or of modern Europe. But every *nation*, as such, is exclusive. Athens was exclusive, Rome was exclusive; nevertheless, we have admitted, all persons admit, that more of humanity came out in the exclusive nations of Athens and of Rome, than ever showed itself in the savage tribes of the earth, which have never attained to a definite polity. Before we can ascertain, whether the exclusiveness of the Jews was an inhuman exclusiveness, we must find out what it excluded; and here the same answer must be given as before. It excluded the worship of sensible, natural things; it excluded the idea of choice and self-will. The covenant with an invisible Being made it treason for men to choose the objects of their worship. This worship of the one Being was the bond of the commonwealth, and, if this were broken, it was dissolved. The covenant with an invisible Being obliged them to look upon all Kings as reigning in virtue of his covenant, as representing his dignity, as responsible to him; upon all other officers, the priestly, the prophetical, the judicial, as in like manner directly receiving their appointments and commission from him. By its first protest it affirmed that there are *not* a set of separate gods over each territory—various, according to the peculiarities of soil and of climate; but that there is one Almighty and Invisible Being, who is the Lord of all. The God of Israel is declared to be the God of all the nations of the earth; the Israelites are chosen out to be witnesses of the fact. By the second protest the exclusive Hebrew witnessed, that no king, no priest, no judge, has a right to look upon himself as possessing intrinsic power; that he is exercising office, under a righteous king, a perfect priest, an all-seeing judge; that, in proportion as he preserves that thought, and in the strength of it fulfils his task, the character of that king, and priest, and judge, and the relation in which he stands to men, reveal themselves to him; that these offices are continued from generation to generation, as a witness of his permanence who is Lord of them all, and who abides for ever and ever.

(pp. 350–2) . . .

But, how did this idea of a human constitution harmonize, or come into collision with those attempts at *universal empire*, which appeared to be the necessary consummation or termination of the ancient polities? . . . (p. 354) . . . The universal monarchs, the Sennacheribs and Nebuchadnezzars, were Men-gods. They took to themselves the attributes of the Invisible: and just in proportion as they did so, just in proportion as they hid the view of anything beyond humanity from the eyes of men, just in that proportion did they become inhuman, separate from their kind, dwelling apart in an infernal solitude.

This black ground brought the perfectly clear bright object more distinctly within their view; they felt that the God-man, in whom the fullness and awfulness of Godhead should shine forth, might *therefore* have perfect sympathy with the poorest and most friendless, and might at the same time enable them to enter into that transcendent region which their spirits had ever been seeking and never been able to penetrate.

Now, when we open the first book of the New Testament, the first words of it announce that the subject of it is the Son of David and the Son of Abraham. As we read on, we find that, according to the belief of the writer, this person came into the world to establish a Kingdom. Every act and word which is recorded of him, has reference to this kingdom. A voice is heard crying in the wilderness, that a kingdom is at hand. Jesus of Nazareth comes preaching the Gospel of the kingdom. (pp. 358–9) . . .

. . . The writers of the New Testament are Jews; language of this kind is essentially Jewish. It belonged to the idiosyncrasy of the most strange and bigoted of all the people of the earth. To a certain extent, the reader will perceive, these statements exactly tally with mine. I have endeavoured to show that the habit of thinking, which this perpetual use of a certain phrase indicates, is Jewish, and why it is Jewish. But there is a long step from this admission, to the one which is generally supposed to be involved in it, that this phrase is merely connected with particular accidents and circumstances, and has nothing to do with that which is essential and human. According to my view of the position of the Israelite, he was taken out of all nations expressly to be a witness of that which is unchanging and permanent, of that which is *not* modal, of the meaning of those relationships which belonged to him in common with the Pagans and with us, and which, as every Pagan felt, and as every peasant among us feels, have a meaning, and of the ground and purpose of national institutions and of law, which the Pagans acknowledged, and which most of us acknowledge, to be the great distinction between men and brutes.

(pp. 360–1) . . .

. . . 'That they all may be one, as thou, Father, art in me, and I in thee, that they may be one in us.'

Either those words contain the essence and meaning of the whole history, or that history must be rejected as being from first to last the wickedest lie and the most awful blasphemy ever palmed upon the world. And if they do contain the meaning of it, that meaning must be embodied in *acts*. The Evangelists therefore go on to record in words perfectly calm and simple, the death of their master and his resurrection. As events they are related; no comment is made upon them; few hints are given of any effects to follow from them. We are made to feel by the quiet accurate detail, 'He certainly died, who, as we believed, was the Son of God, and the King of Israel; he actually rose with his body, and came among us who knew him, and spake and ate with us: this is the accomplishment of the union between heaven and earth; it is no longer a word, it is a fact'. And of this fact, the risen Lord tells his Apostles that they are to go into the world and testify; nor merely to testify of it, but to adopt men into a society grounded upon the accomplishment of it. In connection with that command, and as the ultimate basis of the universal society, a NAME is proclaimed, in which the name that had been revealed to Abraham, and that more awful one which Moses heard in the bush, are combined and reconciled.

(pp. 368–9) . . .

The narrator of such transcendent events, as the ascension of the Son of Man into the invisible glory, or the descent of the Spirit to take possession of the feelings, thoughts, utterances of mortal men, might have been expected to stand still and wonder at that which with so entire a belief he was recording. But no—he looks upon these events as the necessary consummation of all that went before, the necessary foundations of the existence of the church. And therefore, he can quietly relate any other circumstances, however apparently disproportionate, which were demanded for the outward manifestation and development of that church, such as the meeting of the Apostles in the upper room, and the completion of their number. If the foundation of this kingdom were the end of all the purposes of God, if it were the kingdom of God among men, the human conditions of it could be no more passed over than the divine; it was as needful to prove that the ladder had its foot upon earth, as that it had come down out of heaven. As we proceed, we find every new step of the story leading us to notice the church as the child which the Jewish polity had for so many ages been carrying in its womb. Its filial relation is first demonstrated, it is shewn to be an Israelitic not a *mundane* commonwealth; then it is shewn, that though not mundane, it is essentially *human*, containing a principle of expansion greater than that which dwelt in the Roman empire.

And here lies the apparent contradiction, the real harmony of those two aspects in which this kingdom was contemplated by the Apostles of the circumcision and by St Paul. The one witnessed for the continuity of it, the other for its freedom from all national exclusions. These, we may believe, were their respective offices. Yet, as each fulfilled the one, he was in fact teaching the other truth most effectually. St Peter and St James were maintaining the universality of the church, while they were contending for its Jewish character and derivation. St Paul was maintaining the national covenant, while he was telling the Gentiles, that if they were circumcised Christ would profit them nothing. Take away the first testimony and the church becomes an earthly not a spiritual commonwealth, and therefore subject to earthly limitations; take away the second, and the promise to Abraham is unfulfilled. In another sense, as the canon of Scripture shows, St Paul was more directly carrying out the spirit of the Jewish distinction, by upholding the distinctness of ecclesiastical communities according to tribes and countries than the Apostles of Jerusalem; and they were carrying out the idea of the universality of the church more than he did by addressing the members of it as of an entire community dispersed through different parts of the world.

But we must not forget, that while this universal society, according to the historical conception of it, grew out of the Jewish family and nation, it is, according to the theological conception of it, the root of both. 'That', says Aristotle, 'which is first as cause is last in discovery.' And this beautiful formula is translated into life and reality in the letter to the Ephesians, when St Paul tells them that they were created in Christ before all worlds, and when he speaks of the transcendant economy as being gradually revealed to the Apostles and Prophets by the Spirit. In this passage, it seems to me, lies the key to the whole character of the dispensation, as well as of the books in which it is set forth. If the Gospel be the revelation or unveiling of a mystery hidden from ages and generations; if this mystery be the true constitution of humanity in Christ, so that a man believes and acts a lie who does not claim for himself union with Christ, we can understand why the deepest writings of the New Testament, instead of being digests of doctrine, are epistles, explaining to those who had been admitted into the church of Christ their own position, bringing out that side of it which had reference to the circumstances in which they were placed, or to their most besetting sins, and showing what life was in consistency, what life at variance with it. We can understand why the opening of the first of these epistles, of the one which has been supposed to be most like a systematic treatise, announces that the Gospel is concerning Jesus Christ, who was made of the seed of David according to the flesh, and marked out as the Son of God with power, according to the Spirit of holiness, by the resurrection of the dead. The fact of a union between the Godhead and humanity is thus set forth as the one which the Apostle felt himself appointed to proclaim, which was the ground of the message to the Gentiles, and in which all ideas of reconciliation, of a divine life, justification by faith, sanctification by the Spirit, were implicitly contained. (pp. 370–4) . . .

We have observed the traces of a spiritual constitution for mankind. We have observed that the two parts of this constitution, which are united by family relationships and by locality, depend upon a third part which is universal. We have observed that there are two possible forms of a universal society, one of which is destructive of the family and national principle, the other the expansion of them. The first of these is that which in Scripture is called THIS WORLD, the latter is that which in Scripture is called THE CHURCH. We have observed that the principles of the world exist in the heart of every family and of every nation; that they are precisely the natural tendencies and inclinations of men; that they are always threatening to become predominant; that when they become predominant there ceases to be any recognition of men as related to a Being above them, any recognition of them as possessing a common humanity. The other body, therefore, the church, being especially the witness for these facts which it is natural to us to deny, must be a *distinct* body. In losing its distinctness it loses its meaning, loses to all intents and purposes, though the words may at first sound paradoxical, its universality. The question then which we have to examine is, are there any signs in the present day of the existence of a spiritual and universal body upon the earth? Do these signs identify that body with the one spoken of in Scripture? Are they an effectual witness against the world? (pp. 379–80) . . .

XX
KIERKEGAARD

Søren Aabye Kierkegaard (1813–55) was a man of bewildering personal complexity whose philosophical and theological insights, whether they are accepted or not, are of undeniably disturbing profundity. He was born in Copenhagen of parents whose background was originally agricultural. The outward facts of his life are fairly well known, but the interpretation of them is extremely controversial. What strikes some as a sensitivity amounting to that of prophetic genius appears to others as neurotic distortion. But however one assesses his personal life, there can be no doubt of the rigorous honesty and penetrating brilliance of his thought.

He has had a profound influence upon the development of modern existentialist philosophy and upon every form of contemporary theology which gives primacy to faith as decision rather than as theoretical acceptance. Kierkegaard held that there are no 'prior' considerations, philosophical, scientific or historical, on the basis of which one can discover the truth or even the probability of the Christian faith. There is no way in which man can rise above or stand outside the issues of destiny confronting him, in order to assess them rationally and objectively. To do so, he would have to stand where God stands in his absolute sovereignty. To desire to do so is the essence of sin. Therefore one cannot choose between Christ and the world on the basis of knowledge or reason, but only in a trusting, adoring leap of faith. Most conventional religion of Kierkegaard's day seemed to him only to obscure the absolutely serious and critical character of this decision. This led to his increasing estrangement from the church.

It was not until the twentieth century that the full impact of Kierkegaard's extremely radical critique of traditional European theology began to be fully felt. The disturbance he created has not yet settled and the final outcome of his teaching remains to be seen. From the present perspective, it seems unlikely that the climate and method of at least Protestant theology will ever be quite the same after Kierkegaard as it was before.

Some of his main works are: *Either/Or* (1843); *The Concept of Dread* and *Philosophical Fragments* (1844); *Concluding Unscientific Postscript* (1846); *The Sickness Unto Death* (1849) and *Training in Christianity* (1850). His

Journals give considerable help in interpreting his thought (see selection translated by A. Dru, 1938). A variety of translations of his main works are available. The most complete is the series by Walter Lowrie (London and Princeton N.J., 1938 *et seq.*). The passages below are taken from *Philosophical Fragments*, tr. David F. Swenson, Princeton University Press, 1936.

GOD AS TEACHER AND SAVIOUR

Moved by love, God is eternally resolved to reveal himself. But as love is the motive so love must also be the end; for it would be a contradiction for God to have a motive and an end which did not correspond. His love is a love of the learner, and his aim is to win him. For it is only in love that the unequal can be made equal, and it is only in equality or unity that an understanding can be effected, and without a perfect understanding the Teacher is not God, unless the obstacle comes wholly from the side of the learner, in his refusing to realize that which had been made possible for him.

But this love is through and through unhappy, for how great is the difference between them! It may seem a small matter for God to make himself understood, but this is not so easy of accomplishment if he is to refrain from annihilating the unlikeness that exists between them. (p. 19) . . .

Suppose then a king who loved a humble maiden. The heart of the king was not polluted by the wisdom that is loudly enough proclaimed; he knew nothing of the difficulties that the understanding discovers in order to ensnare the heart, which keep the poets so busy, and make their magic formulas necessary. It was easy to realize his purpose. Every statesman feared his wrath and dared not breathe a word of displeasure; every foreign state trembled before his power, and dared not omit sending ambassadors with congratulations for the nuptials; no courtier grovelling in the dust dared wound him, lest his own head be crushed. Then let the harp be tuned, let the songs of the poets begin to sound, and let all be festive while love celebrates its triumph. For love is exultant when it unites equals, but it is triumphant when it makes that which was unequal equal in love.—Then there awoke in the heart of the king an anxious thought; who but a king who thinks kingly thoughts would have dreamed of it! He spoke to no one about his anxiety; for if he had, each courtier would doubtless have said: 'Your majesty is about to confer a favour upon the maiden, for which she can never be sufficiently grateful her whole life long.' This speech would have moved the king to wrath, so that he would have commanded the execution of the courtier for high treason against the beloved, and thus he would in still another way have found his grief increased. So he wrestled with his troubled thoughts alone. Would she be happy in the life at his side? Would she be able to summon confidence enough never to remember what the king wished only to forget, that he was king and she had been a humble maiden? For if this memory were to waken in her soul, and like a favoured lover sometimes steal her thoughts away from the king, luring her reflections into the seclusion of a secret grief; or if this memory sometimes passed through her soul like the shadow of death over the grave: where would then be the glory of their love? Then she would have been happier had she remained in her obscurity, loved by an equal, content in her humble cottage; but confident in her love, and cheerful early and late. What a rich abundance of grief is here laid bare, like ripened grain bent under the weight of its fruitfulness, merely waiting the time of the harvest, when the thought of the king will thresh out all its seed of sorrow! For even if the maiden would be content to become as nothing, this could not satisfy the king, precisely because he loved her, and because it was harder for him to be her benefactor than to lose her. And suppose she could not even understand him? For while we are thus speaking foolishly of human relationships, we may suppose a difference of mind between them such as to render an understanding impossible. What a depth of grief slumbers not in this unhappy love, who dares to rouse it! However, no human being is destined to suffer such grief; him we may refer to Socrates, or to that which in a still more beautiful sense can make the unequal equal.

But if the *Moment* is to have decisive significance (and if not we return to Socrates even if we think to advance beyond him), the learner is in Error, and that by reason of his own guilt. And yet he is the object of God's love, and God desires to teach him, and is concerned to bring him to equality with himself. If this equality cannot be established, God's love becomes unhappy and his teaching meaningless, since they cannot understand one another. Men sometimes think that this might be a matter of indifference to God, since he does not stand in need of the learner. But in this we forget—or rather alas! we prove how far we are from understanding him; we forget that God loves the learner. And just as that kingly grief of which we have spoken can be found only in a kingly soul, and is not even named in the language of the multitude of men, so the entire human language is so selfish that it refuses even to suspect the existence of such a grief. But for that reason God has reserved it to himself, this unfathomable grief: to know that he may repel the learner, that he does not need him, that the learner has brought destruction upon himself by his own guilt, that he can leave the learner to his fate; to know also how wellnigh impossible it is to keep the learner's courage and confidence alive, without which the purposed understanding and equality will fail, and the love become unhappy. The man who cannot feel at least some faint intimation of this grief is a paltry soul of base coinage bearing neither the image of Caesar nor the image of God.

Our problem is now before us, and we invite the poet, unless he is already engaged elsewhere, or belongs to the number of those who must be driven out from the house of mourning, together with the flute-players and the other noise-makers, before gladness can enter in. The poet's task will be to find a solution, some point of union, where love's understanding may be realized in truth, God's anxiety set at rest, his sorrow banished. For the divine love is that unfathomable love which cannot rest content with that which the beloved might in his folly prize as happiness.

A

The union might be brought about by an elevation of the learner. God would then take him up unto himself, transfigure him, fill his cup with millennial joys (for a thousand years are as one day in his sight), and let the learner forget the misunderstanding in tumultuous joy. Alas, the learner might perhaps be greatly inclined to prize such happiness as this. How wonderful suddenly to find his fortune is made, like the humble maiden, because the eye of God happened to rest upon him! And how wonderful also to be his helper in taking all this in vain, deceived by his own heart! Even the noble king could perceive the difficulty of such a method, for he was not without insight into the human heart, and understood that the maiden was at bottom deceived; and no one is so terribly deceived as he who does not himself suspect it, but is as if enchanted by a change in the outward habiliments of his existence.

The union might be brought about by God showing himself to the learner and receiving his worship, causing him to forget himself over the divine apparition. Thus the king might have shown himself to the humble maiden in all the pomp of his power, causing the sun of his presence to rise over her cottage, shedding a glory over the scene, and making her forget herself in worshipful admiration. Alas, and this might have satisfied the maiden, but it could not satisfy the king, who desired not his own glorification but hers. It was this that made his grief so hard to bear, his grief that she could not understand him; but it would have been still harder for him to deceive her. And merely to give his love for her an imperfect expression was in his eyes deception, even though no one understood him and reproaches sought to mortify his soul.

Not in this manner then can their love be made happy, except perhaps in appearance, namely the learner's and the maiden's, but not the Teacher's and the king's, whom no delusion can satisfy. Thus God takes pleasure in arraying the lily in a garb more glorious than that of Solomon; but if there could be any thought of an understanding here, would it not be a sorry delusion of the lily's, if when it looked upon its fine raiment it thought that it was on account of the raiment that God loved it? Instead of standing dauntless in the field, sporting with the wind, carefree as the gust that blows, would it not under the influence of such a thought languish and droop, nor daring to lift up its head? It was God's solicitude to prevent this, for the lily's shoot is tender and easily broken. But if the Moment is to have decisive significance, how unspeakable will be God's anxiety! There once lived a people who had a profound understanding of the divine; this people thought that no man could see God and live.—Who grasps this contradiction of sorrow: not to reveal oneself is the death of love, to reveal oneself is the death of the beloved! The minds of men so often yearn for might and power, and their thoughts are constantly being drawn to such things, as if by their attainment all mysteries would be resolved. Hence they do not even dream that there is sorrow in heaven as well as joy, the deep grief of having to deny the learner what he yearns for with all his heart, of having to deny him precisely because he is the beloved.

B

The union must therefore be brought about in some other way. Let us here again recall Socrates, for what was the Socratic ignorance if not an expression of his love of the learner, and of his sense of equality with him? But this equality was also the truth, as we have already seen. But if the *Moment* is to have decisive significance this is not the truth, for the learner will owe everything to the Teacher. In the Socratic conception the teacher's love would be merely that of a deceiver if he permitted the disciple to rest in the belief that he really owed him anything, instead of fulfilling the function of the teacher to help the learner become sufficient to himself. But when God becomes a Teacher, his love cannot be merely seconding and assisting, but is creative, giving a new being to the learner, or as we have called him, the man born anew; by which designation we signify the transition from non-being to being. The truth then is that the learner owes the Teacher everything. But this is what makes it so difficult to effect an understanding: that the learner becomes as nothing yet is not destroyed; that he comes to owe everything to the Teacher and yet retains his confidence; that he understands the Truth and yet that the Truth makes him free; that he apprehends the guilt of his Error and yet that his confidence arises victorious in the Truth. Between man and man the Socratic midwifery is the highest relation, and begetting is reserved for God, whose love is *creative*, but not merely in the sense which Socrates so beautifully expounds on a certain festal occasion. This latter kind of begetting does not signify the relation between a teacher and his disciple, but that between an autodidact and the beautiful. In turning away from the scattered beauties of particular things to contemplate beauty in and for itself, the autodidact begets many beautiful and glorious discourses and thoughts, *πόλλους καὶ καλοὺς λόγους καὶ μεγαλοπρεπεῖς τίκτει διανοήματα ἐν φιλοσοφίᾳ ἀφθόνῳ* (*Symposium*, 210 D). In so doing he begets and brings forth that which he has long borne within him in the seed (209 E). He has the requisite condition in himself, and the bringing forth or birth is merely a manifestation of what was already present; whence here again, in this begetting, the moment vanishes instantly in the eternal consciousness of Recollection. And he who is begotten by a progressive dying away from self, of him it becomes increasingly clear that he can less and less be said to be begotten, since he only becomes more and more clearly reminded of his existence. And when in turn he begets expressions of the beautiful, he does not so much beget them, as he allows the beautiful within him to beget these expressions from itself.

Since we found that the union could not be brought about by an elevation it must be attempted by a descent. Let the learner be *x*. In this *x* we must include the lowliest; for if even Socrates refused to establish a false fellowship with the clever, how can we suppose that God would make a distinction! In order that the union may be brought about, God must therefore become the equal of such an one, and so he will appear in the likeness of the humblest. But the humblest is one who must serve others, and God will therefore appear in the form of a *servant*. But this servant-form is no mere outer garment, like the king's beggar-cloak, which therefore flutters loosely about him and betrays the king; it is not like the filmy summer-cloak of Socrates, which though woven of nothing yet both conceals and reveals. It is his true form and figure. For this is the unfathomable nature of love, that it desires equality with the beloved, not in jest merely, but in earnest truth. And it is the omnipotence of the love which is so resolved that it is able to accomplish its purpose, which neither Socrates nor the king could do, whence their assumed figures constituted after all a kind of deceit.

Behold where he stands—God! Where? There; do you not see him? He is God; and yet he has not a resting-place for his head, and he dares not lean on any man lest he cause him to be offended. He is God; yet he picks his steps more carefully than if angels guided them, not to prevent his foot from stumbling against a stone, but lest he trample human beings in the dust, in that they are offended in him. He is God; and yet his eye surveys mankind with anxious care, for the tender shoots of an individual life may be crushed as easily as a blade of grass. How wonderful a life, all sorrow and love: to yearn to express the equality of love and yet to be misunderstood; to apprehend the danger that all men may be destroyed, and yet only so to be able really to save a single soul; his own life filled with sorrow, while each hour of the day is taken up with the troubles of the learner who confides in him! This is God as he stands upon the earth, like unto the humblest by the power of his omnipotent love. He knows that the learner is in Error—what if he should misunderstand, and droop, and lose his confidence! To sustain the heavens and the earth by the fiat of his omnipotent word, so that if this word were withdrawn for the fraction of a second the universe would be plunged into chaos—how light a task compared with bearing the burden that mankind may take offence, when one has been constrained by love to become its saviour!

But the servant-form was no mere outer garment, and therefore God must suffer all things, endure all things, make experience of all things. He must suffer hunger in the desert, he must thirst in the time of his agony, he must be forsaken in death, absolutely like the humblest—behold the man! His suffering is not that of his death, but this entire life is a story of suffering; and it is love that suffers, the love which gives all is itself in want. What wonderful self-denial! for though the learner be one of the lowliest, he nevertheless asks him anxiously: Do you now really love me? For he knows where the danger threatens, and yet he also knows that every easier way would involve a deception, even though the learner might not understand it.

Every other form of revelation would be a deception in the eyes of love; for either the learner would first have to be changed, and the fact concealed from him that this was necessary (but love does not alter the beloved, it alters itself); or there would be permitted to prevail a frivolous ignorance of the fact that the entire relationship was a delusion. (This was the error of paganism.) Every other form of revelation would be a deception from the standpoint of the divine love. And if my eyes were more filled with tears than those of a repentant woman, and if each tear were more precious than a pardoned woman's many tears; if I could find a place more humble than the place at his feet, and if I could sit there more humbly than a woman whose heart's sole choice was this one thing needful; if I loved him more sincerely than the most loyal of his servants, eager to shed the last drop of his life-blood in his service; if I had found greater favour in his eyes than the purest among women—nevertheless, if I asked him to alter his purpose, to reveal himself differently, to be more lenient with himself, he would doubtless look at me and say: Man, what have I to do with thee? Get thee hence, for thou art Satan, though thou knowest it not! Or if he once or twice stretched forth his hand in command, and it happened, and I then meant to understand him better or love him more, I would doubtless see him weep over me and hear him say: To think that you could prove so faithless, and so wound my love!

Is it then only the omnipotent wonder-worker that you love, and not him who humbled himself to become your equal?

But the servant-form was no mere outer garment; hence God must yield his spirit in death and again leave the earth. And if my grief were deeper than the sorrow of a mother when her heart is pierced by the sword, and if my danger were more terrible than the danger of a believer when his faith fails him, and if my misery were more pitiful than his who crucifies his hope and has nothing left but the cross—nevertheless, if I begged him to save his life and stay upon the earth, it would only be to see him sorrowful unto death, and stricken with grief also for my sake, because this suffering was for my profit, and now I had added to his sorrow the burden that I could not understand him. O bitter cup! More bitter than wormwood is the bitterness of death for a mortal, how bitter then for an immortal! O bitter refreshment, more bitter than aloes, to be refreshed by the misunderstanding of the beloved! O solace in affliction to suffer as one who is guilty, what solace then to suffer as one who is innocent!

Such will be our poet's picture. For how could it enter his mind that God would reveal himself in this manner merely to subject mankind to a test, the most crucial and the most terrible; and how could he find it in his heart to jest frivolously with the sorrow of God, falsely effacing his love to make room for his wrath!

And now the learner, has he no lot or part in this story of suffering, even though his lot cannot be that of the Teacher? Aye, it cannot be otherwise. And the cause of all this suffering is love, precisely because God is not jealous for himself, but desires in love to be the equal of the humblest. When the seed of the oak is planted in earthen vessels they break asunder; when new wine is poured in old leathern bottles they burst; what must happen when God implants himself in human weakness, unless man becomes a new vessel and a new creature! But this becoming, what labours will attend the change, how convulsed with birthpangs! And the understanding—how precarious, and how close each moment to misunderstanding, when the anguish of guilt seeks to disturb the peace of love! And how wrapt in fear; for it is indeed less terrible to fall to the ground when the mountains tremble at the voice of God, than to sit at table with him as an equal; and yet it is God's concern precisely to have it so.

Now if someone were to say: 'This poem of yours is the most wretched piece of plagiarism ever perpetrated, for it is neither more nor less than what every child knows', I suppose I must blush with shame to hear myself called a liar. But why the most wretched? Every poet who steals, steals from some other poet, and in so far we are all equally wretched; indeed, my own theft is perhaps less harmful, since it is more readily discovered. If I were to be so polite as to ascribe the authorship to you who now condemn me, you would perhaps again be angry. Is there then no poet, although there is a poem? This would surely be strange, as strange as flute-playing without a flute-player. Or is this poem perhaps like a proverb, for which no author can be assigned, because it is as if it owed its existence to humanity at large; was this perhaps the reason you called my theft the most wretched, because I did not steal from any individual man but robbed the human race, and arrogantly, although I am only an individual man, aye even a wretched thief, pretended to be mankind? If this then is the case, and I went about to all men in turn, and all knew the poem, but each one also knew that he was not the author of it, can I then conclude: mankind must be the author? Would not this be a strange conclusion? For if mankind were the author of this poem, this would have to be expressed by considering every individual equally close to the authorship. Does it not seem to you that this is a difficult case in which we have become involved, though the whole matter appeared to be so easily disposed of in the beginning, by your short and angry word about its being the most wretched plagiarism, and my shame in having to hear it? So then perhaps it is no poem, or at any rate not one for which any human being is responsible, nor yet mankind; ah, now I understand you, it was for this reason you called my procedure the most wretched act of plagiarism, because I did not steal from any individual, nor from the race, but from God; or as it were stole God away, and though I am only an individual man, aye even a wretched thief, blasphemously pretended to be God. Now I understand you fully, dear friend, and recognize the justice of your resentment. But then my soul is filled with new wonder, even more, with the spirit of worship; for it would surely have been strange had this poem been a human production. It is not impossible that it might occur to man to imagine himself the equal of God, or to imagine God the equal of man, but not to imagine that God would make himself into the likeness of man; for if God gave no sign, how could it enter into the mind of man that the blessed God should need him? This would be a most stupid thought, or rather, so stupid a thought could never have entered into his mind; though when God has seen fit to entrust him with it he exclaims in worship: This thought did not arise in my own heart! and finds it a most miraculously beautiful thought. And is it not altogether miraculous, and does not this word come as a happy omen to my lips; for as I have just said, and as you yourself involuntarily exclaimed, we stand here before the *Miracle*. And as we both now stand before this miracle, whose solemn silence cannot be perturbed by human wrangling over mine and thine, whose awe-inspiring speech infinitely subdues all human strife about mine and thine, forgive me, I pray, the strange delusion that I was the author of this poem. It was a delusion, and the poem is so different from every human poem as not to be a poem at all, but the *Miracle*. (pp. 20–8) . . .

The Paradox

. . . Will you deny the consistency of our exposition: that Reason, in attempting to determine the Unknown as the unlike, at last goes astray, and confounds the unlike with the like? From this there would seem to follow the further consequence, that if man is to receive any true knowledge about the Unknown (God) he must be made to know that it is unlike him, absolutely unlike him. This knowledge the Reason cannot possibly obtain of itself; we have already seen that this would be a self-contradiction. It will therefore have to obtain this knowledge from God. But even if it obtains such knowledge it cannot understand it, and thus is quite unable to possess such knowledge. For how should the Reason be able to understand what is absolutely different from itself? If this is not immediately evident, it will become clearer in the light of the consequences; for if God is absolutely unlike man, then man is absolutely unlike God; but how could Reason be expected to understand this? Here we seem to be confronted with a paradox. Merely to obtain the knowledge that God is unlike him, man needs the help of God; and now he learns that God is absolutely different from himself. But if God and man are absolutely different, this cannot be accounted for on the basis of what man derives from God, for in so far they are akin. Their unlikeness must therefore be explained by what man derives from himself, or by what he has brought upon his own head. But what can this unlikeness be? Aye, what can it be but sin; since the unlikeness, the absolute unlikeness, is something that man has brought upon himself. We have expressed this in the preceding by saying that man was in Error, and had brought this upon his head by his own guilt; and we came to the conclusion, partly in jest and yet in earnest also, that it was too much to expect of man that he should find this out for himself. Now we have again arrived at the same conclusion. The connoisseur in self-knowledge was perplexed over himself to the point of bewilderment when he came to grapple in thought with the unlike, he scarcely knew any longer whether he was a stranger monster than Typhon, or if his nature partook of something divine.[1] What then did he lack? The consciousness of sin, which he indeed could no more teach to another than another could teach it to him, but only God—if God consents to become a Teacher. But this was his purpose, as we have imagined it. In order to be man's Teacher, God proposed to make himself like the individual man, so that he might understand him

[1] The reference is to Socrates in *Phaedrus*, 229 E.

fully. Thus our paradox is rendered still more appalling, or the same paradox has the double aspect which proclaims it as the Absolute Paradox; negatively by revealing the absolute unlikeness of sin, positively by proposing to do away with the absolute unlikeness in absolute likeness.

But can such a paradox be conceived? Let us not be over-hasty in replying; and since we strive merely to find the answer to a question, and not as those who run a race, it may be well to remember that success is to the accurate rather than to the swift. The Reason will doubtless find it impossible to conceive it, could not of itself have discovered it, and when it hears it announced will not be able to understand it, sensing merely that its downfall is threatened. In so far the Reason will have much to urge against it; and yet we have on the other hand seen that the Reason, in its paradoxical passion, precisely desires its own downfall. But this is what the Paradox also desires, and thus they are at bottom linked in understanding; but this understanding is present only in the moment of passion. Consider the analogy presented by love, though it is not a perfect one. Self-love underlies love; but the paradoxical passion of self-love when at its highest pitch wills precisely its own downfall. This is also what love desires, so that these two are linked in mutual understanding in the passion of the moment, and this passion is love. Why should not the lover find this conceivable? But he who in self-love shrinks from the touch of love can neither understand it nor summon the courage to venture it, since it means his downfall. Such is then the passion of love; self-love is indeed submerged but not annihilated; it is taken captive and becomes love's *spolia opima*, but may again come to life, and this is love's temptation. So also with the Paradox in its relation to the Reason, only that the passion in this case has another name; or rather, we must seek to find a name for it.

. . . .

If the Paradox and the Reason come together in a mutual understanding of their unlikeness their encounter will be happy, like love's understanding, happy in the passion to which we have not yet assigned a name, and will postpone naming until later. If the encounter is not in understanding the relationship becomes unhappy, and this unhappy love of the Reason if I may so call it (which it should be noted is analogous only to that particular form of unhappy love which has its root in misunderstood self-love; no further stretching of the analogy is possible, since accident can play no role in this realm), may be characterized more specifically as *Offence*.

All offence is in its deepest roots passive.[1] In this respect it is like that

[1] The Danish language correctly calls emotion (Dan. '*Affekten*') 'Sinds*lidelse*' [compare Ger. '*Leiden*schaft'].When we use the word '*Affekt*' we are likely to think more immediately of the convulsive daring which astounds us, and makes us forget that it is a form of passivity. So for example: pride, defiance, etc.

form of unhappy love to which we have just alluded. Even when such self-love (and does it not already seem contradictory that love of self should be passive?) announces itself in deeds of audacious daring, in astounding achievements, it is passive and wounded. It is the pain of its wound which gives it this illusory strength, expressing itself in what looks like self-activity and may easily deceive, since self-love is especially bent on concealing its passivity. Even when it tramples on the object of affection, even when it painfully schools itself to a hardened indifference and tortures itself to show this indifference, even then, even when it abandons itself to a frivolous triumph over its success (this form is the most deceptive of all), even then it is passive. Such is also the case with the offended consciousness. Whatever be its mode of expression, even when it exultantly celebrates the triumph of its unspirituality, it is always passive. Whether the offended individual sits broken-hearted, staring almost like a beggar at the Paradox, paralysed by his suffering, or he sheathes himself in the armour of derision, pointing the arrows of his wit as if from a distance—he is still passive and near at hand. Whether offence came and robbed the offended individual of his last bit of comfort and joy, or made him strong—the offended consciousness is nevertheless passive. It has wrestled with the stronger, and its show of strength is like the peculiar agility induced in the bodily sphere by a broken back.

However, it is quite possible to distinguish between an active and a passive form of the offended consciousness, if we take care to remember that the passive form is so far active as not to permit itself wholly to be annihilated (for offence is always an act, never an event); and that the active form is always so weak that it cannot free itself from the cross to which it is nailed, or tear the arrow from out its wound.[1]

But precisely because offence is thus passive, the discovery, if it be allowable to speak thus, does not derive from the Reason, but from the Paradox. The offended consciousness does not understand itself[2] but is understood by the Paradox. While therefore the expressions in which offence proclaims itself, of whatever kind they may be, sound as if they

[1] The idiom of the language also supports the view that all offence is passive. We say: 'to be offended', which primarily expresses only the state or condition; but we also say, as identical in meaning with the foregoing: 'to take offence', which expresses a synthesis of active and passive. The Greek word is *σκανδαλίζεσθαι*. This word comes from *σκάνδαλον* (offence or stumbling-block), and hence means to take offence, or to collide with something. Here the movement of thought is clearly indicated; it is not that offence provokes the collision, but that it meets with a collision, and hence passively, although so far actively as itself to take offence. Hence the Reason is not the discoverer of offence; for the paradoxical collision which the Reason develops in isolation discovers neither the Paradox nor the reaction of offence.

[2] In this sense the Socratic principle that sin is ignorance finds justification. Sin does not understand itself in the Truth, but it does not follow that it may not will itself in Error.

came from elsewhere, even from the opposite direction, they are nevertheless echoings of the Paradox. This is what is called an acoustic illusion. But if the Paradox is *index* and *judex sui et falsi*, the offended consciousness can be taken as an indirect proof of the validity of the Paradox; offence is the mistaken reckoning, the invalid consequence, with which the Paradox repels and thrusts aside. The offended individual does not speak from his own resources, but borrows those of the Paradox; just as one who mimics or parodies another does not invent, but merely copies perversely. The more profound the passion with which the offended consciousness (active or passive) expresses itself, the more apparent it is how much it owes to the Paradox. Offence was not discovered by the Reason, far from it, for then the Reason must also have been able to discover the Paradox; it *comes into being*. Here again we have the Moment, on which everything depends. Let us recapitulate. If we so not posit the Moment we return to Socrates; but it was precisely from him that we departed, in order to discover something. If we posit the Moment the Paradox is there; for the Moment is the Paradox in its most abbreviated form. Because of the Moment the learner is in Error; and man, who had before possessed self-knowledge, now becomes bewildered with respect to himself; instead of self-knowledge he receives the consciousness of sin, and so forth; for as soon as we posit the Moment everything follows of itself.

From the psychological point of view the offended consciousness will display a great variety of nuances within the more active and the more passive forms. To enter into a detailed description of these would not further our present purpose; but it is important to bear fixedly in mind that all offence is in its essence a misunderstanding of the *Moment*, since it is directed against the Paradox, which again is the Moment.

The dialectic of the *Moment* is not difficult. From the Socratic point of view the Moment is invisible and indistinguishable; it is not, it has not been, it will not come. Hence the learner is himself the Truth, and the moment of occasion is but a jest, like a bastard title that does not essentially belong to the book. From this point of view the Moment of decision becomes *folly;* for if a decision in time is postulated, then (by the preceding) the learner is in Error, which is precisely what makes a beginning in the Moment necessary. The reaction of the offended consciousness is to assert that the Moment is folly, and that the Paradox is folly; which is the contention of the Paradox that Reason is absurd, now reflected back as in an echo from the offended consciousness. Or the Moment is regarded as constantly about to come; it is so regarded, and the Reason holds it as *worthy of regard*: but since the Paradox has made the Reason absurd, the regard of the Reason is no reliable criterion.

The offended consciousness holds aloof from the Paradox, and the reason is: *quia absurdum*. But it was not the Reason that made this discovery; on the contrary it was the Paradox that made the discovery, and now receives this testimony from the offended consciousness. The Reason says that the Paradox is absurd, but this is mere mimicry, since the Paradox is the Paradox, *quia absurdum*. The offended consciousness holds aloof from the Paradox and keeps to the probable, the Paradox being the most improbable of things. Again it is not the Reason that made this discovery; it merely snatches the words from the mouth of the Paradox, strange as this may seem; for the Paradox itself says: Comedies and romances and lies must needs be probable, but why should I be probable? The offended consciousness holds aloof from the Paradox, and what wonder, since the Paradox is the Miracle! . . . (pp. 36–42)

. . . .

Let us now picture God going about in the city of his appearance (which city this is, is indifferent). To make his teaching known is the sole necessity of his life; it is his meat and drink. Teaching is his labour, and caring for the learner is his rest from labour. He has no friends nor kindred, but the learner is his brother and sister. It may readily be understood that a web of rumour will soon be woven, catching the curious multitude in its snare. Wherever the Teacher appears the crowd gathers, curious to see, curious to hear, and eager to tell others that they have seen and heard him. Is this curious multitude the learner? By no means. Or if some one of the authorized teachers of that city sought him out secretly, in order to try his strength with him in argument—is he the learner? By no means. If this teacher or that multitude *learn* anything, God serves merely as an occasion in the strict Socratic sense.

God's appearance has now become the news of the day, in the market-place, in the homes of the people, in the council chamber, in the ruler's palace. It gives occasion for much foolish and idle talk, perhaps also for some earnest reflection. But for the learner the news of the day is not an occasion for something else, not even an occasion for the acquirement in Socratic sincerity of a deeper and fuller self-knowledge; for the learner it is the eternal, the beginning of eternity. The news of the day the beginning of eternity! If God had permitted himself to be born in an inn, wrapped in swaddling-clothes and laid in a manger, could the contradiction have been greater than that the news of the day should be the swaddling-clothes of eternity; aye, as in the supposed instance its actual form, so that the *Moment* is really decisive for eternity! Unless God grants the condition which makes it possible to understand this, how is it to be supposed that the learner will be able to discover it! But that God himself gives this condition has been shown above to be a consequence of the *Moment*, and it has also been shown that the Moment is the Paradox, and that without it we are unable to advance, but return to Socrates.

Here at the outset let us take care to make it clear that the question of an historical point of departure arises even for a contemporary disciple; for if we are not careful here we shall meet with an insuperable difficulty later, when we come to deal with the case of the disciple whom we call the disciple at second hand. The contemporary disciple gets an historical point of departure for his eternal consciousness as well as any later disciple; for he is contemporary with precisely that historical phenomenon which refuses to be reduced to a moment of merely occasional significance, but proposes to interest him in another sense than the merely historical presenting itself to him as a condition for his eternal happiness. If this is not so, then (deducing the consequences conversely) the Teacher is not God but only a Socrates, and if he does not conduct himself like a Socrates, he is not even a Socrates.

But how does the learner come to realize an understanding with this Paradox? We do not ask that he understand the Paradox, but only that this is the Paradox. How this takes place we have already shown. It comes to pass when the Reason and the Paradox encounter one another happily in the Moment; when the Reason sets itself aside and the Paradox bestows itself. The third entity in which this union is realized (for it is not realized in the Reason, since it is set aside: nor in the Paradox, which bestows itself—hence it is realized *in* something) is that happy passion to which we will now assign a name, though it is not the name that so much matters. We shall call this passion: *Faith*. This then must be the condition of which we have spoken, which the Paradox contributes. Let us not forget that if the Paradox does not grant this condition the learner must be in possession of it. But if the learner is in possession of the condition he is *eo ipso* himself the Truth, and the moment is merely the moment of occasion.

. . . (pp. 46–7).

INDEX